SUPREME
COMMAND

SOLDIERS, STATESMEN AND
LEADERSHIP IN WARTIME

★ ★ ★

ELIOT A. COHEN

FREE PRESS

This paperback edition first published by Simon & Schuster UK Ltd, 2003
A Viacom Company

1 3 5 7 9 10 8 6 4 2

Simon & Schuster UK Ltd
Africa House
64–78 Kingsway
London WC2B 6AH

www.simonsays.co.uk

Simon & Schuster Australia
Sydney

A CIP catalogue record for this book
is available from the British Library

ISBN 0–7432–4004–9

Typeset by M Rules
Printed and bound in Denmark by
Norhaven Paperback A/S, Viborg

Alvin H. Bernstein, in memoriam

To Shakespeare, robes and crowns and jewels are the garments most appropriate to man because they are the fitting outward manifestation of his inward majesty, but to us they seem absurd because the man who bears them has, in our estimation, so pitifully shrunk. We do not write about kings because we do not believe that any man is worthy to be one and we do not write about courts because hovels seem to us to be dwellings more appropriate to the creatures who inhabit them.

—Joseph Wood Krutch, *The Modern Temper*

ABOUT THE AUTHOR

Eliot A. Cohen is Professor of Strategic Studies at Johns Hopkins University. He previously served on the policy planning staff of the Office of the Secretary of Defense and as an intelligence officer in the United States Army Reserve and taught at the U. S. Naval War College at Harvard University. He has written books and articles on a variety of military and national security related subjects. A frequent consultant to the Department of Defense and the intelligence community, he is a member of the Defense Policy Board, advising the Secretary of Defense.

CONTENTS

	PREFACE	XI
CHAPTER 1	**THE SOLDIER AND THE STATESMAN**	1
CHAPTER 2	**LINCOLN SENDS A LETTER**	17
CHAPTER 3	**CLEMENCEAU PAYS A VISIT**	60
CHAPTER 4	**CHURCHILL ASKS A QUESTION**	110
CHAPTER 5	**BEN-GURION HOLDS A SEMINAR**	154
CHAPTER 6	**LEADERSHIP WITHOUT GENIUS**	201
CHAPTER 7	**THE UNEQUAL DIALOGUE**	242
APPENDIX	**THE THEORY OF CIVILIAN CONTROL**	262
	ACKNOWLEDGMENTS	290
	NOTES	293
	INDEX	323

PREFACE

This is a book about leadership in wartime—or more precisely about the tension between two kinds of leadership, civil and military. In it I have attempted to uncover the nature of strategy-making in war by looking at four great democratic war statesmen, and examining how they dealt with the military leaders who served them. My hope in so doing is to explore some fundamental aspects of leadership. This is, therefore, not merely an historical analysis but a study of issues that remain alive to this day.

This work will appeal, I hope, to those readers who desire to know more about the four statesmen I discuss in the middle of the book and to those who are interested more generally in the problem of how men (or women) confront the greatest challenges that can befall a national leader. There will be other audiences as well, I hope: students of leadership more broadly viewed, soldiers who wish to learn more about the problems of civil-military relations in wartime, scholars interested in this field, and indeed politicians themselves.

The book begins with a discussion of the problem of civil-military relations from a general point of view. Those interested in plunging a bit more deeply into this issue should consult the appendix, "The Theory of Civilian Control." The first chapter sketches out what I call the "normal" theory of civil-military relations—a norm violated in most ways by the subjects of the next four chapters. Lincoln, Clemenceau, Churchill, and Ben-Gurion each receive a chapter-length account, focusing on the problem of civil-military relations. These chapters do not deal with all aspects of wartime leadership (industrial mobilization, for example) except insofar as it affected civil-military relations. Chapter 6 explores civil-military relations after World War II by looking at how the United States has waged war under far less effective leaders than those studied here. A final chapter attempts to draw more generalized lessons for contemporary democracies, and for students of leadership more broadly viewed.

The idea for this book formed when I was teaching at the Naval War College in Newport, Rhode Island, in the mid-1980s. The Strategy Department there, to which I belonged, engaged senior military officers in a discussion of the fundamental issues discussed here through the study of the history of war from ancient to modern times. One day a frustrated officer remarked to me, "This isn't really a course in strategy at all, it's a course on civil-military relations." He had gotten to the heart of the subject, little though it had pleased him to do so. In fact, the study of the relationship between soldiers and *statesmen* (rather different from the relationship between the soldier and *the state*, as a famous book has it) lies at the heart of what strategy is all about. In the book's first chapter we will see how closely related conceptions of strategy are to civil-military relations.

While at Newport I had the opportunity to mull over some of the cases that I discuss here, particularly those of Abraham Lincoln and Winston Churchill, the two greatest war statesmen that the English-speaking world has produced. I should add here that a second impetus for this book came from a long-time fascination with the four statesmen discussed in chapters 2 through 5, particularly Churchill. I was awed, as so many people are, by the courage that enabled him to save Great Britain from surrender to Hitler's Germany. Yet the more widely I read him (particularly his biography of his great ancestor, the duke of Marlborough, published in the 1930s), the more I came to think of him as a certain kind of theorist of the conduct of war. Uniquely, he was not merely a statesman, but a student of statesmanship. Furthermore, the more one learns about his conduct of his war, the more one realizes that the image purveyed by some memoirists and historians of an impulsive, erratic, absurdly romantic aristocrat is, in fact, incorrect. He understood modern warfare better than did his generals, and he acted with far more method than politicians today. Historians of the last twenty years have dealt increasingly unkindly with his conduct of the wars he fought—as, to a lesser extent, they have also criticized Ben-Gurion. I confess to a certain desire to enter the lists on behalf of Churchill and his colleagues in this book.

Such an admission opens me, I well realize, to accusations of hero-worship—a practice out of keeping with the temper of these times, which too often prefers accounts of a politician's sexual peccadillos to reflection on his practice of the political art. Moreover, since great political leaders are by definition unusual, we are unfamiliar with them. "Great men are so rare that they take some getting used to," remarks Henry Kissinger.[1] Furthermore, it seems to me that the scholarly disciplines of political science and, to a lesser extent, history have increasingly distanced themselves from psychological sympathy with their subjects. A belief in the greatness of statesmen puts in jeopardy theories built on descriptions of social forces or institutions, or systemic explanations such as "rational choice." The statesmanship of outstanding individuals was once a popular and legitimate subject of inquiry; this is no longer true. The professionalization of the academy has meant that many scholars have had a narrower range of personal experience, and perhaps a narrower set of social acquaintances, than was the case in the past. Samuel Eliot Morison once said, "The great historians, with few exceptions, are those who have not merely studied, but lived," and he told the veterans of World War II that their war experience would enable them to "read man's doings in the past with far greater understanding than if they had spent these years in sheltered academic groves."[2]

Morison's students, like the master himself, learned much from their personal exposure to the shocks of war. Succeeding generations, however, have become more insulated from a world of practice, and the upshot is often a history that shows remarkably little sympathy for the cares and burdens of political leaders. Edmund Wilson once observed about literary critics that "the relation of the professor to his subjects . . .

is, nine times out of ten, a strained and embarrassing one. The professor would be made most uncomfortable if he had to meet Whitman or Byron; he would not like him—he does not, in fact, like him."[3] *Mutatis mutandis*, the same holds true of many military historians.

The purpose of this book is not, however, to defend the reputations of its principal subjects. The purpose is, rather, to make the nature of the challenges and complexities they faced more comprehensible, and this book does unabashedly accept the notion that there are, occasionally, great statesmen whose skill in the politics of war exceeds those of the average run of political men and women. I will not pretend to encompass the whole of each man's war direction—each has attracted the attention of authors whose works run to many volumes. Rather, this book explores the performance of these four men as war leaders as a way of illuminating the perennial problem of civil-military relations in wartime. It focuses on certain key traits or characteristics, rather than the totality of their experience, and it makes no apology for not providing a comprehensive account of each leader's efforts, which could only produce a superficial text.

Arguments from the experience of exceptional persons make some uneasy. For that reason this book includes a chapter on "leadership without genius," a discussion of what happens when the average run of politicians and generals find themselves at war. It will consider explicitly the argument that the methods and approaches of exceptional leaders cannot serve as the model for their run-of-the-mill counterparts. There I will also examine some of the differences between what historians call total war and more limited conflicts. It turned out, rather to my own surprise, that in their fundamental challenges for civilian leaders the two kinds of war diverge less than one might expect. Extreme circumstances, including war for the most essential national interests, enable us to see more clearly what great leaders do and of what they are made. If one wishes to study the finest steel, best to search for the hottest furnace.

CHAPTER 1

THE SOLDIER AND THE STATESMAN

Few choices bedevil organizations as much as the selection of senior leaders. Often they look for those with high-level experience in different settings: New York City's Columbia University sought out America's most senior general, Dwight D. Eisenhower, to lead it after World War II; President Ronald Reagan made a corporate tycoon his chief of staff in 1985; in the early 1990s, Sears Roebuck, an ailing giant, looked to the chief logistician of the Gulf War to help it turn around. Frequently enough the transplant fails; the sets of skills and aptitudes that led to success in one walk of life either do not carry over or are downright dysfunctional in another. The rules of politics differ from those of business, and universities do not act the way corporations do. Even within the business world, car companies and software giants may operate very differently, and the small arms manufacturer who takes over an ice-cream company may never quite settle in to the new culture.

To be sure, leaders at the top have some roughly similar tasks: setting directions, picking subordinates, monitoring performance, handling external constituencies, and inspiring achievement. And they tend, often enough, to think that someone in a different walk of life has the answers to their dilemmas, which is why the generals study business books, and the CEOs peruse military history. But in truth the details of their work differ so much that in practice the parallels often elude them, or can only be discovered by digging more deeply than is the norm.

The relations between statesmen and soldiers in wartime offer a special case of this phenomenon. Many senior leaders in private life must manage equally senior professionals who have expertise and experience that dwarf their own, but politicians dealing with generals in wartime face exceptional difficulties. The stakes are so high, the gaps in mutual understanding so large, the differences in personality and background so stark, that the challenges exceed anything found in the civilian sector—which is why, perhaps, these relationships merit close attention not only from historians and students of policy, but from anyone interested in leadership at its most acutely difficult. To learn how statesmen manage their generals in wartime one must explore the peculiarities of the military profession and the exceptional atmospheres and values produced by war. These peculiarities and conditions are unique and extreme, and they produce relationships far more complicated and tense than either citizen or soldier may expect in peacetime, or even admit to exist in time of war.

"LET HIM COME WITH ME INTO MACEDONIA"

To see why, turn back to the year 168 B.C. The place is the Senate of the Roman republic, the subject the proposed resumption of war (for the third time) against Macedonia, and the speaker Consul Lucius Aemilius:

I am not, fellow-citizens, one who believes that no advice may be given to leaders; nay rather I judge him to be not a sage, but haughty, who conducts everything according to his own opinion alone. What therefore is my conclusion? Generals should receive advice, in the first place from the experts who are both specially skilled in military matters and have learned from experience; secondly, from those who are on the scene of action, who see the terrain, the enemy, the fitness of the occasion, who are sharers in the danger, as it were, aboard the same vessel. Thus, if there is anyone who is confident that he can advise me as to the best advantage of the state in this campaign which I am about to conduct, let him not refuse his services to the state, but come with me into Macedonia. I will furnish him with his sea-passage, with a horse, a tent, and even travel-funds. If anyone is reluctant to do this and prefers the leisure of the city to the hardships of campaigning, let him not steer the ship from on shore. The city itself provides enough subjects for conversation; let him confine his garrulity to these; and let him be aware that I shall be satisfied with the advice originating in camp.[1]

The Consul's cry for a free hand echoes that of generals throughout history—although the historian Livy records that, as a matter of fact, an unusually large number of senators decided to accompany him on campaign. Still, the notion that generals once given a mission should have near total discretion in its execution is a powerful one.

Popular interpretations of the Vietnam and Gulf wars, the one supposedly a conflict characterized by civilian interference in the details of warmaking, the other a model of benign operational and tactical neglect by an enlightened civilian leadership, seem to confirm the value of a bright line drawn between the duties of soldiers and civilians. Thus the chief of staff to General Norman Schwarzkopf, commander of US forces in Southwest Asia: "Schwarzkopf was never second-guessed by civilians, and that's the way it ought to work."[2] Or more directly, then-President George Bush's declaration when he received the Association of the US Army's George Catlett Marshall Medal: "I vowed that I would never send an American soldier into combat with one hand tied behind that soldier's back. We did the politics and you superbly did the fighting."[3] Small wonder, then, that the editor of the US Army War College's journal wrote to his military colleagues:

> There will be instances where civilian officials with Napoleon complexes and micromanaging mentalities are prompted to seize the reins of operational control. And having taken control, there will be times when they then begin to fumble toward disaster. When this threatens to happen, the nation's top soldier . . . must summon the courage to rise and say to his civilian masters, "You can't do that!" and then stride to the focal point of decision and tell them how it must be done.[4]

Such a view of the roles of civilian and soldier reflects popular understandings as well. The 1996 movie *Independence Day*, for example, features only one notable villain (aside, that is, from the aliens who are attempting to devastate and conquer the Earth)—an overweening secretary of defense who attempts to direct the American military's counterattack against the invaders from outer space. Only after the interfering and deceitful civilian is out of the way can the president, a former Air Force combat pilot who gets back into uniform to lead the climactic aerial battle, and his military assistants (with the aid of one civilian scientist in a purely technical role) get on with the job of defeating the foe. To this comfortable consensus of capital, camp, and Hollywood one can add the weight of academic theory. Samuel Huntington, arguably the greatest American political scientist of our time, in a classic work, *The Soldier and the State*,[5] laid out what he termed a theory of "objective control," which holds that the healthiest and most effective form of civilian control of the military is that which maximizes professionalism by isolating soldiers from politics, and giving them as free a hand as possible in military matters.

THE NORMAL THEORY OF CIVIL-MILITARY RELATIONS

We can call this consensus the "normal" theory of civil-military relations, which runs something like this. Officers are professionals, much like highly trained surgeons: the statesman is in the position of a patient requiring urgent care. He may freely decide whether or not to have an operation, he may choose one doctor over another, and he may even make a decision among different surgical options, although that is more rare. He may not, or at least ought not supervise a surgical procedure, select the doctor's scalpel, or rearrange the operating room to his liking. Even the patient who has medical training is well-advised not to attempt to do so, and indeed, his doctor will almost surely resent a colleague-patient's efforts along such lines. The result should be a limited degree of civilian control over military matters. To ask too many questions (let alone to give orders) about tactics, particular pieces of hardware, the design of a campaign, measures of success, or to press too closely for the promotion or dismissal of anything other than the most senior officers is meddling and interference, which is inappropriate and downright dangerous.

The difficulty is that the great war statesmen do just those improper things—and, what is more, it is *because* they do so that they succeed. This book looks at four indubitably great and successful war leaders, Abraham Lincoln, Georges Clemenceau, Winston Churchill, and David Ben-Gurion. The period of their tenure spans a substantial but not overwhelming period of time and different kinds of democratic polities. These four politicians have enough in common to bear comparison, yet differ enough to exhibit various features of the problem of civil-military relations in wartime. Given the dangers of thinking through these problems exclusively from an American perspective, it makes sense that only one of them should come from the pages of American history.

Lincoln, Clemenceau, Churchill, and Ben-Gurion led four very different kinds of democracies, under the most difficult circumstances imaginable. They came from different traditions of civil-military relations, had had disparate personal experiences, and confronted different arrays of subordinates and peers. The nature of each of their democracies shaped the nature of the leadership that they could exert and that was required of them. They faced much in common, however. Institutions of a more or less free press and legislative bodies constrained their powers, and they had to deal with populations whose temper and disposition could affect their behavior directly. Powerful as each of these men was, he had to consider the possibility that his conduct of the war could bring about his fall from power by constitutional—that is, civilian—means. At the same time, in their dealings with the military they did not need to fear a violent coup. However, military opposition could and did translate into a variety of forms of political opposition, sometimes with a potential to overthrow them.

The period spanned here—a bit less than a century—saw the development of a distinctive style of warfare, sometimes called "total war" but perhaps more accurately described as "industrialized warfare." Success in war depended in large measure on an ability to obtain (through production or importation) mass-manufactured weapons. At the same time, these leaders did not have to cope with one of the distinctive challenges of a later strategic era, that of weapons of mass destruction. Interestingly enough, however, it was Churchill who early on grasped the paradoxical peace-inducing nature of atomic terror, and Ben-Gurion who laid the groundwork for an Israeli nuclear program at a time when Israeli conventional strength was set on a course of prolonged improvement.

These four statesmen conducted their wars during what may come to be seen as the time of the first communications revolution, when it became possible to communicate useful quantities of information almost instantaneously and to move large quantities of men and war materiél at great speed by means of mechanical transportation. In physics, the product of velocity and mass is momentum, and the same is true of warfare. Thus, these statesmen had to conduct wars at a time when the instruments of conflict themselves were changing and gathering speed. One might suggest that a second communications revolution is now upon us, in which a further quantum increase in the amount of information that can be distributed globally has occurred, and the role played by that information in all of civilized life will again transform society and ultimately the conduct of war. Thus these four cases exhibit the problems of wartime leadership during a period of enormous change. By understanding the challenges of those times we may also understand better the nature of the changes that are upon us today, in an age that looks to be quite different. The fundamental problems of statesmanship faced by the leaders of today have not changed as much as one might think. These are matters that I will explore in the conclusion to this book.

Finally, these statesmen were separated in time but linked by deep respect. Clemenceau visited the United States after the Civil War and professed a great admiration for Lincoln; Churchill paid Clemenceau the homage of rhetorical imitation (verging on plagiarism) on more than one occasion. And Ben-Gurion paid a tribute to Churchill's leadership in a note written a few years before the latter's death: "It was not only the liberties and the honour of your own people that you saved," wrote one aged giant to another.[6] Thus a thin but definite personal, not merely conceptual thread links these four men. The personal similarities and contrasts among them will bear examination. Three of them (Clemenceau, Churchill, and Ben-Gurion) assumed the reins of high command at an advanced age; two of them with very little in the way of preparation for the conduct of large-scale warfare (Lincoln and Clemenceau, although one might make a similar point about Ben-Gurion). Each exhibited in different ways similar qualities of ruthlessness, mastery of detail, and fascination with technology. All four were great learners who studied war as if it were their own profession, and in many ways they mastered it as well as did their generals. And all found themselves locked in conflict with military men. When one reads the transcripts of Ben-Gurion's furious arguments in 1948 with the de facto chief of staff of the new Israel Defense Forces—Yigal Yadin, a thirty-two-year-old archaeologist who had never served in any regular army—they do not sound very different from the tempestuous arguments between Winston Churchill and the grim Chief of the Imperial General Staff, Field Marshal Alan Brooke, twenty-five years older than Yadin and with a career spent in uniform. For all of the differences in their backgrounds the backwoods lawyer, the dueling French doctor turned journalist, the rogue aristocrat, and the impoverished Jewish socialist found themselves in similar predicaments: admiring their generals and despairing over them, driving some, dismissing others, and watching even the best with affection ever limited by wariness.

"WAR IS NOT MERELY AN ACT OF POLICY, BUT A TRUE POLITICAL INSTRUMENT."

If these four could have had a collective military adviser, one suspects that it would have been an older figure yet, Carl von Clausewitz, the greatest theorist of war, whose *On War* remains a standard text for aspiring strategists to the present day. For the Prussian general, who spent most of his adult life on active service fighting against the French Revolution and Napoleon, the attempt to separate the business of politicians and soldiers was a hopeless task. For that reason, early in the nineteenth century he rejected the "normal" theory. To understand why, at the deepest level, these statesmen did not delegate war fighting to the generals, one turns to Clausewitz's famous dictum, that war is merely the continuation of politics by other means. But by this he has something far more radical in mind than is commonly thought.[7]

"We see, therefore, that war is *not merely an act of policy but a true political instrument*, a continuation of political intercourse, carried on with other means."[8] The first part of the sentence ("not merely an act of policy") illuminates the second and suggests its radical nature. For Clausewitz there is no field of military action that might not be touched by political considerations. In practice, politics might not determine the stationing of pickets or the dispatch of patrols, he writes, but in theory it could (and, one might add, in the day of CNN often does). Although Clausewitz fully recognizes the power of war untrammeled to overwhelm political rationality—by intoxicating men with blood lust, or through the sheer difficulty of making things happen, which he termed friction—he thought that all activity in war had potential political consequences and repercussions, and that every effort must therefore be made to bend war to serve the ends of politics.

The Clausewitzian view is incompatible with the doctrine of professionalism codified by the "normal" theory of civil-military relations. If every facet of military life may have political consequences, if one cannot find a refuge from politics in the levels of war (saying, for example, that "grand strategy" is properly subject to political influence, but "military strategy" is not), civil-military relations are problematic. The Clausewitzian formula for civil-military relations has it that the statesman may legitimately interject himself in any aspect of war-making, although it is often imprudent for him to do so. On most occasions political leaders will have neither the knowledge nor the judgment to intervene in a tactical decision, and most episodes in war have little or no political import. But there can be in Clausewitz's view no arbitrary line dividing civilian and military responsibility, no neat way of carving off a distinct sphere of military action. "When people talk, as they often do, about harmful political influence on the management of war, they are not really saying what they mean. Their quarrel should be with the policy itself, not its influence. If the policy is right—that is, successful—

any intentional effect it has on the conduct of the war can only be to the good."[9]

The political nature of war drives the Clausewitzian to this conclusion. So too does the curious nature of military professionalism. The peculiarities of that calling (see the appendix "The Theory of Civilian Control") mandate more action by the politician than may be customary among the clients or employers of other professionals. The selection of and dismissal of generals is one such activity. Generals rarely enter a war having commanded for any length of time forces comparable to those assigned them on the outbreak of a conflict; hence they are almost always unproved. It often falls to the political leadership to determine the competence—the narrower tactical ability, in fact—of the military leaders in the face of ambiguous information, for not all defeated generals are inept. Furthermore, it often occurs that generals fit for one type of operation fail dismally at another; the slashing, attacking commander may lack the talents of his more stolid brethren for conducting a defense or those of his more tactful colleagues for handling allies. Of course, contenders in lawsuits occasionally fire their attorneys, patients seek new doctors, and companies look for different engineers. But the problem of selecting military leadership is altogether more acute. Not only is it more pervasive (most patients, after all, do not in fact fire their doctors—or if they do decide to do so, they often come to that conclusion too late), but the problem of selecting military leadership frequently covers a far wider field. Rather than picking a single professional or firm to handle a task, politicians must select dozens, even scores. Often enough they cannot know that the next man they pick will be any better than his predecessor, for all alike are inexperienced at the task before them. Except at the end of a very long war, there is no recognized expert at hand with a proven record in the managing of complex military operations against an active enemy.

And there is little parallel in civilian life to the problems of morale and domestic political disharmony that beset a politician considering dismissal of a general. In daily life the professional's employment is understood to be simply at the sufferance of his client; but in the world of war, generals become semi-independent political figures of considerable importance. Soldiers are not merely neutral instruments of the state but warriors, and in wartime warriors elicit respect and admiration. Most generals know this, and many are human enough to act accordingly. Rarely in wartime are senior military leaders cut off from the highest echelons of politics; rather they mingle (rather more than they do in peacetime, in fact) with legislators, journalists, and senior bureaucrats. They appear on the front pages of newspapers and are lionized by social élites, and they may even attempt to undermine their nominal superiors in the forum of public opinion.[10] A dismissed lawyer or doctor does not normally seize such opportunities.

It is not, however, only the selection and dismissal of generals that constitute a politician's chief responsibility in war, nor is it even (as the military textbooks would suggest) the articulation of goals or the allocation of resources. Rather, a politician finds himself managing military alliances, deciding the nature of acceptable risk, shaping operational choices, and reconstructing military organizations. During World War II, for example, the British War Cabinet found itself called upon to make decisions on matters as minute as whether certain trans-Atlantic convoys should travel at thirteen as opposed to fifteen knots, because although their naval advisers could tell them about the pros and cons of a decision on either side, the assumption of risk to Britain's lifeline to the outer world required a political decision.[11] Or, to take an even more telling case, in June 1943 it was a prime-ministerial decision whether or not to introduce WINDOW—radar-jamming chaff—to help British bombers break through to Germany. The Royal Air Force was divided: Bomber Command favored such a measure, but those responsible for the air defense of Great Britain, expecting enemy imitation of such a move, feared that for half a year they would lose all ability to defend the night skies over Britain.[12] Once again, the balance of risk required a political decision. In both these cases (and there are many more) the politicians had to resolve important questions not only because of the scope of the issues at stake, but because the professionals could not agree. Divided among themselves not merely by opinion but by professional background, military leaders often differ sharply about the best course of action. Ben-Gurion, for example, had to arbitrate between the homegrown socialist élites of the Palmach and the more stolid veterans of the British Army. As Stephen Rosen has noted, military organizations may be understood not simply as professional organizations but as political communities that struggle internally over fundamental issues. "They determine who will live and die, in wartime, and how; who will be honored and who will sit on the sidelines when war occurs."[13]

In all four of the cases we will examine here, there was little debate about the fundamental subordination of soldiers to civilian control. Coexisting, however, with that subordination—that acceptance of the legitimacy of civilian dominance—is a deep undercurrent of mutual mistrust. In practice, soldiers and statesmen in war often find themselves in an uneasy, even conflictual collaborative relationship, in which the civilian usually (at least in democracies) has the upper hand. It is a conflict often exacerbated by the differences in experience and outlook that political life and military life engender. These differences are not ideological but temperamental, even cultural.

"THIS MAN TOO HAS ONE MOUTH AND ONE HAND"

The memoirs of two soldiers turned politicians illustrate this. Ariel Sharon, prime minister of Israel as this book goes to press, was a uniformed hero of Israel's 1956, 1967, and 1973 wars, but subsequently became, in the eyes of many of his countrymen, a civilian villain as minister of defense during the 1982 war in Lebanon. His memoirs capture the essence of a general's mistrust of politicians, and render (perhaps disingenuously) his own wonderment at his entry into politics. He reflects on joining the Israeli parliament, the Knesset, for the first time:

> Like politics, military life is a constant struggle. But with all the difficulties and bitterness that may develop, at least there are certain rules. In politics there are no rules, no sense of proportion, no sensible hierarchy. An Israeli military man setting foot in this new world has most likely experienced great victories and also terrible defeats. He has had moments of exultation and moments of deepest grief. He knows what it is to be supremely confident, even inspired. But he has suffered the most abject fear and the deepest horror. He has made decisions about life and death, for himself as well as for others.
>
> The same person enters the political world and finds that he has one mouth to speak with and one hand to vote with, exactly like the man sitting next to him. And that man perhaps has never witnessed or experienced anything profound or anything dramatic in his life. He does not know either the heights or the depths. He has never tested himself or made critical decisions or taken responsibility for his life or the lives of his fellows. And this man—it seems incredible—but this man too has one mouth and one hand.[14]

Charles de Gaulle, writing more than half a century earlier, captured these fundamental differences no less starkly:

> The soldier often regards the man of politics as unreliable, inconstant, and greedy for the limelight. Bred on imperatives, the military temperament is astonished by the number of pretenses in which the statesman has to indulge. . . . The impassioned twists and turns, the dominant concern with the effect to be produced, the appearance of weighing others in terms not of their merit but of their influence—all inevitable characteristics in the civilian whose authority rests upon the popular will—cannot but worry

the professional soldier, broken in, as he is, to a life of hard duties, self-effacement, and respect shown for services rendered.

Inversely, the taste for system, the self-assurance and the rigidity which, as the result of prolonged constraint, are inbred in the soldier, seem to the politicians tiresome and unattractive. Everything in the military code which is absolute, peremptory and not to be questioned, is repugnant to those who live in a world of rough and ready solutions, endless intriguing and decisions which may be reversed at a moment's notice.[15]

De Gaulle goes on to argue that this contrast explains the preference of politicians in peacetime for complaisant and docile military leaders, who frequently must be replaced at the outset of a war. Allowing for the differences in time and nationality, there is a kernel of truth here.

Yet the ultimate domination of the civilian leader is contingent, often fragile, and always haunted by his own lack of experience at high command, for he too is usually a novice in making the great decisions of war. For a politician to dictate military action is almost always folly. Civil-military relations must thus be a dialogue of unequals and the degree of civilian intervention in military matters a question of prudence, not principle, because principle properly opens the entire field of military activity to civilian scrutiny and direction. Perhaps the greatest of all leaders, Winston Churchill, noted in his reflections on World War II that "It is always right to probe."[16]

"THE SURPRISING CAPACITY OF HUMAN INTELLIGENCE FOR ERROR"

A fictional general famously remarked:

... do you recall what Clemenceau said about war? He said war was too important to be left to the generals.

When he said that, fifty years ago, he might have been right.

But today, war is too important to be left to politicians. They have neither the time, the training, or the inclination for strategic thought.

The words, one suspects, would win approval from more than a few practitioners and observers of contemporary civil-military relations—until they realized that they were expressed by the half-crazed Brigadier General Jack D. Ripper, of Stanley Kubrick's *Dr. Strangelove, Or: How I Learned to Stop Worrying and Love the Bomb* (1964). There are few, if any, General Rippers in the American military, but the sentiment surely persists, and indeed is even shared by some politicians. "The notion that it is inappropriate for civilian leaders to involve themselves in the details of military operations is pervasive in the military," writes Scott Cooper, a Marine captain troubled by the views of the generals. "It is also misguided."[17]

The generals and politicians who nonetheless cling to the "normal" theory do so for understandable reasons. It has much to be said for it. The "normal" theory reaffirms our belief in a distinctive "military way," a compelling if somewhat anachronistic code by which most military officers live. There are military values that are indeed distinct from those of civil society: self-abnegation, altruism, loyalty, and of course, courage. To set aside those differences or to ignore their importance would be not merely unwise, but devastating to military effectiveness. Nor should anyone cast aside the ideal of political neutrality, which has, if anything, grown in importance in an age when politicians populate political staffs with officers, be it on Capitol Hill or in the White House.[18] But where the "normal" theory goes awry is in its insistence on a *principled*, as opposed to a *prudential* basis for civilian restraint in interrogating, probing, and even in extremis, dictating military action. Taken to extremes, it would free politicians of real responsibility for the gravest challenges a country can face, and remove oversight and control from those whose job most requires it.

Only the surprising capacity of human intelligence for error can explain the opinion of prominent authorities who, although they acknowledge the role of politics in preparing for war and drafting the initial plan, rule out the possibility that politics can affect strategy once a war has started . . . A politics that would renounce the retention of its authority over the leadership of a war and acknowledge the primacy of military specialists and silently conform to their requirements would itself acknowledge its own bankruptcy.[19]

Thus the words of a shrewd Russian strategist, a victim of Stalin's purges, who had studied closely the disaster that had befallen his country and the rest of Europe in 1914–1918, partly as a result of faulty civilian control of military operations.

It is not a popular view. The former Supreme Allied Commander Atlantic, Admiral Harry Train, wrote in an analysis of the 1982 Falklands War, "when the duly accountable political leadership assumes the military role of deciding *how* the armed forces will perform their duties, the nation has a problem."[20] On the contrary, the truth is that when politicians abdicate their role in making those decisions, the nation has a problem. In the words of a wise observer of an earlier generation, reflecting upon the disaster of Vietnam and the role of weak civilian and unimaginative military leadership in bringing it about, "The civil hand must never relax, and it must without one hint of apology hold the control that has always belonged to it by right."[21]

Thus far the theory; we now turn to the practice.

CHAPTER 2

LINCOLN SENDS A LETTER

"FOR A RANK AMATEUR ASTONISHINGLY GOOD"

On 30 April 1864 Abraham Lincoln wrote a letter to Ulysses S. Grant, his newly selected general in chief, soon to embark on the campaign that would, during a single bloody year, crush the Confederacy.

> Not expecting to see you again before the spring campaign opens, I wish to express, in this way, my entire satisfaction with what you have done up to this time, so far as I understand it. The particulars of your plans I neither know, or seek to know. You are vigilant and self-reliant; and, pleased with this, I wish not to obtrude any constraints or restraints upon you. While I am very anxious that any great disaster, or the capture of our men in great numbers, shall be avoided, I know these points are less likely to escape your attention than they would mine. If there is anything wanting which is within my power to give, do not fail to let me know it.

And now with a brave Army, and a just cause, may God sustain you.[1]

Like so many of Lincoln's letters, this one has achieved fame for its eloquent simplicity. And like the man himself it is utterly deceptive in that regard, for Lincoln's letters to his generals reflected the workings of a subtle and cunning mind. In studying them, and the man behind them, one sees an example of war leadership that departs very far from the seeming detachment from military detail that he promised—but did not always deliver—to Grant.

For many years, though, historians have not taken this view. Two of the best-known books on Lincoln as commander in chief, T. Harry Williams's *Lincoln and His Generals* and Kenneth P. Williams's massive (but unfinished) *Lincoln Finds a General* have taken the view that Lincoln's challenge and achievement as commander in chief consisted of finding a general or generals who could do the bloody work of reuniting the country. In this common account, Lincoln deserves credit (or, according to a few, blame) for working his way through a list of incompetent commanders until finally he struck gold with Grant, at which point he stopped meddling in military affairs.

In an unintentionally patronizing passage, T. Harry Williams says that Lincoln's "strategic thinking was sound and for a rank amateur astonishingly good," but that "he was willing to discard his judgment of what was good strategy and take the opinion of any general whom he considered to be able. He was willing to yield the power to direct strategic operations to any general who could demonstrate that he was competent to frame and execute strategy."[2] This is, in some ways, the "normal" theory of civil-military relations applied to history: a political leader who won a war by defining objectives, mobilizing the public, picking the right leader, and handing the war over to him.

More recent authors have challenged this version of Lincoln's tenure as commander in chief. Indeed, the more closely one examines the record, the more difficult it becomes to sustain the thesis that the problem of high command in the Civil War boiled down to the problem of merely finding a general, as opposed to guiding and directing the one Lincoln found. Hence the need to read carefully these missives—some powerfully clear, others equally misleading. In this particular case, for example, Lincoln sent this message to Grant only after the general had spent *two months* in the capital, not far from the president, who must have had some notion of what he was about. Furthermore, within a week of composing this letter disclaiming any wish to know Grant's plans, Lincoln sent a special emissary to report back regularly—daily, in some cases—on what Grant was doing.[3]

Although it is hard to say that any part of Lincoln's career has received insufficient attention, it remains the case that most students of the war have tacitly yielded the field to the "Lincoln finds a general" school of historiography and therefore have paid less attention to his direction of military operations and his handling of even his successful generals than they might.[4] In fact, Lincoln exercised a constant oversight of the war effort from beginning to end. On 1 April 1861, only a few weeks after taking office, he instructed the commander in chief of the Army, the ancient but shrewd Winfield Scott, to provide "short, comprehensive, daily reports to me of what occurs in his department, including movements by himself, and under his orders, and the receipt of intelligence."[5] Scott obeyed this request—and on those few occasions on which he failed to do so, Lincoln noted that fact in his own memoranda. Lincoln did not hesitate to overrule his military advisers—not just after he had found his feet as commander in chief, but at the earliest stage in the war, when many contemporaries and not a few historians have regarded him as tentative, unsure of himself, even indecisive.[6] Nowhere is this more clear than when the newly elected president confronted the problem of what to do about the harbor forts on the periphery of the seceding Southern states. This was a prime case of how military detail and political decision came together, and of Lincoln's ability to do much more than pick a general.

On 15 March 1861 Lincoln asked his subordinates whether or not an effort should be made to resupply the isolated garrison at Fort Sumter. It was a time of crisis: the tiny military forces of the United States were falling apart as officers departed for the emerging Confederacy. (Enlisted men, by and large, remained loyal.) Seven states had seceded and others were preparing to do so. The departed states had inaugurated a president and vice president, and adopted a constitution; federal arsenals in those states had fallen (or been abandoned) to the secessionists. Masses of men were gathering weapons and drilling, but war had not broken out and many, on both sides, still hoped to avoid it.

Both the secretary of war, Simon Cameron, and the commanding general of the Army, Winfield Scott, argued against attempting to relieve the isolated garrisons on the Southern coast. General Scott declared that it would be best to evacuate both Sumter and Fort Pickens, making his case on the grounds of both the indefensibility of the forts and the desirable political consequences that would follow from voluntary evacuation.[7] Lincoln turned to considerably more junior officers (including a rising captain, Montgomery C. Meigs, who would become the Army's great quartermaster general) for alternative views.[8] Then, overruling his senior advisers, Lincoln ordered the nonviolent resupply of Sumter. Understanding as he did that the South would rise to the bait, he would place the onus of firing the first shots in a civil war on the Confederacy. It was a characteristically cunning move, for underneath Lincoln's apparent uncertainty and hesitation lay a steely willingness to accept the hazards of war. "The tug has to come, & better now, than any time hereafter,"[9] he had written to a friend in December 1860. He understood, better than most, what "the tug" would mean. He chose an act of military imprudence—refusing to either withdraw or reinforce outnumbered garrisons—to achieve a broader political effect. In so doing, he rejected the unanimous advice of his senior military advisers, and not for the last time.

By war's end Lincoln was allowing Grant and his close colleague, William Tecumseh Sherman, a fair degree of operational latitude, but only after they had devised a plan that matched his fundamental strategic concept of how the war would be won, a concept that dated back to the earliest stage of the conflict. His selection of Grant as general in chief of the Armies of the United States was preceded by years of careful watching and judgment. More importantly, from our point of view, that watching did not end with Grant's ascension to supreme command—nor did Lincoln's active scrutiny of military operations, which he undertook by means more subtle, but no less effective, than the issuance of direct orders. Lincoln did not merely find his generals; he controlled them. He molded the war to its last days, and he intended to dominate the making of peace at its end.

THE UNLIKELY COMMANDER IN CHIEF

Lincoln's qualifications to serve as commander in chief were, on paper, infinitely inferior to those of his antagonist, Jefferson Davis. Davis graduated from West Point in 1828 and served seven years on active duty, returning to the colors in 1846 to lead a volunteer regiment gallantly and successfully at the battles of Monterrey and Buena Vista. After service in the Senate he became secretary of war in 1853 and served for four years; in that capacity he pressed for the widespread introduction of the new Minié ball (an improved bullet) and the adoption of the rifle as a standard arm in the military. He then returned to the Senate and remained deeply engaged in military matters there. Lincoln, by way of contrast, had done only a few months' token service as a junior militia officer in the Black Hawk war of 1832, where his military experience included a (lost) wrestling contest with another captain for whose company would occupy a choice campground. Few would deny, however, that Lincoln was easily the greater war leader. Davis—unbending in his attitudes and stiff in his manners—did not have the reservoirs of humor, of patience, and of sympathy that allowed his opponent to put up with the misbehavior and failures of military commanders. It was easy for Davis to make use of a superlative officer like Robert E. Lee, who was not only a superb field commander but a deferential subordinate. The better test of Davis's abilities appears in his ability to make use of the capable but short-tempered and unsociable Braxton Bragg. Davis attempted to smooth over the wrangling among generals that paralyzed the Army of Tennessee outside Chattanooga in October of 1863 and failed. Not decisive enough either to fire or transfer those who opposed and resented Bragg, or to relieve the commander himself, he tolerated a climate of command that led to disaster in the West only two months after an overwhelming victory at Chickamauga.[10]

Lincoln was by far the abler manager of men. A far more revealing letter than that to Grant in April 1864 is his 26 January 1863 letter of appointment to the blustering General Joseph Hooker:

> I have placed you at the head of the Army of the Potomac. Of course I have done this upon what appear to me to be sufficient reasons. And yet I think it best for you to know that there are some things in regard to which, I am not quite satisfied with you. I believe you to be a brave and a skillful soldier, which, of course, I like. I also believe you do not mix politics with your profession, in which you are right. You have confidence in yourself, which is a valuable, if not an indispensable quality. You are ambitious, which, within reasonable bounds, does good rather than harm. But I think that during Gen. Burnside's command of the Army, you have taken counsel of your ambition, and thwarted him as much as you could, in which you did a great wrong to the country, and to a most meritorious and honorable brother officer. I have heard, in such a way as to believe it, of your recently saying that both the Army and the Government needed a Dictator. Of course it was not *for* this, but in spite of it, that I have given you the command. Only those generals who gain successes, can set up dictators. What I now ask of you is military success, and I will risk the dictatorship. The government will support you to the utmost

of its ability, which is neither more nor less than it has done and will do for all commanders. I much fear that the spirit which you have aided to infuse into the Army, of criticising their Commander, and withholding confidence from him, will now turn upon you. I shall assist you as far as I can, to put it down. Neither you, nor Napoleon, if he were alive again, could get any good out of an army, while such a spirit prevails in it.

And now, beware of rashness. Beware of rashness, but with energy, and sleepless vigilance, go forward, and give us victories.[11]

This letter, which remained private until Hooker's death, shows Lincoln at his best. It is, indeed, a model for a leader dealing with a flawed, willful, but energetic and useful subordinate. It showed Hooker that the president saw through him, understanding his faults no less than his virtues, and it administered both rebuke and encouragement with a paternal air of concern that seems to have engendered neither resentment nor misunderstanding. Perhaps it is no coincidence that Hooker, whatever his other defects as a leader and despite his squabbles and feuds with other generals, thereafter obeyed Lincoln without a murmur.

Lincoln had the art, which he shared with the greatest of all Civil War field commanders, Robert E. Lee, of making use of able but flawed subordinates who could not abide one another. Lee managed to create an efficient team of the fanatical Stonewall Jackson, the dour James Longstreet, the flamboyant J. E. B. Stuart, and others, all united only by a common devotion to their commanding general and the larger cause. Lincoln managed an even more difficult task, harnessing the energies not only of a wide variety of military officers but of his wily and manipulative secretary of state, William Seward, his abrasive secretary of war, Edwin Stanton, and other members of a Cabinet that included his political enemies and rivals as well as his friends. Seward, who had intended to serve as de facto prime minister to the gawky Western president, became instead his most devoted servant; Stanton, who had mocked Lincoln as president—and in his previous career, treated him shabbily in the legal profession—became his chosen instrument; Salmon P. Chase, who had his own presidential aspirations, found himself maneuvered from the Cabinet to the Supreme Court, but only after ably managing the finances of the war. It is an easy thing for a politician to find docile, second-rate subordinates who will serve him loyally; it is a far more impressive achievement to mold fractious, ambitious, even disloyal but first-rate subordinates into a winning team.

At the same time Lincoln was no less willing than Davis, and in fact rather more so, to dismiss men who failed to perform. By comparison with our recent presidents, Lincoln was an exceptionally unforgiving boss. His first commander of what would become the Army of the Potomac, Irwin McDowell, lasted barely five months; George McClellan did better (roughly a year); John Pope scarcely two months. McClellan in his second tour of duty lasted a bit more than a month; Ambrose Burnside less than three months; Joseph Hooker, five months; and George Meade nominally almost two years, although in truth he was effectively superseded by Ulysses S. Grant within nine months.

Despite Lincoln's humanity he not only tolerated but fostered the ruthlessness needed to wage a total war. His injunction to the dogged Grant in the late summer of 1864 to "hold on with a bulldog grip, and chew and choke as much as possible,"[12] was but one indication of the same resolve that manifested itself in an insistent demand to his commanders that they close with and destroy the enemy. It was manifested as well in General Orders 252, which declared that for every Union soldier executed by the Confederates one rebel prisoner would be killed by the Northerners, and for every Negro Union soldier enslaved, one Southerner would be put to hard labor.[13]

Lincoln brought to war leadership a thoroughly disciplined and educated mind. Though not formally educated, he had mastered not only the texts of his legal profession but Shakespeare and, to a lesser extent, the language of the Bible. A moment's reflection will recall that both are steeped in military knowledge—of the agonies of warfare, of the character of warriors, and of the choices war leaders must make. He borrowed books from the Library of Congress to learn about war, although just how much he read remains a matter of dispute.[14] Unlike many autodidacts, Lincoln had not merely a powerful intellect but an extraordinarily orderly and balanced one. More important yet, it had a quality invaluable to anyone who must lead in difficult circumstances: one of his more important subordinates, Assistant Secretary of War Charles Dana, described it as a mind with the remarkable peculiarity that it had no illusions. "He had no freakish notions that things were so, or might be so, when they were not so. All his thinking and reasoning, all his mind, in short, was based continually upon actual facts, and upon facts of which, as I said, he saw the essence."[15] Lincoln's old law partner William Herndon remarked on the combination of cunning and cold, remorseless intellect in Lincoln's prewar law practice: "Any man who took Lincoln for a simple-minded man would very soon wake up with his back in a ditch."[16]

For all the pathos and power of Lincoln's great speeches and letters, his papers often reveal an utterly unsentimental reasoning about human affairs. Consider for example his unpublished opinion on the draft, which begins with a dispassionate analysis of the reasons that impel men to enlist: "Among these motives would be patriotism, political bias, ambition, personal courage, love of adventure, want of employment, and convenience, or the opposites of some of these."[17] In wartime this quality of having no illusions is particularly valuable, yet rare. Clausewitz asserts that "War has a way of masking the stage with scenery crudely daubed with fearsome apparitions,"[18] an observation as true for those in the highest headquarters as for those in the field. The history of warfare reveals many leaders who before a clash of arms have wildly unrealistic mental images of catastrophe or triumph. By contrast, one of Lincoln's peculiarities was an unwillingness to forecast the consequences of military operations, to indulge in either illusion. His secretaries observed:

Throughout the tedious four-years' war he pretended to no prophecy and recorded no predictions. When souls of little faith and great fear came to him with pertinacious questioning, he might possibly tell them what he had done; he never told them what he intended to do. "My policy is to have no policy," was his pithy axiom oftentimes repeated; whence many illogically and most mistakenly inferred him to be without plans or expedients.[19]

He had his hopes and his desires, but he did not commit the strategic sin that Napoleon once described, of "making pictures" of the world as one wishes it to be, rather than as it is.

"HE ALMOST LIVED IN THE TELEGRAPH OFFICE."

Lincoln's skills at managing men, and the power of his intellect in understanding his predicament, were all the more crucial because of the peculiar challenge of high command during a time of upheaval in military affairs more generally. The Civil War has often been described as a pivotal conflict in military history because it witnessed a transformation of warfare driven by three elements: the rifle, the railroad, and the telegraph.[20] This transformation had large consequences for the high command of the war, because it meant that the generals were operating with unfamiliar tools. The impact of the communications and logistical revolutions, in particular, would have enormous consequences for the high command of the war—both as to whom Lincoln would select to lead the armies and as to how he himself would conduct the conflict. The generals and the untested president alike faced, in other words, the challenges of war waged with tools that they did not understand and that were carrying their war in directions they could not predict. This transformation of war made Lincoln's art of supreme command both more difficult and more necessary for the Union to win the war.

Indeed, the transformations of the middle and late nineteenth century ushered in the modern era of high command, in which political authority can monitor and direct far-flung military forces in real time. That development, vastly increased today by the advent of telephone, e-mail, and video teleconferencing, was in itself epochal. The no less dramatic transformation of weapons and logistics meant that henceforth every war would present a new set of problems to statesman and general alike. No matter what game they had practiced in peacetime, henceforth every match would take place on an unfamiliar field with new rules and different implements.

The technological quantum leap of Civil War weaponry extended not only to the rifle but to a variety of weapons, including mines (both contact and electrically detonated), primitive submarines, proto--machine guns, rifled artillery, incendiary shells, and improved artillery fuses of various types. The war took place as the world's armies were completing the change from the smooth-bore musket, familiar since the end of the seventeenth century, into a far more formidable firearm. Rifling (i.e., the manufacturing of a firearm's barrel with a groove cut in it, causing the projectile to spin) and the use of the cylindro-conoidal Minié ball, rather than the spherical musket ball of the old days, meant that the individual soldier's weapon now had an effective range of several hundred yards or more, as opposed to a fraction of that in former times. Massed attacks by infantry on well-defended positions, particularly if they were protected by a minimum of field entrenchments, were guaranteed to be exceptionally sanguinary affairs. The rise of the rifle helps account for the difficulty of Civil War generals in consummating their victories. Their drill manuals remained those of the Napoleonic age, with tight formations for the offense and inadequate attention to the importance of entrenchments covered by obstacles and entanglements. At Cold Harbor on 3 June 1864 some seven thousand federal troops fell in less than an hour to Confederate rifles and artillery. On 29 November 1863 James Longstreet, the Confederate commander with perhaps the greatest respect for the power of the rifle in the defense, nonetheless launched an assault against a small but obstacle-strewn Union position (including wire entanglements) at Fort Sanders, Tennessee. The defending Northern force of perhaps 250 men and a dozen artillery pieces inflicted over eight hundred casualties on the attacking Confederate force of several thousand, at a cost of scarcely a hundred Union casualties, of whom all but thirteen were in supporting units outside the fortification. In this and numerous other cases assaults on field fortifications proved ruinous, in large part due to the power of the new weapons available to defending infantry.

Moreover, the Civil War saw the introduction of more powerful weapons yet, particularly the breech-loading, magazine-fed carbine and rifle, which enabled troops to load and reload while lying down and fire at a rate hitherto considered impossible. These weapons, never introduced in great enough quantity to be decisive, nonetheless had a powerful effect towards the end of the war; Confederate forces were stunned by the volume of fire produced by relatively small numbers of Union troops equipped with them. One Union officer at the end of the war took part in an infantry-style rush by cavalry armed with Spencer repeating carbines. He recalled being told by prisoners "that it was useless to try to stand against our seven shooters. . . ." One rebel officer confessed, "The men are really afraid of the seven shooters, they dread them, a panic seems to possess them as soon as they see them coming."[21] By and large, only the cavalry had these guns, and usually as carbines, which had less range and accuracy than heavier rifles. Even so, at short ranges the psychological as well as the material impact of these weapons was devastating.

Lincoln took a personal interest in the development of Civil War firearms, including test-firing the main types, establishing personal contacts with the responsible officers, and even meeting the occasional oddball inventor who was pressing his discoveries upon the irritable and overworked officers of the Ordnance Department.[22] Particularly, early in the war Lincoln repeatedly pressured Ordnance and its hidebound chief,

Brigadier General James W. Ripley, to mass produce breech-loading weapons. Lincoln also intervened to protect and advance the career of one of the more remarkable military technologists of the war: John A. Dahlgren, the Navy's premier ordnance expert. The Union's technological superiority over the Confederacy did not determine the outcome of the war, but it carried increasing weight as the conflict unfolded. Without it, at the very least, the United States Navy could not have maintained its blockade of the Southern coastline and contributed to the deterrence of foreign intervention. Had the war lasted, moreover, the pressure of Northern technology (particularly the repeating breech-loading rifle) would have put the remaining armies of the Confederacy at a crippling disadvantage.

No less important, and in some respects rather more so, was the impact of the railroad on military operations. The railroad system of the United States had grown from less than 3,000 miles of track in 1840 to 10,000 miles in 1850, and to some 30,000 miles by the beginning of the Civil War; despite the destruction wrought by war, an additional 5,000 miles of track were brought into service by the war's end.[23] The railroad exercised a pervasive effect on the war from the outset, when Confederate forces shuttled General Joseph Johnston's forces (including Stonewall Jackson's brigade) from the Shenandoah Valley to Manassas Junction some 35 miles from Washington, where they enabled the South to win the confused battle of First Bull Run (or First Manassas) on 21 July 1861. The railroad allowed both sides, but particularly the Union, to sustain large armies in the field year round, and to resupply those forces relatively quickly after large battles. By the Antietam campaign of September 1862 the Union's logistical superiority had begun to tell, in large part as a result of an intelligent use of the railroads.[24] During the Gettysburg battle in 1863, for example, Union railroads were running 1,500 tons of supplies a day over the Western Maryland line. To get some notion of this achievement: this rate of supply would have sufficed to keep better than two World War II divisions sustained in combat. By the day after the battle, the great Union railroad engineer

Herman Haupt had established a railhead to the battlefield. As Turner, the historian of the role of railroads in the war, points out, "It is farther from Baltimore to Gettysburg than from Richmond to Fredericksburg, yet in four days during the heat of desperate battle Haupt accomplished for Meade what the Confederate organization could not do for Lee in four months of quiet."[25] Throughout the war neither army suffered a crippling lack of munitions, and that is at least partially attributable to the railroad.[26]

On occasion, as at First Bull Run, it was even possible to make operational moves by rail. The most impressive examples, on both sides, of the operational possibilities of the railroad appeared during the Chattanooga campaign of September 1863. In advance of that battle the Confederacy attempted over several weeks to move two Confederate divisions under James Longstreet to Chattanooga, a journey of a thousand miles over ten different railroads. Only half his men arrived in time to participate in the fight. Only a week or two later, on 23 September, Secretary of War Stanton, learning of the crisis around Chattanooga, proposed sending 30,000 men there from the Army of the Potomac, and doing so in five days. He bullied his doubtful military subordinates into agreement, and the XI and XII corps were soon on their way. Twelve days after the decision 25,000 men and their impedimenta, including artillery and baggage, had made the 1,100-mile trip to the West.[27] The Union had the infrastructure and—no less important—the organizational talent to move a force several times as large as the Confederates could muster twice as fast over the same distance.

The railroad could limit armies even as it sustained them. General William Tecumseh Sherman's painful advance to Atlanta from May through November 1864 could not have occurred without the construction and maintenance of a 472-mile supply line stretching all the way back to Louisville. It was a Herculean undertaking, the advance from Chattanooga to Atlanta alone requiring the building of no fewer than eleven bridges for the railroad. On the other hand, Sherman found himself hampered by the need to sustain rail lines to the north, where they lay vulnerable to Confederate guerrillas and cavalry. Modern generals had, therefore, a new problem of supply with which to cope, and the result was innovation in a number of areas, including the creation of new organizations to construct and maintain the railroads.

The third element of revolutionary change in the conduct of war was the advent of the telegraph, which transformed not only field command itself but, more importantly, the relationship between national command authorities and military leaders in the field. The telegraph had had only negligible military effects on the Mexican War, although there were some communications from Washington to New York (where General Winfield Scott had his headquarters) early in that war.[28] By January 1848 over 2,000 miles of telegraph lines were in operation—their expansion driven, at least in part, by the insatiable hunger of newspapers for war news.[29] The exponential growth of telegraph lines, however, occurred after the Mexican war. By 1850 12,000 miles of telegraph lines were in operation, and perhaps five times that much at the time of the outbreak of the Civil War. During the war the Confederacy had difficulty maintaining its prewar telegraph lines. The Union, however, not only expanded its civilian telegraphy (completing the first transcontinental telegraph in early 1862), but created a separate military telegraph system, which by war's end operated some thousands of miles of line, including underwater cables.[30] By 1864 field telegraph units were keeping army commanders in touch with corps headquarters, and generals found themselves using the telegraph scores of times a day within their own commands.[31] The volume of telegraphed communications during the war was enormous. In one year alone the military telegraph system handled some 1,800,000 messages, a phenomenal volume of traffic for the time. In 1864 alone, a thousand men worked constructing, maintaining, and operating over 5,000 miles of military telegraph lines.[32]

Perhaps the most important effects of the telegraph, however, were felt on the higher direction of the war. Already at the beginning of the war telegraphy transformed the role of high-level political authority in monitoring events on the battlefield. On Sunday 21 July 1861 an anxious

President Lincoln received telegrams every ten or fifteen minutes from Union forces engaged in the first large battle of the war, First Bull Run.[33] Military telegraphy at the level of high command remained under the control of Secretary of War Edwin Stanton, who had rebuffed efforts by the US Army Signal Corps to gain control of the military telegraph system. The US Military Telegraph was a hybrid of civilian and military authority, arising from the initial confusion of the early period of the war, during which the American Telegraph Company gave the government six months of free use of the wires before Congress belatedly reimbursed it. Lincoln's first secretary of war, the corrupt and incompetent Pennsylvania politician Simon Cameron, allowed the terminus of the emerging telegraph system to go to the headquarters of Major General George McClellan. His successor, the driving and imperious Edwin Stanton, removed the head of the military telegraph from McClellan's headquarters and directed him to connect the wires to the War Department headquarters, with only enough independent wires to allow McClellan to direct his army.[34]

Next door to Stanton's office, the telegraph room was a refuge for Lincoln, who would pay almost daily visits to read dispatches from the front and to compose replies. The telegraph office was also an intelligence center, since the telegraphers doubled as cryptanalysts, a field in which Union officials believed with some reason that they excelled. Indeed, by 1864 the head of the Signal Corps could report to the secretary of war that "It has now been proven beyond all doubt that the enemy uses the plans of signals first introduced into our armies. His system has stood still, whereas ours has been so improved as to render it secure against any treachery. This enables us to read his signals, while ours can never be deciphered by him."[35] In many respects, then, Lincoln's telegraph office was the direct predecessor of the elaborate Situation Room, with its video screens and computers, that constitutes the command center of the modern American presidency at war. During particularly active days, Lincoln might send a dozen or more messages to generals in the field, and as a battle unfolded he would often spend the night reading message traffic describing it. "He almost lived in the telegraph office when a battle was in progress," recalled the office's manager.[36] And of course Lincoln's immediate subordinates, Secretary Stanton and General Halleck, used the telegraph even more frequently, informing field commanders of newly arrived intelligence regarding their theater of operations.[37] Now senior leaders in the capital could, in at least some limited way, have a better sense of the big picture of the ongoing operations in a theater of war than the local commander—a change fraught with implications for the relationship between the center and the periphery in war.

The combined impact of the rifle, railroad, and telegraph—not just one of these inventions alone—transformed warfare. The rifle made it ever more difficult to consummate victories on the field, and gradually extended the size and scope of combat. The railroad kept armies in the field for longer periods of time, permitted continental movements of large forces with relative speed, and allowed armies to conduct sustained operations without relying exclusively on local supplies of food. The telegraph made the coordination of movements a continent apart a possibility and, because of its connection with the dissemination of news, heightened the political impact of individual battles and engagements. Indeed, it is difficult to imagine the development of the mass newspaper without the telegraph to feed its craving for information. The loose coupling of battle events and political reactions was tightened by the immediacy of telegraphic communication. Collectively, the new technologies increased the importance of high command at the political center: a single field commander could not now hope to duplicate the feats of a Napoleon or Wellington, much though they indeed aspired to do so. There would be no Jena or Austerlitz that could bring this war to an end, nor was it possible for one man to control operations from the field alone. The logistical requirements of modern war, including mass production, centralized acquisition of hardware and supplies, and the movement of vast numbers of men and goods great distances by rail, further reinforced the need for central authority to coordinate and allocate priorities.[38]

Lincoln may not have forged a modern command system, as some historians would have it, but he did preside over one of the first wars in which high command at the center of government would exercise a daily and immediate influence on the conduct of war in the field. No less important, he had to build a military organization adapted to the new conditions of war. Such an organization, however, would have mattered little without a broader set of notions about how the Union should fight its war.

"THESE ALL AGAINST US, AND THE JOB ON OUR HANDS IS TOO LARGE FOR US."

Lincoln's largest responsibility as commander in chief was that of devising a strategy for winning the war—a role that fits, to some extent, the "normal" theory of civil-military relations. He did this at the outset of the war, not in so many words, but in a series of memoranda and letters and through conversations with his key advisers. His fundamental concept was simple, and may be reduced to the following five interlocking propositions.

1. *The war's fundamental aim was the restoration of the Union, but only on the condition that slavery could not be expanded beyond the states in which it existed in 1860.* There would be no Constitutional compromise to secure peace. "Have none of it. Stand firm," he wrote to a political colleague in the aftermath of the election of 1860, referring to potential compromises on the extension of slavery. Lincoln would stand ready to make peace on generous terms, but none that would allow the real cause of the war—the insistence of the South on the right to expand slave-holding territory—to prevail. The desire of the Southern states to reverse a natural and desirable trend toward the extinction of slavery was, in his view, the cause of the war.

2. Although war was inevitable in the absence of Southern yielding on this point, *the war had to begin with acts of Southern aggression*, if only to keep an initially fragile coalition in the North together. For this reason, the South had to fire the first shot at Fort Sumter. Furthermore, the Union could not afford to antagonize the pro-Union slave states—including Delaware, Maryland, and Kentucky. Explaining to Orville Browning why it was necessary to reverse John C. Frémont's premature acts of manumission in the West, he wrote, "I think to lose Kentucky is nearly the same as to lose the whole game. Kentucky gone, we can not hold Missouri, nor, as I think, Maryland. These all against us, and the job on our hands is too large for us."[39]

3. *The Confederacy must be deprived of external support, and the active intervention of European powers—Britain above all—prevented, either by accommodation or by threat.* In this respect Lincoln diverged sharply from the view of his secretary of state, William Seward, who during the crisis of 1860–61 suggested using a foreign crisis to restore national unity. To the extent that this meant accepting some infringements of American rights of war at sea, Lincoln would do so. The so-called *Trent* affair of November–December 1861, in which the United States repudiated the action of an overzealous naval officer who had taken two Southern commissioners from a British ship, was probably the most delicate moment in Anglo-American relations during the war.

4. *To achieve ultimate victory Union armies would have to crush their Confederate counterparts.* "The strength of the rebellion is its military—its army," Lincoln wrote—and not, he implied, its capital, its territory, or even its population.[40] Lincoln adhered to this view consistently, beginning with his insistence on operations against the Confederate army around Manassas in the summer of 1861 and continuing to the end of the war. "I think *Lee's* army and not *Richmond*, is your true objective point."[41] The

war would not be won by maneuver but by hard fighting; it would not end with the fall of Richmond or any other geographical location, but with the collapse of the enemy's army.

5. *The most efficacious means of achieving the destruction of the Confederate armies was by a concerted offensive around the circumference of the South, thereby allowing the numerical and material superiority of the Union to come into play.* In a number of memoranda written in the early part of the war Lincoln made this point.[42] The blockade, accompanied by simultaneous offensives, would be the key to victory—not necessarily an offensive in any single part of the country.

Put thus, the Union strategy seems clear enough. In fact, however, four of these propositions would require modification in the course of a prolonged and difficult war. As often occurs in war, the fundamental objectives changed as a result of the interactions that the fighting brought about. The "normal" theory of civil-military relations presents the statesman as the setter of goals and the designer of the outline of the war, but fails to take into account the ways in which the conduct of war causes objectives and strategic methods alike to change. Lincoln's original strategic concept, reasonable though it was, could not and did not stand the test of struggle. The changes that he found necessary reflect not the inadequacy of his original conceptions but the nature of war itself, which compels those who wage it to change their goals and courses of action no less than their techniques. It is, indeed, in his ability to adapt, and not in the capacity for grand design, that a war statesman finds his largest test.

Although the war was not initially a war to end slavery—"If I could save the Union without freeing any slave I would do that"[43]—it became such. It thus became a revolutionary struggle, against Lincoln's will. As James McPherson put it, "It was *the war itself,* not the ideological blueprints of Lincoln . . . that generated the radical momentum that made it a second American revolution."[44] Scholars disagree as to whether

Lincoln embraced this change or resisted it as long as possible. It is, in any event, clear that the war assumed a character which he had anticipated but had not desired. Once that had occurred—certainly by the late summer of 1862—Lincoln did not look back. Accepting the expansion of the Union's objectives he did not cling to his original, more limited goal, which could no longer suffice to mobilize domestic support or to deter foreign intervention.

The second and third elements of Lincoln's strategy—the preservation of Union control of the border states and the isolation of the Confederacy abroad—succeeded, albeit with great difficulty. His hope of clinging to the border states through a combination of restraint and judicious use of force, particularly in the first six months of the war, came under strain. Particularly in Missouri, zealous Unionists radicalized an already pro-Southern population, guaranteeing years of guerrilla warfare. The exploitation of anti-slavery sentiment in Britain to prevent that country (and with it France) from intervening in the war required, ultimately, emancipation of the slaves. Lincoln would probably have chosen this route in any event, but it contributed to a further and unwelcome intensification of the war.

The fourth tenet of Lincoln's strategy, the destruction of the Confederate army, proved far more difficult than the president ever anticipated. After First Bull Run, it was clear that the suppression of the army of the rebellion would take years. Moreover—and this did not become clear until 1863—the indispensable crushing of the Confederate armed forces would have to be complemented by a strategy of raiding, directed at the morale and will to fight of the Confederacy's civilian population.[45] Lincoln appears to have thought that in many sections of the South the appearance of federal forces would allow pro-Union populations to rise up and overthrow the rebel government. With notable exceptions, however, such spontaneous uprisings did not occur. The war had to become "the hard war" of 1864–1865.[46]

Finally, a concerted offensive, though desirable in theory, proved impossible to execute in practice until 1864. Even then, only two of the five thrusts envisioned—Grant's pursuit of Lee and Sherman's march through Georgia and later South Carolina—were successful. Earlier efforts to act aggressively in the West, and in particular to link up with a Unionist population in the mountains of western Tennessee, failed.

Thus, although the principal tenets of Lincoln's strategy—his "theory of victory"—proved sound, they required substantial modification in practice. As James McPherson points out, sometimes the changes were matters of timing—most notably the Emancipation Proclamation, which freed Southern slaves as a war measure, and which was exquisitely timed to produce the desired effect at home and abroad.[47] But the central point remains: even the soundest strategic concept could not survive the crucible of war unmodified. Even a man with Lincoln's political wisdom could not foresee the course of a great war; he would have to adjust and change course although his ultimate objectives remained the same. To do this, he would need to do much more than merely find the right leaders—but find them he must.

"THE GOVERNMENT DID NOT KNOW HOW TO UTILIZE THE PROFESSIONAL SKILL AT ITS DISPOSAL."

Lincoln's tasks, then, extended far beyond picking generals—but that does not diminish the importance to him of finding the generals who could adapt to the new means of war and follow his evolving strategic design. No American general other than the octogenarian Winfield Scott had commanded even so large a force as ten thousand men in wartime, let alone the armies of a hundred thousand or more that were now forming. As is the case in most wars, generals faced problems of leading organizations quite different from those they had known in peacetime. More than one critic of Lincoln has berated him for appointing "political generals" and failing to make adequate use of his military advisers. "The government did not know how to utilize the professional skill at its disposal," were the bitter words of Major General Emory Upton in 1880, reflecting at least in part the antipathy of West Pointers for civilian generals; this criticism has persisted.[48]

In fact, the quality of the professional military officers in the Civil War requires some close examination. Those who reached general officer rank in the Union Army fell into four groups: long-service professionals; veterans who had left the military after five or ten years of service; young men who rose through the ranks during the war itself; and civilians without military experience. Each of the four groups displayed a mixture of ability and incompetence. The veterans—men who had joined the Army and never left—included some stalwarts of the Union Armies. Winfield Scott Hancock and John Reynolds, for example (USMA '40 and '41), saved the day at Gettysburg; they were the best of the old school, in some ways—staunch, alert disciplinarians who led corps in the Army of the Potomac through a series of bloody engagements and sustained its morale during long stretches of frustrating setbacks. George Thomas (USMA '40) performed similar services in the West, earning the sobriquet "the Rock of Chickamauga" for his stubborn defense of the Union line after a lucky Confederate breakthrough shattered William Rosecrans's Army of the Cumberland at the battle of Chickamauga in September 1863. These and other professional officers were not shunted aside at the beginning of the war: in fact, Lincoln turned to them first to lead the new armies. Most of them had served with distinction in the Mexican War. None of them, however, had had military education beyond their undergraduate training at West Point, which had focused on engineering. Moreover (and unlike the case of Lee in the South), few of them had come to the most senior levels of command during a war, which would have weeded out incompetents with remarkable swiftness. Furthermore a fair number of the professional soldiers, including some of those most highly regarded at the outset of the war, proved themselves inept at high command.

Samuel Heintzelman (USMA '26), for example, though personally brave, blanched at the thought of attacking the sham Confederate fortifications on the peninsula of Virginia in 1862, and proved so clumsy at the handling of a corps at the second battle of Bull Run (29–30 August 1862) that he was relegated to administrative commands thereafter. Don Carlos Buell (USMA '41) successfully thwarted a Confederate invasion of Kentucky in the autumn of 1862 but failed to pursue a beaten foe, and was replaced in October of that year. A younger man, Oliver Otis Howard (USMA '54), had a seemingly successful career despite a series of corps commands in which his forces were overrun (Chancellorsville), shattered (Gettysburg), or merely undistinguished (Chattanooga). The record of the pure professionals, then, was mixed. On balance one would have to say that their contribution to the Union cause was steadiness and organization. Interestingly, some of the most able generals who had never left the military were younger men who started the war as lieutenants newly out of West Point. Emory Upton (USMA '61) ended the war as a major general and a corps commander in the Army of the Potomac. James Wilson (USMA '60), also ended as a major general, commanding William Tecumseh Sherman's cavalry. This group of very young men provided much of the dash wanting in the older group.

More interesting, perhaps, are the semiprofessionals, generals who spent time in the military and then left it for some substantial period of time before returning to active duty. Grant (USMA '43) resigned from the service in 1854; Sherman (USMA '40) doffed the uniform the year before, as did Ambrose Burnside; McClellan (USMA '46) resigned in 1857; Rosecrans (USMA '42) quit the Army in 1854; and Hooker (USMA '37) left in 1853. It was from this class of officers that the armies drew their senior leaders—good, bad, and indifferent. Why this was the case is an interesting question. Perhaps the most ambitious and aggressive men had left the peacetime military; perhaps their experiences in the world beyond the Army had made them more fit for command in the age of transformed armies and logistical systems. (It is no accident, for example, that McClellan was an extremely successful railroad executive in the four years after he left the Army.)

Lincoln's appointment of politicians as general officers excited the anger of writers like Upton after the war. Its importance, however, has been exaggerated. To be sure, some of them proved hopelessly incompetent. Nathaniel Banks, for example, former speaker of the Massachusetts House of Representatives and governor of that state, was twice thrashed by Stonewall Jackson and in 1864 led the abortive Red River expedition. But other civilians had considerably more impressive careers. Some were not politicians at all: Joshua Lawrence Chamberlain, whose importance in history may have been magnified beyond appropriate proportions as a result of Michael Shaara's novel *Killer Angels* (1974) about the battle of Gettysburg, was a professor before the war who became a major general and corps commander. Chamberlain received Lee's surrender at Appomattox, an honor conferred on him by Grant personally. Nelson Miles, a Massachusetts farm boy, rose from the ranks to become a corps commander immediately after the war; ultimately he became general in chief of the Army. John Logan, a Free Soil Democrat from Illinois, served with distinction in the West, commanding a corps and eventually serving as acting commander of the Army of Tennessee. Jacob Cox, an Ohio politician, fought with distinction as a corps commander in the Army of the Potomac and later on out West in the battles of Franklin and Nashville.

Even some of the more notorious politician-generals have a more complicated story to them. Daniel Sickles of New York—who in 1859 had shot his wife's lover (the son of the author of "The Star Spangled Banner," no less) in front of the White House and successfully defended himself using the plea of temporary insanity—has gone down in history as an insubordinate amateur who needlessly exposed the Union left flank to disaster at Gettysburg, where he lost a leg in the action. In truth, he was well liked and respected by his men and their officers in III Corps, which he commanded, and at Chancellorsville he showed both a sound appreciation for terrain and steadiness in his ability to conduct a battle. The egregious Ben Butler, another Democrat who had served as governor of Massachusetts, acquired a reputation for gross incompetence in the siege of Richmond, and for possible corruption earlier in the war. But whatever his faults, it was Butler who had led a Massachusetts regiment to the rescue of Washington in 1861, who conducted several amphibious operations successfully, and who served effectively as military governor of New Orleans. Butler, more than any other general, was eager to exploit the new technologies, including Gatling guns, repeating rifles, flamethrowers, wire entanglements, and armored railroad cars; he was "the first American general to employ aerial reconnaissance" by using a balloonist in the summer of 1861.[49] If he ended up being bottled up by Confederate forces outside Richmond, he was not the only Union general, professional or amateur, who suffered humiliation at the hands of the likes of Lee and Beauregard.

Even Grant, who was generally prejudiced against civilians-turned-generals, turned to a lawyer, John Rawlins, to serve (very successfully) as his chief of staff. Similarly, Joseph Hooker picked as his chief of staff another civilian, Daniel Butterfield, who introduced the system of badges and insignia that gave each corps in the Army a distinctive identity. Moreover, the administrative systems of the Union armies rested on the services of men like Herman Haupt, who organized the Union railroads at the outset of the war, thereby performing an invaluable service—and Haupt had resigned his commission three months after graduating from West Point in 1835.

Politician-generals occasionally received patronage from Lincoln, but rarely without a reason. In many ways the Union resembled a coalition more than an integral state, and often in order to sustain support for the war the president had to turn to political representatives of important constituencies. Pro-war Democrats and German-American immigrants were particularly important, and received much of the preferment. Furthermore more than one politician complained, and with some reason, that incompetent West Pointers often received preferment over more talented civilians. The case of John Logan, who was passed over for command of the Army of Tennessee in favor of the notably less competent Oliver O. Howard, was a case in point.

Lincoln did not have a competent cadre of generals at his disposal, and indeed *competence* itself was and is a slippery term. When the war came, none of them (with the possible exception of Scott) had the comprehensive military experience Lincoln required. Nevertheless some of these men, such as McClellan, were excellent drill masters, suitable for organizing an army and teaching it the fundamentals of its business, but no more. Others could provide outstanding service, but only in particular tasks (cavalry raiding, for example) or particular operational contexts (e.g., defense). Still others would show their talents only after a series of errors and mishaps that called their abilities into question. This is most notably true of Sherman and Grant. The former's mental instability and the latter's alcoholic bouts and failure on the first day of Shiloh raised doubts about their military qualities that took some time to dispel. Lincoln had to develop his own military judgment in order to know which personal traits and military failures to ignore and which bespoke a fundamental unfitness for the job. None of these military leaders were perfect: all made mistakes from rashness (Grant at Cold Harbor) or caution (Sherman in the Atlanta campaign) and late in the war as well as early.[50] For Lincoln, as for most leaders in wartime, picking generals was bound to be a process of cultivation and weeding rather than, as in peacetime, one of selection from a small, well-defined pool.

"WATCH IT, EVERY DAY AND HOUR, AND FORCE IT."

Finding the right generals was only a prerequisite for strategic success; directing them proved for Lincoln, as for other war statesmen, the critical matter. The strategic principles that Lincoln had laid out required modification in practice, and their execution required his active monitoring and intervention. It would not be enough to articulate these principles once or twice: they would have to be inculcated in commanding officers who often thought, and occasionally acted, in opposition to them. In no case is this more clear than in Lincoln's repeated interventions to deal with the problem of spontaneous acts of emancipation by Union commanders operating in the South. From the outset of the war slaves ran away to the safety of the Union garrisons as they began to be established in the territory of the Confederacy. More than one overeager commander used this as an occasion to begin a process of emancipation; that process would radicalize the war well before Lincoln was prepared for such a move. On a number of occasions Lincoln moved to thwart such efforts, as in May 1862, when he issued a formal proclamation repudiating a putative emancipation of all slaves in Georgia, Florida, and South Carolina by Major General David Hunter, commanding on the Carolina coast.[51]

In what Lincoln probably viewed as a more insidious threat to his strategy, too many Union commanders refused to believe that the war would be won by defeating the enemy in the field. "Lee's army, and not Richmond, is your true objective point," he told the third commander of the Army of the Potomac, Fighting Joe Hooker, who would fail him like the rest.[52] Small wonder the palpable sense of relief in his dispatches to Grant upon discovering a general who acted in accordance with this fundamental understanding of the war.

More sinister in Lincoln's view than the defensiveness of his early generals—which, after all, had something to do with the quality of the opponents they faced—was his fear that many officers, particularly in the Army of the Potomac, were not merely timid but actually opposed to his policies. More than a few, he thought with good reason, wanted to see a compromise peace with the South. McClellan's views were not that far from this point of view, of course; but it had spread further than that. On 26 September 1862 Lincoln wrote personally to Major John J. Key, aide-de-camp to the general in chief, Henry Halleck, and brother to Colonel Thomas M. Key, one of the closest aides to General McClellan, a former Senator and prominent Democrat. The president said that he had been informed that Major Key had, in private conversation, been asked by a fellow officer, Major Levi C. Turner, "Why was not the rebel army bagged immediately after the battle near Sharpsburg?" and that Key had replied,

> That is not the game. The object is that neither army shall get much advantage of the other; that both shall be kept in the field till they are exhausted, when we will make a compromise and save slavery.
>
> I shall be very happy if you will, within twenty-four hours from the receipt of this, prove to me by Major Turner, that you did not, either literally, or in substance, make the answer stated.[53]

Key and the officer with whom he had spoken (who strongly vouched for Key's loyalty to the Union cause) appeared the next day before Lincoln. They could not deny that Key had made those remarks. Lincoln gave Key a letter, which read in part that "it is wholly inadmissible for any gentleman holding a military commission from the United States to utter such sentiments as Major Key is within proved to have done." He forthwith dismissed Key from the service, observing grimly to a secretary "that if there was a 'game' ever among Union men, to have our army not take an advantage of the enemy when it could, it was his object to break up that game." On 24 November 1862 Lincoln wrote a second letter to Major Key, who had just submitted a collection of letters pleading for reinstatement in the service, forwarded (and probably endorsed) by General Halleck.

One may easily imagine that the time had come for a show of Lincoln's well-known clemency. McClellan was dismissed from command, replaced by the more pliant Ambrose Burnside. Key's contrition was no doubt real, and he had, in addition, made the greatest sacrifice a man could to the Union cause: his son, an eighteen-year-old captain of the Ohio Volunteers, had died of battle wounds only two weeks earlier. Lincoln knew that. His letter to Key began by expressing condolences to the grieving, cashiered major on the death of his son. But the president followed those words of sympathy with these:

I did not charge, or intend to charge you with disloyalty. I had been brought to fear that there was a class of officers in the army, not very inconsiderable in numbers, who were playing a game to not beat the enemy when they could, on some peculiar notion as to the proper way of saving the Union; and when you were proved to me, in your own presence, to have avowed yourself in favor of that "game," and did not attempt to controvert the proof, I dismissed you as an example and a warning to that supposed class. I bear you no ill will; and I regret that I could not have set the example without wounding you personally. But can I now, in view of the public interest, restore you to the service, by which the army would understand that I indorse and approve that game myself? If there was any doubt of your having made the avowal, the case would be different. . . .

I am really sorry for the pain the case gives you, but I do not see how, consistently with duty, I can change it.[54]

It was a hard letter to write to a man who, after all, had just made the greatest sacrifice imaginable to the Union cause, but Lincoln remained adamant. He reviewed the case one last time, two days after Christmas, and concluded, "On full reconsideration, I can not find sufficient ground to change the conclusion therein arrived at."[55] Thus the iron resolve that undergirded Lincoln's well-known kindliness and human sympathy.

Lincoln's ruthlessness in the Union cause was, however, balanced by his judgment about what could be expected. When the Army of the Potomac's General George Meade defeated the Army of Northern Virginia under Robert E. Lee at Gettysburg, the general spoke of driving "the invaders from our soil"—a phrase that infuriated the president.

This is a dreadful reminiscence of McClellan; it is the same spirit that moved him to claim a great victory because "Pennsylvania and Maryland were safe." Will the generals never get that idea out of their heads? The whole country is our soil. . . . Our army held the war in the hollow of their hand and they would not close it. . . . We had gone through all the labor of tilling and planting an enormous crop, and when it was ripe we did not harvest it.[56]

Meade, in a fit of pique, submitted his resignation after learning of Lincoln's desperate disappointment at the failure to completely destroy the retreating Confederates, who had let themselves be trapped with their backs to the flooded Potomac. Lincoln wrote:

. . . my dear general, I do not believe you appreciate the magnitude of the misfortune involved in Lee's escape. He was within your easy grasp, and to have closed upon him would, in connection with our other late successes, have ended the war. As it is, the war will be prolonged indefinitely. If you could not safely attack Lee last Monday, how can you possibly do so South of the river, when you can take with you very few more than two thirds of the force you then had in hand? It would be unreasonable to expect, and I do not expect you can now effect much. Your golden opportunity is gone, and I am distressed immeasurably because of it.[57]

Lincoln never sent the letter. Halleck prevailed upon Meade to withdraw the resignation, and Lincoln refrained from raising the matter again. But when Meade failed to come to grips with Lee in a renewed campaign in September, Lincoln shifted a large part of the Army of the Potomac to the West, there to consummate a victory at Chattanooga, and in the winter of 1863–64 he brought Ulysses S. Grant to the East, to serve not only as general in chief of the armies, but as de facto commander of the Army of the Potomac.[58] Courteous and protective of Meade, whom he probably recognized as a solid, fighting general who would never drive an army to the last clinch, Lincoln did not trust him to fight the final campaign unsupervised—and neither did Grant.

From the first Lincoln tended not to order, but to question, prod, and suggest. He did this, however, after soliciting various sources of military advice. We have mentioned above his willingness to consult junior officers regarding the possibility of relieving Fort Sumter, much to the annoyance of General Scott. When in turn General Scott was replaced by General McClellan, Lincoln continued to consult the retired military leader for advice, visiting him for that purpose at West Point on 24–25 June 1862, in the midst of the Peninsula campaign. Another, more constant military adviser was Ethan Allen Hitchcock. The grandson of the Revolutionary War hero Ethan Allen and author of more than half a dozen books on alchemy and Swedenborgian philosophy, Hitchcock had had an exemplary career, including service as inspector general of Scott's army in Mexico. Lincoln turned to him at several crucial points, including when the president and Secretary of War Stanton suspected that McClellan had left Washington insufficiently protected from Southern attack while the Army of the Potomac sailed for the Peninsula. On that occasion Hitchcock and the adjutant-general, Lorenzo Thomas, reported to the president that McClellan had failed to meet Lincoln's requirement that Washington be kept "perfectly secure" while the Army of the Potomac tried to take Richmond from the Peninsula.[59]

Lincoln also learned directly about the conduct of military operations from personal observation and interviews with senior military leaders. In July of 1862, for example, he visited the Army of the Potomac on the Peninsula, questioning not only McClellan but his chief subordinates on the Army's health, morale, and operational prospects.[60] He repeated such visits to the front on a number of occasions, including on 1–5 October of that year after the battle of Antietam, in April of 1863 before General Hooker's abortive Chancellorsville campaign, as well as immediately thereafter (on 4–6 and 19 April and again on 7 May). He also inspected the front lines during Jubal Early's march on Washington, experiencing hostile fire as he did so (11 July 1864), and shortly thereafter visited Grant at Fortress Monroe to confer with him, bringing him back to Washington for the first week of August, until he had sorted out the command there. Lincoln continued to speak with corps commanders throughout the war, at least until Grant became commander in chief of the Army. Although he often did not like what he heard—he warned Hooker of the cliques that had formed among the senior generals of the Army of the Potomac—he thereby kept his finger on the Army's pulse.[61] And on occasion he acted on the advice of subordinate generals, as when he imposed a corps-level organization on an unwilling George McClellan, who preferred not to see such an aggregation of divisional commands below him.[62]

Perhaps most interesting of all Lincoln's mechanisms of control was his use, together with Stanton, of Charles Dana, assistant secretary of war, as a personal observer of Union armies in the field. Dana, aged forty-four when the war broke out, was assistant managing editor (and owner of a one-fifth share) of the *New York Tribune*. Dismissed by the formidable Horace Greeley because of his political views, he had met Stanton and Lincoln before the war and was, early on, dispatched West as part of a commission "to audit unsettled claims against the quartermaster's department in Cairo, Illinois."[63] In light of his later activities one wonders whether this was the true purpose of his mission.

Be that as it may, after exploring business ventures in cotton trading along the shifting borders of the Union and the Confederacy (a practice he subsequently roundly condemned) Dana was summoned to Washington in March 1863 by Stanton and given a mission. Stanton told Dana that he and the president wanted such information "as would enable Mr. Lincoln and himself to settle their minds as to Grant, about whom at that time there were many doubts, and against whom there was some complaint."[64] Dana's cover was that of "special commissioner of the War Department to investigate the pay service of the Western armies, but your real duty will be to report to me every day what you see." To this end Dana received his own private cipher to use in communications with Stanton. Dana went West and attached himself to Grant, who wisely hid nothing from Dana, despite the misgivings of his staff. In short order Dana became attached to Grant and, in fact, became one of his most articulate defenders in Washington.

Stanton directed Dana to refrain from giving advice to any of the commands to which he was subsequently attached—a prudent order, as Dana subsequently realized.[65] Following the successful Vicksburg campaign, Stanton dispatched Dana to keep an eye on General William Rosecrans and the Army of the Cumberland, which he followed throughout the harrowing Chattanooga campaign. In December of 1863 Dana returned to Washington, where he was subsequently appointed assistant secretary of war. When, in May of the next year, Grant had begun the long campaign that would lead from the Wilderness to the siege of Petersburg and ultimately to the final defeat of the Confederacy, Lincoln personally dispatched Dana to Grant's headquarters—again, with the mission of reporting back regularly on Grant's movements. Dana remained with Grant through the summer, returning to the capital to serve as a liaison between Grant and the War Department during the scare of Jubal Early's march on Washington. From there to the end of the war he was retained in Washington, investigating "defaulting contractors and dishonest agents, and . . . ordering arrests of persons suspected of disloyalty to the Government," as well as running spies against the Confederacy.[66] He was one of the first people Stanton summoned following Lincoln's assassination to help supervise the massive manhunt for the conspirators involved in the murder.

Dana's training as a journalist made him a superb tool for the purposes that Lincoln and Stanton had in mind. A regular and faithful correspondent, his depictions of battle were both accurate and evocative. More valuable, however, was his ability to discern character. Thus his description of Rosecrans at Chattanooga:

> It is my duty to declare that while few persons exhibit more estimable social qualities, I have never seen a public man possessing talent with less administrative power, less clearness and steadiness in difficulty, and greater practical incapacity than

General Rosecrans. He has inventive fertility and knowledge, but he has no strength of will and no concentration of purpose. His mind scatters; there is no system in the use of his busy days and restless nights, no courage against individuals in his composition, and, with great love of command, he is a feeble commander. He is conscientious and honest, just as he is imperious and disputatious; always with a stray vein of caprice and an overweening passion for the approbation of his personal friends and the public outside.

Under the present circumstances I consider this army to be very unsafe in his hands; but do know of no man except Thomas who could now be safely put in his place. Weather pleasant but cloudy.[67]

For the most part, however, Dana simply provided Stanton and Lincoln with a stream of reliable accounts of operations, allowing them to form judgments of the commanders concerned. His positive view of Grant, which shone through his dispatches, must have gone a considerable way to dispel mistrust of the general based upon his real errors in the Shiloh campaign and the reports—again, based on fact—of his occasional binge drinking.[68] Lincoln, ever a careful reader of dispatches, had a source of information that he could trust, and which could be more copious, blunter, and less self-serving than the usual reports of generals on their own activities.

Even after Grant had won Lincoln's and Stanton's trust, the president kept Dana attached to Grant's headquarters, reporting back on the Union general's movements, a further piece of evidence that Lincoln did not simply turn the higher direction of the war over to Grant. Dana had become a great backer of Grant by this time, but this did not diminish his usefulness. Not only did he remain an acute recorder of military operations, with a journalist's pen but a senior government official's access; as a sympathetic observer he provided Grant insight into the political environment in which the general had to operate. For example,

Dana bluntly warned General Rawlins, Grant's chief of staff, of "the interior truth" of the political realities in the summer of 1864, following a bloody campaign that had cost 70,000 casualties and that had left the capital uncovered against a Confederate raid. Although the responsibility for many of the disasters that had befallen the Army belonged to Generals Butler and Meade, Grant, as general in chief, had chosen to relieve neither. "That is true & there is no answer to it," Dana noted.[69]

As the end of the war approached, Lincoln maintained a close oversight on Grant's activities. On 3 March 1865 he gave Grant strict instructions (through Stanton) that he was to "have no conference with General Lee, unless it be for the capitulation of Lee's army or on solely minor and purely military matters . . . you are not to decide, discuss, or confer upon any political questions. Such questions the president holds in his own hands; and will submit them to no military conferences or conversations. Meanwhile you are to press to the utmost, your military advantages."[70] The president's concern was far from being merely theoretical. A few days after Lincoln's death, on 18 April 1865, Sherman agreed to extremely generous surrender terms for General Joseph Johnston's army, the last major Confederate force in existence. The terms of the agreement included such provisions as the recognition by the United States government of the Southern state governments, including an agreement that where conflicting claims to state powers existed these would be submitted to the Supreme Court; full political rights to all Southerners; and a general amnesty—all policies that had not been countenanced by the Lincoln administration.[71] On Stanton's orders Grant promptly instructed Sherman to revoke this armistice agreement; and Secretary of War Stanton issued a public repudiation of it which left Sherman outraged—to the point that he publicly refused to shake Stanton's hand at the Grand Review of the Armies in Washington a month later.[72]

For his part, Grant was nothing if not deferential in his submission to Lincoln's authority, both in deed and in his remarkably thin direct correspondence with the president.[73] A typical expression occurs in a letter of 19 July 1864, in which he pleaded for an additional 300,000 men with whom to prosecute the war: "I give this entirely as my view and not in any spirit of dictation, always holding myself in readiness to use the material given me to the best advantage I know how."[74] Revealingly, Lincoln replied that Grant must not have seen his call for 500,000 more the previous day. Grant showed, more than any other of Lincoln's generals, an astonishing docility in any matter touched by politics, and a similar lack of impatience at the president's queries, suggestions, and observations.

Lincoln's involvement in current operations did not end with Grant's appointment as general in chief. During the last Confederate invasion of the North, Jubal Early's raid on Washington in July 1864, Lincoln again took an active role. It was Stanton and Lincoln who first became uneasy about Early's whereabouts, in contrast to the more optimistic view in Grant's headquarters that the Confederates had not yet moved very far north.[75] Lincoln suggested that Grant return to Washington not so much to put the city's defenses in order as to arrange the destruction of Early's army. Grant dispatched the troops but remained in Petersburg, and Lincoln continued to monitor operations, corresponding with various generals involved. The pursuit was complicated by divided lines of authority and by the unwillingness or inability of General Halleck, the Army's chief of staff, to unify the various forces assembled in the Washington area as ordered by Lincoln.[76] Lincoln then summoned Grant to a meeting at Fort Monroe on 31 July, the day after an abortive assault on Lee's army at Petersburg. Still dissatisfied with the vigor of the Union operations against the Confederate forces—which had just burned down the town of Chambersburg during a raid into Pennsylvania from positions in the Shenandoah Valley—he followed up with a stiff message to Grant.

I have seen your dispatch in which you say "I want Sheridan put in command of all the troops in the field, with instructions to put himself South of the enemy, and follow him to the death.

Wherever the enemy goes, let our troops go also." This, I think, is exactly right, as to how our forces should move. But please look over the dispatches you may have received from here, ever since you made that order, and discover, if you can, that there is any idea in the head of any one here, of "putting our army *South* of the enemy" or of following him "to the *death*" in any direction. I repeat to you it will neither be done nor attempted unless you watch it every day, and hour, and force it.[77]

Grant came to Washington the next day. In the course of the next few days he reorganized the multiple military jurisdictions of the Atlantic states, creating the Army of the Shenandoah and placing it under Major General Philip Sheridan, who did indeed follow Early to the death.

"CAMPAIGN AND STATECRAFT ARE SIAMESE TWINS, INSEPARABLE AND INTERDEPENDENT."

Lincoln's oversight of military operations did not end until his death. It changed over time, to be sure: his confidence in Grant, although not absolute, was strong enough to allow him to relax the supervision which he had exerted over the general's predecessors. Nonetheless, in the matter of peace negotiations and during an operational crisis he had no hesitation about asserting his authority. He remained, as he had been at the beginning of the war, deeply immersed in the details of military operations, following to the end the actions of armies and the dispatches of commanders. To the end, his reading of military operations was usually as good as, and often better than, that of his generals.[78]

Like many political leaders Lincoln often preferred to work indirectly, using Henry Halleck and Edwin Stanton as intermediaries, although rarely disguising his own role. One often finds in the dispatches of both men to generals in the field references to the president's instructions to them. Although Stanton embraced authority where Halleck all too often evaded it, both knew who the master was in the White House. For his part, Lincoln used both men for their strengths while accepting their weaknesses. Halleck provided Lincoln with technical expertise, serving as a kind of military translator to the commander in chief. Although often caricatured as a fussy and evasive administrator—"an emptiness surrounded by an education" as one critic put it—Halleck had genuine merits. He had the respect of more than one major commander. Sherman wrote to his brother, Senator John Sherman, in December 1863: "Halleck has more capacity than anybody in the Army. Grant has qualities Halleck doesn't, but not such as would qualify him to command the whole Army. The war hasn't developed his equal as a commander in chief."[79] A man who had won the sobriquet "Old Brains," he was a sound soldier of an earlier generation, who perhaps never quite came to terms with the revolution in warfare of his time.[80] The author of well-thought-of texts on military affairs and international law, he was, in the harsh words of Lincoln's secretary of the Navy, Gideon Welles, "a pretty good critic of other men's deeds and acts," but incapable of acting with vigor through a want of "readiness, courage and heart."[81] Not a strong man in an emergency—Lincoln clearly believed that he had failed him during the Army of the Potomac's crisis of self-confidence in December 1862, and again in the alarming days of Early's raid on Washington in the summer of 1864—he nonetheless provided useful service as a man to handle the flow of messages between the civilian leaders and their far-flung armies.[82] When Grant became general in chief he had no desire to replace Halleck as chief of staff, although Halleck had not treated Grant overly well earlier in the war. "One of the greatest men of the age," Grant called Halleck in April 1862, although he surely changed that view by the war's end.[83]

Halleck served Lincoln as a conduit of communication, a translator, and an administrative supervisor—not a unique role, as we shall see in later chapters. Edwin Stanton was an altogether different figure, a man of enormous energy, ambition, and temper. A War Democrat who had done his best to preserve the government during the crisis of the winter of 1860–61, when the administration of James Buchanan was dissolving in a welter of conspiracy and disunion, Stanton had previously been a successful professional rival of Lincoln. He had, until his appointment, shared the same disparaging view of the president widely held in Washington circles. From that moment on, however, he gave Lincoln the full measure of his considerable talents.[84] Lincoln dominated—"[the president] was the War Minister," Secretary of State Seward remarked after the war—but the relationship was one of exceptional closeness.[85]

Stanton mistrusted most military officers, believing that they lacked the full zeal needed to finish the work of reunion. His explosion at Sherman's outrageous violation of instructions in his armistice with Johnston must be understood in that context.[86] Lincoln and Stanton developed a close relationship, and Lincoln often strolled into Stanton's office to examine the telegrams and confer on military operations at all hours of the day or night. Stanton made more than his share of enemies in Lincoln's Cabinet and among general officers, but that did not diminish his utility to the president, whose most urgent requirement was energy in the war effort. That Stanton provided, from the day of his appointment to the end of the conflict.

We have seen in our previous chapter a conventional understanding of the traditional role of a civilian war leader: setting the broad outlines of policy, mobilizing resources, and selecting the most senior commanders. Lincoln faced these tasks, which were weighty enough, not least because they required conflicting choices. The senior commanders who adhered most wholeheartedly to the policy of the president did not necessarily have the greatest military talents, or vice versa. In part for that reason, Stanton and Lincoln—reasonably enough—demonstrated some partiality to politicians-turned-generals, amateur soldiers who had both the energy and desire to crush the rebellion that some of the more skilled experts lacked. At the same time, they had to mobilize the energies of the North through actions that did not necessarily translate into the most efficient allocation of resources. Thus the North's pernicious habit of raising new regiments to supplement forces depleted by combat, rather than drafting individuals to rebuild the old units. This practice created an excessive number of understrength units and deprived the new soldiers of the stiffening they would have acquired from the presence of veterans. At the same time, however, it allowed political leaders in the North, including the all important war governors, to use their political patronage and to capitalize on the political impact of the raising of new regiments.[87]

Yet difficult as these traditional tasks of civilian war leadership may have been for Lincoln, they constituted only part of his understanding of his responsibilities as commander in chief. In practice, he did much more: Lincoln had not merely to select his generals, but to educate, train, and guide them. To this end he believed that he had to master the details of war, from the technology to the organization and movement of armies, if only to enable himself to make informed judgments about general officers. At a time of tremendous flux in the art of war itself, military professionals could not be relied upon to make infallible judgments on the means and methods best suited to the tasks at hand. Like any individual, they sometimes favored old friends and colleagues: Sherman's and Grant's prejudice against citizen soldiers and in favor of regulars led to an injustice to John Logan, who certainly deserved corps command, and indulgence to the incompetent David Hunter, who was crushed in the summer of 1864 by Jubal Early.[88] Outstanding military leaders such as Grant or Lee did not always fully appreciate the impact of the new military technologies (in particular, the Minié-ball-firing rifle) nor did military administrators such as Halleck appreciate the potentialities of the new civilian technologies such as the railroad. And even when the war had settled into a more or less comprehensible tactical and technical pattern, commanding generals could misread the military situation. Grant's failure to appreciate early enough Early's intentions in the attack on Washington, and his delays in taking the appropriate organizational and personnel decisions to create the force that would destroy the Confederate raiders, provide an instructive example. Focused, as generals often are, on the immediate theater and the task at hand—in this case the siege of Petersburg, and the synergy of his own efforts to destroy Lee while Sherman's army devastated the heartland of the South—Grant temporarily lost a broader picture of the war. And if this happened to Grant, who more than any other general had the vision and will to see the war on a continental basis and to prosecute it accordingly, it could happen to lesser men.

Lincoln had to educate his generals about the purposes of the war and to remind them of its fundamental political characteristics. He had not merely to create a strategic approach to the war, but to insist that the generals adhere to it. His subordinates did not always agree with him or with one another, and indeed, he often found himself having to arbitrate disputes among general officers at odds with each other over matters weighty or trivial. He received, in short, very little in the way of unified military advice, and indeed, on more than one occasion found himself confronted with advisers deeply unwilling to provide any advice at all.

Perhaps the best biography of Lincoln was written by two of the men who knew him best during the war, his secretaries John Nicolay and John Hay. Their account of the war does not fit the "Lincoln finds a general" interpretation of Lincoln's tenure as commander in chief. Rather, their description of his struggle to control the conduct of the war most strongly echoes the words of Carl von Clausewitz on the relationship between politics and war. After explaining why Lincoln had found it necessary to order an early offensive against the Confederacy in July 1861, despite the misgivings of his generals, Nicolay and Hay comment:

> Historical judgment of war is subject to an inflexible law, either very imperfectly understood or very constantly lost sight of. Military writers love to fight over the campaigns of history exclusively by the rules of the professional chess-board, always

subordinating, often totally ignoring, the element of politics. This is a radical error. Every war is begun, dominated, and ended by political considerations; without a nation, without a government, without money or credit, without popular enthusiasm which furnishes volunteers, or public support which endures conscription, there could be no army and no war—neither beginning nor end of methodical hostilities. War and politics, campaign and statecraft, are Siamese twins, inseparable and interdependent; and to talk of military operations without the direction and interference of an administration is as absurd as to plan a campaign without recruits, pay, or rations.[89]

It was Lincoln's understanding of the interplay of war and politics, no less than his ability to absorb military detail and to read human character, that made him the greatest of American war presidents.

CHAPTER 3

CLEMENCEAU PAYS A VISIT

On 30 March 1918, at the height of a devastating German offensive in France, the new British minister of munitions, Winston Churchill, went to France at the request of Prime Minister Lloyd George. The heaviest blows had fallen on Britain's Fifth Army, but the French had also fallen back, yielding to a German attack of unprecedented ferocity and technical skill. Allied lines were crumbling and a cataclysmic battle outside Paris loomed. Accompanied by premier Georges Clemenceau, the small party visited the British high command, which asked urgently for French reinforcements.

"Very well," said Clemenceau in English to the company, "then it is all right. I have done what you wish. Never mind what has been arranged before. If your men are tired and we have fresh men near at hand, our men shall come at once and help you. And now," he said, "I claim my reward."

"What is that, sir?" asked [British Fourth Army commander, General Sir Henry] Rawlinson.

"I wish to pass the river and see the battle."

The army commander shook his head.

"It would not be right for you to go across the river," he said.

"Why not?"

"Well, we are not at all sure of the situation beyond the river. It is extremely uncertain."

"Good," cried Clemenceau. "We will re-establish it. After coming all this way and sending you two divisions, I shall not go back without crossing the river. You come with me, Mr. Winston Churchill . . . and you, Loucheur. A few shells will do the general good," pointing gaily to his military *chef de cabinet*.

Bowing to *force majeure*, General Rawlinson provided an escort and the party set off, reaching a position from which they could see the last British soldiers—a thin line about three hundred yards away on a ridge line. Clemenceau descended from his car, and with him the rest of the party.

We remained for about a quarter of an hour questioning the stragglers and admiring the scene. No shell burst nearer to us than a hundred yards. Loucheur and Clemenceau were in the highest spirits and as irresponsible as schoolboys on a holiday. But the French staff officers were increasingly concerned for the safety of their prime minister. They urged me to persuade him to withdraw. There was nothing more to see, and we had far to go before our tour of inspection was finished. The old Tiger was at that moment shaking hands with some weary British officers who had recognized and saluted him. We gave these officers the contents of our cigar-cases. I then said that I thought we ought to be off. He consented with much good humor. As we reached the road a shell burst among a group of led horses at no great distance. The group was scattered. A wounded and riderless horse came in a staggering trot along the road towards us. The poor animal was streaming blood. The Tiger, aged seventy-four, advanced towards it and with great quickness seized its bridle, bringing it to a standstill. The blood accumulated in a pool upon the road. The French general expostulated with him, and he turned reluctantly towards his car. As he did so, he gave me a sidelong glance and observed in an undertone, *"Quel moment délicieux!"*[1]

Even for Churchill, no stranger to flying bullets and in an odd way partial to them ("there is nothing so exhilarating as being shot at without result"), it was a moment to remember. For Clemenceau, however, it was hardly a remarkable occasion; during the year in which he directed France's supreme effort during the war, he visited the front lines roughly once a week. He did so, as we shall see, not out of mere bravado or irresponsible delight in the noise and drama of war—not that he, or any politician, is ever immune to such temptations. Rather, Clemenceau's visits, like Lincoln's letters, reflected a style of wartime civilian leadership as carefully considered as any state paper or formal address, and no less effective. What prompted the old man to spend one day out of seven dodging shells and chatting with soldiers in their trenches? And what did he achieve by it?

THE TIGER

"War is too important to be left to the generals," remains Georges Clemenceau's chief legacy to English-speaking students of military affairs; few of them, however, know anything about how he arrived at or implemented that view. They may know vaguely that he breathed a spirit of resistance into an exhausted France in 1918, and that he attempted to win for a blood-drained country a hard peace with Germany in 1919, but beyond this he is too little known to us. In his own country, the story is different—although there too the trials and triumphs of France after 1919 have tended to put his accomplishments in the shade.

The Tiger, as he was known by 1903, came to power late in life. He had three and a half generally unhappy years as France's minister of the interior and then premier from 1906 to 1909, entering government again only on 17 November 1917, scarcely a year before the end of World War I. He served as premier until January of 1920, having decided to run for the less powerful but more honorific position of president of France, for which office he was defeated. In 1917, when he came to power in France's greatest crisis to that point, he was already seventy-six years old. He had made more than his share of enemies, and would gladly make more. Late in his life he told General Edward Spears, the elegant British liaison officer with the French armies: "I had a wife, she abandoned me; I had children, they turned against me; I had friends, they betrayed me. I have only my claws, and I use them."[2]

Clemenceau, unlike Lincoln, Churchill, or Ben-Gurion, made both war and a fragile but real peace. He struggled with remarkably determined and pronounced personalities—France's two leading soldiers, Philippe Pétain and Ferdinand Foch, and a brilliant but only intermittently cooperative president, Raymond Poincaré, not to mention a host of no less formidable foreigners, including British figures such as the prime minister, David Lloyd George, and the British commander Field Marshal Douglas Haig, and Americans such as the commander of the American Expeditionary Force, General John J. Pershing. Clemenceau led a country that had suffered, as few democracies ever have, the scourge of war. France sustained casualties of 1,385,000 killed and 3,044,000 soldiers and civilians wounded in World War I, in all more than one-tenth of its total population of something under forty million.[3] In purely military terms, the losses were unbelievably great. In 1914 France, with a peacetime army of 823,000, had mobilized a total of 3,781,000 men: its casualties during the entire war, therefore, amounted to virtually the whole of its initial military strength. German troops occupied approximately 10 percent of France's national territory, including its most important coal and iron fields. Twice German forces seemed within reach of the capital, Paris—the undisputed center of French political, social, and economic life—and indeed showered bombs and shells upon it in a display of ferocity that, though a mere irritation by the standards of the Second World War, was nothing less than horrifying and astounding by the standards of the First.

During his time as premier Clemenceau had to shore up the will to fight of an army bled white for three years. The battle of Verdun alone cost France, between February and December of 1916, 162,000 killed or missing in action and at least 200,000 more wounded; as Guy Pedroncini notes, a bell chiming once a minute for each French loss there would ring for four months without pause.[4] Put differently, in that *one* battle, which took place during *one* year of the war, France lost almost three times as many men as the United States did in all of the Vietnam war. It suffered those losses from a population one sixth of that of the United States in the 1960s. One may think of French losses at Verdun alone, in other words, as the equivalent of eighteen Vietnams, suffered in one year.

When Clemenceau became premier Russia was exiting the conflict, allowing Germany to turn its full force on the staggering Allies in the West. The United States had yet to appear in force; Britain had suffered its own hideous losses in the mud of Passchendaele, in a battle that lasted roughly three months—from August through November 1917— costing Field Marshal Haig's British and imperial troops 70,000 dead of their own and 170,000 wounded.[5] Clemenceau saw France through the German offensives of the spring and early summer of 1918—attacks employing, with devastating effect, techniques developed and perfected in the course of the great defensive battles on the Western Front—battles which prefigured the deep thrusts of the war that would break out in Europe twenty years later. He helped maintain the troubled coalition with Britain and the United States (the latter an "associated power," and hence not technically even an ally), to eventual victory. Finally, he presided over the negotiation of a peace treaty that, however flawed, restored to his country the lost provinces of Alsace and Lorraine, left Germany constrained though not crippled, and provided France, if she had the will to maintain them, positions on the bank of the Rhine to repel a possible future German bid for power.

These achievements had many aspects. Three will occupy us here: first, Clemenceau's style of command, which involved a remarkable degree of firsthand examination of the battlefield; second, his management of the triangular relationship between himself, Foch (who eventually became the supreme allied commander), and Pétain (commander in chief of France's armies on the Western Front), including his disputes with Foch over how to handle American reinforcements; third, his handling of the civil-military relations of peacemaking, culminating in his clash with Foch over the terms of the eventual peace treaty. These tasks involved Clemenceau deeply in the management of a coalition in which no country really played a dominating role, and required the control of soldiers whose mastery of the technique of their profession no one could doubt, and themselves least of all.

Clemenceau was born in Brittany in 1841, the son of a fierce opponent of the rule of Napoleon Bonaparte's nephew, Napoleon III. Receiving his medical degree in 1865, Clemenceau journeyed to the United States in that year, stayed for four years, acquired a great respect for the recently assassinated Abraham Lincoln, married an American wife (from whom he divorced in 1892) by whom he had three children, and began a literary career. Returning to France, he was elected to the National Assembly in 1871 and was mayor of one of Paris's *arrondissements* during the uprising that became known as the Commune. From then on he mixed medicine (to a diminishing degree) with politics and journalism, serving in the Chamber of Deputies from 1876 to 1893 and later in the Senate.

Clemenceau was a Radical Socialist, which meant something quite different from what the words imply today in English. He argued passionately for freedom of the press and of assembly, denounced the death penalty, mocked France's colonial policy, and in the all-consuming Dreyfus affair took the side of the Jewish army captain Alfred Dreyfus, who had been falsely accused of espionage. It was his newspaper *L'Aurore* that on 13 January 1898 published Émile Zola's magnificent denunciation of the anti-Dreyfusards, *J'accuse*. A very large part of "the affair" lay in the uncovering of the General Staff's efforts to frame Dreyfus and then to prevent the truth—the treason of a well-connected aristocratic officer named Ferdinand Esterhazy—from coming out. Clemenceau was fiercely anticlerical—so much so that in contradiction to his liberal principles he opposed the extension of suffrage to women, on the grounds that they would yield too easily to the influence of the Church.

For most of his career, Clemenceau had viewed the French army with mixed emotions. As the thirty-year-old mayor of the Montmartre district in 1871, he failed in an attempt to rescue two generals caught by the Paris mob during the bloody Commune uprising following France's defeat by Prussia and her German confederates the previous year. It was an episode that marked him forever with a disgust for mobs and blood lust; it revealed as well a willingness to stand alone that would characterize him throughout his life. One of the officers whom he did manage to rescue subsequently told the National Assembly in Versailles, "If you had seen how he lashed into the murderers, you could not have imagined how he managed to escape being shot himself."[6]

Clemenceau liked to tell American troops during World War I that he arrived in Richmond just before Ulysses S. Grant. He had managed to interview the American general and was struck by his submissiveness to civilian authority.[7] A Jacobin of the old school, he believed in an army firmly subjugated to civilian authority, but politically neutral. Thus Jean-Baptiste Duroselle sums up Clemenceau's views at the time of the Dreyfus affair: "Long live the Army! Of course, but submissive to civil power; a patriotic and republican army; condemnation of statism (*raison d'État*); rejection of all oligarchical power, particularly that which emanates from the military."[8] It mattered not to the Tiger what the direction of politicization: he abhorred it on the left as much as on the right. He was, for example, disgusted by the *affaire des fiches*, in which French republicans had, through the good offices of the Freemasons, kept files on the affiliations of the officer corps—in particular their religious beliefs. Thousands of slips of paper went to the anticlerical and antimonarchist French Minister of War, who resigned from office in 1904 when the program—which ruined many military careers—became public knowledge. Nevertheless it was the anti-Catholic Clemenceau who, in his first term as premier, appointed Ferdinand Foch, of whom more later, to the important and prestigious command of the French war college, the École Superiéure de la Guerre. According to one account their discussion went as follows:[9]

> "I am offering you command of the Staff College."
>
> "I am grateful to you, M. le Président, but I am sure you know that one of my brothers is a Jesuit."
>
> "I know and I don't care a damn; you will turn out good officers for us and nothing else counts."

A professional man himself, Clemenceau respected professional ability in others, but he was not impressed by uniform or rank per se. "It takes more than a hat with gold braid to turn an imbecile into an intelligent man."[10] Like Ben-Gurion later, he believed that "no science escapes the superior laws of good sense," and acted accordingly.[11] As for the French army as an institution, he wrote at the time of the Dreyfus affair in 1894:

> There is no honor of the army, honor of the judiciary, or the Council of State any more than there is an honor of farmers or cigar sellers. There are personal faults whose consequences should fall only on the guilty. . . . The army is composed of civilians, clothed in a certain fashion and subordinated to a special regime for a certain purpose. Men are neither better nor worse if they wear red pants or gray, a képi or a bowler hat.[12]

No pacifist—how could he be, talented as he was with sword and pistol, and veteran of a dozen duels with rivals in politics and love?— Clemenceau abhorred military adventurism. A consistent critic of French colonial expansion, he helped bring down cabinets that had begun creating a French empire in Indochina, and he denounced French participation in the anti-Boxer expedition in China. Devoted to the cause of the lost provinces of Alsace and Lorraine, he was not a *revanchiste*, although once war came their liberation was one of his chief goals.

Clemenceau knew the French army fairly well; during the war until 1917 he made it his business to know it even better. His newspaper, *L'Homme libre* (*"The Free Man"*) was scathingly critical of the French army's handling of its own wounded, and soon came under the severe scrutiny of military censors, leading Clemenceau to change its name to *L'Homme Enchâiné* (*"Man in Chains"*). In December 1914 he became vice chairman of the Senate's military affairs committee, and three months later assumed the same position on the Senate's foreign affairs committee. In November 1915 he assumed the chair of both committees. He was a strong believer in parliamentary oversight of the war effort, focusing primarily on problems of acquisition, troop morale, and the like; he deplored the failure of the French military to respond adequately to the introduction of chemical weapons, for example, and the unwillingness of the French government to arrest subversives.

Clemenceau's rise to power followed the fall of the Painlevé government in November 1917. Paul Painlevé, a talented mathematician, three times premier and minister of war since March 1917, had assumed the premiership in September of that year following the disastrous Nivelle offensives and the ensuing mutinies in the French army. His outlook in some respects mirrored Clemenceau's, although he was perhaps more defensive in outlook. But in the fashion of the French Republic he succumbed to a wave of scandals. (These included the Bolo Pasha affair, which culminated in the execution of an adventurer who, it turned out, had been a conduit for German money going to a French newspaper owned by one of the senators on the military affairs committee.) The previous governments of René Viviani, Aristide Briand, and Alexandre Ribot had proven unable to control the military or retain public confidence, headed as they were by well-meaning men utterly unsuited to the stresses of war. The war began, in fact, with what Jere Clemens King, the closest student of French civil-military relations during the war, terms a "military dictatorship."[13] Minister of War Alexandre Millerand did his best to prevent any parliamentary visits to the front lines, and went so far as to rebuke the president of the Republic for speaking to army officers without his approval. Not until mid-1916 did parliament begin successfully to assert its right to monitor and call to account the armed forces of France—and even then it faced continuous obstruction in so doing.[14]

General Spears knew the politicians well, and described them accurately if unkindly:

The men to whom the people were used to look for guidance found themselves just like other men, small, puzzled, bewildered, facing a cataclysm their minds could not grasp. Ministers had a little the aspect of marionettes presented without the familiar surroundings of footlights and wings. Their usual animators, well-drilled civil servants, were powerless to actuate them on a stage for which neither experience nor training had equipped them, and the strings usually taut in their hands lay in skeins tangled beyond all unraveling. . . . They seem very inconsequent, very well-meaning, dealing with the war as they would have dealt with unexpected, tiresome or alarming happenings in their own lives. . . .[15]

Clemenceau, but for his accumulation of enemies, might have come to power earlier. Now, however, the highly intelligent but personally hostile president, Raymond Poincaré—whose election Clemenceau had opposed—had little choice but to call on the Tiger.

He did so because the military situation was parlous. The blood-letting had been staggering: the initial battle of the frontiers in 1914 alone had cost the French something like a quarter of a million casualties. This was but a foretaste, for to this were added such débacles as the offensives of the French army in Champagne (September–October 1915, 144,000 casualties), on the Somme (July–November 1916, 195,000 casualties), and the grinding battle for Verdun. The last straw had been the Nivelle offensives of April–May 1917, which had exacted a further 187,000 dead, wounded, and missing Frenchmen. Mutinies had begun to occur in French units, which, though not on the scale often described, were frightening enough. Perhaps 35,000 men were affected by the mutinies (which the troops themselves often referred to more often as strikes), leading to more than five hundred sentences of death (only fifty carried out) and more than 1,300 sentences to five or more years of imprisonment.[16] The Allied expedition to the Dardanelles (in which, one frequently forgets, French troops took part) had failed. Subsequent Allied offensives in the Balkans had led to the creation of a bridgehead based at Salonika, ironically referred to by the Germans as their largest internment camp of the war. British operations in Iraq had bogged down, and the commander there had just died of cholera. British imperial forces were advancing into Palestine, to be sure, and had taken Baghdad, but the collapse of the Ottoman Turks was a long way off. The Italian front had the potential for disaster. In a furious assault from 24 October through 9 November the Austrians and Germans had shattered an Italian army at the battle of Caporetto (also known, more grimly, as the twelfth battle of the Isonzo), inflicting 60,000 casualties (three times as many as their own) and taking a quarter of a million prisoners and more than three thousand artillery pieces.

To this one had to add the collapse of Russia, which meant that Germany might soon be able to turn large forces—42 divisions, more than half a million men—to the West.[17] The only good news lay in the new participation of the United States in the war. But although the

United States had become an associated (not an allied) power in April 1917, its weight was still far from being felt. Not until April 1918 would the Americans hold more of the front line than did the exhausted Belgian army; and although the promise of vast American armies was real (nearly two million would eventually show up in Europe), as yet only between 25,000 and 50,000 men had sailed for France every month from June to November 1917.

It was in these unpromising circumstances that Clemenceau came to power. On 19 November 1917 he addressed the Chamber of Deputies: "[E]verything for France bleeding in its glory . . . the hour has come to be French, and simply French, with the pride to say that that suffices."[18] But would it? Clemenceau would, in later years, be seen simply as the spirit of roaring defiance—*Père la Victoire*, "Father Victory"—rather like Churchill, whom he resembled in many ways. And to be sure, he breathed resolution and determination. On 8 March 1918 he delivered a speech whose refrain, "*je fais la guerre*"—"I make war"—reverberated throughout France:[19]

> You want peace? So do I. It would be criminal to have any other thought. But howls for peace will not silence Prussian militarism.
>
> My formula is everywhere the same. Domestic politics? I make war. Foreign policy? I make war. Always, I make war.
>
> I seek to maintain trust with our allies. Russia betrays us? I continue to make war. Unfortunate Rumania is forced to surrender? I continue to make war, and I will continue to the last fifteen minutes, because it is we who will have that last quarter of an hour!

It was in the same spirit that he growled at his military *chef de cabinet* in May 1918, when Paris itself was in danger, "Yes, the Germans can take Paris, that won't stop me from making war. We will fight them on the Loire, then on the Garonne if we have to, and even on the Pyrénées. And if, finally, we are chased out of the Pyrénées we will continue the war overseas, but as for making peace, never! They will never get that from me!"[20] A few weeks later, he said as much to the Chamber of Deputies: "I will fight in front of Paris, I will fight in Paris, I will fight behind Paris."[21] And, as he remarked in private to his military aide, "As for the two of us, my little one, we will of course be the last to leave on an airplane and rejoin the armies."[22] The spirit of this grizzled seventy-six-year-old was magnificent—and sorely needed. France had, for more than three brutal years, poured its blood into the mud of the trenches. It began the war making a far greater effort in terms of manpower than its main ally, Great Britain. In the spring of 1915, for example, after nine months of war, their forces outnumbered their British counterparts by five to one.[23] Unlike the British, the French could boast neither triumphs at sea nor romantic, if strategically insignificant, conquests abroad; also unlike the British, their strength had begun to wane. Where the British Empire could continue to mobilize divisions and extend its front, France had come to the end of its resources. By December 1917, in fact, the French high command had concluded that it might have to disband as many as twenty-two divisions.[24] French will, furthermore, had weakened—the corrosive effect of mediocre political leadership and a succession of scandals that, in wartime, had lost the darkly amusing quality that had once enlivened peacetime French politics. Clearly, then, Clemenceau would have to put heart back in his exhausted countrymen. But, as we shall see, he did much more than inspire a battered nation and its dispirited leaders.

JOURNAL OF A WITNESS

Clemenceau was an orderly man.[25] He had maintained a rigorous regimen throughout most of his life, and despite occasional medical problems, was a remarkably healthy and vigorous man. Rising at four o'clock in the morning, he would perform a calisthenic routine and receive a massage from what we might today call a personal trainer. He dictated letters constantly, and retained a voracious appetite for the written word. He would dine at home, and retire early, at 9:00 P.M. An irascible man who understood his own character, he would hold off on any personnel decision for twenty-four hours, allowing his judgment to dominate his temper.

For his work as premier and as minister of war, Clemenceau relied on two men: Jean-Jules-Henri Mordacq and Georges Mandel. Mordacq had come to his attention before the war, as a thoughtful soldier who already had several books to his name, including one on politics and strategy in a democracy. Shortly before assuming office, Clemenceau had visited Mordacq at the front, where he was commanding the 24th Division. He asked the general to serve as his military chief of staff (*chef de cabinet*)—which would mean forgoing the promotion to corps command and beyond to which Mordacq seems to have aspired.

Mordacq was a strategic thinker in his own right, but devoted himself to his chief. "We require the closest alliance of politics and strategy," he noted; unlike many officers of his time, he did not see the two as separate.[26] He served, much as Halleck had served Lincoln, but with greater force of character (and possibly greater skill as a diplomat), as an interpreter of military matters and a go-between with the generals. An acute observer of men and of history, he maintained a detailed journal, and given that Clemenceau destroyed many of his own papers before his death, it is upon the "Journals of a Witness" of Mordacq that much of our knowledge of Clemenceau during the war rests.

As his *chef de cabinet* for civil matters, Clemenceau picked Georges Mandel. Born Louis Rothschild, Mandel was cold, discreet, and efficient, a man with a card-index mind—"the kind you could not 'rattle,' whose pulse and mind remained unaffected by events however unforeseen, sudden or shattering," a man suffused with a "reptilian" kind of courage, commented one arch Englishman, "not endearing but wholly enviable."[27] Mandel was Mordacq's equal as an administrator, and it was through him that Clemenceau deployed France's police in the crackdown on defeatism that began almost immediately upon his entry to power. He was responsible for the arrest of Joseph Caillaux, one of France's most prominent politicians, who sought a negotiated peace during the war and was imprisoned and tried for treason after it. Mandel's own end would be tragic. His intelligence and abilities should have brought him to the highest rank, and indeed during the 1930s he served as a minister in the Cabinet, but a combination of fear and anti-Semitism blocked him. A resolute opponent of Hitler, he favored carrying on war despite the calamities of May–June 1940, but could not prevail. Escaping to North Africa, he was returned to France, there to be imprisoned by his enemies in the Vichy regime. Ultimately, in 1944, he was shot by them, saying only, "Dying is nothing; the sad thing is dying before seeing liberation and the restoration of the Republic."[28]

Clemenceau's personal discipline and organization were unusual, but not extraordinary. Where he did depart from the practice of most other war leaders was in his habit of visiting the front lines, which he had begun to do early on in the war while still serving as a senator. The proximity of the front lines to Paris facilitated this, of course, and France's excellent railroad system made trips to other sectors of the front line easy as well. Even so, Clemenceau spent more time on the front lines—within machine-gun range in some cases—than any other war leader of whom we have a record. From January 1918 on he spent an average of one day a week at the front, and sometimes more.

Why did he do this? In part he wished to communicate with general officers at their headquarters, not only to save them a trip to Paris but to take their measure in the field. Mordacq recalls his belief in the imperative of replacing a cadre of general officers who were in many cases exhausted by the strain of war or mutually sheltered by ties of comradeship.[29] Clemenceau was ruthless in purging the army's high command. "It was necessary to cut down generals who were incompetent, tired, or merely unfortunate."[30] He reviewed the selection of generals down to the level of divisional commander, believing that that was the key level of command, and that many of the generals occupying those positions were too old and exhausted to lead properly.[31]

To some extent Clemenceau's visits may be attributed to his desire to see whether or not directives that had been given were being implemented—particularly in the matter of organizing defenses in depth to meet the German onslaughts expected in the spring and summer.[32] As we shall see, he had reason to fear that this change would not be adopted—a fear that led him to order the preparation of detailed maps of the new defensive positions every two weeks.[33] These visits had, as well, broader political purposes. Clemenceau made a point of taking with him senior members of the Senate and the Chamber of Deputies: he hoped thereby to forestall the kind of parliamentary intrusions that had characterized French war direction after the fall of Joffre, France's first commander in chief—a reaction to the military's resistance to civilian control at the outset of the war. Clemenceau's visits revealed seemingly minor breakdowns in the French military's administrative system that had large morale consequences—tobacco shortages and the like.[34] Clearly, his visits were intended to boost morale—both that of the troops and that of the leader himself. The sight of the white-haired old man stomping through the trenches, cane in hand, moustaches bristling, was a tonic to the men. Indeed, years later Clemenceau's coffin contained a single keepsake, a bouquet of dried flowers that he received from soldiers during one of his visits to the front, and that he had kept on his dresser throughout the rest of his life.[35] The French *poilus* wanted to know that at long last there was firm leadership of the war, and this impression Clemenceau certainly gave. This worked both ways; Clemenceau often said that the visits were good for his own morale as well.

The term "management by walking around" was not yet invented—it would take another sixty or seventy years for that—but the concept was in place. Clemenceau, perhaps because of his years as a journalist and before that as a clinician, understood the importance of detailed information—the kind acquired not by reading reports but by looking people in the eye, observing the way they held themselves, hearing their small complaints—sharing, however briefly, the way they lived.

He, like the other war leaders discussed here, felt a powerful urge to mingle with the men at the front. One may speculate on the reasons why: to some extent shared risk validates leadership, but in most wars politicians can only sporadically undergo the trials of soldiers. Clemenceau communicated somehow that these visits were not perfunctory acts of obligation but central to his character as war leader. An inefficient use of his time in one sense, they were perhaps his most powerful technique for acquiring information and influencing events.

"LOOK, TO OBTAIN ANYTHING, THERE IS ONLY ONE METHOD: FIGHTING."

Clemenceau played a role in many aspects of the French war effort in 1918, including mobilization of the war economy, selection of senior commanders, and suppression of domestic opposition to the war. He did not, interestingly enough, set great store by the setting of objectives for the war, a key task under what we have called the "normal" theory of civil-military relations. Nor would that have made much sense: the objectives of such a war were bound to fluctuate with the fortunes of arms, and in the winter of 1917–1918 there was little reason to expect that France would, together with its allies, find itself dealing with a prostrate Germany. His minimum aims were clear: the expulsion of the German army from French territory, the recovery of the lost provinces of Alsace and Lorraine, the imposition of some kind of reparations upon Germany, and some measures—ill-defined until the war ended—for France's future security. That could wait until the war was won, however; in the meantime there was much work to be done to stave off the German offensives of the first half of 1918 and to wrest the initiative from them. The fine-tuning of political objectives meant little for a France that until the middle of 1918 could well have lost the war and with it a large measure of its national independence.

Clemenceau's management of France's two top generals, Foch and Pétain, showed his qualities as a war leader most clearly. Both became Marshals of France; both attracted the unstinted admiration of their subordinates; both were thoroughly trained senior officers. Unfortunately, as one author shrewdly notes, they had "nothing in common beyond France and the profession of arms."[36] And what is worse, they disagreed on the fundamentals.

Ferdinand Foch, born in 1851, first donned the uniform just as the Franco-Prussian War was ending. He remembered vividly the presence of German soldiers in Metz, and the careless way in which the French high command treated the recruits of that generation. He became the antithesis of the rough, ill-educated generals who thought that the methods that had won France a colonial empire in North Africa—toughness and small-unit tactical skill—would suffice to gain her victory in a war against the scientifically schooled, well-drilled masses of Prussian infantry. Foch attended the École Polytechnique and graduated fourth in his class. Mastering German and Italian, he rose through the laborious promotion system of the pre-1914 French army, becoming the commander of the French war college in 1908 at the age of fifty-six. There he preached a doctrine of the carefully wrought offensive. French doctrine before World War I has occasionally been misunderstood. Foch did not believe that French *élan* and the cry *"À la baionnette!"* would carry the day. Rather, in his lectures and subsequent book on the principles of war (first published in 1903 and repeatedly reprinted thereafter) he laid out a more complicated if in some ways confused doctrine.[37] He *did* believe in the dominance of the offensive in war, as do most soldiers at most times in history; only the offensive, after all, can finally decide a contest of arms. He emphasized the psychology of combat, prefiguring, as did other French writers, the kind of sociopsychological writings which are now a central element of the social science of war. His focus on the higher theory of war (a theory often remarkably detached from politics) drew heavily not on French philosophy, but on German military authorities such as von Moltke and von der Goltz. If he is to be faulted it is for an unhealthy obsession with the achievements of Napoleon Bonaparte, and an attempt not so much to imitate them as to find the enduring principles that underlay them—a military quest that was peculiar neither to his time nor his country. But Foch retained a healthy respect for technology that was, in fact, reinforced by the opening experiences of World War I:

> The aspects of war are ever a function of the engines placed at its disposal. Man alone, however gallant he may be, cannot change them; for without his machines he is powerless. And, since in war, machines change constantly and become ever more abundant, one of the first duties of the soldier at the front is to animate and serve them. These were things we had learned before the year 1914 closed.[38]

Foch retained a belief in the imperative of the offensive as the ultimate operational tool—the sole means to cause Germany to give up the war, and to be driven from French soil. But he was considerably more prudent about matters of technique than is often suggested.[39]

Foch's first moment of glory came in September 1914 when, as commander of the Ninth Army, an improvised formation used to fill a dangerous gap in the French lines—which had been twisted open by the German onslaught through Belgium—he contributed to the "miracle of the Marne" that broke the German momentum. For this feat, on 18 September 1914 he was made a *grand officier de la Légion d'honneur*.[40] He became the commander of the northern Army group, but a combination of health problems, a car accident, and the unsuccessful Somme campaign of the summer of 1916 led to his being withdrawn from command in December of that year. Clemenceau, who knew and admired him, wrote a note of condolence: "Dear friend: In the test one is squeezed. I am struck down with you. Yours ever . . ."[41]

Disciplined, outwardly imperturbable—his memoir makes only a glancing reference to the death of his only son and his son-in-law within a few days of each other in August 1914—Foch in command always displayed a superbly confident spirit. The remark often attributed to him, "My right is penetrated, my left yields, all is well: I attack," is probably apocryphal, but captures something of his fighting spirit.[42] At the conference of Doullens, which on 26 March 1918 made him supreme allied commander, Foch was asked about his plans:

> Oh, my plan is not complicated. I want to fight. I will fight in the north, I will fight on the Somme, I will fight on the Aisne, in Lorraine, in Alsace, I will fight all the time and everywhere; from now on by force of striking I will finish by smashing the Boche.[43]

It was a spirit that matched Clemenceau's own: "Look, to obtain anything, there is only one method: fighting."[44]

To professional skill, incurable optimism, and sheer strength of character Foch added two further qualities: tact with fellow professionals and an abiding mistrust of civilian politicians. Coalition warfare, Churchill once remarked, "is a tale of the reciprocal complaints of allies." World War I was no different: French and British soldiers, for example, often had more regard for their German foe than for their partners, whom they regarded as incapable of digging a decent trench, let alone concocting a sound scheme of attack. Indeed, one French general, Albert Sarrail, is reported to have remarked with some asperity that after his experience of coalition command "I have lost something of my respect for Napoleon"—who, of course, only fought coalitions.

For France in World War I the strain of working with the Allies was even more acute. France bore the heaviest burden in the West. Its small Belgian ally trembled on the verge of collapse; the British mobilized late and, by the standards of a country with a large standing army, with appalling inefficiency; the Americans showed up later still, suffused with an arrogance for which they would pay dearly. "If the Americans do not permit the French to teach them," Clemenceau is said to have remarked, "the Germans will do so."[45]

Foch, whether from an innate sense of tact or from historical study, which reminded him that every army faced its own peculiar predicaments, was unusually sensitive to those of the Allies. "Each army has its own spirit and tradition; each has to satisfy the requirements of its own government; and the latter, in its turn, has its own particular needs and interests to consider."[46] This forbearance, however, extended to soldiers, not civilians. As for politicians, Major T. Bentley Mott, General John Pershing's liaison to Foch, recalled after the war, "He was instinctively distrustful of three categories of men: orators, politicians, and journalists, for he believed that they all did more harm in the world than good."[47] If he had a fault it was arrogance, of the kind that led him to tell Mott, who had asked him why so many professors at the French war college had gained eminence in the war,

> "To successfully teach a doctrine," he answered, "you have got to be absolutely sure it is right. This means profound study and a long meditation upon all the objections advanced against it. Once sure, you can proceed with confidence and you carry conviction with your pupils. The men who had taught at the War College went through this process. The early disasters of the conflict could not shake their faith in our doctrine. They continued to apply it, and we finally won."[48]

That those disasters may, in fact, have had something to do with their faith in their doctrine, Foch does not seem to have countenanced. Still, in May 1917 Foch came back into prominence as chief of staff of the French army, with renewed powers as a general adviser to the government.

Philippe Pétain has come down in popular memory as the doddering, senescent old man who in 1940 chose to collaborate with Hitler's Germany, establishing a regime that would forever tarnish the name of the pleasant spa town of Vichy. It is curious that the deeds of a man in his mid-eighties—he was born in 1856—should so overshadow the rest of his career. In truth, until 1914 that career had been solid but hardly distinguished. A northern peasant, Pétain lacked family connections; this inhibited his rise through the ranks. He attended Saint-Cyr (the French West Point) and worked his way up to the rank of colonel in 1914, a fit, sturdy fifty-eight-year-old already contemplating retirement. As an instructor at the École de Guerre he was out of step with those who, like Foch, favored the offensive and meditated deeply on the wars of Napoleon and Moltke; Pétain's interest lay rather with the Boer and Russo-Japanese wars and with the gloomy fact, which he made a motto, "Fire kills." It was not so much that he opposed the offense, but rather that he believed that machines well served, not will or operational virtuosity by themselves, were necessary to make it work.[49] Without any particular warmth of character, he demonstrated a care and regard for the average French soldier that won him their affection to a degree achieved by few other generals. He visited the wounded in hospitals, and exerted himself without cease to make sure that when his men went into battle they did so armed and equipped, rested and fed. Small wonder they revered him. A humorless, reserved man, he hated publicity and despised politicians. He went so far as to tell the president, Raymond Poincaré, that "nobody was better placed than the president himself to be aware that France was neither led nor governed."[50]

Suddenly, at age fifty-nine, Pétain began a meteoric rise. The aging colonel of 1914 became within months a general commanding a division, then a corps, then an army, and within three years of the opening shots of the war, of the entire French army opposing Germany. In late February 1916 he was dispatched to restore the perilous predicament of the army at Verdun, which is where he first attracted national attention. A meticulous organizer, he personally supervised the artillery and, most important of all, the construction of a supply line to keep the vast force of almost half a million men fed and equipped. He subsequently became chief of staff of the army, a post that he held until May 1917, when he was relieved by Foch. During that year he subdued the mutinies that had begun to erupt in the French army. He did so with a characteristic combination of caution, firmness, and accommodation: fifty executions and nearly fourteen hundred sentences of five years or more in prison suppressed the revolts, which were short-lived and localized.[51]

In a situation such as that of 1918 there was bound to be some friction between Pétain and Foch. Their personalities were quite different. More importantly, it is normal for the chief of staff—the military head of the armed forces and chief adviser to the civilian government—to come into conflict with the most powerful commander of troops in contact with the enemy. When, as in the situation of 1918, the chief of staff can easily see and influence matters directly it becomes even more likely. But in this case other forces were at work, particularly once Foch had been appointed supreme allied commander in the spring of 1918.[52]

World War I posed, on a greater scale than ever before, the problem of coalition warfare. It always presents a difficult problem, but the tactical conditions of warfare in 1914–1918 created new and even more baffling challenges. Because of the growth of armies and their firepower in the last years of the nineteenth and the first years of the twentieth century, World War I saw the development of a continuous front from the Swiss border to the English Channel. The development of gaps between the four Allied armies (Belgian, French, British, and American, plus the minor foreign contingents such as the Portuguese) would prove ruinous, and had to be avoided at all costs. The elaborate logistical requirements of modern armies meant that armies were more solicitous than ever of their well-organized rear areas, and would tend to fall back upon them or to operate at as short a distance from them as possible. To these challenges were added the traditional ones of concerting the action of armies trained to different standards, led by commanders whose pride and mutual suspicion caused them to seek autonomy whenever possible, and directed by governments with subtly different ends in view.

The handling of coalitions at war is one of the most difficult tasks of supreme command. In any coalition bargaining power shifts over time, and according to three different sets of calculations. One might think that the ally providing the greatest amount of military power dominates; this is not always the case, however. The ally who has paid, or is paying, the heaviest price in blood and effort may have the upper hand; and one must also consider the element of risk. That ally most in peril has the least degree of choice, and may have correspondingly great bargaining power. On all three counts France dominated the Allied coalition of 1914–1918 for at least the first three years of the war. As the British and American contributions to the war effort grew, however, France's leverage weakened. Thus Clemenceau and his marshals were playing the game of inter-alliance poker with a hand that was bound to deteriorate over time.

Since the beginning of the war political leaders, and some military leaders as well, had called for a unified coalition command. The British high command, spearheaded by Douglas Haig and backed by the chief of the Imperial General Staff, Field Marshal William Robertson, were the most skeptical:

> I submit that, except in very special circumstances, the placing of armies permanently under the control of a foreign General, having no responsibility to the Parliament of the country to which they belong, can never be a measure that any soldier will recommend, or any Government will sanction, without reluctance. The presumption is that armies fight better under a Commander in Chief of their own than under a foreigner, and there are other obvious objections to the latter in respect of such questions as casualties, discipline, and appointments. It is essential, too, before trying to establish "unified command" that the allied Governments should be agreed amongst themselves as to the general policy to be pursued, and be satisfied that the agreement will not be disturbed, since without unity of policy unity of command may lead to the operations being conducted in the interests of one ally rather than of the others, and so defeat its own ends.

On more than one occasion unity of policy as between some of the Entente Governments was far from being either definite or stable.[53]

The forced resignation of Robertson in late February 1918 removed one major obstacle to the creation of a unified command.[54] The crises of the German attacks of March 1918 obliterated those that remained. Grudgingly, British and American generals came to see the value of having a single man to coordinate the overall fight, and above all to allocate reserves among the different fronts.

Foch, sympathetic and quick, was the natural choice for supreme allied commander. He quickly established a good rapport with both Haig and Pershing, whose American contingents could ultimately prove the decisive element in the war, even though they were as yet raw and rather disorganized. He understood their problems and, acutely conscious of the limits of his powers, hesitated to give them orders. He had, beyond these skills in managing people, one other great virtue: he had a vision of victory. Foch believed that once the fury of the German assault had spent itself, the Allies would be able, at long last, finally to break through the German line in the north, provided that they could assemble a substantial reserve—a *masse de manœuvre* as the French called it.

Pétain had a very different view. Inclined to promise much less than he could deliver, he preferred, as he put it, to "wait for the tanks and the Americans." He favored, in time, a series of short, limited-objective offensives with a view to imposing attrition on the overstretched Germans. A patient master of technique, he shook his head at the unformed and reckless American units that he saw, and believed that they required seasoning by being distributed to French divisions for tours in the front lines. A skeptic about the Anglo-Saxons, he preferred, when the time came, to launch an offensive in Lorraine rather than in Flanders, where the German lines were exceptionally strong and the ground reduced by bombardment to a slimy mass of mud and putrefaction. Pétain was particularly troubled during the winter of 1917–1918 by the thought of the weight the Germans could bring to bear on the French front. He had a solution, simple enough in theory but fraught with larger implications: defense in depth.

During the first stages of World War I the opposing armies tenaciously fought over every inch of ground; having been expelled from their trenches by a combination of bombardment and assault, they would expend any effort, often taking enormous casualties, in order to regain their front line. This inflexible tactical doctrine cost both sides enormous casualties. It meant that heavy preparatory bombardments could kill, wound, or stun most of the defenders or any given front. It required counterattacks in the open, and it precluded the abandonment of inferior terrain—e.g., that overlooked by enemy positions on higher ground.

The Germans came earlier to the solution that appears, in retrospect, to have been obvious—the defense in depth.[55] Rather than clinging to a crowded first set of trenches they would create battle zones between a thinly posted forward area and a second (and some times a third) system of trenches and outposts four or five kilometers back, often concealed behind the reverse slope of a gradual rise in the ground. The defenders would disperse in bunkers or shell holes, wait out the invariable preliminary bombardment, and counterattack in small groups as the attackers came forward, ambushing the enemy from the side and behind. The Germans were willing, moreover, to yield ground. Their large withdrawals in March 1917 to the Hindenburg Line gave them shorter and more easily defended lines. The system proved itself less than a month later, in April 1917, when France's Nivelle offensive collapsed after taking a further 130,000 casualties. Pétain, drawing on his experience of Verdun, likewise favored a defense in depth, and on 22 December 1917 he issued an order, Directive Number 4 (amplified in a follow-up order of 24 January, 1918), which mandated the new defensive scheme.

Such a decision seems, at first, the quintessentially tactical choice—a matter with which politicians would be wise to have nothing to do. In fact, the very reverse was the case, and Clemenceau was soon deeply immersed in the consequences and implications of Pétain's doctrine. Three in particular stood out.

First, defense in depth meant something very different for French soldiers, and for France, than it did for Germany. Ten percent of the most productive territory of France had been occupied by the enemy, and Paris was only a couple of days' march from the front lines; to cede more ground was psychologically difficult, if not impossible. All the more did this apply in the aftermath of the calvary of Verdun, where 162,000 Frenchmen had given their lives for a meaningless fortress—one which had, in fact, initially been abandoned by its defenders. Second, to defend in depth meant a very different use of reserves than that implicit under a system of unified French and British command. Whereas under defense in depth French forces would prepare for local counterattacks once the enemy's assault had begun, a more unified approach would require the use of large reserves for the general good—as in fact became necessary. At the inter-Allied conference of January 1918 Foch and Pétain clashed repeatedly over the question of the creation of an inter-Allied reserve—favored by the former, opposed by the latter.[56] Finally, defense in depth was bound to prove more manpower intensive than manning a single system of trenches. Inevitably, this brought into play the question of what the French, as opposed to their British allies, would defend. In January 1918 the French held 520 kilometers of front out of a total of 754—some 69 percent of the total, after nearly four years of war. A doctrine of defense in depth, if adopted by both the British and the French, would reinforce the desire of both to shorten their lines, each insisting that their ally pick up the slack. The French sense of grievance would grow in the summer of 1918 when, after British reverses, the percentage of front line held by France would grow to 73 percent.

Pétain was not, as he has often been portrayed, a purely defense-minded general. He favored an eventual resumption of the offensive, and indeed prepared the mirror image of his defensive doctrine. Historians of the Western Front often distinguish between the concepts of "breaking through" and "breaking in." The former accorded with a Napoleonic concept of war, in which powerful concentrations of artillery and determined assaults by infantry eventually cracked open an enemy line, allowing the use of cavalry to pour into the gap and complete the rout of a broken foe. This idealized version of battle certainly shaped much of the operational art of the first years of the war, including the retention of (useless, as it turned out) cavalry divisions to exploit the success that never came.[57] By the end of the war two different approaches had emerged. The Germans adopted a style of attack that involved very brief but intense preparatory fire (including extensive use of chemical agents) followed by infiltration tactics that bypassed enemy strong points and penetrated as deeply as possible. This concept, including the use of élite "storm troops" was a precedent, in many ways, for the style of German operations that would annihilate Polish and French forces twenty years later. The alternative, preferred by the Allies, involved precisely choreographed attacks aimed at limited objectives, and involving the maximum use of machines—chiefly tanks and aircraft. This methodical "breaking in" was the method advocated by Pétain. To the end, he wanted to demolish the German lines piece by piece, tearing down the trench systems rather than pursuing the mirage of a decisive battle that had tantalized and eluded the soldiers of 1914.[58] But here too there were larger issues. Pétain had learned the simple lesson, *"Le feu tue"*—"Fire kills." Enthusiasm, physical fitness, and courage would avail nothing against barbed wire, machine guns, and rapid-fire artillery. Training, the right weapons (and proficiency in their use), and high-quality staff work were what counted. In particular, the American Army could not play a useful role in the battles of 1918 until its training had been perfected, preferably under French tutelage. The incompetence of American staff work—manifested in the vast traffic jams behind American lines—raised doubts about the ability of the American Expeditionary Force to function as an independent army. Clemenceau, commenting on American insistence on having a unified army under General John Pershing's control (rather than, as he wished, a force broken up and allocated to the Allies, noted after the war:

All the representatives of the higher American military authorities openly inclined to the views of Pershing—General Bliss being the one exception. They wanted an American Army. They had it. Any one who saw, as I saw, the hopeless congestion at Thiaucourt will bear witness that they may congratulate themselves on not having had it sooner.[59]

Pétain favored, in the strongest terms, the integration of American divisions and even regiments into larger French units—a position bound to be at odds with the desire of the Americans to prove their worth, and to establish their diplomatic weight, through independent military effort. This was a view shared by Clemenceau and his military adviser Mordacq, who argued that the American "obstinacy" about refusing French advice "cost, in the Argonne, in September 1918, more than 25,000 killed."[60]

Thus, as frequently occurs in war, a seemingly tactical or even technical issue was fraught with the largest implications for French national morale, manpower policy, strategy, and alliance relations. Pétain's tactical doctrines were embedded—as doctrine often is—in a host of broader assumptions often left unstated, but potent nonetheless. Not surprisingly, political intervention would be required to make such doctrines reality.

Clemenceau was initially doubtful about Pétain's doctrine; the general's dour personality and his willingness to yield yet more French territory accorded ill with Clemenceau's considerably more ardent spirit. Pétain was, Clemenceau remarked to President Poincaré, better at the second rank than the first.[61] Yet Clemenceau was convinced, in part by Mordacq (who agreed with Pétain's views), and in part by his own good sense.[62] His visits to the front now became efforts to monitor the implementation of Pétain's directive, which did not sit well with all French commanders and which demanded considerable labor on the part of weary troops who now had, by pick and shovel, to construct extensive new systems of field fortification in accordance with the new doctrine. Indeed, he ordered the high command to begin reporting to him biweekly about the progress of the new defenses under construction.[63]

From the first, Foch looked to conduct an attack—an immediate counteroffensive to block the German attack, and then to achieve "decisive results" with a combined Allied offensive in 1918.[64] Foch's chief objection to Pétain's new doctrine rested on the former's wish to control French reserves, to shore up weak spots in the line as they appeared, and to lay the groundwork for his massive counterattack. In a series of sharp clashes at the newly created Supreme Allied War Council, Pétain and Haig argued strenuously against both ideas: mounting an offensive and building up a large inter-Allied reserve.[65]

Pétain, doubtful of the technical skill of his British and American counterparts, would favor an ultimate counteroffensive—but in Lorraine, remote from the Flanders battlefields where the British and French linked up. Offensives in Lorraine also, of course, had the advantage in France's eyes of furthering the liberation of one of the two lost provinces of 1870. Furthermore Foch was, by temperament, far more sensitive than Pétain to the concerns and needs of his coalition partners. He did not believe that it was possible to strong-arm the Americans into yielding up their independence to suit French views of tactics; and he sympathized with the plight of the British armies, which had borne the brunt of the initial German attacks in the spring of 1918. Furthermore, by the fall of 1918, sensing the cracking of German morale and cohesion, he favored attacks that would resemble the "break-through" far more than the "break-in."[66]

Clemenceau's personal intervention secured the success of Pétain's tactical doctrines.[67] At the same time, he concluded that Foch's desire to wield the reserves of the French army as a bloc for larger offensive purposes was right. He agreed as well to the shift of offensive operations away from Lorraine, where Pétain wanted them, to Flanders. Regarding the Americans he sympathized with Pétain but yielded, with increasing irritation, to Foch's representations.

Clemenceau's management of competing military advice and philosophy required a stream of decisions, not an overall choice in favor of one or the other. He understood that both generals' positions had merit, even though they were ultimately incompatible. To the end of the war he tilted first to one, then the other. To some extent he had to deal with the effects of two powerful personalities: Foch forceful, optimistic, and dashing, Pétain dour and competent. After the Doullens conference of the Supreme Allied War Council in March 1918 Mordacq ruefully observed that "Pétain, with his fine conscience and habitual loyalty, thought it his duty to make known the bad side of the situation, while doing everything necessary to repair it."[68] Small wonder that Pétain, who habitually delivered more than he promised, acquired the reputation of a defeatist.

Clemenceau almost surely favored Foch, both because of his own unquenchably determined spirit and out of a belief that the Allies would and could win the war. He recognized too Foch's superior skill at handling allies, for although the French premier could be a prickly ally, he understood the British and the Americans well enough to appreciate the need for cooperation with them. Pétain, on the other hand, clearly had the greater mastery of matters of tactics and technique, and Clemenceau's good sense saw the merits of the new defensive doctrine, which stood the test in the first wave of German attacks that began in March 1918.

On Monday 27 May 1918 the second great test came. In a week-long attack German forces broke through on the Aisne river, along the Chemin des Dames in the direction of Paris. A 4,000-gun bombardment for two and a half hours preceded an assault by two dozen German divisions against eight weak French and British divisions, as the Germans achieved an astonishing twelve-mile penetration of the French and British front. American units came on line at this, the second battle of the Marne, helping to staunch the German offensive, but for a time it seemed as if Paris itself might be in danger.

Clemenceau, furious that the commander of the French Sixth Army, General Duchêne, had failed to implement Pétain's defense in depth, promptly relieved him and began a purge of the senior ranks of the Army.[69] Some of the blame rested with a senior leadership that had resisted Pétain's direction; some with Foch, who was bent on an early offensive and who, as support to the British, had moved reserves off to the north, where he expected the next German blow to fall. Clemenceau later recalled:

> In reply to my first inquiries I was briefly told that such things are inevitable in war, that any one, soldier and civilian alike, may be found at fault, and that it was no good dwelling upon the fact . . .[70]
>
> I had defended the High Command in the House [of Deputies], but I knew very well, from having seen it close up on my visits to the Front, that an important group of leaders had grown old and ought to be replaced. Foch certainly knew it as well as I did, perhaps even better, but, as with many chiefs, the phrase "old comrade" was a very potent charm with him . . . The Generalissimo did not challenge in one single instance; he knew too well each one's deficiencies. At certain names I saw him shrug his shoulders with the murmur, "An old friend!" The sacrifice was consummated with but few exceptions.[71]

Clemenceau respected the staunchness of Pétain—who, taking responsibility that was not entirely his, offered his resignation, which the premier rejected. A cloud lingered over Foch, but the crisis had passed.

"DO YOU KNOW THAT I AM NOT YOUR SUBORDINATE?"

A greater conflict with the supreme allied commander, however, arose as the Allies had begun the counteroffensives which would eventually bring Germany to its knees. The issue turned on the role that the vast

American armies would play in the coming battles. Clemenceau's view of the problem was straightforward:

> The problem lay in the single fact that we had already been fighting for a long time when the first American contingents, which were of necessity inexperienced, joined us. The true function of the American allies was first and foremost to help us to make up for lost time by joining the fray as they arrived, whereas the natural vanity of the great democracy inclined her to throw in her full power for the supreme victory on the last battlefield. . . .
>
> Just one black spot: the fanatical determination of the great chiefs of the American Army to delay the arrival of the star-spangled banner on the battlefield. The slow organization of the great American Army was costing us, and our Allies too, seas of blood, but it was destined, so they kept telling us, to solve the whole mass of military problems at one stroke. Thus it happened that the war was practically over when the Argonne proved to those handsome, gallant soldiers of valiant America that death-defying courage was not enough to win a strategical success.[72]

There were multiple issues: whether the Americans would be committed in the emergency of the spring and summer of 1918 as reinforcing units for the tattered French and British units, and later whether they would launch a semi-independent offensive as an army, rather than as divisions assigned to Allied sectors. Beyond this, Clemenceau believed that Pershing must be subject to Foch's orders as the general in chief of the Allies.

Foch, perhaps the prototypical Allied commander, saw things differently. The term "unified command gives a false idea of the powers exercised by the individual in question—that is, if it is meant that he commanded in the military sense of the word . . ."[73] Somewhat more realistically than Clemenceau, he contended that his was the power to persuade and suggest, not to order. Germany's sudden collapse in the fall of 1918 saved the two men from a much worse clash. Clemenceau insisted that Foch should prepare to ask President Wilson to relieve Pershing of his command for failure to cooperate with the French. On 21 October he wrote to Foch:

> . . . thanks to his [Pershing's] invincible obstinacy, he has won out against you as well as against your immediate subordinates. . . .
>
> Constitutionally, I am the head of the French army.
>
> The interests of this army lie only too obviously in the parallel organization of all the troops under your command.
>
> I would be a criminal if I allowed the French army to wear itself out indefinitely in battle, without doing everything in my power to ensure that an Allied army which has hurried to its aid was rendered capable of fulfilling the military role for which it is destined.[74]

One sees in this letter an awareness of France's deep weariness. Underneath the Tiger's defiance lay a keen sense of the weakness, the fragility even, of French morale and will.

Foch's sympathy for Pershing and his skepticism about politicians led him to side more with the American general than with his own premier. He was pleased with his new colleagues, noting with pride that at the end of the war, "I was gratified to find myself the personal friend of all the American generals, beginning with Pershing."[75] "Having a more comprehensive knowledge of the difficulties encountered by the American Army, I could not acquiesce [in] the radical solution contemplated by Monsieur Clemenceau."[76] Here too, Clemenceau had cause for complaint, for the laggardly and unsatisfactory performance of the Americans was largely of Pershing's making. Pershing had run terrible and unnecessary risks to preserve a large, unwieldy, and not terribly effective but unified American army in the field. His obsession with individual marksmanship and fieldcraft—coupled with a disdain for trench warfare—ignored the hard lessons about combined-arms fighting so painfully learned by the French. "Had the war ended on October 31 instead of eleven days later," Pershing's biographer notes, the American general's postwar reputation would have been "quite diminished." Its breakthroughs in the last ten days of the war reflected chiefly "the deterioration of the enemy" rather than growing AEF competence in field operations. These latter included such mishaps as the farcical lunge by the First Division across a neighboring National Guard division's front in order to take Sedan—scene of France's defeat in 1870—before the outraged French could liberate the city.[77]

The clash between Foch and Clemenceau over dealing with the Americans reflected a greater tension, not uncommon in the civil-military relations of great coalitions at war.

> "Do you know," the marshal said to me one day, "that I am not your subordinate?"
>
> "No I don't," I replied, with a laugh. "I don't even want to know who put that notion into your head. You know that I am your friend. I strongly advise you not to try to act on this idea, for it would never do."
>
> There was no answer.[78]

There may have been no answer, but the matter did not rest there. Even as the war drew to a close, Foch complained bitterly to Mordacq that Clemenceau was not keeping him fully informed of negotiations with the Central Powers as one by one they sued for terms.[79] The stage was set for even sharper disagreements.

"THE GOOD LORD MADE DO WITH TEN."

The Allied offensives of September–November 1918 broke the back of German resistance. One by one, Germany's allies collapsed: Turkey opened armistice talks on 26 October and came to terms four days later; Austria-Hungary had proposed negotiations more than a month earlier, in mid-September, and had virtually disintegrated before the war's end. On 3 October the German army had itself told its leadership that it needed an immediate armistice; it was in a parlous state, with hundreds of thousands of deserters (nearly a million by the last weeks of the war) and a general staff that had quite lost its nerve.[80]

It was now, in the forging of a peace, that Clemenceau faced the greatest challenge to civilian control of the military. The first issue to be addressed was the terms of an armistice with the Germans. Clearly, a longer-term settlement would require an international conference, but equally clearly there needed to be terms upon which a cessation of fighting could occur. Here there were two schools of thought. One, shared by Pershing and, interestingly enough, Pétain, and supported by the French president, Raymond Poincaré, favored a march on Berlin and the occupation of Germany, from which point the Allies could dictate terms to a prostrate foe. The other, favored by Foch and Haig, was for stiff terms that would nonetheless leave the German army intact, if enfeebled, and the German government in control of most of its territory. The difficulty of the choice was compounded by the German decision to open armistice negotiations through the Americans, whom they expected to prove more tractable than the Europeans. The Americans, after all, had entered the lists as an Associated rather than an Allied power, and Wilson's Fourteen Points gave hope for leniency on their part. The negotiation was protracted and difficult.

The quandary was one seen in most wars that end in apparent victory in the field: does one accept a cease-fire that leaves the opponent weakened but intact, or press for a complete submission of the devastated foe? The case for the latter is always obvious in retrospect, but rarely so at the time. One may think of the end of the First World War as a study in competitive collapse; the Allied commanders, with the important exception of Pershing, whose army had not yet been fully committed to the fight, were all too aware of how fragile their forces were, and of the enormous human price their countries had paid for success thus far. That Germany was defeated was clear; but there was also reason to think that an attempt to force the Allies' way to Berlin would cause hundreds of thousands of additional casualties that could be avoided.

There was, in addition, a powerful political argument for an early termination of the fighting. The German government had approached President Wilson, whose 8 January 1918 speech to Congress announcing the Fourteen Points ("The good Lord made do with ten," Clemenceau is reported to have growled) had been remarkably gentle. It offered a number of countries (France, Belgium, Romania, Serbia, and Montenegro) a return to their old borders, and autonomy or independence to other peoples (those of Austria-Hungary and Poland), but it contained no indication of harsh treatment for Germany, and it included this statement:

> We have no jealousy of German greatness, and there is nothing in this program that impairs it. We grudge her no achievement or distinction of learning or of pacific enterprise such as have made her record very bright and very enviable. We do not wish to injure her or to block in any way her legitimate influence or power. We do not wish to fight her either with arms or with hostile arrangements of trade if she is willing to associate herself with us and the other peace-loving nations of the world in covenants of justice and law and fair dealing. We wish her only to accept a place of equality among the peoples of the world,— the new world in which we now live,—instead of a place of mastery.[81]

Once the German imperial regime had collapsed, Wilson was strongly disinclined to dictate a peace on terms that would merely ratify the rights of the victor rather than create, as he wished, a new order in international politics. And already in the discussion of the terms of the armistice the tensions among the victors were becoming apparent.

Although all agreed that Germany should withdraw from Alsace-Lorraine as part of the terms of the armistice, France wanted the larger Alsace-Lorraine of the short-lived peace of 1814; the Allies agreed only to the borders of the Alsace-Lorraine of 1815.[82]

Foch and Clemenceau alike favored an armistice, albeit on terms that would prevent Germany from resuming the fight. Clemenceau, in particular, wished to see the German army completely demobilized. Foch, for his part, had already written to Clemenceau arguing for armistice terms that included a repatriation of populations in Alsace-Lorraine, and above all, maintenance of the French border at the Rhine. "If France has a firm hold of the Rhine, she may be at rest, for she can be sure of reparations and security; without the Rhine she has neither."[83] Clemenceau shared Foch's view on the desirability of securing the Rhine, with bridgeheads on the right or German bank, as a means of temporarily disarming Germany; he agreed as well that the conditions should include the evacuation of all occupied territory (Belgium, France, and Alsace-Lorraine) and the restoration of French and Belgian railroad equipment.[84] More important, Clemenceau agreed with Foch (and disagreed with Poincaré and the Americans) that there was no point in attempting to drive to Berlin if adequate armistice terms could be achieved in France. But Clemenceau was irritated at Foch's letter of 19 October complaining about not being fully informed of the political negotiations that were bringing the war to an end.[85] It augured poorly for what was to follow.

Trouble in Clemenceau's relationship with Foch had been brewing for some time, particularly over Foch's reluctance to ask Wilson for Pershing's relief.[86] Foch had, moreover, insisted that in their armistice negotiations the politicians bypass the Supreme War Council (composed of military representatives of the Allies) in favor of himself and the other field commanders. On 16 October he wrote to Clemenceau, "The only military counselors qualified to deal with the conditions of an armistice are the commanders in chief. They alone are responsible to their governments for the safety of their armies and the conditions under which hostilities should be resumed in case of rupture. They alone are thoroughly informed as to the state of their armies and of the enemy forces confronting them."[87] Clemenceau, who believed that civilian leaders could ask for military advice as they wished, had little use for soldiers telling him whom he might consult.

Beyond this, Mordacq is correct in describing this as "the eternal question of politics and strategy."[88] Politics pervades all of war: the notion that politicians step aside during it is empirically untrue and theoretically undesirable. Armistice negotiations offer the most sensitive moments for civil-military interaction. In November 1918 the dividing line between operational considerations (rendering the Germans incapable of further resistance in the event of a resumption of hostilities) and political questions (what the Allies would tolerate by way of actions that might predetermine the outcome of the peace negotiations) became exceptionally delicate. Foch, as supreme allied commander, seems to have been unwilling to see a clear difference between offering expert advice and counsel and exercising excessive control over what were, in the end, political problems.

The deterioration of the relationship between Foch and Clemenceau reflected several phenomena common in civil-military relations at the top. Foch was, as we have noted, disdainful of politicians. He did not view military commanders in general, and himself in particular, as the executors of policy but as partners in its creation. His comment to a friendly journalist about the war and its aftermath is revealing:

> War is not a dual object, but a unity; so, for that matter, is peace. They are not divided into military and civil departments. The two aspects are closely and inseparably linked. Because the Allies did not recognize that, for years they committed a series of mistakes that considerably delayed victory. Statesman and general were acting each on his own account; they did not try to coordinate their efforts, and so they alighted upon the surest way of doing harm.[89]

Note that there is nothing here of the subordination of the general to the statesman. The ideal that Foch sets up is "coordination," not "advice," much less "subordination." He was even more explicit in his observation that "the political and diplomatic realms are in certain cases inseparable from the domain of military matters; so that my first incursion into those realms was eminently legitimate."[90]

Foch was, moreover, acutely aware of his status not only as the supreme allied commander (although he realized better than anyone else the limits on his ability truly to command, rather than persuade), but as a war hero. On 5 August 1918 he had been made a Marshal of France—well before Pétain, who had arguably done as much to win the victory, received the same honor (which was awarded him on 19 November). Foch had received the same accolades from the Chamber of Deputies on 11 November, which rendered a "sacred and eternal homage" to the armies, to the government, and to only two men by name—"citizen Georges Clemenceau" and "Marshal Foch."[91] As often occurs at the end of a war, a prominent soldier can be far more popular than his political master, and Foch knew it. Having, moreover, the prestige of the supreme command behind him, he believed that he deserved an independent role. Nowhere did this become more clear than in his attempt to impose upon the Allied governments the only settlement that he believed could ensure French security: a military occupation of the west (or French) bank of the Rhine, and with it the support of separatist governments there.

"I FEAR THE MARSHAL IS MIXING POLICY WITH STRATEGY"

In the long run no set of guarantees, no system of disarmament imposed upon Germany, no vigilance on the part of the French army could, in Foch's view, compensate for the weight of German manpower and industry. A physical border, however, would—hence, in his view, the imperative of keeping the French army on the left bank of the Rhine, be it through occupation, annexation, or the establishment of a Rhenish protectorate. This obsession reflected an understandable but narrow view of security, narrow chiefly because it ignored political realities. A war whose objectives had been set, for most of the peoples of Europe, in the Fourteen Points could not leave a large German-speaking population under perpetual French rule. Yet, even years after the event, Foch still believed that the Rhine frontier had been achievable—and that it had been missed only by the stubbornness of Clemenceau.

> It is really extraordinary that M. Clemenceau did not think of me in the first place as a suitable person to overcome the resistance of President Wilson and Lloyd George. He was fortunate in that the Supreme Commander who led the Allied armies to victory was a Frenchman. Neither Lloyd George nor Wilson could be surprised that the *generalissimo* should give his opinion on military matters; and the future security of France and the Allies, as well as the avoidance of more aggression from Germany, who had willed and lost the war, were eminently military in nature. It was the right and the duty of a commander to express his views. France's representatives at the conference could use him to illustrate his theory and overcome resistance. He could say: "I am obliged to accede to Foch in all that pertains to security. Foch will not hear of any solution other than the Rhine as a military frontier. Anything you could offer us in exchange—the disarmament of Germany, pacts, temporary occupation—he considers entirely inadequate. I cannot ignore his resistance or combat his state of mind. For it is obvious that on this point he has the country at his back."[92]

It is difficult to know what is more remarkable here—Foch's naïveté about the peace conference, or his greater naïveté about the propriety of a politician declaring himself to be incapable of disagreeing with his military adviser.

Clemenceau, of course, would have none of this. He excluded Foch from much of the negotiations at Versailles—which lasted from mid-January through June of 1919. Foch was outraged. Quite apart from the wounds to his self-esteem, Foch believed that the planned treaty would sacrifice the only true security France could find after the war. Although Clemenceau agreed with Foch's view that the Rhine frontier was desirable for France, he believed, more realistically, that he could not gain it over the opposition of the British and the Americans. A frontier seized unilaterally would involve a rupture with the British and Americans that France—now stripped by the Bolshevik revolution of its erstwhile Russian ally—simply could not afford.

Foch did not, however, stop at protests directed against Clemenceau. Instead, he resorted to a variety of tactics, including obstructionist behavior of various kinds, appealing to other French politicians, covert action by the French military in the Rhineland itself, and a press campaign orchestrated against his own government.[93] He attempted to bypass Clemenceau by working with the considerably more sympathetic president, Raymond Poincaré, who shared both his hard-line views and a growing dislike for their mutual enemy, Clemenceau.[94]

This is as good a place as any to note the way in which generals, particularly successful generals, often may choose which politicians they wish to work with. Foch could and did exploit the division between France's brilliant but less than effectual president and its dominating premier, and Poincaré could collaborate with Foch against Clemenceau. In a like manner William Maxwell Aitken, Lord Beaverbrook, disparaged the British First Lord Sir Edward Carson, a grim Ulsterman who in 1917 stood with the Admiralty in its opposition to the introduction of convoys even as British trade was being strangled. "As long as I am at the Admiralty the sailors will have full scope. They will not be interfered with by me, and I will not interfere with them," Carson said. To which Beaverbrook noted:

Carson thus stood in defiant hostility to any pressure from the politicians upon the admirals. When analysed, his attitude was strange and even self-contradictory. He would see that the admirals were allowed to go their own way and pursue their own strategy. And if things went wrong—who were to be criticized? Not, it seemed, the admirals. Criticism could fall only on politicians.[95]

One great lesson of the history of World War I, particularly in Great Britain and France, is that civil-military tension only rarely takes the form of a pure civil-military division. Rather, some political figures will side with the soldiers (who themselves may be divided) against other politicians. It may be, as it was in the British case, an alliance of mutual convenience, or it may reflect genuine agreement. At its root, however, the issue remains one of civil-military tension.

On 10 February 1919 an interview with Foch appeared in the British newspaper *The Daily Mail*—which, unlike French newspapers, could not be censored by the French government. In it Foch declared that the Germans could raise three million soldiers in three months, against whom the Allies could field scarcely more than half as many. It was another effort to pressure the Allies to give France the strategic frontier he believed that it required.[96] On 17 April he came close to outright disobedience when he declared that it was impossible to bring the German delegation to Versailles to receive the terms agreed upon by the Four. In the ensuing crisis—smoothed over by Mordacq—President Wilson remarked that he found it impossible to imagine consigning the United States Army to a general who would not obey his own government.[97] Foch backed down, but the damage had been done; Clemenceau had, in fact, ordered Mordacq to prepare for Foch's dismissal and replacement with Pétain. A few weeks later the crisis took its full form. In April 1919, after the Council of Four had already decided against separating the Rhineland from Germany, Foch's staff inspired and edited an article in *Le Matin* that quoted French staff sources as insisting on the need for a military frontier on the Rhine. Foch himself bypassed French censors by turning again to the sympathetic *Daily Mail* in an interview that appeared on 19 April 1919.

> "And now, having reached the Rhine, we must stay there," went on the marshal very emphatically. "Impress that upon your fellow countrymen. It is our only safety, their only safety. We must have a barrier. We must double-lock the door. Democracies like ours, which are never aggressive, must have strong natural military frontiers. Remember that those seventy millions of Germans will always be a menace to us. Do not trust the appearances of the moment. They are a people both envious and warlike. Their natural characteristics have not changed in four years. Fifty years hence they will be what they are today."[98]

The premier twice gave Foch an opportunity to have his say, once before the "Big Four," as the political leaders of the United States, Great Britain, France, and Italy were known, on 31 March and once before the French Council of Ministers on 25 April. Clemenceau refused, however, to allow Foch to be present at the deliberations of either the French government or the Allied powers. Foch had already attempted other means of influencing the Four. On 2 May Foch told Poincaré that he considered the treaty "a surrender," even "treason." On 6 May he addressed the Allied chiefs denouncing the treaty and insisting that it be vetted by the appropriate military experts, failing which he would resign his position.[99] The British, in particular, were furious; Bonar Law remarked that if a British officer had "taken the same attitude, he would not have remained in his position for five minutes."[100] Clemenceau summoned Pétain to replace Foch, remarking to Mordacq:

> After having struggled so much during these past weeks in the interest of my country, it is really too much to get this kind of letter from someone who never wished to understand that, in

order to make peace with Germany, we could not be more alone than when we were fighting her. And even so he needs to recall that at the end of the war, when he was the commander in chief, who had every right to give orders, he could not make the Americans obey. I had to make a peace treaty with no authority to give orders, and even so I got almost everything that one could. What more does he want?[101]

Clemenceau regretted that his impossible relations with Poincaré had given room to Foch for these and other maneuvers, including planting other articles in the French press. Clemenceau had no desire to deal with the political storm that would follow the resignation of the most famous French general since Napoleon, but he would accept it. "So much the worse for Foch," he remarked. The marshal, however, failed to make good on his threat.

Foch did, however, make one more attempt to sway Allied policy. On 16 June 1919, the Council of Four—the leaders of the United States, France, Britain, and Italy—summoned him to inquire about his plans in the event that Germany refused to sign the treaty. Although Germany was disarmed, Foch declared that the task of occupying Germany would absorb such a large force that his armies would reach Berlin "too anemic to deliver the decisive blow."

In order to avoid this ruinous occupation . . . the only way is to put southern Germany out of action, that is, to think about a separatist strategy. But in order for this separatist strategy to obtain results, it must be completed by a separatist policy, which imposes a separate peace and disarmament on the states of the South.[102]

Lloyd George replied angrily, "I fear the Marshal is mixing policy with strategy and allowing his judgment about political matters to create doubts in his mind about purely military questions."[103] Later that day, he, Wilson, and Clemenceau got together and commiserated with one another. "He has seen his plans collapse and doesn't want to help in the execution of ours," Wilson remarked. Clemenceau was more blunt yet.

> If he has it in his head not to go to Berlin, he won't go. What troubles me is that in our last meetings, Marshal Foch has not always proved entirely frank. I recently spoke to him about a newspaper article that I knew was inspired by him; he denied it. Then I said to him: "Do you want me to give you the name of the officer on your general staff who corrected the proofs?" He couldn't reply.[104]

Grimly, Clemenceau asked for twenty-four hours to clear matters up, saying only that he intended to speak with Pétain—whom, it is clear, he would have used to replace Foch. A week later, however, after a tense standoff, Germany acceded to the terms of the treaty, and Foch (who usually backed down from all-out confrontation with the Tiger) never confronted the ultimate test of military subordination to policy.

"YOU CHALLENGE ME. HERE I AM."[105]

Foch continued the battle after the war, however, through interviews that he granted and approved with friendly journalists, criticizing Clemenceau as a "domineering Jacobin" who had a morbid distrust of the military. His final shot—a posthumously published memoir dictated to Raymond Recouly—prompted Clemenceau to respond with a furious denunciation in his own memoirs, *Grandeur and Misery of Victory*. "The Parthian, as he fled at full gallop, loosed one more shaft behind. At the moment when he was swallowed up in the night of the tomb Marshal Foch seems to have left a whole bundle of stray arrows to the uncertain bow of a chance archer."[106]

Clemenceau had discovered that the civil-military relations of peace-making can be as difficult as the civil-military relations of waging war. Victorious generals are heroes. Particularly in a coalitional war, but indeed in virtually any conflict, high-ranking soldiers have close contact with political leaders; accordingly they develop their own concepts of politics, and come to feel more familiar in that realm than they normally do in peacetime. Having seen, and in some cases felt closely, the sacrifices made to win a war, these general officers are dismayed, even horrified at the prospect of losses shrugged off for what seem to be low or unworthy motives. Domineering personalities for the most part—for they could not have succeeded in war without tremendous force of character—they believe it their right, indeed their duty, to win the peace for their countries. General Maxime Weygand, Foch's chief of staff, shrugged off Clemenceau's irritation by saying there was nothing wrong in Foch's opposition to the premier. "Discipline is not servility. A man is a man, after all."[107] One should set these apparently mild words against Weygand's military career (including four years as commander in chief of the French military) that included involvement in reactionary politics throughout the interwar period and that culminated in his intimate involvement with France's surrender and collaboration with Nazi Germany in 1940.

Clemenceau, whose commitment to the supremacy of civilian power and the political neutrality of the army was absolute, would have none of this. He made few concessions to Foch's inflated picture of his proper role in the peace negotiations, and he yielded little to the importunate general's claims of his own importance or his view of the proper settlement at this war's end. France had a weak hand to play, and Clemenceau knew it. British anxieties about Germany had declined sharply with the destruction of the German fleet and the naval disarmament clauses, which were far easier to enforce than those on land. He shared with the British a fear of a Communist revolution in Germany itself, as well as in Russia, and he had to contend with a United States that commanded vast wealth and resources and was nearly untouched by the war. Meanwhile his own country, ravaged and bled white, had, he knew, no stomach for a renewal of the war.

Clemenceau, despite his ferocity and unyielding determination to fight for France, knew the art of not overreaching. He was, in the words of Woodrow Wilson's biographer Arthur Link, "the wisest and most far-sighted of the Four."[108] The terms he obtained for France were, on the whole, good ones. Germany was disarmed; its military was reduced to 100,000 long-service volunteers and denied most of the advanced technology needed for modern warfare. The left bank of the Rhine was demilitarized (as was its right bank to a depth of fifty kilometers), and its remilitarization designated a *causa belli*. Heavy reparations payments were levied upon Germany, and a band of successor states naturally hostile to Germany created to its east. Britain and the United States gave France commitments—subsequently withdrawn—to come to her aid in the event of another German challenge. Clemenceau was surely right when he wrote:

> I am bitterly censured for having refused to give my country a strategic frontier. How can I take seriously those who, both great and small, reproach me with this, since they know that I could not—apart from any question of the rights of the peoples—annex the Rhineland without breaking off our alliance, *which no one dared to suggest to me?*[109]

Foch never confronted this issue, save to dismiss it. Yet quite apart from the impractical nature of his demands—and the impropriety of his method of making them—his strategic judgment appears even in retrospect to be lamentable.

France, as Clemenceau knew, could not ensure its security by the Rhine frontier alone. A peace based on the principle of self-determination could not deny that right to millions of Germans in the Rhineland, who—the agitation of a minority for a separate republic notwithstanding—clearly wished to remain German. French security would rest on two critical considerations: the creation of a French military force that could compensate for France's weakness in manpower—taking advantage of German disarmament to create a long-term lead in military power—and a close relationship with the Allies. To that end, an even more punitive peace with Germany would not serve. However, a France more willing to act decisively in the 1930s, a Britain less blinkered by its own troubles, a United States more open to its global responsibilities, and above all, a Germany resistant to the infection of Nazism could have avoided the calamity that followed the rise of Hitler.

By then, however, the valiant old man who had saved his country from one scourge had, at last, passed from the scene. Wounded in an assassination attempt during the peace negotiations, harried by longstanding enemies and erstwhile friends, he was repudiated by France when he ran for the presidency in January of 1920. He retired, but not before performing one last service to his country: he toured the United States in 1922 urging the country that he admired and knew well not to abandon France. He died in 1929, having left a grim warning to his countrymen:

> There are nations that are beginning. There are nations that are coming to an end. Our consciousness of our own acts entails the fixing of responsibilities. France will be what the men of France deserve. . . . There will be days of horror, and then the appeal to Fate, who from our scattered limbs will re-create another champion of Destiny.[110]

He was all too correct in his prophesy.

Although Clemenceau departed life depressed by what he foresaw for France—its allies' perfidy, its enemies' hostility, and its own weakness of spirit—he left it with a positive legacy as well, a legacy of courage in the worst of circumstances to which other Frenchmen would turn in years to come. A quarter of a century later, an army of a defeated and yet reborn and victorious France passed again under the Arc de Triomphe. Its leader—Clemenceau's "champion of Destiny," perhaps?—loved France and mistrusted Frenchmen as deeply as he had. Charles de Gaulle marched at the head of the battle-scarred veterans of Free France down the avenue where four years earlier stunned Parisians had watched Hitler's victorious armies goose-step by. De Gaulle looked up and greeted the statue of Clemenceau, thinking for a moment as he marched by that the old man "looked as if he were springing up to march beside us."[111] In a sense the Tiger had done just that.

CHAPTER 4

CHURCHILL ASKS A QUESTION

"THE GREATEST EXHILARATION OF ALL"

On 21 June 1940, an anxious twenty-eight-year-old London scientist who had spent something less than a year working in the field of scientific intelligence (itself a rather new field) arrived at his office to find a message from a friend, telling him to report to the Cabinet Room at 10 Downing Street. R. V. Jones—a practical joker who delighted in giving others plausible excuses to plunge telephones into buckets of water—took some time to realize that the summons was, in fact, altogether serious. He hurried over to Downing Street and was ushered into the Cabinet Room. There he found Winston Churchill, prime minister and minister of defence, flanked by his scientific adviser, the minister of aircraft production, the air minister, and the uniformed high command of the Royal Air Force: the chief of air staff, the commanders in chief of both Fighter Command and Bomber Command, and their scientific advisers. The meeting concerned the possibility that the Germans had developed a means of all-weather precision navigation—and with it, the ability to drop bombs through cloud cover—that would give them a decided advantage in the battle of Britain, the German air offensive against Britain then under way. The evidence was fragmentary, including enigmatic radio intercepts such as "Cleves Knickebein is established at position 53° 24' North and 1° West," a curious radio receiver retrieved from a German bomber shot down a few nights earlier, a prisoner of war's claim that the Germans had a new navigation system, and some odd-shaped towers photographed on the North German island of Sylt.

Churchill asked Jones to explain what it all meant. "For twenty minutes or more he spoke in quiet tones, unrolling his chain of circumstantial evidence, the like of which for its convincing fascination was never surpassed by tales of Sherlock Holmes or Monsieur Lecoq."[1] For a moment lines from the *Ingoldsby Legends* came to the old man:

> *But now one Mr. Jones*
> *Comes forth and depones*
> *That, fifteen years since, he had heard certain groans*
> *On his way to Stone Henge (to examine the stones*
> *Described in a work of the late Sir John Soane's)*
> *that he'd followed the moans,*
> *And, led by their tones,*
> *Found a Raven a-picking a Drummer-boy's bones!*

The poem flashed by, because after hearing him out Churchill quizzed the young man, who made the case that the Germans were using radio beams to find their way to their targets. The others present, eminent scientists and marshals of the Royal Air Force, doubted his evidence—the physics was too difficult, and after all British pilots were trained to navigate by the stars, and found their targets very reliably that way—or so they believed, until the evidence proved otherwise.[2] Jones stood his ground and made the case for the beams. Churchill probed. What could be done? Could the existence of the beams be verified? Could aerial mines be sowed along their path? Could they be deceived or jammed? Jones replied to the direct questioning. He was, he later recalled, filled with

> the elation of a young man at being noticed by any prime minis-
> ter, but somehow it was much more. It was the same whenever
> we met in the war—I had the feeling of being recharged by con-
> tact with a source of living power. Here was strength, resolution,
> humor, readiness to listen, to ask the searching question and,
> when convinced, to act. He was rarely complimentary at the time,
> handsome though his compliments could be afterwards, for he
> had been brought up in sterner days. In 1940 it was compliment
> enough to be called in by him at the crisis; but to stand up to his
> questioning attack and then to convince him was the greatest
> exhilaration of all.[3]

As for Churchill, "Being master, and not having to argue too much, once I was convinced about the principles of this queer and deadly game, I gave all the necessary orders that very day in June for the existence of the beam to be assumed, and for all counter-measures to receive absolute priority. The slightest reluctance or deviation in carrying out this policy was to be reported to me."[4] In short order, by a combination of jamming and deception, the British deprived KNICKEBEIN of most of its usefulness.

"WHAT A PUBLIC MENACE HE IS!"

Few historical figures escape revisions of their worth as statesmen; this is particularly true of wartime leaders, and especially true of Winston Churchill. Although some presidents and prime ministers have had their reputations rise (Harry Truman, most notably) or remain the same (Lincoln comes to mind), such re-examination usually chips away at the historical statuary rather than polishing it. In the case of Churchill the critique is particularly interesting, because it goes not only to the question of the character and personality of the British leader but to the essence of the activity in which he engaged—the creation of strategy. The revision downward of Churchill's worth as a war leader implies not only a changed view of the man but a changed view of what strategy is in wartime and how it is fashioned, for Churchill is the twentieth-century war statesman *par excellence*.

"There are times when I incline to judge all historians by their opinion of Winston Churchill—whether they can see that, no matter how much better the details, often damaging, of man and career become known, he still remains, quite simply, a great man."[5] Judged by historian G. R. Elton's standards, many contemporary historians fail. For the last several decades Churchill's war leadership has come under increasingly severe attack, culminating in John Charmley's savage biography of him.[6] Actually, the current spate of criticism represents merely the latest of several waves of postwar attacks on Churchill as warlord.

The first surge of criticism came primarily from military authors, and in particular from Churchill's own chairman of the Chiefs of Staff and Chief of the Imperial General Staff, Alan Brooke. The publication of portions of his diaries in the late 1950s shocked readers, who discovered in entries that Brooke himself later described as "liverish" that all had not gone smoothly between Churchill and his generals. In fact, Brooke had withheld some of the more pointed criticisms of the prime minister, which he often wrote after late-night arguments with Churchill. If anything, his anger at the prime minister grew as the war went on. On 10 September 1944 Brooke wrote in his diary (in an entry not present in the first, published version):

[Churchill] has only got half the picture in his mind, talks absurdities and makes my blood boil to listen to his nonsense. I find it hard to remain civil. And the wonderful thing is that 3/4 of the population of this world imagine that Winston Churchill is one of the Strategists of History, a second Marlborough, and the other 1/4 have no conception what a public menace he is and has been throughout the war! It is far better that the world should never know and never suspect the feet of clay on that otherwise super-human being. Without him England was lost for a certainty, with him England has been on the verge of disaster time [and] again. . . . Never have I admired and despised a man simultane-ously to the same extent.[7]

Brooke was not alone. Others expressed themselves in more temperate language but had, one suspects, opinions no less severe. One chroni-cally jaundiced military adviser quoted approvingly Robert Menzies, Australia's prime minister early in World War II: "Only Churchill's magnificent and courageous leadership compensated for his deplorable strategic sense."[8] As the war went on their discontent with their polit-ical master seems, if anything, to have grown. At the end of the war in Europe, General Hastings Ismay recalled a decade later, Churchill hosted a victory celebration for the chiefs of staff at 10 Downing Street. The prime minister "handed out extravagant praise to the three Chiefs of Staff as having been the architects of victory. Not one of them responded by saying that Winston had also had a little to do with it."[9]

Many of the field marshals and admirals of World War II came away nursing the bruises that inevitably came their way in dealing with Churchill. They deplored his excessive interest in what struck them as properly military detail; they feared his imagination and its restless probing for new courses of action. For them, as for some historians who have sympathized with their point of view, Churchill's greatest flaw as warlord was that he meddled, incurably and unforgivably, in the pro-fessional affairs of his military advisers. "The prime minister had no understanding of operational details, nor of logistic constraints and opportunities; but he had a great passion for them. He pestered com-manders in the field for information and bombarded them with exhortations which went well beyond his responsibilities."[10]

A second wave of criticism comes from those who have pored over the documents at some distance from the actual events. Thus David Reynolds writes of Britain's "decision" (his quotes) to fight on in 1940 as "right policy, wrong reasons." Writing of Churchill elsewhere as "a romantic militarist," Reynolds deplores with mock pathos the fate of "young whippersnappers who have the temerity to read the documents and then ask awkward questions!"[11] Other historians have had less resort to humor. Churchill was "seldom consistent and was easily carried away."[12] Small wonder, then, that "the conduct of war emerged, not from any one 'grand plan' or strategy, but out of a series of conflicting and changing views, misunderstandings, personal interests and confusions."[13] In the end, in this view Churchill, "like all men, however great, was powerless to alter the great decisions of history."[14] Thus, for the new historians Churchill's sins have to do less with bullying and meddling—few late-twentieth-century scholars are inclined to carry a brief for generals—than with lack of foresight or inability to bring any plan to fruition. When Churchill was right, it was for the wrong reasons; if he changed his mind, and he did so frequently, it was a sign of febrile instability; if he described the strategic position to the Allies in compelling prose, it was a sham that covered up chaotic forces that he had neither the wisdom nor the fixity of purpose to master.

Thus we have another indictment, no less severe than that of the generals: Churchill failed as a strategist because he did not devise a coherent strategy for the war. Perhaps no one can, some of these historians might argue; in that case, Churchill deserves removal from his pedestal because he misled his contemporaries and at least one succeeding generation into believing otherwise. Even at his best, contemporary historians frequently contend, Churchill did no better than would any other statesman in his place. Churchill devoted an enormous amount of attention, for example, to his personal relationship with President Franklin D. Roosevelt, which he regarded as central to the Anglo-American alliance, and with it, to victory. Historian

Warren Kimball, however, dismisses the importance of the Churchill-Roosevelt relationship. "Had it been Neville Chamberlain and Wendell Willkie—a plausible prospect—wartime relations between the two nations would not have been fundamentally different."[15]

One may sympathize with both groups of critics. The generals, after all, suffered the indignities of working with a man who kept them up late night after night, while hounding them with questions of detail. Even less forgivable, one suspects, were such barbs as his remark about confronting, in the person of his Chief of the Imperial General Staff, "the dead hand of inanition," or his observation, on watching the chiefs of staff file out of a meeting. "I have to wage modern war with ancient weapons."[16] Strolling past a new bomb-proof shelter at the Admiralty he is reported to have remarked, "They have put up a very strong place there—masses of concrete and tons of steel. Taking into account the fact that their heads are solid bone, they ought to be quite safe inside."[17] Bearing the responsibilities they shouldered, knowing better than anyone else the strains suffered by a force all too often fighting at a disadvantage, small wonder that they seethed with discontent. Nor did Churchill's work habits make their lives any easier. Working to a military routine they had to rise early, but serving a master who transacted much business after a late dinner they often had to stay up until the small hours of the morning.

Surrounding their caustic and aggressive master were a host of odd characters: acerbic professors like Frederick Lindemann, piratical politicians like Max Beaverbrook and Brendan Bracken, and maverick soldiers like Orde Wingate of Burma fame or Percy Hobart, a pioneering tank general reinstated to active duty after Churchill found him languishing as a corporal in the Home Guard. It was Hobart's recall to service that prompted Churchill's remark to Field Marshall Dill, who opposed the move, "It isn't only the good boys who help to win the wars; it is the sneaks and the stinkers as well."[18] To this a modern British officer, pledged to resurrect Dill's reputation and reflecting nearly fifty years after the event the wounded feelings of that decent but limited man:

Churchill had a weakness for sneaks and stinkers of all kinds. . . .
Perhaps only a stinker *manqué* manages to be his own biographer.
He should not be allowed to have the last word.[19]

The historians as well have some excuse for their impatience. The
stifling weight of pro-Churchill orthodoxy that dominated not only historiography but public opinion for decades after the Second World War
eventually provoked a reaction from the academics, who are naturally
skeptical of political leaders. Churchill's own World War II memoirs,
appearing shortly after the war and bolstered by large quantities of official documents, held the field for many years in shaping popular as
well as scholarly understanding of the war. Here too was a source of discontent for professional students of the past, who by both training and
temperament look askance at the self-serving accounts of political leaders, and who rebel automatically against conventional wisdom and pat
interpretations of great events. Moreover, some of them are deeply sus-
picious of the vivid and generally favorable accounts of those politicians,
officers, and civil servants who worked most intimately with Churchill
and maintained an unaccountably high regard for him—"an exclusive,
close-knit, troglodytic group," as Alex Danchev calls them.[20]

All the more irritating to many professional historians have been the
political leaders of our own day who have declared their reverence for
Churchill. Churchill's popularity with the likes of conservative politicians such as Dan Quayle, Caspar Weinberger, or Margaret Thatcher has
not improved his standing with professors on either side of the Atlantic.
A popular icon as much as an historial figure, Churchill excites the
kind of intense admiration in narrow circles usually reserved for sports
stars in broader ones. The existence of an International Churchill
Society (complete with annual conferences, a glossy magazine, and a
souvenir shop selling "Action This Day" stickers) embodies the kind of
hero worship that most historians instinctively reject—this is all the
more upsetting in view of Churchill's indubitably checkered career.
Even as sympathetic a historian as Michael Howard remarks that "the

problem for the historian" is "how it was that a man with so unpromising a background and so disastrous a track record could emerge in 1940 as the savior of his country."[21]

The generals may have suffered from their excessive closeness to a man who made excruciating demands upon their energies, time, and patience. The dons may have let the temptations of the donnish life, which rewards swipes at historical orthodoxy and deprecates the Great Man theory of history, get the better of them. Both groups were abetted by murmurs of dissent from within Churchill's camp. Of these none was more important than the diary/memoir of Churchill's personal physician, Lord Moran, who described the ailments that began to affect the prime minister during World War II.[22] (Another member of Churchill's inner circle cuttingly remarked of Moran, "He was not, of course, present when discussions of political and military importance took place; but he was often invited to luncheon afterwards.")[23] The legend of a Churchill debilitated by heart ailments and exhaustion, woozy with liquor and showing the signs of early senility still persists, although the truth seems to be that he survived the stresses of the war in far better physical condition and with greater mental acuity than younger political leaders and general officers.

Churchill's critics, both contemporary and subsequent, hold a common view of the central flaw in his makeup as a statesman: instability. In their view he was the creature of his enthusiasms, a genius, to be sure, but a whimsical and erratic fantasist. His passion for the Dardanelles expedition of 1915, his quixotic defense of Edward VIII (later made duke of Windsor), his imperialist opposition to Indian independence, his relentless pursuit of strategic dead ends in World War II—including an invasion of Norway early in the war and a lunge for Vienna through the Ljubljana gap at its end—display a lack of political and military sobriety dismaying in a head of state. His odd working hours and exuberant life style (including his reputed taste for Chablis with breakfast and his consumption of whisky throughout working hours), his love of uniforms and his hounding of military subordinates about tactical and technical details well beyond his purview (proposals for antiaircraft defenses based on rockets rather than guns, for example, or his minute proposals for artificial harbors to be installed on the French coast immediately following an invasion) seem to reinforce these views. In this light, and increasingly to modern students of Churchill, he appears a brilliant orator but one whose reactionary views and wild imagination, whose incessant meddling and irrational enthusiasms made him as much a menace as a source of salvation to a beleaguered Britain. Indeed, it is fair to say that this is now very much the scholarly view of Churchill.[24]

"IT IS ALL THE FAULT OF THE HUMAN BRAIN BEING MADE IN TWO LOBES."

In fact, the above impression, common though it be, is false to the core, for Churchill was a man of system—unorthodox and exuberant system, but system nonetheless. A shrewd Royal Navy captain, Percy Scott, himself a pioneer in naval warfare, observed after meeting a twenty-five-year-old Winston Churchill in 1899, "I am very proud to have met you. . . . I feel certain that I shall some day shake hands with you as prime minister of England. You possess the two necessary qualifications, genius and plod."[25] The plod was no less important than the genius. Churchill, far from being an aristocratic lounger, was a glutton for work; his motto to his secretaries during the Second World War was "KBO"—"Keep Buggering On."[26] Only disciplined work habits allowed him to pursue a crowded career that included leading positions in politics, a steady stream of journalistic output, and the writing of at least five multivolume works, as well as single-volume books of history and personal narrative. His staff usually consisted of at least one private secretary and three or more other secretaries, who had to work in relays to keep up with the blizzard of letters, articles, and books that he dictated to them. His working hours were, it is true, hard on his subordinates, extending as they frequently did into the small hours of the morning. But here too he exhibited not self-indulgence but a regimen that enabled him to handle a crushing burden of work. Rising at eight, he would read for several hours in bed—scanning newspapers, intelligence reports, and cables. Meetings and dictation of minutes would be followed by lunch and then a nap of an hour or more, allowing him to work on until early morning. "By this means I was able to press a day and a half's work into one," he recalled; he maintained this routine throughout the war.[27] That he enjoyed leisurely lunches and dinners is true; one must ask, however, whether this did not show a shrewd understanding of the need for some relaxation in sociable circumstances from the extraordinary pressures of war. Indeed, in this respect as in others—for example, his orders not to be woken up for news save in the most dire circumstances—Churchill exhibited a wise sense of pacing that allowed him, a man of seventy in 1944, to sustain a program of work and travel that would have killed a much younger man.

Churchill's appetite for information included a shrewd ability to ensure its delivery to him in usable form. He turned to "the Prof," Professor Frederick Lindemann of Oxford (later Lord Cherwell), who had the outstanding gift of being able to explain briefly and lucidly some of the chief technical issues associated with modern warfare—an invaluable service for a chief who had an abiding interest in technology but no background in science. The Prof, moreover, ran a small statistical office that prepared accurate and comprehensible charts and tables for the prime minister, enabling him to retain a good picture of those aspects of the war (especially the battle of the Atlantic) which could only be measured and judged in this way, rather than by the movement of battle lines. The Prof's data often served the prime minister better than did the more tendentious presentations prepared by various departments of the government. And the Prof provided an independent—occasionally misguided, but nonetheless useful—source of military analysis. It was, for example, Lindemann who first suspected in 1941 that Bomber Command had had far less success in hitting its targets than it claimed, prompting Churchill to launch a series of studies and reforms that led to a far more capable Royal Air Force by 1944.

System, not whim, dominated Churchill's government machinery. His immediate staff throughout the war consisted primarily of men who had worked for and admired his predecessor Neville Chamberlain. His strict injunction to conduct business in writing ("Let it be very clearly understood that all directions from me are made in writing, or should be immediately afterwards confirmed in writing, and that I do not accept any responsibility for matters relating to national defence on which I am alleged to have given decisions, unless they are recorded in writing") stands in remarkable contrast to the work habits of Roosevelt, Hitler, and Stalin, all of whom relied chiefly on the spoken word, with all its increased possibilities for ambiguity and misinterpretation.[28] At his orders, a small but diligent staff followed up the blizzard of memoranda that issued from his office, making sure that orders were followed, questions answered, and data assembled. Of orders, however, there were actually very few, particularly in military matters, as we shall see. Moreover, throughout the war Churchill relied on his staff to maintain a smoothly working machinery of war direction. General Sir Hastings Ismay, the secretary to the Chiefs of Staff, served as the indispensable link between the irascible prime minister and his harried chieftains. As Ismay later described his role: "I felt that my job was to interpret, repeat to interpret, the prime minister to the Chiefs of Staff, and the Chiefs of Staff to the prime minister."[29] This task he performed superbly. One suspects that in his absence the undeniable rancor between Churchill and the chiefs might have exploded disastrously. Indeed, Ismay recalled in 1964 that in advance of the second Quebec summit the Chiefs of Staff were on the verge of a collective resignation. Ismay "stepped into the breach" and formally resigned, only to have the resignation ripped up and relations at least temporarily restored.[30]

Churchill's work habits reveal far more order and discipline than is commonly thought; the same holds true for the zigs and zags of his policymaking. In an historical work, Churchill wrote of the first duke of

Marlborough's contemporary, Lord Halifax, that "a love of moderation and a sense of the practical seemed in him to emerge in bold rather than tepid courses. He could strike as hard for compromise as most leaders for victory."[31] Whether or not this description accurately captured the eighteenth-century statesman, it surely did his twentieth-century student.

> I thought we ought to have conquered the Irish and then given them Home Rule: that we ought to have starved out the Germans, and then revictualled their country; and that after smashing the General Strike we should have met the grievances of the miners. I always get into trouble because so few people take this line. . . . It is all the fault of the human brain being made in two lobes, only one of which does any thinking, so that we are all right-handed or left-handed; whereas if we were properly constructed we should use our right and left hands with equal force and skill according to circumstances. As it is, those who can win a war well can rarely make a good peace, and those who could make a good peace would never have won the war.[32]

This was a theme to which Churchill gave attention on more than one occasion.[33]

> To understand history the reader must always remember how small is the proportion of what is recorded to what actually took place, and above all how severely the time factor is compressed. Years pass with chapters and sometimes with pages, and the tale abruptly reaches new situations, changed relationships, and different atmospheres. Thus the figures of the past are insensibly portrayed as more fickle, more harlequin, and less natural in their actions than they really were.[34]

Churchill brought to the Second World War an exceedingly rich knowledge, direct as well as vicarious, of military affairs. Indeed, unique among statesmen, he experienced many of the great wars of his lifetime twice—once in reality, a second time in study, as he reflected upon their structure and meaning. During his early career as a junior officer and newspaper correspondent (roles that he combined, to the distress of his superiors) he saw combat on several continents—in India, Cuba, the Sudan, and South Africa. Some historians have suggested that these colonial campaigns gave him a romantic picture of war. Had he not taken part in, and subsequently described with obvious relish and exuberance, one of the last great and successful cavalry charges, at the battle of Omdurman in 1898? And did he not write, in retrospect, that "there is nothing so exhilarating as being shot at without result"?

In truth, however, a closer examination of both the published work and the private letters even from this period of his career reveals a far more sober and penetrating student of war. In his one-volume book *The River War*, for example, he pays eloquent tribute to the importance of the Anglo-Egyptian force's lines of communications, and to the remarkable feats of transport and supply that were crucial to Lord Kitchener's campaign up the Nile.

> Victory is the beautiful, bright-colored flower. Transport is the stem without which it could never have blossomed. Yet even the military student, in his zeal to master the fascinating combinations of the actual conflict, often forgets the far more intricate complications of supply.[35]

Making good this rhetorical flourish, Churchill proceeded to devote an entire chapter to a meticulous and lucid account of the complicated logistics of Kitchener's operations.

In these conflicts, of course, Churchill was a junior participant, his writings still those of a promising young man. In the years leading up to the First World War he was a leading figure, serving as First Lord of the Admiralty from 1911 to 1915, taking a brief turn in the trenches, and then returning to public office as minister of munitions and later secretary of state for war. His four-volume work, *The World Crisis,* although supposedly dismissed by George Bernard Shaw as "a memoir masquerading as a history of the cosmos," contains extended reflections on all features of war, including the processes of technological innovation, tactics, and the problem of coalition warfare. His chapter on "The Romance of Design," for example, carries a reader from the problem of gun size on battleships to the larger trade-offs (speed, armor, and firepower) in warship design, to the issue of propulsion, which in turn bore on the momentous decision to change the Royal Navy over from coal to oil as its principal fuel—a seemingly technical decision pregnant with vast political consequences.[36]

To those wars that Churchill both fought and lived one must add those that he experienced as an historian only.[37] Of these, the most important were the War of the Spanish Succession, conducted by his ancestor the first duke of Marlborough, and the American Civil War. His biography of Marlborough, again too easily dismissed as a mere apologia for his great ancestor, is best understood not only as history but also as a treatise on statesmanship.[38] It is, in particular, a study of the problem of coalition warfare—and "the history of all coalitions," he told his readers, "is a tale of the reciprocal complaints of allies."[39]

The American Civil War formed a central feature of Churchill's last major work, his *History of the English-speaking Peoples,* much of which was composed before the Second World War.[40] He devoted less time and energy to its study than he had to the other conflicts that he examined, but it too informed his understanding of war. When, for example, he recalled the skepticism (substantial in English military circles) about American military potential, he wrote that his firm conviction to the contrary was based at least in part on his knowledge of the Civil War.[41] On more than one occasion in his account of World War II analogies to the American Civil War develop, as they did in his speeches—particularly, of course, those directed to Americans. He reminded Congress in May 1943 that "No one after Gettysburg doubted which way the dread balance of war would incline, yet far more blood was shed after the Union victory at Gettysburg than in all the fighting which went before." In this he saw, quite properly, an analogy with the Allies' circumstances in that watershed year.[42]

"THE SUM OF ALL FORCES AND PRESSURES OPERATIVE AT A GIVEN PERIOD"

What did Churchill take from this massive experience of and reflection upon war? Oddly, perhaps, the key may be found in a pamphlet—an essay, really—published about his chief hobby, painting, which he explicitly compared with the art of war: "It is the same kind of problem as unfolding a long, sustained, interlocked argument. It is a proposition which, whether of few or numberless parts, is commanded by a single unity of conception."[43] Churchill, a talented amateur painter, brought an artist's perspective to bear on war. The selection of broad themes (a word which he used often in both contexts) and the marshaling of detail to support those large ideas formed an important part of his war statecraft as much as it did of his palette. Painting cannot be done to hard and fast rules or to a rigid schedule; it must be adapted to the scene before it; and room must remain for creativity and adaptation to shifting lights and the artist's own flashes of insight—such artistic truths applied no less to Churchill's war leadership than to his essays in oils. Churchill's frequent use of the word "proportion" is revealing. Often he would remind his colleagues during World War II of the need to set particular operations into the larger context of the scheme of the war. Indeed, much of his genius for war lay in his ability to see the relationship between the large and the minute elements of conflict and to make the latter, where possible, fit the former. He welcomed his sea voyage to the United States following Japan's attack on Pearl Harbor because "it is perhaps a good thing to stand away from the canvas from time to time and take a full view of the picture."[44]

War statesmanship, in Churchill's view, focused at the apex of government an array of considerations and calculations that even those one rung down could not fully fathom. War, he wrote in *The World Crisis*, "knows no rigid divisions between . . . Allies, between Land, Sea and Air, between gaining victories and alliances, between supplies and fighting men, between propaganda and machinery, which is, in fact, simply the sum of all forces and pressures operative at a given period. . . ." Churchill's profound sense of the uncertainties inherent in war suggests that he would have found the notion that one could produce a blueprint for victory at any time before, say, 1943 an absurdity bred of unfamiliarity with war itself.

> War is a constant struggle and must be waged from day to day. It is only with some difficulty and within limits that provision can be made for the future. Experience shows that forecasts are usually falsified and preparations always in arrear. Nevertheless, there must be a design and theme for bringing the war to a victorious end in a reasonable period. All the more is this necessary when under modern conditions no large-scale offensive operation can be launched without the preparation of elaborate technical apparatus.[45]

Here was a view that he had long held as a result of experience and study. "Every set of assumptions which it is necessary to make, draws new veils of varying density in front of the dark curtain of the future."[46] Churchill's awareness of the ironies of politics and the limits of human foresight was grounded not only in the experience of a long life in public affairs, but in a close study of history. Commenting at the end of his biography of the first duke of Marlborough on the shifting relations between Britain and France over the centuries, he observed soberly that "even the most penetrating gaze reaches only conclusions which, however seemingly vindicated at a given moment, are inexorably effaced by time."[47]

Churchill thus struck a middle position between those who would deny any possibility of strategy (as opposed to mere military opportunism, with which he has been charged) and those who would reduce it to a blueprint. In the latter category fell the American military leadership, which bitterly resisted any attempt to deviate from the basic strategy of an invasion of Northwest Europe in 1943. Churchill successfully opposed them, persuading President Roosevelt to adopt first the invasion of North Africa in 1942 and then the follow-up campaigns in Sicily and Italy in 1943.

In part because he mistrusted all foresight, including his own, Churchill believed that the formulation of strategy in war did not consist merely in drawing up state documents sketching out a comprehensive view of how the war would be won, but also in a host of detailed activities which, when united and dominated by a central conception, would form a comprehensive picture.[48] This attention to detail stemmed as well from his unwillingness to put full reliance on military expertise. This skepticism, which he did not hide, provoked the deepest resentments in Churchill's lieutenants. They knew that although he might respect them individually for their knowledge, courage, and qualities of leadership, he regarded his military subordinates with no small amount of professional mistrust. Some of this stemmed from his suspicion of bureaucratic processes. "You may take the most gallant sailor, the most intrepid airman, or the most audacious soldier, put them at a table together—what do you get? The sum total of their fears!"[49] Hence too his mordant remarks about military staffs, even at one point a suggestion that "The best thing would be to form a Sacred Legion of about one thousand staff officers and let them set an example to the troops in leading some particularly desperate attack."[50]

To a degree that is today insufficiently realized, all the high-ranking combatants of the Second World War, at least in its early phases, operated on the basis of personal memories of the First. It is striking indeed how often analogies with World War I experiences crop up in official memoranda and minutes of discussions. In Churchill's case one dominant memory, of course, was of having attempted to force through a strategy, the attack on Turkey via the Dardanelles, which collapsed as a result of what he considered to be insufficient military enthusiasm for the project. Certainly the First World War dominated British thinking about acceptable levels of casualties in major military operations on the Continent—hence Lindemann's 1942 remark to General George C. Marshall, chief of staff of the United States Army, as the latter pressed for an early landing on the European Continent, "It's no use—you are arguing against the casualties on the Somme."[51] From Churchill's point of view, however, the most important feature of the First World War was the cold and glaring light it cast on the limitations of senior military leaders.

Norman Brook, secretary of the Cabinet under Churchill in the 1950s, wrote to Hastings Ismay, the former secretary to the Chiefs of Staff, a revealing Churchillian observation: "Churchill has said to me, in private in conversation, that this [a more harmonious pattern of civil-military relations than in 1914–1918] was partly due to the extent to which the generals had been discredited in the First War—which meant that, in the Second War, their successors could not pretend to be professionally infallible."[52] Churchill did not share the simple view, common after the First World War, that the top brass had been mere incompetents, callous dullards oblivious to human suffering. Rather, it was that they persisted in a theory of war that could only be conducted at enormous cost. British and French generals "were throughout consistently true to their professional theories, and when in the fifth campaign of the war the facts began for the first time to fit the theories, they reaped their just reward."[53] In his sophisticated if severe criticism of the generals he anticipated the conclusions of historians writing some seventy years later; they had, of course, far greater advantages of time and documentation with which to work.[54]

Commanders in chief, Churchill wrote, are, like emperors, surrounded "by smiling and respectful faces" of staffs that "are often prompted to use smooth processes" rather than bring harsh facts to the

fore. "The whole habit of mind of a military staff is based on subordination of opinion."[55] If there was one failure in war direction during the
First World War, in Churchill's view, it was a fault that he ascribed to
the political leadership in dealing with Lord Kitchener, who was secretary of state for war but really, in the first years of the war, a
generalissimo in all but name: "The War Council, instead of coming to
grips with him and making him come to grips with his problem, mutely
and supinely awaited the mysterious workings of his mind."[56]
Politicians should make no apologies for putting their military subordinates under severe pressure, because "war is a business of terrible
pressures."[57]

Churchill expressed his view most directly in a comment deprecating
an American proposal in 1943 for appointing a single supreme commander for the war in Northwest Europe.

> This all looks very simple from a distance and appeals to the
> American sense of logic. However in practice it is found not suf-
> ficient for a government to give a general a directive to beat the
> enemy and wait to see what happens. The matter is much more
> complicated. The general may well be below the level of his task,
> and has often been found so.[58]

Churchill, to be sure, admired many military leaders, including some of
those whose views he contested bitterly. But at no point was he willing
to simply take their judgments on faith—especially not on some of the
higher isues of strategy, but not on technical matters either. Nor should
he have. The spotlight that today is focused on Churchill's errors of
operational and strategic judgment all too often ignores the extent to
which these were shared, sometimes with greater enthusiasm, by his
professional advisers—such as his exaggeration of the possibilities in
Greece in the spring of 1941, or his more dangerous underestimation of
Japanese military and naval abilities later in that year, or his exaggeration of the strategic possibilities open in the eastern Mediterranean

and Italy in 1944. This selective reading of the record also leaves unil-
luminated the mistakes, no less grave or frequent, of his professional
advisers when they ran counter to Churchill's judgments. At different
points, let it be remembered, his senior military leaders were unwilling
to run risks at home to save the Mediterranean in 1941, fully expected
Russia to collapse in that year (as they did Germany in 1944), underestimated the military potential of the United States in 1942, entertained
the gravest reservations about the Normandy operation ("It may well be
the most ghastly disaster of the whole war!" wrote Brooke on June 5
1944),[59] disbelieved in the possibility of strategic bombing of anything
other than cities, and refused to concede, as late as 1944, that the day
of the battleship had passed. Were their views to come under a scrutiny
as severe as that they and others accorded Churchill's, one might well
wonder how their reputations would stand up. What would the anti-
Churchill historians do, for example, with misjudgments as egregious
as that of the chief planners of the British Chiefs of Staff who in
September 1941 expressed the view "that the entry of Russia into the
war made no fundamental change in our major strategy"?[60]

The core problem with much of the historical critique of Churchill
does not lie in its details, many of which are indeed right. Rather, and
more fundamentally, the hollowness of the critique results from its lack
of an adequate standard for judging statesmanship, and war statesmanship above all. Forgetting that most human beings usually err in
predicting the future, too many historians seem to grade statesmen
(and Churchill in particular) as if they were scrutinizing the footnotes
of a sloppy undergraduate's term paper. It is perhaps wiser to remember
how often judgments in war are wrong, and to assess a statesman's or
a soldier's qualities by the number and importance of the situations that
he evaluates correctly, rather than by those in which he errs.
Furthermore, the sum total of a statesman's work in a war situation
often has more importance than his specific choices. To say, as is probably correct, that in 1940 Churchill pressed too hard for antisubmarine
tactics that were unlikely to succeed should not blind us to the drive

and coherence he gave to Britain's war against the U-boat by constituting the Battle of the Atlantic Committee, to which he gave unremitting attention throughout the hard years in the North Atlantic until 1943. Furthermore, in considering incidents of personal harshness (and Churchill was no more rough with his subordinates than Roosevelt could be with his, including the ailing Harry Hopkins) some allowance must be made for pressures that the scholar, or even the memoirist, can only dimly conjure up in the comfort of an author's chair. The moods of peace and contemplation differ in the most fundamental way from the crucible of wartime leadership. The difficulty writers have in putting themselves in the place of a wartime political leader, who bears manifold responsibilities and carries stresses that they have never borne, is the gratest obstacle to sound historical judgment on wartime statesmanship. Indeed, even the immediate subordinates of the man at the top only dimly understand, much less share, the acute pressures or the perspective of a prime minister or a president.

When examined with a broader and truer set of standards, Churchill's record is astonishingly good. Consider his largest political and strategic judgments. In 1938 he judged aright the importance of opposing Hitler early, at a time when the odds were against the German dictator. Arguments that he exaggerated the German air menace and underestimated the strain on Britain's financial resources miss the central point, which was that firm opposition to Hitler by a coalition led by Britain, with France and at least one of the East European powers, made sense before Hitler had completed his rearmament and laid his hands on the resources of Eastern Europe. He was right too in the weight he assigned to the American relationship, and in the assiduousness with which he and Roosevelt constructed the closest alliance in history. And he was right as well in his concern about Soviet intentions in Europe, little though he could do to thwart them.

Churchill's record at the operational level is more mixed. His appreciation of the requirements of elaborate air defense systems in 1940 and again in 1944 to counter the German manned and unmanned aerial assaults on London owes something, of course, to his prewar experience. He deserves some credit for the concept of a landing at Anzio in 1944 (which, though badly executed, was potentially an important strike in the Italian campaign). On more than one occasion, to be sure, he advocated courses of action that could have proved a desperate error; these include his willingness to commit some of the scant reserves of the RAF to the fighting in France in June 1940, his belief in JUPITER (an amphibious assault on northern Norway), and his fascination with a similarly extravagant plan for British landings in the Netherlands East Indies in 1944 or 1945. Weighed against these undoubted errors is the cardinal fact that despite having the supreme power to act as he wished, he allowed himself to be talked out of every one of them. More important, one can find numerous examples of sound operational judgment—his drive for a technologically sophisticated set of solutions to the problems of a cross-Channel invasion, his belief in the eventual success of daylight precision bombing by the US Army Air Forces, and his support for an early amphibious strike in Italy in 1944. Moreover, Churchill acted as the patron of odd and eccentric agencies of war— from the cryptanalysts of Bletchley Park to the Commandos and Chindits to a small technological research establishment responsible for such inventions as the PIAT light antitank grenade thrower and the antiship limpet mine.[61] More importantly, his constant questioning and prodding of his generals undoubtedly led to far greater activity on their part than they would otherwise have shown. Churchill's war leadership rested in part on his broad strategic vision, and in part on the effect of his probing questions and efforts to animate each of the many parts of the war effort.

One of Churchill's greatest contributions to the war lay in his ability to define as battles the vague, generalized domains of a prolonged and murky struggle. It was he who coined the terms "Battle of Britain" and "Battle of the Atlantic," which have remained in use among historians more than a half century after the event. More than mere ringing phrases, these terms drew an encompassing circle around varied military activities that were functionally related but that did not lie in the province of any one theater commander or any single service. In each case Churchill would convene a special committee, which he chaired, to bring together every part of the government with responsibility for the task at hand, to sort out priorities and tasks, and to define critical problems. The specially created committees to deal with D-Day sped up the development and production of the specialized equipment (from mobile harbors to amphibious tanks) needed for the assault on Fortress Europe. The Crossbow Committee monitored the development of the German revenge weapons—the V-1 flying bomb and the V-2 missile—and supported the various countermeasures (air defense, bombing of launch sites, and deception plans) devised to contain the threat. Perhaps most successful of all was the Battle of the Atlantic Committee, which gave unparalleled coherence to the British side of the air and naval campaign to secure the Atlantic sea lanes.

One of Churchill's greatest tasks in the Second World War, and one for which his previous experience had uniquely fitted him, was the management of the great Allied coalition against Hitler. Composed of disparate and to some extent antagonistic elements, the Grand Alliance could easily have come apart in any of a number of ways. Churchill faced a three-tiered problem. After 1940 nothing mattered more than the ties between Britain and its two most important potential, and then real, partners, the Soviet Union and the United States. The participation of these two powers in the war, he told Parliament after the fall of Singapore in the dark days of February 1942, "are two tremendous fundamental facts which will in the end dominate the world situation and make victory possible in a form never possible before."[62] His readiness to support the Soviet Union, despite his long-standing opposition to Communism, and his ardent pursuit of the American alliance laid the groundwork for eventual victory. In these relations Churchill had an exceedingly weak hand to play, particularly vis-à-vis the Americans. In 1940 and 1941 Britain nearly bankrupted itself, even as its forces were driven from the Continent in one débacle after another. As a result of British defeats in

France, Greece, and North Africa, Americans entertained the gravest doubts about British military capacities, and many Americans, including the president, viewed with a mixture of skepticism, distaste, and suspicion British imperial policy. It is therefore all the more remarkable that Churchill and his advisers had their way on virtually every major strategic decision—until the end of June 1944, when he was forced to yield to the American insistence on executing the long-planned (and in his view superfluous) invasion of southern France (DRAGOON) as well as the assault on Normandy. The invasion of North Africa in 1942, followed by the attack on Italy in 1943 and follow-on operations there until the winter of 1944, represented the unfolding of a Churchillian strategic design not too different from that laid out in his memoranda prepared for the first Washington conference in 1942. Even later in 1944 Churchill retained his freedom of action, cajoling some modicum of American support for a wildly unpopular policy of intervention in the Greek civil war.

Churchill cultivated the Americans through personal relationships, including his friendship with Harry Hopkins, Roosevelt's intimate adviser and with the president himself, with whom he they exchanged an extraordinary sequence of messages throughout the war. With the Soviets no such relations were possible. Nonetheless, Churchill managed to support the Soviet Union in the war, while yielding neither to the enthusiasm of some of his Cabinet for a premature Second Front to aid Russia nor to the pessimism of his military advisers, who doubted Russia's ability to survive. Relations with the great Allies were never far from his mind, as in April 1943 when he exploded in fury at the news that General Eisenhower was contemplating canceling HUSKY (the invasion of Sicily), if it turned out that two German divisions were in the area of the assault objective.

If the presence of two German divisions is held to be decisive against any operation of an offensive or amphibious character open to the million men now in North Africa, it is difficult to see how the war can be carried on. Months of preparation, sea power and air power in abundance, and yet two German divisions are sufficient to knock it all on the head. . . . I trust the chiefs of staff will not accept these pusillanimous and defeatist doctrines, from whoever they come. We have told the Russians that they cannot have their supplies by the Northern convoy for the sake of "Husky," and now "Husky" is to be abandoned if there are two German divisions (strength unspecified) in the neighborhood. What Stalin would think of this, when he has 185 German divisions on his front, I cannot imagine.[63]

At the same time Churchill fended off the more outrageous demands of the Soviet government and understood, earlier than any other Allied statesman, the threat a Communist Russia would pose to those East European states liberated from one horror by the Red Army only to find another imposed upon them.

A second tier of relationships that absorbed Churchill's time and attention was that with the Empire and the Commonwealth, which also required adroit handling. India and the self-governing dominions (Canada, Australia, New Zealand, and South Africa) provided resources, strategic depth, and manpower, including much of the front-line combat strength of the Imperial ground forces. The Empire required management as well. India was convulsed by internal struggles against British rule; South Africa had a large isolationist element and barely joined the war in 1939; Canada could not impose conscription on its French-speaking population (and therefore not on its Anglophones either); Australia and New Zealand clamored to have their forces under a united command, and to withdraw them to the Pacific immediately upon the outbreak of war with Japan. To navigate his way through these relationships Churchill had to struggle with Middle East commanders who, for example, opposed the unification of Australian forces under a single commander, or with dominion prime ministers who had to be consulted and cajoled, but who could not be given formal decision-making power in the British Cabinet.

A third level of coalition relations was that of lesser Allies and neutrals. Of these none was more important, or more difficult, than the management of the Free French under Charles de Gaulle. Unlike President Roosevelt, who loathed de Gaulle, Churchill understood that the prickly, vain, and uncontrollable general had, unlike other putative French leaders, a real following among the French people. In a similar vein, he did his best to stand by the exiled governments of Greece and Poland, in the face of overwhelming pressures from Communist movements that were determined to wrest power from them in the wake of liberation from Nazi rule. Regarding the neutral powers he was, with some exceptions (Switzerland, most notably), far more ruthless. Seeking to expand the war against Hitler in 1939, he favored violating the neutrality of Norway by mining its territorial waters, arguing that "small nations must not tie our hands when we are fighting for their rights and freedom."[64] Perhaps the grimmest example of his determination was his ordering the assault on the French fleet at Oran in Algeria only a few weeks after France's surrender to Germany in 1940.

Churchill's conduct of the diplomacy of war reveals an extraordinary blend of techniques and approaches. When compared with the cross-purposes at which, for example, the Allies of the First World War operated, the cohesiveness of the Grand Alliance stands out as a remarkable feat. Churchill's personal control of those relations— through extensive correspondence and frequent overseas trips for private meetings and the large conferences that dominated the strategy of the war—accounts for much of their success.

CHURCHILL'S ART OF INTERROGATION

Churchill, of course, served one major function as a war leader by shaping some of the largest decisions of war: for example, when to launch the invasion of France, what weight to place on strategic bombing as a means of defeating Germany, and how much emphasis to put on aid to the Soviet Union. But undergirding these high-level strategic decisions, on which historians traditionally lavish a great deal of attention, are other less visible but no less important activities. They involve decision-making about matters of detail—important detail, but detail nonetheless.

Perhaps the most important of these activities was a continuous audit of the military's judgment. Lord Ismay, the secretary to the Chiefs of Staff and an indispensable figure in the war machine, recalled in his memoirs that "not once during the whole war did [Churchill] overrule his military advisers on a purely military question."[65] He exercised his control over events, rather, by incessant close questioning of the staffs. Churchill, as his generals often complained, kept a close eye on many matters of military detail, querying not only actions but their larger significance. A good example of this is Churchill's scrutiny of an exercise, called VICTOR, which had occurred from 22 to 25 January 1941, under the auspices of the then commander of Home Forces, General Alan Brooke. On 30 March Churchill sent a note to Ismay about VICTOR. It was one in a series of large-scale exercises designed to illuminate the problems of, and prepare for, a German invasion across the Channel. This remained the preeminent military challenge confronting the British, despite their close-run success in the air battles of the fall of 1940, which delayed the invasion threat—forever as it turned out, though no one could know this at the time. Churchill's query went as follows:

1. In the invasion exercise VICTOR two Armoured, one Motorised and two Infantry Divisions were assumed to be landed by the enemy on the Norfolk coast in the teeth of heavy opposition. They fought their way ashore and were all assumed to be in action at the end of 48 hours.

2. I presume the details of this remarkable feat have been worked out by the Staff concerned. Let me see them. For instance, how

many ships and transports carried these five divisions? How many armoured vehicles did they comprise? How many motor lorries, how many guns, how much ammunition, how many men, how many tons of stores, how far did they advance in the first 48 hours, how many men and vehicles were assumed to have landed in the first 12 hours, what percentage of loss were they debited with? What happened to the transports and store-ships while the first 48 hours of fighting was going on? Had they completed emptying their cargoes, or were they still lying in-shore off the beaches? What naval escort did they have? Was the landing at this point protected by superior enemy daylight fighter formations? How many fighter airplanes did the enemy have to employ, if so, to cover the landing places?

The purpose of Churchill's query became clear in the third paragraph:

3. All this data would be most valuable for our future offensive operations. I should be very glad if the same officers would work out a scheme for our landing an exactly similar force on the French coast at the same extreme range of our fighter protection and assuming that the Germans have naval superiority in the Channel. . . .[66]

Clearly, Churchill feared that such exercise assumptions fed an altogether excessive assessment of enemy capabilities, one that if taken seriously could paralyze the British high command and prevent it from acting in any way save defensively. Brooke replied on 7 April, giving the figures noted by Churchill, including estimates of enemy loss rates (10 percent in crossing, 5 to 10 percent on landing), plus the curious assumption that the Germans would sustain themselves with petrol and food captured on British soil.

Churchill responded a few weeks later, noting how much more difficult than this the British landings in Greece had proven, and continuing to press his inquiries.[67] British forces had trickled ashore in Greece in March 1941—under the watchful eye, it must be noted, of the German military attaché, whose country was still at peace with Greece. It took a full month for the British to transport 31,000 lightly equipped soldiers, a force perhaps half the size of the notional German invaders of VICTOR. When the British landed without opposition they still found themselves logistically taxed by the difficulty of simply setting up a base in a foreign country. With that recent experience (admittedly in far rougher terrain and in an undeveloped country) in mind, Churchill found the assumption of the Germans flinging ashore a far larger force in two days, in the teeth of sustained conventional and irregular opposition, to be questionable at the very least. He noted, for example, that on the last two days of the exercise the British were credited with 432 fighter sorties, and the Germans with 1,500—three times as many sorties, although the Luftwaffe had further to fly than did the Royal Air Force. He inquired about how much warning of this invasion was assumed, and asked (without receiving an answer) why the Germans should have been assumed to capture large quantities of petrol on landing in Britain. Gamely enough, Brooke continued to reply until the exchange ended in mid-May.

What is the significance of this episode? It is revealing in what it tells about Churchill's manner of dealing with his subordinates: a relentless querying of their assumptions and arguments, not just once but in successive iterations of a debate. It is noteworthy that the commander in charge of the exercise, Brooke, stood up to Churchill and not only did not suffer by it, but ultimately gained promotion to the post of chief of the Imperial General Staff and chairman of the Chiefs of Staff Committee. It is abundantly clear that Churchill could bear men who disagreed with him, so long as they were neither fools nor silent about it.

Churchill conducted his interrogation with an awareness of the broader implications of any technical issue. Indeed, much of his genius for war lay in his ability to link seemingly mundane or routine matters to much broader problems of policy and strategy. So too in the case of exercise VICTOR. "It is of course quite reasonable for assumptions of this character to be made as a foundation for a military exercise. It would be indeed a darkening counsel to make them the foundation of serious military thought." At this very time, the Chiefs of Staff were debating the dispatch of armored vehicles to the Middle East. Churchill was arguing—against the position of several of his military advisers (including the CIGS, Sir John Dill)—that the risks of invasion were sufficiently low to make the TIGER convoy worth the attempt. TIGER went through, losing only one ship to a mine and delivering some 250 tanks to the hard-pressed British forces in the Middle East.

By no means did Churchill always have it right. Early in the war, for example, he persistently exaggerated the damage done to U-boats by the Royal Navy, although he did so in part as a way of keeping British morale up. More seriously, he initially supported offensive operations against German submarines rather than the sounder course of escorting convoys and picking off the U-boats as they attacked their prey. His persistent attempts to bring Turkey into the war—a policy that absorbed a great deal of diplomatic effort, as well as substantial sums of cash and amounts of military matériel—came to naught. Many of his schemes, and in particular his persistent clamor for operations against northern Norway, could not meet the test of military practicability, and if he is to be faulted it is for pressing them well beyond the point at which their infeasibility had become clear.

But it is no less true that Churchill often caught his military staff when they had it wrong. Sir Alan Cunningham, who succeeded Sir Dudley Pound as First Sea Lord, has established a reputation as a critic and victim of Churchill, without Brooke's bile.[68] The Royal Navy's chief historian, S. W. Roskill, quoted approvingly Cunningham's judgment that Churchill was "a bad strategist but doesn't know it, and nobody has the courage to stand up to him."[69]

The second part of the statement is demonstrably false; at various points Brooke, Portal, and Cunningham himself all showed just such courage. As for Churchill's technical judgments, which Cunningham deplored, the record shows that his own and his service's naval judgment could prove no less defective than that of his political superior.[70] In the spring of 1944, for example, Churchill beat back a Royal Navy plan, based on a 1 May 1944 paper by the First Sea Lord, "The Empire's Post-War Fleet," for a postwar force based on the bizarre premise that "the basis of the strength of the Fleet is the battleship. . . . This war has proved the necessity of battleships and no scientific development is in sight which might render them obsolete. . . . A heavier broadside than the enemy is still a very telling weapon in a Naval action."[71] Churchill, who had pioneered the development of naval aviation, who had followed closely the dramatic aero-naval battles of the Pacific War, and who had strongly doubted the merits of this view for several years, demurred. The evidence of years of naval warfare seemed overwhelming; Churchill referred as well to a paper by Professor Lindemann that deprecated the ability of the battleship to survive (and, among other things, presciently forecasted the maturation of radio-, television-, and infrared-homing guided bombs). Churchill threw back in the Navy's teeth the judgment that "the laws of nature put the battleship at such a disadvantage compared with the aircraft that I fear it will not survive in the evolutionary race."[72] Throughout the war Churchill had deplored the Navy's preoccupation with a battleship fleet, which persisted even after the entrance of the United States into the war and the destruction of most of the heavy units of the German Navy. It was, as he put it, the result of an obsession with the battle of Jutland, a repetition of which "is certainly never going to happen."

Some of the most uncomfortable moments for Churchill's military interlocutors came when he probed the war resources that they had or were claiming. A fine example of this is his reaction to the Royal Navy's submission of its manpower requirements for 1944:

The admiralty are now demanding 288,000 more men for the fleet in 1944 and 71,000 for the shipyards totalling about 360,000. This is at a time when the manpower shortage enforces heavy cuts on every form of national war activity. The question arises, why does the Admiralty require more men in 1944 than in 1943, observing that the new facts are:

(a) the decisive defeat of the U-boats, largely through Air assistance;

(b) the surrender of the Italian fleet

(c) the accession of the *Richelieu* and many lesser French units to active service

(d) the establishment by the United States of two-to-one strength over the Japanese in the Pacific;

(e) the immobilization for a good many months to come of the *Tirpitz*, the only hostile capital unit in the Western world (unless the new German carrier is ready).

Why should you ask for so much more when your opponents' force is so much less and your Allies so much stronger?[73]

Churchill's questions did not, of course, completely thwart the Navy, which managed to get along with considerably less than half the increase that it had requested.[74]

In a similar vein, Churchill regarded the products of the superb British intelligence system with a combination of interest and skepticism rare in political leaders. When the Joint Intelligence Committee suggested in September 1944 that Germany would collapse by December, Churchill disagreed vigorously and, as it transpired, correctly.[75] The intelligence professionals of the JIC had, by this point in the war, access to outstanding information and had had the experience of five years of war in which to sharpen their judgment. After noting that the Germans had suffered approximately a million casualties in the first half of 1944 alone, and pointing to reverses around the circumference of the German position in Central Europe, they argued that Germany would probably not be able to sustain the war to the end of the year. They were proven wrong, as had been their operational colleagues. Churchill's acidic reply to the JIC on 8 September is a masterpiece of critical analysis of an intelligence estimate by a policy maker, beginning with the opening line: "I have now read the Report and have not noticed any fact in it of which I was not already aware." Churchill forecasted the attenuation of Allied logistics, the improvement in German fighting spirit on home ground, the adverse consequences of worsening weather, and concluded with the correct prediction: "It is at least as likely that Hitler will be fighting on the 1st January as that he will collapse before then."

This is not to say that Churchill's military judgment was invariably, or even frequently, superior to that of his subordinates, although on occasion it clearly was. Rather, Churchill exercised one of his most important functions as war leader by holding their calculations and assertions up to the standards of a massive common sense informed by wide reading and experience at war. On numerous occasions his queries to the joint planning staffs resulted in answers of which he disapproved and which he could probe sharply. For example, in advance of the invasion of Europe he asked for an evaluation of the military consequences of using chemical weapons in support of the landings. "I want the matter studied in cold blood by sensible people and not by that particular set of psalm-singing uniformed defeatists."[76]

From Churchill's pen (or, more precisely, his mouth, since he dictated almost all of his work) emanated, throughout the war, an unstinting stream of inquiries, probes, and questions to various parts of the government. Norman Brook, a member of the Cabinet secretariat from 1941 to 1962 and secretary to the Cabinet from 1947 to 1962, recalled the effects of Churchill's queries.

Knowledge of these messages, sometimes peremptory in tone but always pertinent and timely, quickly spread through the administrative cadres in Whitehall. They did much to confirm the feeling that there was now a strong personal control at the center. This stream of messages, covering so wide a range of subjects, was like the beam of a searchlight ceaselessly swinging round and penetrating into the remote recesses of the administration—so that everyone, however humble his rank or his function, felt that one day the beam might rest on him and light up what he was doing. In Whitehall the effect of this influence was immediate and dramatic. . . . A new sense of purpose and of urgency was created as it came to be realized that a firm hand, guided by a strong will, was on the wheel.[77]

The probing did not confine itself to questions of operations or military technology, but extended to matters of seemingly routine administration that, in Churchill's view, bore a larger significance. A fine example of this is the affair of the regimental patches. On 21 November 1942 Churchill, fresh from visiting the 53rd Division, wrote a note to the secretary of state for war reporting that he was "shocked" to learn that an order had been issued by the Army Council (the Army's senior leadership) banning regimental shoulder patches.

Both the general commanding the division and the commander in chief Home Forces expressed to me their surprise and regret. There is no doubt that it will be extremely unpopular and tend to destroy that regimental *esprit de corps* upon which all armies worthy of the name are founded. I was also told that the Army Council instruction was accompanied by a notification that no discussion of it was to be allowed. Who is responsible for this? I fear it is the Adjutant-General. If so, it would confirm much that I have heard of his outlook upon the army.

I hope you will give directions to cancel the instruction before great harm is done.[78]

Receiving no reply, ten days later Churchill's staff reminded the secretary of state for war of the need to answer this note. Responding the next day, the secretary of state for war, P. J. Grigg, informed the prime minister that the order prohibiting regimental patches for all units save the Guards and Household Cavalry had been sent out a year ago but imperfectly enforced. Moreover, Grigg said, the Board of Trade had declared that the provision of such patches would "mean a serious further reduction of the already inadequate tailoring facilities to civilians."

Characteristically, the prime minister then asked the president of the Board of Trade for details of "the actual dimensions of the demand on the tailoring trade" of providing cloth regimental patches for the army. In response, the head of the Board of Trade replied that one of his staff, when asked by the army staff (on 30 November—nine days after the original query from Churchill) whether manufacturing and sewing on regimental patches would be a waste of labor, had indeed replied affirmatively to the army's inquiry, albeit only "in a general sense." The official continued, however, that the Board of Trade had no firm views on what would, after all, be only a minor drain on the tailoring trade's resources: 85,000 yards of cloth in total from a national consumption of eight million yards a week. In short, Churchill discovered that the Army Council had attempted to hide behind an assumed clothing shortage to prop up a decision that was wildly unpopular with the army, as well as with the prime minister and minister of defence.

The secretary of state for war next fell back on the argument that it would be adverse to good discipline to reverse a ruling on the basis of the prime minister's intervention. Churchill was not satisfied: the ban on patches had, he learned, been in place for a year, but enforced only in the last few months. Churchill's "Action This Day" response continued the dialogue with some pointed questions: "What is General Paget's [commander in chief Home Forces] explanation of the nonenforcement of this instruction until the order sent out by him in July 1942?" Why were some units favored with permission to wear patches and others not? He concluded: "I can quite see that the difficulty is one into which you have got yourself by making the enforcement of this wrong principle a matter of prestige," and declared that he would be willing to allow some lapse of time before resuming the wearing of patches by line units.

Secretary of State Grigg made one last desperate attempt to persuade Churchill to set aside his interest in fostering regimental spirit through the wearing of patches (23 December 1942), only to receive a crushing reply five days later from the prime minister. Churchill noted that the practice of permitting units to wear patches had not hampered discipline, that the regulation stripping them off "ought not to have been settled by the military members [of the Army Council] alone. This was exactly one of those cases which affect morale and nationalist and territorial feelings, in which the parliamentary ministers should have been consulted." Moreover, the new regulations, which would have allowed some units (the Guards and Household Cavalry) to wear patches, but prohibited all others from doing so, would have detrimental effects on army morale. Churchill offered to take the whole matter up at the War Cabinet but concluded, "I trust however that you will not think it necessary to inflict this upon us at so busy a time." Early in the new year, the secretary of state for war submitted a new scheme for reissuing regimental patches to the troops.

The case of the regimental patches is a revealing one. At first glance it looks like mere meddling by a military romantic, undermining the military chain of command and looking after details best consigned to soldiers. In fact, however, Churchill's intervention (as much in his capacity as minister of defence as prime minister) shows a far shrewder understanding of war leadership. First, this intervention must be set in the context of his concern for maintaining fighting spirit in an army which had known mostly defeat until this point, and the bulk of which had been inactive in the British Isles for several years—and would remain so for another eighteen months. In keeping up the morale of such an army—which was built, more than that of any other European force, on powerful regimental traditions and identities—the matter of distinctive patches and badges was no trivial matter.

Secondly, Churchill realized that in such a mass military the attempt to protect even minor privileges for some units at the expense of others would be injurious to morale. Churchill, despite his aristocratic background, was keenly aware that Britain would become a far more egalitarian country after the war than it had been before it—and he did not find the prospect troubling. Speaking of the products of grammar schools (in American terms, public-school graduates) he said to his private secretary in 1941, "They have saved this country; they have the right to rule it."[79] Even minor discrepancies in privilege were, he well understood, likely to cause discontent in a society transformed by war.

Thirdly, Churchill had uncovered at least one bureaucratic subterfuge—an attempt by the Army Council to shift responsibility for an unpopular decision to the Board of Trade—thereby teaching a no doubt uncomfortable lesson to the military officers involved. Finally, it is noteworthy that Churchill did not merely order the restitution of the patches, but followed through, in a sustained exchange during which one argument after another crumbled under sharp questioning. Grigg did not merely yield to superior authority: he gave way in the face of queries to which neither he nor his military subordinates could provide good answers.

It should not be thought that Churchill's questioning consisted merely of a bullying interrogation. Churchill's desire to see, test, and probe for himself led to escapades that may appear foolish (such as his crossing of the Rhine with Montgomery), but also to more than one important decision. For example, after a visit to Bletchley Park, home of the British code-breaking service, to see the cryptanalysts, he received a direct plea for assistance from a number of the leading figures working there, including the renowned mathematician Alan Turing. They told the prime minister that their work of breaking German codes was being held up because they were terribly short of staff and even basic supplies. The next day, 22 October 1941, Churchill minuted Ismay in an "Action This Day" memorandum: "Make sure they have all they want on extreme priority and report to me that this has been done." Within several weeks seemingly intractable bureaucratic obstacles had dissolved.[80]

Churchill's uneasy relationship with his generals stemmed in large part from his willingness to pick commanders who disagreed with him—and did so violently. The two most forceful members of the Chiefs of Staff, Brooke and Cunningham, were evidence of that. If he dispensed with Dill he did so with the silent approval of key officers, who shared his judgment that the CIGS did not have the spirit to fight the war through to victory.[81] As Ismay and others privately admitted, Dill was a spent man by 1941 and hardly up to the demands of coping with Churchill. "The one thing that was necessary and indeed that Winston preferred, was someone to stand up to him—instead of which Jack Dill merely looked, and was, bitterly hurt." If Churchill were to make a rude remark about the courage of the British Army, Ismay later recalled, the wise course was to laugh it off or to refer Churchill to his own writings. "Dill, on the other hand, was cut to the quick that anyone should insult his beloved Army and vowed he would never serve with him again, which of course was silly."[82] One may compare, by contrast, the recollection of Sir Charles Portal, chief of staff of the Royal Air Force:

> I had to disagree very forcibly with some proposal of his and used language which would have been more polite if I had had more time to choose my words. During my tirade he fixed me with a glassy stare and at the end when I said I was sorry if I had seemed rude, a broad smile appeared across his face and he said: "You know, in war you don't have to be nice, you only have to be right."[83]

Churchill's relationship with Brooke was the most explosive of all his dealings with his military subordinates, but he and Cunningham, the First Sea Lord who replaced the ailing Dudley Pound in 1942, developed a relationship almost as tense. And some of Churchill's field commanders suffered particularly from his impatience, above all Archibald Wavell and Claude Auchinleck, the hapless commanders in the Middle East in 1939–41 and 1941–42 respectively. Although Wavell presided over a successful campaign against the Italians in 1941, his silence in the face of Churchill's barrage of memoranda urging action, together with the failures in Greece and in Libya, doomed him. Like his predecessor Auchinleck found himself axed by Churchill, and in large part for the same reason: an apparent reluctance to engage the enemy. The tension between Churchill and his Middle East commanders stemmed in part from differing perspectives. The prime minister was preoccupied with the sacrifices made to sustain the armed forces in the Middle East, including the dispatch of convoys sent at great risk through the Mediterranean; the local commanders saw chiefly the difficulties in assimilating the new equipment into their forces. Churchill, because of his awareness of the imperatives of coalition warfare—keeping both Russians and Americans convinced that Britain could and would bear its share in defeating the Axis—needed success in the desert. Local commanders saw chiefly the operational task before them, and pleaded for time. Churchill, an avid consumer of intelligence, particularly decrypts of Rommel's communications, knew just how badly off the *Afrika Korps* was (or claimed to be), which made his irritation at the failure of his commanders to crush the Germans all the more intense and, in retrospect, understandable.[84] They, for their part, were mesmerized by an enemy crowned repeatedly with success.

It was not enough, of course, to pick good military leaders: as a civilian war leader Churchill found himself compelled to prod them as well—an activity that occasioned more than a little resentment on their part. Indeed, in a private letter to Auchinleck shortly before the latter assumed command in the Middle East in June 1941, Dill warned of this, saying that "the commander will always be subject to great and often undue pressure from his government."[85] Clearly, Churchill viewed as one of his most important responsibilities the goading of his commanders into action; and if Alan Brooke resented this pressure, he at least responded to it better than did Dill.

The permeation of all war, even total war, by political concerns should come as no surprise to the contemporary student of military history, who has usually been fed on a diet of Clausewitz and his disciples. But it is sometimes forgotten just how deep and pervasive political considerations in war are. Take, for example, the question of the employment of air power in advance of the Normandy invasion. In late 1943 and early 1944 the Anglo-American Allies prepared for their greatest operation of the war—the crossing of the English Channel and the invasion of Europe. In this desperate effort, whose success was considered uncertain to the very date of its launching, few preparations counted for more than the deployment of the vast air power of the Allies to prepare the way for the assaulting forces. Not only did the Allies wish to stun the German defenders in the immediate vicinity of the beachhead: they thought it essential to delay, disrupt, and where possible destroy German reinforcements flowing to the bridgehead. Getting ashore might well be costly and difficult, but Allied planners worried no less, and in some respects more, about the potential for German reinforcements swarming to seal off the Normandy landing grounds, and even counterattacking in overpowering force against Allied armies pinned against the coast.

Expert opinion split, as it often does, on the most proper use of both the tactical air forces (the shorter-ranged fighters and light and medium bombers of the British and American Allied Expeditionary Air Force) and the heavy bombing forces of the Eighth Air Force and the Royal Air Force's Bomber Command. One group favored the employment of only the tactical air forces against targets in the Normandy area, while the bomber forces would continue their strategic assault on vital targets in the heart of Germany, including synthetic fuel plants and military industry. The best targets for the former would be road bridges and rail lines in western and northern France, to isolate the battlefield. Others proposed a systematic attack on the French rail network, which would prove crucial for the German forces.[86] This second group urged the use of heavy bombers to attack the marshaling yards of the French rail system, on the theory that under repeated attacks it would, after a period of time, simply collapse.

This seemingly technical military issue had, however, political ramifications because any attack (but particularly one targeted against French marshaling yards) promised to kill French civilians. Churchill therefore intervened in the bombing debate to secure a promise that French civilian casualties would be held to a bare minimum. "You are piling up an awful load of hatred," Churchill wrote to Air Chief Marshal Arthur Tedder, insisting that French civilian casualties be kept to a maximum of 10,000 killed (versus initial projections of as many as 160,000). Reports were submitted throughout May that listed the number of French civilians killed and (callously enough) "Credit Balance Remaining."[87] By the end of May German reporting indicated that some 6,000 Frenchmen had perished in the bombing—considerably fewer than Churchill had feared.

"At the summit, true strategy and politics are one," Churchill wrote in *The World Crisis*. From a close study of his career, particularly his tenure as prime minister and minister of defence in the Second World War, one may learn just how inextricably the civil-military relationship and the formulation of strategy are intertwined. It reveals as well the power of hard, intelligent questioning, based less on professional expertise than on wide reading and massive common sense—the quality that Carl von Clausewitz described as the bedrock of military genius.

Churchill's incessant probing was harnessed to his understanding of the war as a whole. Perhaps nowhere did this become clearer than in his effort, during the war, to mold the peace that would follow the conflict. It is in this light that one may best understand his desperate and unsuccessful arguments with the American high command in 1945. Even as victory approached, he later wrote, this climax of apparently measureless success was to me a most unhappy time. I moved amid cheering crowds, or sat at a table adorned with congratulations and blessings from every part of the Grand Alliance, with an aching heart and a mind oppressed by forebodings.[88]

Churchill saw early on the threat posed by Soviet Communism to Eastern Europe. (Already in the summer of 1943 he had informed President Roosevelt that the Soviets were the probable perpetrators of the Katyn Forest massacre of thousands of Polish officers and intellectuals.) Therefore he pressed for the alignment of military operations with political action.[89] His pleas for the Allied liberation of Prague and the thrusting forward of Anglo-American armies to Vienna and Berlin rested on a true judgment of the political value of arriving first in the heart of the erstwhile Third Reich. Even so shrewd a political general as Eisenhower failed to grasp this, at the end of March 1945 dismissing Berlin as "no longer a particularly important objective."[90] Churchill achieved only partial successes (for example, through his intervention in the brewing Greek Civil War in 1944–45) in his effort to make the final, convulsive operations of war serve the ends of peace. By the winter and spring of 1945 his hand was weak; barely a quarter of the troops in Western Europe were British or British-controlled, and the Empire's financial, human, and material resources had been stretched to their limits and beyond by five and a half years of struggle. And yet, to a degree remarkable in the annals of war statesmanship, he struggled to have the final operations of the war conform to a broader set of political calculations than those which began the conflict.

To these twin gifts—the ability to probe, and the ability to shape a larger vision and fight for it in adverse circumstances—were added the indispensable third, which even his sharpest critics concede to him. This was, of course, a mastery of political rhetoric, an ability to, as John F. Kennedy later put it, "mobilize the English language and send it into battle." He had other political gifts, to be sure. It is insufficiently remarked, for example, how deftly he managed to keep an all-party coalition together throughout the war, despite some bitter conflicts among personalities and in the face of more than one challenge to his authority. Even his speeches contained far more than the ringing perorations that are usually associated with them. It is often forgotten to what extent he described, with remarkable detail, the conduct of the war thus far and, without revealing future plans, the shape of things to come. Concealing no defeats and minimizing no reverses, he realized the importance of keeping as many people as possible "in the picture," as the wartime phrase had it.[91]

Still, Churchill's cardinal political virtue was his ability to touch the hearts of men and women with words that reflected his own unique and indomitable spirit. The British people, he later wrote about 1940, had the lion's heart; he was merely privileged to give the roar. He was, uncharacteristically perhaps, overly modest. He had many strengths as a war leader sitting in a Cabinet room or around a table with a handful of advisers. He had, as few men have ever had, the gift of composing trenchant state papers and penetrating memoranda. His art of leadership included, as we have noted, a skill at questioning and challenging professional subordinates that few others have mastered. But all these skills would have availed nothing had they not rested on a courage that, even at the distance of fifty years, is nothing less than magnificent. That indomitable spirit, when coupled with his skills at higher war leadership, made him the greatest war statesman of the century.

CHAPTER 5

BEN-GURION HOLDS A SEMINAR

IMAGES IN A HUT

David Ben-Gurion retired twice from public life, once in 1953 and again, finally, in 1963. In both cases he went not to the Tel Aviv apartment from which he conducted business as the leader of the Jewish community of Palestine, and later as Israel's first and most important prime minister. Rather he retired to a new and struggling *kibbutz,* or collective settlement, Sde Boker, in Israel's Negev desert. There he lived in what became known as his *tsrif,* or hut—a modest one-floor bungalow, crammed with books, where his formidably abrasive wife Paula kept a vigilant eye on him and the awed kibbutzniks kept their distance. There are four pictures or images in the *tsrif.* One, on his work desk, is a picture of Berl Katznelson, one of the leading figures in Palestinian Jewish politics in the 1930s, and one of Ben-Gurion's earliest comrades. He was as warm and lovable a man as Ben-Gurion was forbidding and distant, proof that in political as in more intimate life, opposites sometimes attract. Opposite that desk, on a wall lined with books, stands a replica of Michelangelo's Moses, with whom some might compare the doughty father of the Israeli state—not only for his achievements, but for the incessant battling he did with a recalcitrant people and stubborn dissenters in the course of his labors. (One of Ben-Gurion's intimates, when asked late in 1953 why the Old Man had resigned, remarked: "The Messiah arrived, he gathered in Israel's exiles, he triumphed over all the peoples around, he conquered the Land of Israel . . . and then he had to take his seat in a coalition."[1] In the tiny living room, where distinguished visitors came to visit Ben-Gurion, the wall was graced by a third image: a portrait of Abraham Lincoln inset in a micrograph of the Emancipation Proclamation. And, most surprising of all for this pugnacious battler, in his bedroom is a fourth picture—of Mahatma Gandhi, the pacifist who forced the British Empire to yield.

These four images capture much of the complexity of Ben-Gurion's personality—Katznelson, his immersion in the fierce internecine struggles of the Labor movement of Palestine, and the even more ferocious contests with political rivals outside it; Moses, his roots in Jewish history and identity and his messianic aspirations for the Jewish people; Lincoln, his admiration of the English-speaking world and its greatest leaders in their most bitter contests for freedom and democratic rule; Gandhi, his appreciation of spiritual power even when its expression took a form so completely different from his own. His own greatness resided, in great measure, in his ability to harmonize these contrasting and in some respects contradictory sides of his personality.

Surrounding these images are vast quantities of books, which line the walls of the hut as they do the walls of his apartment in Tel Aviv. Totaling some 12,000 volumes in both locations, they reflect the interests of a man who read at least eight foreign languages, and include numerous volumes on military history as well as philosophy, science, literature, and Jewish lore.[2] A hard-bitten political activist since his earliest years (he had to flee Russia and later Palestine itself early in the century), he was, as well, a widely read man of insatiable intellectual curiosity, who in his old age would explore Eastern philosophy with the same zest that he studied European history and military science. The world has never seen a more astonishing autodidact among its great statesmen. The qualities of intellectual breadth and application apparent in this extraordinary library manifested themselves no less clearly in his preparation for war.

In December 1946 David Ben-Gurion, aged sixty, became the shadow defense minister of the embryonic Jewish state; with Israel's independence a year and a half later he became the real thing, as well as prime minister. During that time he transformed an already impressive underground military establishment, the Haganah; absorbed smaller but better organized dissident guerrilla and terrorist organizations; created one of the most formidable armies in the world for its size; and handled the conduct of a war that created a state—a state that has, willy nilly, occupied center stage in international politics ever since. He did all this with fragmentary material resources and a tiny population, in the face of the organized opposition of every neighboring state and the dominant force of Great Britain, and only tepid approval—occasionally, little better than indifference—from the emerging superpowers. It is as remarkable a story of statecraft in its way as that of Washington or Lincoln, and under circumstances no less adverse.

PRELUDE TO INDEPENDENCE

For a time after World War I, the ambition of creating an autonomous national home, even a state, seemed within the reach of the fledgling Jewish community in Palestine. In the early 1880s the Jewish population of Palestine numbered barely 25,000; by the beginning of World War I that number had risen to 85,000. Rebounding from losses by emigration during the war, Palestine absorbed another 100,000 by 1925, for a total of perhaps 160,000. By the late 1920s, however, the environment had changed. Arab riots in Hebron in 1929 revealed the intensity of local opposition to Jewish immigration into Palestine, and the 1936 eruption of the Arab Revolt confirmed to Palestine's British masters the dangers of allowing unimpeded Jewish immigration into the country. By then some 400,000 Jews (many recent refugees from Germany and Poland) were calling Palestine home. In May 1939, after a series of investigating commissions and conferences, Great Britain published a White Paper providing for the eventual creation of an Arab-dominated Palestinian state after ten years. The most terrifying part of this White Paper, not only for the Zionists' prospects of overcoming their demographic disadvantage vis-à-vis the Arabs of Palestine, but for the sheer survival of the multitudes of Jews trapped in Hitler's Europe, was a proviso limiting Jewish immigration to 75,000 over five years, with any future Jewish entry depending on Arab acquiescence—certain, of course, to be denied.

Desperate not only to save the Zionist project but to create a refuge for the imperiled Jewish populations of Eastern Europe, the leadership of the Jewish community struggled against the strictures of Great Britain. In the midst of the world war Ben-Gurion coined the slogan, "We will fight the war as if there were no White Paper, and the White Paper as if there were no war." But despite such valiant talk the Jewish community of Palestine was, in fact, powerless to do much to rescue European Jewry or to convince Great Britain to provide it sanctuary in Palestine. On the whole the Palestinian Jewish community, numbering by the war's end some 500,000 souls, could make only feeble and unsuccessful efforts to rescue their brethren in Europe. Tens of thousands of Palestinian Jews served in the British Army, and a handful of Jewish agents heroically but ineffectually infiltrated occupied Europe, but on the whole the Jewish community in Palestine could only watch with horror the catastrophe that was overwhelming European Jewry.[3]

Through 1945 Ben-Gurion had, of course, paid attention to security matters, but he had not made them his principal concern; the establishment of Zionist institutions, the creation of a consensus in support of the idea of a Jewish state, and the increase of immigration, legal or not, into Palestine absorbed all of his energies. The war, calamitous as it had been, renewed Jewish hopes for an independent state; masses of Jewish refugees were ready to come to Palestine, and American (and to a lesser degree, British and European) sympathy for their plight and horror at the Nazi extermination campaign smoothed the way for them. A struggle between Britain and the Jews of Palestine took shape, conducted on the political front through American pressure to admit immediately 100,000 Jewish refugees to Palestine, and through an Anglo-American Commission of Inquiry in the spring of 1946 and later a UN Special Committee on Palestine (UNSCOP) in 1947. These battles on the diplomatic and political fronts led to the collapse of the policies (particularly those limiting Jewish immigration) enshrined in the White Paper of 1939, and the eventual British decision in September 1947 to end the mandate, turning the problem of Palestine over to the United Nations.

If the Zionists' political struggle against the British mandate constituted one front—albeit one that extended to the front pages of the *New York Times* and the back benches of Parliament—their overt armed struggle in Palestine itself constituted a second front. Early in the 1940s two Jewish guerrilla and terrorist groups—the Irgun Zvai Leumi, or IZL (also called "the Irgun" in English) and Lohamei Herut Yisrael (Lechi)—embarked on a violent campaign against the British authorities. Their use of assassination and sabotage took a dramatic and politically disastrous turn with the assassination of Lord Moyne in Cairo in 1944. The Jewish community, horrified by these deeds yet desperate to open the gates of Palestine to the remnants of the slaughtered communities of Europe, wavered between repugnance at the deeds of these groups and a tentative cooperation with them. At a certain point, the mainstream Jewish community took part in the struggle as well. In October 1945 Ben-Gurion induced the Haganah to begin a series of attacks on British installations (avoiding, where possible, causing

British casualties) in order to force Britain to acquiesce to increased immigration to Palestine.[4]

British countermeasures—including the June 1946 "Black Sunday" mass arrest of Jewish leaders, and raids on Haganah arms depots—and the excesses of the extremists (including, in particular, the spectacular bombing of the King David Hotel in Jerusalem in July 1946) ended the general community's armed resistance to British rule. Ben-Gurion had, as the main Jewish leader in Palestine, urged a course of moderate opposition to British rule, including the use of force but in a controlled way. Enraged at the actions (and, let it be said, the independence) of the IZL and Lechi, he twice (from late 1944 through March 1945, and again in April 1947) supported collaboration with the British to help suppress those organizations. Throughout this stormy period, Ben-Gurion and the Jewish community's other leaders favored a combination of confrontation and negotiation with Great Britain, yielding neither to those who thought all direct struggle with the mandate authorities to be futile nor to those who thought that Britain could only be dynamited out of Palestine. Some of the patterns of his later war leadership—ruthlessness and flexibility, most notably—began to appear during this grim apprenticeship. Ben-Gurion adopted a mixture of violence and compromise, confrontation and accommodation that made him neither popular with nor entirely trusted by his comrades in arms, but which served him well in his dealings with a British government that had lost whatever interest it had once had in promoting Jewish settlement in Palestine.

The end of World War II marked the beginning of far higher levels of violence in Palestine. The anti-British IZL and Lechi began active operations against the British, while Arab hostility to the Jews of Palestine and Arab fear of Jewish statehood grew enormously. The Palestinian Arabs, numbering between three quarters of a million and a million, consisted of diverse populations.[5] Although still divided by clan and local loyalties, they had a number of popular leaders, and in particular the Grand Mufti of Jerusalem, Haj Amin al-Husseini, who saw the rise of a Jewish state as an intolerable development for the Arabs of Palestine. Husseini, a shrewd agitator, had been both installed and exiled by the British and had aligned himself with the Germans during World War II. He had returned to the Middle East determined to lead the Arabs of Palestine in a struggle to the death with the Jews.

At the end of 1946 Palestine was in crisis. British military efforts to suppress both an increasingly vicious Jewish guerrilla campaign within Palestine and Arab-Jewish communal violence coincided with pressure from the West to do something about Palestine. Public opinion in the United States, and to some extent in Britain itself, was distressed by what Winston Churchill, now on the Opposition benches, described as "this squalid war against the Jews." The sight of Jewish refugees from Europe, survivors of Hitler's massacres, being manhandled, held behind barbed wire, or even shipped back to the sites of their families' extermination was repellent. More concretely, the desperate financial circumstances of the Empire simply could not support the deployment of nearly a hundred thousand troops a year to keep hold of Palestine. Only a massive American loan had averted British bankruptcy in 1946; economic ruin, piled on Imperial crises around the globe (including most notably in India, where the viceroy no longer believed the Indian Army to be a reliable instrument for maintaining order), persuaded the now willing British leaders to leave Palestine to its own devices.[6]

When the representatives of the international Zionist movement met at the Twenty-Second Zionist Congress in Basel in the fall of 1946 they found themselves struggling with a radically new situation. The horrors of the Holocaust were now fully known. In Europe, there was a pool of hundreds of thousands of desperate refugees anxious to come to Palestine; in the Jewish community there (now numbering over 600,000) a no less desperate determination to open the gates to immigration; and in the prosperous Jewish community in the United States, an eagerness (absent in many quarters before the war) to support the Zionist endeavor. In many countries as well (the United States most notably, but others too) there was sympathy on the part of non-Jewish leaders and peoples for the Jews and their dream of a state.

On all other counts, however, the situation for the Zionist leadership was grossly unfavorable. The British government, in the hands of a hard-pressed Labour leadership, manifested an animosity toward the Zionist cause that went, in some cases, beyond mere policy to something more personal and darker. In particular Foreign Secretary Ernest Bevin seemed to have become hostile to the point (as it appeared to leaders of the Jewish community in Palestine, the *yishuv*) of anti-Semitism. The British government seemed to the Zionist leaders to be implacably hostile to their aspirations. The Arab states had emerged from World War II in positions of increasing independence, both formal (in the case of Jordan and Syria) and substantive. As tension between East and West grew, so too did Arab leverage with both Britain and the United States, because the Great Powers needed bases, oil, and quiet for their remaining colonial positions. American support for the Zionists was, to an alarming degree, a matter of personal sympathy rather than collective interest: the coldness with which the State and War (later Defense) Departments viewed the Jews of Palestine reflected not so much antipathy as an absence of any sentiment at all.

The presence in the Jewish camp of Communists and their sympathizers only reinforced this preference on the part of the Western Great Powers for nations numbering thirty million over one nation counting all of 600,000 souls. At the same time, paradoxically, the predominance of democratic socialists among Palestinian Jews, together with the fact that they were led by a man who had early become disillusioned with Communism and whose movement could not but reject Communist claims of universalism, created a certain distance from the Soviet Union. It was in these desperate conditions that David Ben-Gurion, the acknowledged leader of the Jewish community in Palestine, asked for the "Defense portfolio," becoming in effect, the quasi-state's minister of defense as well as its prime minister.

THE OLD MAN

What manner of leader had now taken upon himself responsibility for the physical security of the Jewish community in Palestine?[7] David Gruen had immigrated from Poland to Palestine in 1906, at the age of twenty. By the early 1930s, through a combination of hard work and dedication to political activism, David Ben-Gurion had become the first secretary-general of the Histadrut, the Jewish labor organization, which soon combined union activity with ownership of key economic and social activities in the Jewish community. In 1935 he became the chairman of the Jewish Agency, the semi-official self-governing organization of Jewish Palestine. Although he had participated in some of the Jewish community's earliest self-defense efforts before World War I, and had served in the British Army during it, his active military experience was slight. His service during World War I he had regarded primarily as an opportunity for political work, to which he devoted his entire being. His goal throughout was clear and simple: the creation of a Jewish state, despite all obstacles.

He was, in personal habits, frugal save in the matter of buying books—a practice which, combined with a fierce rectitude in financial matters, more than once forced his wife to scrimp on meals in order to make ends meet. Ferociously argumentative, implacable in his animosities, but possessed of a powerful sense of political realism, he knew when and how to check the harshness of his personal feelings in battles with political foes—be they Jews, Britons, or Arabs. His sociopolitical and economic views, and those of his movement, were essentially those of Russian socialists from the turn of the century, but with a twist. He saw himself, as did so many of the early Zionists, as one of a new kind of Jews: farmers, laborers, and soldiers, proud of their people's history and achievements on the one hand, yet disdainful of ghetto-bred meekness and physical softness on the other.

Ben-Gurion's Jewish patriotism and rough humanitarianism, together with his grudging but sincere admiration of British and American political institutions, trumped his socialism. By the late 1920s he doubted that the world's only socialist state, the Soviet Union, could provide a model for the state-in-the-making. As the years went on he came to regard the USSR with the wariest of respect, taking advantage of its support where offered, but never supposing that its universalistic claims and tyrannical system of government would, in the long run, coexist with Jewish nationalism and the civil liberties he admired in the Anglo-Saxon world.

Ben-Gurion brought to the task of supreme command scant military experience and, one might have thought, little aptitude for the job. He had, however, the tenacity and cunning bred of decades of political work, the talent of an orator driven by belief and in full command of the language he used, and the intellectual discipline and depth of a scholar. Throughout his adult life he kept a voluminous diary, not merely as a personal journal but as a working tool for absorbing and digesting vast quantities of information. Slowly writing near-verbatim accounts of interviews and conversations, copying statistics and making careful notes for later review, Ben-Gurion kept a unique record of what passed across his desk and through his mind, in these as in other matters.[8]

Ben-Gurion's place in the leadership of the Jewish community, although central, was not without its challengers. He had his opponents within the Jewish labor movement, including a pro-Soviet Left based in the collective settlements (*kibbutzim*) that were dominated by what would become the United Workers' Party or Mapam. He faced bitter opposition from the "separatists" (*porshim*), and in particular the National Military Organization (IZL) of the Revisionist movement, and he had uncertain relations with the bourgeois, religious, and Eastern communities of the *yishuv*. He contended successfully for supremacy with leaders of the Zionist movement who resided outside Palestine, most notably Chaim Weizmann, the brilliant scientist who had managed relations with Great Britain for years and who would subsequently become the first president of the State of Israel. Finally, and not least important, although Ben-Gurion dominated his own party, Mapai, he operated within a socialist tradition of collective decision-making and leadership that made him something considerably less than the dictator of legend. Indeed, his colleagues' resentment of his high-handed ways on more than one occasion brought the nascent Israeli government to a condition of internal crisis.

Against such an array of rivals and under such a set of constraints Ben-Gurion had only the power of persuasion and, no less important, the ultimate lever of his own indispensability. His bitterest enemies could call him dictatorial and manipulative; they could not impugn his intelligence, his energy, or his devotion to the cause of a Jewish state in Palestine. "The Old Man," people called the diminutive man with unruly wings of white hair setting off a large bald head. Few, even among his closest colleagues, liked him; even his enemies had to respect him. Willing to resign over matters of principle (not least of the principles being his own supreme authority), Ben-Gurion played a complex domestic political game of pleas, threats, and bargains. It would absorb his energies almost as much as the far deadlier grapples with foreign enemies.

By the end of 1946 it had become clear to Ben-Gurion that those struggles would likely broaden well beyond confrontation with the British Empire, whose days were obviously numbered and whose resolve ebbed daily. As harsh and even cruel as that contest was, it had taken place against a civilized and on the whole restrained power, which Ben-Gurion admired in many ways. He had seen London during the Blitz, had British friends (including a mistress), and respected all that the civilization of the great Empire had to offer in cultural, political, and military terms. The struggle that loomed ahead was with an Arab world that he knew far less well, although he had traveled in it and met some of its leaders.[9] It was a world from which he had no desire to borrow institutions or any aspect of culture. It was, he feared, a world which might exercise very little of the self-restraint and compunction of even the more malign inhabitants of the governor-general's residence in Jerusalem.

Unlike many if not most of his colleagues, Ben-Gurion had always believed that the Zionist program would lead not merely to unlimited Jewish immigration to Palestine and the creation of a semi-autonomous British protectorate there, but to the creation of a full-fledged Jewish state. He had been instrumental in the passing of the so-called Biltmore program of May 1942, which, during some of the darkest days of World War II, proclaimed the Zionist objective to be statehood. His desire to take direct control of defense matters flowed from his belief that the time had come—even before the British had concluded that the time had come for them to leave Palestine—to prepare the underground army for new tasks.

THE SEMINAR: "WE HAVE TO START VIRTUALLY EVERYTHING AFRESH."

As preparation, Ben-Gurion conducted, from the end of March to the end of May 1947, what became known in the history of the underground army, the Haganah, as "the Seminar." For two months he suspended his normal duties and instead undertook to interview systematically the entire high command of the Haganah (and many of its subordinate officers as well), so as to review its state of preparedness. Writing slowly but unweariedly in his diary, he probed the quality of the commanders, the nature of their training, the state of their equipment, the position of the budget, the structure of the high command, the quality of intelligence collection—all the facets of the Haganah's activities. Underlying the Seminar lay one simple, massive, and as it turned out, entirely correct political premise: that the upcoming confrontation between Jews and Arabs would not be like the disturbances of 1921, 1929, and 1936–1939; it would not be a contest between a semilegal voluntary defense organization on the Jewish side and gangs of Palestinian Arab villagers or clansmen on the other. Rather, it would be a contest with the Arab states and their armies, and it would take place in the context of the creation of a Jewish state, which would require an army of its own.[10] Ben-Gurion's judgment at the end of the Seminar, in a speech to the Mapai central committee, was typically harsh and direct. By the end of the Seminar he had concluded that the Haganah was profoundly unfit for the challenge looming ahead—and worse, its leadership was reluctant to admit as much.

> I know that I am saying very hard things. In my heart are even harder views, and I speak therefore the minimum . . . We have to start everything virtually afresh, because the Arab front is becoming serious, and it is no longer a front of robbers.

Here was the central problem, to which Ben-Gurion would return throughout the ensuing two years, and even after, as a profound lesson in military statecraft. The Haganah was a generally successful adaptation to one problem—the threat posed by the Palestinian Arabs, both in organized units and as gangs of marauders, to the security of the Jewish settlements. This very success, however, had rendered the Haganah in many ways unfit for the challenges of the future, not least because its leadership refused to admit the fundamental differences in the nature of the future threat.

> There is an organized Arab world, states, armies. Of course, as compared to European armies they have no value, but compared to a non-army they have value, while what we have is a non-army. We have to undertake difficult work—to uproot from the hearts of men who are close to the matter the belief that they have something. In fact, they have nothing. They have good will, they have hidden capacities, but they have to know: to make a shoe one has to study cobbling.[11]

On the eve of the Seminar the Haganah (or "The Organization" as Ben-Gurion and his collaborators called it) was a complex organization. It operated under the general supervision of the *Mifkadah Artzit* (National Command), headed by a civilian leader *(Rosh Mifkada Artzit, or Rama)* who looked primarily to budgetary and general policy matters. It had a general staff, although without quite the usual staff elements that one would expect in a regular army. Six regional commands (Jerusalem, Tel Aviv, Haifa, plus the South and the Upper and Lower Galilee for the smaller cities) coexisted with the three battalions of the Palmach, or commando units, which had their own staff and separate chain of command. The general staff of the Haganah had units for planning, training, and other functions. But they did not control the intelligence service, which reported both to the Jewish Agency and to the chief of the National Command *(Rosh Mifkada Artzit, or Rama)*, who acted as a kind of quasi-defense minister but without comparable authority. Organizations for illegal immigration and overseas acquisition and recruitment networks were also outside the Haganah's direct chain of command, reporting instead to the *Rama*. It was a confusing, anomalous structure.[12] By the end of 1947, however, the Haganah consisted of perhaps four hundred full-time personnel, 2,000 semi-official Jewish police, the reserve Palmach battalions (3,000 in all), roughly 10,000 infantry plus various home guard and youth units.[13]

The underground army had existed in a kind of legal twilight—generally tolerated by the British although subject to repression by them when it opposed the mandate government directly. Voluntarily recruited, sparsely funded, and staffed—for the most part—by home-grown talent with little or no formal military training, it was, for an underground, a remarkably sophisticated organization. It conducted regular training and had a fledgling arms industry, an excellent and improving intelligence service (which was already supplying the leadership with telephone intercepts of high-level Arab conversations, as well as agent reports), and a daring commando force. Later in 1947 a

Security Committee of the embryonic national assembly provided civilian oversight and control. Throughout its history the Haganah was, in fact, subject to supervision of some kind by the shadow government of the *yishuv*. The depth and intensity of that control was, however, as much a matter of personality as of institutional arrangement; nominally a nonpartisan body, the Haganah was, in fact, largely under the control of the moderate socialist faction led by David Ben-Gurion.

Ben-Gurion's own position in this already diffuse hierarchy was in some ways unclear. As the chairman of the Jewish Agency and the leading political figure in Palestine, he exercised considerable power, but he was, as well, at the mercy of a Jewish community riven into a number of political groupings. His own party, Mapai (*Mifleget poalei yisrael*—Israel Workers' Party) was the largest, but he had to contend with right-wing Zionists as well as groups considerably further to the left, not to mention non-Zionist groups and several religious parties. Moreover, as a result of the socialist traditions of Mapai and many of the early Jewish settlers of Palestine, who provided its leadership elite, he had to contend with a tradition of collective leadership, which viewed with suspicion the domination of any one man.

The Seminar took place in the "red house"—Haganah headquarters in Tel Aviv, and it covered all aspects of the defense structure of the Jewish community, including "structure, organization, exercises, education, planning, training, equipment, storage, manufacturing, acquisition, budget, *shai* (intelligence), youth, [foreign] relations."[14] Ben-Gurion's first interest appears to have been the personalities and qualities of the senior Haganah commanders. He seems to have crystalized, at this point, his assessments of various leading personalities, saying, for example, of Yitzhak Sadeh, one of the Haganah's pioneers in offensive operations, that he was unsuited to serve as chief of staff because "he's an artist."[15] Ben-Gurion was already selecting some of the field commanders for Israel's war of independence, and among those whom he praises (Moshe Carmel, for example, later to serve as the commander of the Northern Front) are foreshadowed the high command for the latter phases of that war.

Two broader leadership concerns troubled Ben-Gurion greatly. The first was the lack of overall preparedness for leadership at the higher level. Early on, for example, he noted the absence in Palestine of higher schools for Jewish commanders and he deprecated what he took to be the amateurish quality of the Haganah's leadership. With a trace of the autodidact's exaggerated respect for the formally educated, he doubted the ability of homegrown leadership to perform the tasks required of the true professional. His second concern centered on an administrative structure that, already at this period, appeared to him anomalous and unclear. In particular, the role of the chief of the National Command inserted an unwelcome layer of authority between himself as shadow defense minister and the chief of staff. He replaced the current *Rama*, Ze'ev Feinstein, with Israel Galili, an able organizer prominent in left-wing political circles. But within weeks he was chafing at the tendency he thought he had discovered for the *Rama* to serve as a layer of insula-tion between the civil and the military authority rather than as a conduit for it.[16]

The fundamental organizational problem Ben-Gurion saw in the Haganah was one of scale. The former *Rama*, Moshe Sneh, gave him a long account of the dispute in Haganah circles about whether the fun-damental unit of organization was the platoon or the company—and indeed, the course for platoon leaders was then the highest level of effective military education offered in the Haganah.[17] The embryonic state's military leaders, therefore, were thinking in terms of units of thirty-five or at most 150 men. Ben-Gurion believed that they should be thinking in terms of brigades of several thousand, and indeed that they needed to begin plans to acquire tanks, airplanes, artillery—in short, all of the equipment of a regular armed force. He set that standard explic-itly: when Moshe Carmel, who subsequently became one of the first generals in the Israel Defense Forces, praised the fighting qualities of the Jewish soldier vis-à-vis his Arab opponent, Ben-Gurion asked whether the Haganah could stand up to a single British battalion in the field.[18] Carmel admitted that he did not know. Ben-Gurion had no intention of starting a war with the British, of course, but he wished to establish the standard.

Ben-Gurion explored not only the fighting organization of the Haganah but its support functions as well—noting, for example, the essentially static communications system of the Jewish settlements in Palestine, which would need considerable improvement if the Haganah were to shift to mobile operations.[19] Only in the area of intelligence did the underground meet Ben-Gurion's standards. His diaries contain long discussions of the program for acquiring arms overseas. The underground arms industry of Palestine was impressive enough, turning out crude small arms (particularly the homemade Sten submachine gun), mortars, some high explosives, ammunition, and even improvised armored cars and buses. But it could not hope to come up with the tanks, airplanes, and heavy weapons like machine guns and artillery pieces needed by a regular army.

Ben-Gurion learned during the Seminar that the Haganah was very far from being a fully mobilized underground force. The *yishuv* was, by intention or good fortune, reputed to have a much more substantial force than it actually possessed: British unclassified estimates in January 1948 assigned the Haganah a strength of 70,000 and the Palmach 15,000—numbers off by factors of two and five, respectively; American and French intelligence sources were, interestingly enough, even further off base.[20] The publicly reported numbers of men and women in the underground military were fictitious. Even the internal number (30,000–35,000) was, Ben-Gurion learned, "an exaggeration."[21] The Haganah was, of course, a voluntary organization, and it competed with the IZL and Lechi for manpower. But the relative shortage of manpower, in Ben-Gurion's view, stemmed from a failure to tap the 25,000-odd Jewish men who had joined the British military during World War II and served in a variety of capacities, both in combat and, no less important, in the support services. The personnel branch of the

Haganah had copies of the demobilization certificates of many of these soldiers but, he noted in his diary, two-fifths of the addresses on them were no longer correct.[22]

The root of the problem, Ben-Gurion believed, was a willful provincialism on the part of the Haganah's leadership, almost all of whom had stayed in Palestine during World War II and who scorned the lessons to be learned from a regular army. A complex psychology seemed to be at work: a doubt that the regimentation of British army life could meld with the anarchic egalitarianism of Palestinian Jews, a more reasoned rejection of the applicability of the practices of a large, well-equipped, and traditionally organized military to the problems of an impoverished and only semilegal militia, and perhaps as well a measure of resentment and envy of those who had taken part in the greatest struggle of the time. Moreover, as one Haganah commander correctly observed, most of the British veterans had not served in the combat arms, and the Haganah leadership's view was that the greatest and most urgent need was for more and better-trained infantry.[23]

Compounding the difficulty was the élitism of the Haganah's proud striking arm, the Palmach (a Hebrew acronym for *plugot machatz*, "storm companies"). The Palmach, founded in 1942, were the Jewish Palestinians' equivalent of eighteenth-century America's Minute Men. Supporting themselves by working part time on *kibbutzim,* they were the only standing—actually only semi-standing—force of Palestinian Jewry. Led for the most part by representatives of the left-wing *kibbutz* movement, they had a strong streak of socialist egalitarianism. A light infantry or commando force, they had both superior training and high morale, and were entrusted by the Haganah high command with various operations against both the British and local Arab populations. But much though he valued the Palmach's superior effectiveness, Ben-Gurion had already become alarmed at its élitism and its autonomy; it had a separate staff and a budget whose details proved remarkably opaque to outside scrutiny.[24] He could not deal with it immediately, but its time would come.

"THEY DON'T HAVE REAL MILITARY EXPERIENCE, AND THEY DON'T WANT IT."

Shortly after the event, Ben-Gurion described to colleagues his assessment of June 1947: "[Here are] the faults I found: lack of equipment; for years no adequate thought about the needs of security and the Arab danger; the "Organization" sees itself as an end and not a means (the task for which it was created was not sufficiently in the forefront of their minds); the Haganah has a corporate spirit; they don't have real military experience, and they don't want it."[25] In the meanwhile, events had continued to move. In the winter of 1946–47 the British authorities concocted a proposal for dividing Palestine into Jewish and Arab zones, supervised by a lingering British presence. Formally offered in February 1947, the proposal encountered stout opposition by all concerned, and it collapsed. In April 1947, in the midst of the Seminar, the British government referred the problem of Palestine to the United Nations. By the summer of 1947 it was clear that the climactic struggle was at hand: Ben-Gurion, above all, recognized that a UN vote for partition of Palestine would almost immediately unleash a war. In November of that year the Security Council did indeed vote in favor of partitioning Palestine into two independent states, one Arab and one Jewish.

Anticipating these events, and immediately following the Seminar, Ben-Gurion embarked upon three broad policies. He began by overhauling the high command of the Haganah. In addition to replacing the ineffectual chief of the National Command, Ze'ev Feinstein, with Israel Galili, he made changes in the military command as well.[26] He did not replace Ya'akov Dori, who had served since 1939 as the Haganah's chief of staff, but he did install the youthful Yigal Yadin as chief of the operations branch. This was, as yet, a provisional change: more would come later on, but for the moment he wanted at the head of the Haganah men who would not challenge his authority and who shared his view that the organization was inadequate and complacent. Ben-Gurion remarked in October 1947 that the most serious problem he faced was "a lack of civilian control of the Organization [the Haganah]. Civilian control of the Organization was," he declared, "without a doubt, fictitious."[27] His selection of new leaders for the Haganah already reflected his intention to assert civilian control: neither Dori nor Yadin had independent followings in the Haganah. The former had served in the Haganah for many years and was an engineer by training and outlook; ailing, he did not dominate a military staff. Yadin, the younger man, was a member neither of the Palmach nor of the old Haganah establishment, having taken a leave from the organization for a year and a half until the spring of 1947.[28] The son of a self-trained archaeologist, Yadin prided himself on his military professionalism although he had never served in the British Army. Well read in military theory, he had played an important role in the creation of the Haganah's officer training program, and actually ran the school; there he came into conflict with the freer spirits of the Palmach. The immediate disputes were incredibly petty—should platoons train for independent action or in company formations? should squads gain experience with medium machine guns?—but the larger issues of personality and style were serious.[29] Ben-Gurion interviewed Yadin during the Seminar, and probed him particularly carefully about his leaving the Haganah. By the fall of 1947, Yadin was back in the center of the organization, setting up an operations branch and developing the staffs that the previous chief of staff, Yitzhak Sadeh, had sorely neglected.

Ben-Gurion thus began by inserting a more professional kind of underground soldier into the army. He also moved to clarify the chain of command. In particular, he moved swiftly to insist that Galili, as chief of the National Command (Rama), serve not as a buffer between himself and the general staff but as, if anything, a kind of executive officer. An open clash was deferred, but its outlines had become clear, and Ben-Gurion had already begun to describe the National Command as an organizational anomaly, to be disposed of (by implication) when the pressure of events would allow.[30]

Secondly, Ben-Gurion reached out to the British veterans, and particularly a serious young major, Haim Laskov, who had enlisted in the

British Army in 1940 and taken every course available to him during the course of World War II.[31] Laskov, who in 1958 became chief of staff in the postwar IDF, was languishing as the security officer in an electric company when Ben-Gurion picked him to become chief training officer of the Haganah in August 1947. Ben-Gurion had interviewed him during the Seminar. The Old Man, who had sworn all those who spoke to him to secrecy, heard Laskov give him exactly the same requirement for the number of rifles per battalion as another former British officer. After a sharp exchange in which Ben-Gurion accused Laskov of having found out more than was proper from other officers, Laskov patiently explained the concept of a table of organization and equipment—something that any well-trained British officer had committed to memory.[32] It was the beginning of a long and fruitful relationship; Ben-Gurion turned to Laskov for concepts of organization and training that he could impose upon the Haganah—which viewed Laskov and other returned British officers with considerable suspicion.[33]

Thirdly, Ben-Gurion accelerated the programs for mobilization and acquisition upon which the military structure of a potential Jewish state would rest. Indeed, Ben-Gurion's achievements in this area—his selection of leaders, his insistence on thinking big, his drive and ceaseless scrutiny—match his better understood role as a decision maker in the war of independence. Israel's survival—and more than that, its victories—against the armies of the Arab states reflected not only the determination of a people with their back against the wall but a redressing of the quantitative balance in the war. The Arab states would make no all-out national effort to mobilize against the Jews: they had neither the experience nor the institutions that would have allowed them to do so. Their expeditionary armies, for better or worse, would neither grow in size nor improve much in proficiency. The Jewish state, on the other hand, much like revolutionary France in the 1790s or the Union in the American Civil War, could mobilize human and material resources for total war in ways that its opponents simply could not match.[34] The mobilization problem had two sides: manpower and materiél.

Ben-Gurion's intuition, backed up by close inquiry during the Seminar, that the Haganah had done a poor job of identifying and registering usable manpower was correct. Once a serious effort was made to register and induct men of military age in Palestine and, increasingly, in the refugee camps in Europe from whence new immigrants would come, the quantitative increase in manpower was staggering. In February 1948, on the eve of Israel's independence, the Haganah numbered 16,000 men and women, in May roughly twice that, or 35,300. In December 1948, at the peak of mobilization, the IDF included over 92,000 soldiers.[35] To be sure, some of the increase probably came from the absorption of the dissident military groups and the Palmach, and so represented reorganization and consolidation rather than growth. But even allowing for that, Ben-Gurion and his helpers paved the way for a mobilization of manpower that easily quadrupled the military manpower available to the Jewish state between the time of the Seminar and the end of the war of independence two years later.

The underground army had developed an impressive clandestine manufacturing capability, but the acquisition of arms from overseas would prove decisive for Israel's survival, as the table indicates.

LAND FORCES EQUIPMENT OF THE IDF, 1947–48[36]

	April '47	Nov '47	May '48	Oct '48	Mar '49
Rifles	10,073	10,678	21,886	59,389	62,200
Submachine guns	1,900	3,662	10,264	21,343	31,049
Machine guns	444	775	1,269	6,436	6,494
2" mortars	672	670	682	618	1,706
3" mortars	96	84	105	389	678
Artillery pieces*		25	25	253	492

*All types, including, by March 1949, 150 field pieces and 89 antitank guns.

The breakthrough developments were the nascent state's arms deals with Czechoslovakia in the first half of 1948, which provided the Jewish state with the fruits of the Czech arms industry as modified by the Germans for their own use during World War II. Ironically, many survivors of Hitler's extermination camps went into battle against the Arabs carrying German-designed Mauser rifles and light machine guns, under air cover from modified Bf-109 fighters—all fruits of the arms deals. These agreements, which combined finance (above all, fundraising in the United States), diplomacy (as the Soviet Union established Communist rule in Prague), and organization (to bring the arms in despite a British quasi-blockade and in the midst of UN-sponsored truces), absorbed much of Ben-Gurion's energy.

Ben-Gurion moved swiftly not only to reorganize the high command of the Haganah, but to provide it strategic guidance. This vision he expressed in a series of speeches to senior political and military leaders. Like Churchill, he believed in the importance of systematic surveys of the situation as a way of preparing colleagues and subordinates for the tasks ahead. Speeches, for Ben-Gurion, served not merely to rouse others to new efforts, but to explain to them—sometimes in deliberately harsh terms—the problems that remained to be confronted. Perhaps the most important of these speeches, "The Haganah in the days to come," delivered on 18 June 1947, bears particularly close scrutiny, both for its substance and for what it reveals of the working of Ben-Gurion's mind.[37]

Ben-Gurion began, as he often did, with a historical survey of the Jewish community's struggle in Palestine, describing the conflict as one of changing stages, in which the yishuv had at different times faced different enemies on different fronts. At the turn of the century, the problem had been protecting their property and lives against the depredations of bandits; after the First World War the threat became organized groups of local Arabs whose motivation was, at least in part, political. There had come into existence, following the White Paper, a "British front" as well, as the yishuv had fought the efforts of the British to restrict immigration to Palestine. Now, however, the final and most important test would arise: "the aggressive hostility of the rulers of Arab states, and we must prepare for this front with all seriousness and urgency."

After exploring the links between the British and Arab fronts, Ben-Gurion argued that the impending struggle would pit the Jews of Palestine against forces expected to be superior in numbers and having, furthermore, the benefit of belonging to ordered armies; the *yishuv* would need to strive for qualitative superiority by tapping the military experience of its World War II veterans and by tapping the technological superiority of the Jewish population of Palestine. The Jews required three kinds of forces: a static militia for territorial defense (the *cheyl mishmar*, or CHIM); a mobile force organized along regular principles; and an élite arm for special operations. No less important than this tripartite division of the Haganah (an assignment of functions that has persisted throughout the post-independence history of the Israel Defense Forces) was his insistence on preparing the way for larger units and a regular army. He concluded with an injunction to the leaders of the Haganah to set up schools to train leaders at the battalion level and above, as well as the staffs that would be needed for the control of large units in field operations.

Ben-Gurion, like Churchill, spent much of his time goading and energizing subordinates who, even if they could never achieve what he desired, nonetheless complied with his wishes. His critics, then and thereafter, insisted that in most respects—regarding arms acquisition, for example, or the organization of large units—he had merely accelerated trends already under way. The old-line leadership of the Haganah argued that the British-trained officers favored by Ben-Gurion often lacked the flexibility of their Palestinian-trained counterparts, and that they favored British-style formal discipline and rigid tactics, which were suited neither to the psychology of the fiercely independent Jews of the *yishuv* nor to the requirements of light infantry warfare in the Judaean hills. There was no doubt some substance to these criticisms, but they are not entirely accurate, nor do they touch the heart of the matter. Like Lincoln, Clemenceau, and Churchill, Ben-Gurion drove and inspired his subordinates to do those things which, left to their own devices, they might have known to be desirable but also might not have carried out.

He got results because, like Churchill, he expected to hear about the details of compliance with his instructions. Ben-Gurion paid close attention, for example, to the establishment of courses for the Haganah's small signal corps, which, though well suited for maintaining links among widely separated civilian settlements, had had neither the equipment nor the personnel to staff complex mobile military organizations.[38] His monumental diary served as a means of keeping track of the changes that he had ordered, and of the transformation under way. The prospect of standing before the irascible Old Man, as he was already known, his bald head crowned with wings of unruly white hair, his questions short, sharp, and peremptory, and his pen always writing, may have recalled even to the less devout who stood before him a line from an ancient Jewish text: "Know what is above you: an eye that sees, an ear that hears, and a book in which all your deeds are recorded."[39]

"A WAR OF COMMANDERS"

The test of Ben-Gurion's labors came with frightening speed, because Israel's war of independence began well before the formal declaration of a state in May 1948. On 29 November 1947 a wave of celebration swept the *yishuv*—the United Nations had decided, by a vote of 33 to 13 with ten abstentions, to partition Palestine and to create a Jewish state out of three barely contiguous areas west of the Jordan. The streets of Tel Aviv filled with dancing crowds—but Ben-Gurion, anticipating a bitter war to come, stayed in his room. He could not join the street celebrations, as he remarked somberly to his daughter, knowing that some of those now dancing would before long fall in battle.[40]

His words proved correct. The decision of the United Nations inaugurated the first phase of a war that would last some thirteen months, through three phases, each bringing its own array of struggle and hardships. In the first, which began the very next day, the *yishuv* suffered continuous attacks from local Palestinian Arab groups, while the Arab states began to mobilize against it. In this war of ambush and raid, the British mandate authority played an ambiguous role—occasionally intervening to stop the fighting and occasionally tilting to one side or the other—although generally more favorable to the Arabs, particularly after bloody attacks by Lechi and IZL on their forces withdrawing from Palestine. Arab villagers and irregulars struck particularly hard against the roads that linked Jewish population centers, above all the road to Jerusalem from the coastal plain. For four months the *yishuv*, still mobilizing its resources, remained on the defensive. In April 1948, however, it launched powerful counterattacks, temporarily opening the road to Jerusalem and defeating Arab forces in key cities, including Tiberias, Haifa, and Jaffa.

Israel's declaration of independence on 14 May 1948 brought about the second phase of the war and its most severe crisis—the invasion by Arab armies. In less than a month of bitter fighting Jerusalem (where the exiguous garrison of the Old City surrendered to the professional soldiers of the Arab Legion) was again cut off, while the Syrian army seized small pockets of territory allocated to the new Jewish state and Egyptian forces occupied Beersheba and advanced to within thirty miles of Tel Aviv. Although by early June the Israelis had won some victories and thwarted the immediate onslaught, the first truce, which came on 11 June, seemed to some observers to have barely averted disaster.

During the month-long hiatus in fighting, however, the Israel Defense Forces, as they were now called, reorganized and equipped themselves for renewed fighting; this constituted the war's third phase. On 8 July a ten-day struggle between the Israelis and their Arab enemies cleared much of the central part of the country of Arab forces and restored the initiative in the south against Egypt. A second truce, begun on 18 July, broke down and in a series of episodic campaigns, including a major outbreak of fighting in mid-October 1948, the Israelis swept the Egyptians out of the Negev and Arab irregular forces out of the Galilee, and they now seemed poised to renew the battle for all of Jerusalem. The last sharp fighting of the war occurred in the last week of 1948 and the first week of 1949 when Israeli forces thrust into the Sinai peninsula, very nearly precipitating a major armed clash with the British forces there.[41]

The sheer size of a military action—the numbers of soldiers involved, casualties suffered, or ground conquered—is no measure of its strategic and operational complexity and hence its value to the student of war. The Israeli war of independence, fought though it was in an area no larger than the state of New Jersey, provides a capital demonstration of this fact. Strategically, the conflict began as a war of survival, at least from the Israeli point of view: the leaders and people of Israel believed that upon their victory depended not only the existence of an independent Jewish state but the physical survival of its citizens. They fought, therefore, a total war, as all-embracing in its efforts (however much smaller in its dimensions) as the conflict that had swept the world in the preceding ten years. The Israelis mobilized, or attempted to mobilize, every last man and woman capable of bearing arms; they strained every nerve to produce their own weapons of war and to smuggle in equipment from abroad. In particular the battles to relieve Jerusalem, or the fights to hold on to isolated settlements such as Yad Mordechai, Negba, and Mishmar HaEmek, though no more than skirmishes beside World War II battles, were fought with no less a sense of enormous stakes.

Yet the war had another strategic aspect, as a coolly conducted struggle for limited ends among powers who had in mind a peace settlement of a moderate kind. Even at the outset, the leaders of the provisional government of Israel declined to describe the borders of the Jewish state, suspecting that by force of arms they might secure more territory from favorable adjustments to the partition plan of 1947—as indeed they did. Yet even during this phase, when survival itself was at stake, Ben-Gurion had perplexing choices to make. He had not merely to guarantee the security of the core Jewish population in the coastal enclave from Tel Aviv to Haifa, but to keep open lines of communication with major settlements in the north and in the south, and above all with Jerusalem. He sought as well to bring in the hardware and supplies (everything from uniforms to medicine) needed for the expanding Israeli military, while creating the state institutions that could make good use of them.

Following the first truce Israel's leaders no longer worried about their prospects of simple survival. From the very first their opponents had not offered up a solid and implacable front. The Lebanese and Egyptian commitment to the war was, at the most, half-hearted, and in King Abdullah of Transjordan the Israelis had an opponent who had, in the past, been a collaborator—and possibly a recipient of Jewish Agency funds. Negotiating with Abdullah up to the very outbreak of the war, the Israeli leadership never seems to have lost hope that it could come to terms with the emir of Transjordan, who had command of the most formidable of all the Arab fighting forces, the Arab Legion. Indeed, it soon became apparent that Abdullah, who had little interest in conquering the Jewish state but every desire to retain the old city of Jerusalem and fend off his Arab rivals, was anything but a fanatical opponent. He was, rather, to some extent at the mercy of younger, nationalist officers such as Abdullah el-Tel, the commander of one of the four regiments of the Arab Legion.[42] Similar rivalries and internal discord hampered the relations between Egypt and Iraq—rivals for leadership in the Arab world—and even the relations among Palestinian groups. Jewish factionalism also broke out in violence on occasion during the war, but on the whole the crisis of 1948–49 produced unity in the yishuv. On the Arab side the story was just the reverse, as initial unity gave way to increasing dissension in the loose anti-Jewish coalition. Furthermore the Arab side, with its small regular armies of mixed quality, was hampered by problems of distance and hence resupply to a far greater extent than the more compact Jewish state; nor did the Arabs have the potential to mobilize for war that the Israelis had. They had experienced neither the pressure of necessity that the *yishuv* had faced, nor the strain of the European powers in mustering forces for the great struggle of World War II; their bureaucracies were inefficient and slow, their armies by and large untested in war.

The paradoxical nature of this war—an unconditional struggle for survival, and yet a limited war for borders and minor advantage— became even more complex as one considered the role of the external powers. Great Britain favored its Arab dependencies, yet resentfully sustained an arms embargo on them; the United States, like several key European states, sympathized with the Israelis yet had its interests in the Arab world; the Soviet Union and its clients were willing to thwart British imperialism and hasten the collapse of pro-Western Arab regimes, yet mistrusted Jewish nationalism and the democratic social-ism of the Israeli state. Furthermore, each of the great powers had their admirers and adherents in the Zionist camp. The Palmach was, to a remarkable degree, pro-Soviet; and some of Israel's middle-class Anglophiles still looked to Britain while others saw in the distant United States, with its vast economic power and influential Jewish pop-ulation, Israel's most important ally.

Resolving the contradictions in the war's strategic essence proved to be but one of Ben-Gurion's challenges. No less daunting were its oper-ational features. The means of conflict included aerial operations (the capitals of most major combatants came under bombing at different points in the war), guerrilla activities (focusing on road ambushes), and conventional assaults by combined arms formations up to brigade and sometimes divisional strength. Each of the three fronts—northern, cen-tral, and southern—posed distinct geographical and demographic challenges, even though they lay little more than thirty or forty miles apart. In the mountainous north isolated Jewish settlements were pre-cariously linked by roads plagued by the irregulars of Fawzi el-Kawukji's Arab Liberation Army, and threatened by the thrusts of the Syrian and to a lesser extent the Lebanese armies. In the center, the coastal plain provided the "Zionist redoubt" as one American observer called it, the center of gravity of the Jewish population and war-making potential. In the heart of the north–south Judaean hill mass, however, lay Jerusalem, the political heart of the Jewish state, surrounded by Arab villages and easily accessible to the Arab Legion, reinforced by the Iraqi army. In the south, Egyptian forces operated in a rolling desert region where Israel had only a few scattered fortified settlements to serve as staging areas for large-scale operations. There were no natural obstacles to Egyptian advances through the Sinai into the heart of the country and indeed, before the tide turned, the Egyptians came close to both Tel Aviv and Jerusalem.

Hard fighting (and the morale and mobilization of resources behind it) no doubt determined the outcome of this, like any war, but the Kimche brothers, one of whom fought in the war while another covered it as a journalist, have a point when they write that

> [W]hat really mattered was the clash of wills, the battle of com-
> mands. . . . In fact, the actual fighting of the war (certainly until
> October 1948) played a much smaller part in the wider aspect of
> the conflict than one would conclude from the somewhat stylized
> accounts of the military side of the war which have become famil-
> iar by repetition, each according to his needs: the Israeli, the
> Arab, and the British. . . . If ever there was a war of commanders,
> this was it: supreme commanders, field commanders and local
> commanders. They were decisive. . . .[43]

On the Israeli side the "war of commanders" was all the more difficult because it was a war conducted by a high command often at odds with itself, not only about personalities, policy, and goals, but about structure as well.

Thus, although the war of Israeli independence may have appeared a puny affair by the standards of the epic struggles just ended in Europe and Asia less than five years earlier, it was, in fact, a struggle of extraordinary strategic complexity. No government can conduct war by rule of thumb, and this situation was no exception. Thus, for example, at the outset of the war Ben-Gurion made a strategic decision that violated or seemed to violate a cardinal principle of war: he ordered the general staff to defend every Jewish settlement throughout Palestine, rather than abandoning some in order to concentrate their forces for counteroffensives. At the same time he authorized local commanders to undertake counteroffensives.[44] This presents an interesting case of the intersection between operational and strategic decision-making.

Ben-Gurion's decision had two rationales. First, by defending every location the Jews of Palestine would delay and absorb attacks by both local Arabs and the armies of the Arab states, gaining time for the mobilization of people and materiél within Palestine and abroad. This ability of the Jewish state to amass resources was central to his concept of the war. The agricultural settlements of Jewish Palestine were organized for self-defense; although a number fell throughout the country, most held, and even those that could not withstand Syrian, Egyptian, or Jordanian assaults made the enemy pay a price in time and space. His second reason for not yielding an inch of ground without a fight was psychological: it would deny the enemy the satisfaction and encouragement of seeing the Jews flee. Disdaining the Jews as a subject and nonwarrior race, many Arabs were unprepared for a fierce fight. To the Jewish side it was an equally important statement: that flight was no longer a possibility; now, unlike during the hideous years just passed, Jews could—indeed must—stand and fight.

Ben-Gurion's perilous decision came at a cost. The Etzion settlement bloc south of Jerusalem was wiped out by the Arab Legion; Zemach and Mishmar Hayarden fell to the Syrians; Yad Mordechai fell to the Egyptians. By the end of the first truce the newborn Israel Defense Forces, awkwardly positioned as they were, had been stretched to the limits of their endurance. But the Israelis had blunted the initial attacks, secured important pockets within the borders assigned to them (particularly in the cities), and were far better prepared than their opponents to take advantage of the truce—to smuggle in weapons and volunteers, to reorganize, and to seize the initiative, which they did as soon as the truce ended.

Ben-Gurion's peculiar mixture of ability to think big, ruthless determination, and flexibility shows to greatest advantage in his strategic decisions about Jerusalem. Under the terms of UN Resolution 181, which authorized the creation of the Jewish state, Jerusalem was to "be established as a corpus separatum under a special international regime . . . administered by the United Nations." With its Jewish population of roughly 100,000 and the holy sites (above all the Western Wall) Jerusalem had enormous significance to the *yishuv* both as a symbol and as a major population center. Although barely thirty miles from the coastal plain the city was at the mercy of its sole supply line, a winding mountain road dominated by Arab villages. Well before Israeli independence, convoys carrying supplies to Jerusalem came under fire from local Palestinian Arabs, ably led by Abd el-Kadr al-Hussaini. As British forces withdrew, they tended to cover only their own convoys, and gave less and less protection to the Jewish convoys.

At the outset of the war, therefore, Ben-Gurion focused his attention on Jerusalem. By January 1948 he had in mind a multistage campaign for the city, timed to coincide with the British departure, and to include an operation to secure the road to the coast.[45] On 31 March the general staff came to his house to discuss several matters.

> I told them that at this moment there is only one burning question—the fight for the road to Jerusalem, and the manpower that Yigal [Yadin] has prepared—400–500 men—is inadequate. This is now the decisive fight. The fall of Jewish Jerusalem would be a death blow to the *yishuv*, and the Arabs understand that and have concentrated many forces to cut our communications, and we must take all unused manpower [for this purpose]. . . . We immediately went back to the office to organize the operation.[46]

The result of Ben-Gurion's order was the largest operation the Israelis would undertake until late in the war—NACHSHON, named after the first Israelite to plunge into the Red Sea during the Exodus from Egypt. The brigade-sized operation, the Jews' first, involved 1,500 troops from 3–16 April; its desperate combat included a fight for the hilltop known as Kastel, in which the best Palestinian guerrilla leader, Abd el-Kadr Hussaini, fell. Three large convoys got through to the city, providing the wherewithal to allow it to hold on—barely—through the first bitter month of all-out warfare, which erupted a month later. The Jewish population of Jerusalem had, just as importantly, now gained the confidence to hang on during a desperate siege. The Arab villagers, on the other hand, never recovered enough offensive spirit for another try.

Once the war had fairly started, Ben-Gurion insisted that the defense of Jerusalem must take first precedence, even over the dire needs of Israeli settlements in the north and south that were under attack from regular Arab armies. As so often occurs in war, seemingly minor choices had large repercussions. At one point, Ben-Gurion argued with the chief of the operations department of the Israel Defense Forces, Yigal Yadin, over whether four obsolete 65-millimeter cannon should go north to the Galilee or to Jerusalem (as Ben-Gurion preferred). Yadin, who seems to have exaggerated in retrospect his willingness to defy the Old Man, reported that he slammed his fist down so hard on Ben-Gurion's table that the glass broke. It seems that after all the two compromised.[47]

The eruption of the interstate war threw Jerusalem once again into contention. Once the interstate war began, the Arab Legion's police fortress at Latrun sealed the road far more firmly than the villagers had. Ben-Gurion ordered repeated, costly assaults on Latrun; they were some of the bloodiest battles of the war, and they remain deeply controversial to the present day.[48] In some of these assaults untrained waves of new immigrants were reported (inaccurately, as it turned out) to have borne the brunt of the assaults, suffering large losses for no gain. In any event the well-trained, British-led Arab Legion beat back the Israeli attacks on Latrun while Jordanian forces within Jerusalem reduced the Jewish Quarter in the walled Old City. Ben-Gurion turned to an American officer, Mickey Marcus, to deal with the problem of Jerusalem. Marcus, a graduate of West Point, had served with distinction during World War II as a US Army lawyer, albeit a lawyer with a penchant for finding his way to the front line. In keeping with the principle of thinking big, Ben-Gurion made him Israel's first *aluf,* or general officer commanding a front. Marcus was unable to take Latrun, but he did, on the day just before the onset of the truce, succeed in constructing a bypass road that allowed convoys to move up to Jerusalem and relieve the near-starvation conditions there.

Ben-Gurion's determined campaign to control Jerusalem had been largely but not entirely successful. The city held, and Jewish forces within the city had taken important Arab neighborhoods; the Old City, however, including the Temple Mount, had fallen to the Arab Legion. Yet when the truce ended and the period of Jewish offensive operations resumed, Ben-Gurion no longer devoted the bulk of the Israel Defense Forces' efforts to Jerusalem; it became a relatively quiet front. He turned, rather, to the conquest of the Galilee and the clearing of Egyptian forces from the Negev.[49]

Ben-Gurion, seemingly inflexible in negotiation and action, had, in fact, the gift of knowing when to content himself with half a loaf—as he had in accepting the UN partition resolution, which left the proposed Jewish state looking like three indefensible blotches of ground touching at only two points. If the Jewish state was to be viable it needed the empty spaces of the Negev desert, and some degree of depth in the north as well. Moreover, Ben-Gurion knew well that Jerusalem was a matter of international concern, and he had already begun to feel pressure on that score from the international community. Furthermore, like other Jewish leaders, he continued to entertain hopes of a pragmatic deal with King Abdullah of Transjordan, who was restraining his more ardently nationalistic subordinates and would content himself with control of the Muslim holy places in Jerusalem—which were virtually identical to the Jewish ones.

For half a year, from July 1948 through January 1949, David Ben-Gurion directed a war characterized by short, intense episodes of fighting followed by truces often violated in letter or spirit by both sides. Throughout this second half of the open war between Israel and its Arab neighbors the Israel Defense Forces grew in size, sophistication, and self-confidence. Its short, sharp offensives allowed the IDF to recover virtually all the territory assigned to the state of Israel under the original United Nations partition plan, and to gain more at the expense of its neighbors. By the time final truce talks began on Rhodes in January Israeli forces had penetrated into the Sinai peninsula, isolating a large Egyptian force, and had clear superiority over Jordanian, Syrian, and Iraqi forces in the country's center and north. Ben-Gurion managed the Israeli war effort carefully, favoring the aggressive exploitation of Arab truce violations, but knowing when to refrain from pushing too far.

Thus, in September 1948 Ben-Gurion was contemplating a thrust at Hebron, just south of Jerusalem. A successful operation might have given Israel all of the West Bank south of Jerusalem, and perhaps brought it back to the Old City itself. The Cabinet opposed the move, so, reluctantly, Ben-Gurion set aside the proposal, later calling it a matter of "weeping for the generations" that the newly created state would not dominate all of the Judaean hills to the Jordan River.[50] But in light of the hostility of Great Britain, only lukewarm support from the United States and the Soviet Union, and his own anxiety about the Palestinian refugee problem—already a source of ill will for the new state—prudence dictated otherwise, and on 27 September he told his government, "We are not free to use our military power. Even more powerful states than ours are not completely free in this way. In this world everything depends on everything else. . . ."[51] Acutely conscious though he was of the new state's military superiority over its enemies, and desirous though he was of expanding its borders, Ben-Gurion accepted the limits imposed by international politics.

 We can win in war and strike our enemies and smash the armies
of Abdullah and Syria, and Iraq and Egypt, and drive them from the
land—and we can still lose the diplomatic battle if as a result we
create decisive state interests against us in the rest of the world.[52]

Visiting the southern front in 1949, he asked Yigal Alon and Yitzhak
Rabin how they would conquer the area south of Hebron.

Alon began explaining in some detail how he would conduct the
operation. Suddenly he stopped and asked in wonder, "Listen
Ben-Gurion, do you really want to conquer this area?" There was
a lightning flash in Ben-Gurion's eyes. He replied, "It's not possible now, but maybe, some day. . . ."[53]

Ben-Gurion would have gladly taken the entire western bank of the
Jordan for the new Jewish state, and he grieved for the loss of the eastern half of Jerusalem. But prudence triumphed over ambition. The
enmity of a British government that had opposed partition and supported Israel's chief military opponents (Egypt, Jordan, and Iraq),
coupled with the flood of Palestinian refugees fleeing the fighting to
neighboring countries, made Israel's international situation precarious.
He neither desired nor could he expect the embrace of the Soviet Union
as a patron, and the United States, although sympathetic, had no desire
to further alienate the Arab world by supporting the expansion of the
Jewish state.

"OF ALL THE DEFICIENCIES OF OUR MILITARY, LACK OF DISCIPLINE IS THE MOST SEVERE."

Ben-Gurion, like many war statesmen, found himself not only
immersed in the problem of strategy as normally understood—the challenge of applying force to achieve political ends—but compelled to

construct institutions at the same time. He was a self-conscious state-builder, who described his political philosophy as one of *mamlachtiut* (statism). Acutely aware of the extraordinary diversity of the Jews of Palestine and of the many more diaspora Jews who, he hoped, would stream in following independence, he was determined to create a state with strong institutions. This began most simply with the mandatory use of Hebrew, an ancient language only recently revived from its status as a tongue of prayer and religious instruction to one of daily use. One of his first orders as defense minister, for example, was to require of general officers that they Hebraicize their names: he understood well the importance of symbols in shaping a new state.

Of most pressing importance was the creation of a military organization that would serve as a neutral servant of the new Israeli state, responsive to the duly constituted political authority alone and possessing an unquestioned monopoly on the use of force. A week after the beginning of the first truce (which commenced on 11 June and lasted through 8 July) Ben-Gurion wrote in his diary, "Of all the deficiencies of our military, lack of discipline is the most severe, and above all at the highest levels."[54] He wrote this after a ten-hour meeting with all the brigade commanders in the IDF, in which he quizzed them closely about the conduct of operations to this point.[55] Ben-Gurion blamed the unwillingness of the high command to devote an unreserved effort to the seizure of Latrun for the tenuousness of a secure line of communications to Jerusalem, but his worries included not only the creation of a responsive general staff but the incorporation of both the pre-independence guerrilla and terrorist movements and the absorption of the autonomous left-wing Palmach into the new Israel Defense Forces.

These internal political battles, which sometimes took place in smoky conference rooms but occasionally spilled out onto the Tel Aviv seafront, were every bit as bitter as any operational decision about where and how to deploy the scanty forces of the new Israeli military. No doubt Ben-Gurion's autocratic style and temper contributed much to their acerbity and to the extreme quality of some of his decisions, and it is not always easy to distinguish between his concerns as a state-builder and his mere insistence on having his way. Nevertheless the result was an Israel Defense Forces that, despite its peculiar qualities as the embodiment of a nation in arms, was an essentially professional and politically neutral, if not completely subordinate, military force.

The IDF came into existence on 26 May 1948, its leadership and central staffs simply moving over from the Haganah and Palmach. The leaders of the two competing underground units, the Lechi and the IZL, pledged to merge with the new IDF—a relatively trivial problem for the tiny Lechi, which had only a few hundred activists at most. The IZL, which had perhaps 3,000 men under arms, in accordance with an agreement in March 1948 became part of the IDF in most parts of the country upon independence. It had fought under the general direction of the Haganah in the period immediately before independence, with the important exception of Jerusalem, where its base of support had been particularly strong, and where its men made up a substantial fraction of the city's defenders—a strong battalion of perhaps 700.[56]

There remained bad blood between the IZL and the Haganah/Palmach. Memories of "the season," when the Haganah had helped hunt down IZL activists, still lingered. The Haganah blamed the IZL for the April 1948 massacre of Arab villagers at Deir Yasin outside Jerusalem, when a misconceived and botched assault on a village that was marginal to the struggle for the roads around the city turned into a bloodbath. The IZL felt aggrieved at being blamed, given that the attack had been approved by the Haganah commander in the city. Furthermore, most IZL members viewed with suspicion the hard left-wing ideology of the Palmach, which in turn looked upon the IZL as a potential source of ideological contamination of the new state. The clash came to a head in the *Altalena* affair.

The IZL, like the Haganah, had run an extensive arms-acquisition and illegal-immigration operation in Europe immediately after World War II. In early June 1948 the ship *Altalena* headed for Israel from southern France, crammed with arms (some 5,000 rifles, 250 machine guns, mortars, and large quantities of shells, grenades, and high explosives) and some 900 overseas volunteers. She approached the shore on 19 June, eight days after the first truce began. It was a substantial increment of supplies and manpower, and it was clearly the intention of the IZL high command to reserve much if not all of the incoming ship's cargo for the use of IZL units, particularly in Jerusalem. Ben-Gurion was equally determined that the ship and all it contained should be put at the disposal of the IDF. After a series of miscommunications between ship and shore, and misunderstanding between the two sides over who would have control of the ship's unloading, on 19 June the *Altalena* stood in to shore, first at Kfar Vitkin and then off the Tel Aviv shoreline. IZL men left their units to help with the unloading. Ben-Gurion ordered Palmach units under the command of a twenty-six-year-old Yitzhak Rabin to open fire upon the *Altalena*, with the result that eighteen IZL men were killed and ten wounded.[57] It was a heart-rending and horrifying scene. Barely containing his fury Menachem Begin, leader of the IZL, ordered his men not to retaliate, however, and the absorption of the IZL into the IDF was completed shortly thereafter. In a pugnacious phrase that outraged and infuriated many a right-wing Israeli in years to come, Ben-Gurion insisted that when the Jews finally built the Third Temple (the First having been destroyed in 586 B.C.E., and the Second in 70 C.E.), the "holy cannon" that sank the *Altalena* would find its place at the side of the altar.[58]

The end of the *Altalena* affair, however, was a long way from the end of the challenges that David Ben-Gurion faced in creating a united and politically responsive IDF. The continuation of a semi-independent Palmach posed, in his view, an equal threat to the solidity of the military institutions of the Jewish state. The Palmach had come into existence in 1941 as a way of keeping small standing units available, particularly for guerrilla operations, in defense of a Palestinian Jewish community menaced by the march of Rommel's army in Egypt. In time the Palmach, based largely on friendly *kibbutzim*, became the semi-standing force of the *yishuv*. When the war with the Arab states broke out, the Palmach consisted of three brigades (out of an IDF total of ten), with a separate command structure, even though Ben-Gurion had intended its battalions to be distributed among the regular brigades of the army.[59] It was most definitely a home-grown organization—socialist, informal, and proud of an independent military style, disdaining the spit-and-polish of regular armies. Its leaders were some of the best the IDF had, most notably Yigal Alon, its overall commander, and Yitzhak Rabin, commander of the Harel brigade on the Jerusalem front.

Ben-Gurion used the Palmach to suppress the IZL. He now undertook, in a far more measured way, the dismantling of the Palmach itself.[60] The possibility of conflict with the high command of the Palmach, and to some extent with the Haganah overall, had emerged much earlier, beginning with Ben-Gurion's firing of Galili as chief of the National Command on 3 May 1948, less than two weeks before independence and all-out war. He yielded to the military's protests at this—they much preferred to work with the more even-tempered Galili—but although Ben-Gurion reinstated Galili in an anomalous status thereafter, he established his own control by insisting that he must have full authority as defense minister, i.e., the right to issue orders directly to the general staff. On 12 May the shadow government yielded to his demands.[61]

Ben-Gurion's authority, however, came under fierce attack from his political enemies and from some quarters in the military itself. During the first truce Ben-Gurion wanted the appointment of British-trained officers, including Mordechai Makleff, to take over the all-important central front. He looked as well to experienced officers like Ben Dunkelman (a Canadian Jew who had served with distinction in the Canadian army in Europe throughout World War II) to take command of the dispirited, newly formed 7th Brigade, which would eventually become the first armored formation in the Israel Defense Forces.[62] Like many foreign-trained officers, Dunkelman had encountered suspicion and even condescension from home-grown Israeli soldiers. When Dunkelman commented on the lax staff work in the Palmach brigade to which he was first attached, he received a sharp rebuke from the plans officer. "In the Palmach, we have to see the ground—we don't do our planning from *maps!*"[63]

Matters came to a head on 24 June when Ben-Gurion rejected Yadin's plan for reorganizing the high command, which would have kept the primacy of senior Palmach officers and men of the left-wing Mapam party. On 1 July Yadin and Mapam members of the general staff tendered their resignations—although just how serious that gesture was remains a matter of dispute. In one of the truly astonishing episodes of the war, the new Israeli government, in a country on the verge of renewed hostilities on the southern front, set up a five-man commission including the ministers of Foreign Affairs, Justice, Health and Immigration, and Agriculture, from a range of political parties chaired by Interior Minister Yitzchak Greenbaum, a long-time Zionist functionary, to inquire into Ben-Gurion's conduct of the war.[64] From 3 through 6 July it met, hearing the testimony of bitter generals—including Yadin, who, though somewhat more moderate than the others, criticized Ben-Gurion's intrusion into the details of war. "Matters of war are separated into two parts," Yadin argued, "one part strategic decisions, the highest politics of the war, but the army has a second part—the actual operational part."[65] One could not ask for a more perfect statement of the "normal" theory of civil-military relations. "Tell me what you want me to do, not how to do it," he said in effect, echoing the sentiments of soldiers throughout the ages.

Ben-Gurion offered a spirited response. He noted the politicization of the army and was sharply critical of the Haganah and the Palmach for their bias against British-trained officers and for general indiscipline. He declared that his intrusion into matters of detail resulted from the failure of the military to follow through on his orders. He asserted his right to oversee all aspects of war, which were interconnected. When the Greenbaum committee recommended curtailing Ben-Gurion's powers by inserting an intermediate level between the defense minister and the chief of staff (re-establishing, in other words, the chief of the National

Command), and suggesting that all disputes between the two come to the War Cabinet, Ben-Gurion offered his resignation. With only a day to spare before the end of the first truce, the Cabinet caved in, and Ben-Gurion retained his overwhelming authority.

Ben-Gurion timed his move against the Palmach carefully. On the eve of the resumption of hostilities against the Egyptians in late October 1948 he had the IDF disestablish the Palmach's high command while retaining its units in their three brigade-sized formations. It was a shrewdly chosen juncture: Yigal Alon was busy as commander of Israel's southern front; he succeeded in taking the whole of the Negev desert, sending a flying column to take possession of Eilat, Israel's future Red Sea port, and even penetrating as far as El Arish in the Sinai. Still, Palmach members protested the decision, foreseeing that this would lead to the ultimate dissolution of the Palmach itself. Ben-Gurion denied this, but made a case that pointed in the direction of such a move. Writing to a wounded Palmachnik, he disavowed (disingenuously, of course) any intention of breaking up the Palmach itself.[66]

Again Ben-Gurion chose his moment carefully. In May 1949 he ordered the final absorption of the Palmach into the IDF by dissolving the three Palmach brigades. There were protests and much bitterness.[67] Ben-Gurion shunted aside the charismatic Alon, who was a natural candidate to become the first peacetime chief of staff of the IDF; he turned instead to Yigal Yadin, the ascetic young archaeologist turned soldier who had never served in the Palmach, as a replacement for the ailing Ya'akov Dori. Yadin had complained about Ben-Gurion but never turned as bitterly against him as other commanders, and he was neutral in the disputes between the different schools of thought in the new IDF. Ben-Gurion retained the promising young commanders, including Moshe Dayan and Yitzhak Rabin, who would subsequently become chiefs of staff themselves, but he made quite clear his intention to create a unified IDF culture. The selection of Yadin was shrewd: organized and precise, Yadin resembled the British-trained officers that Ben-Gurion favored, without having been one himself.

Yadin possessed great talent as an organizer and briefer, if not as a combat commander. His crisp military analyses impressed more than one foreign observer, including the British military journalist and historian Basil Liddell Hart; and to Yadin belongs the credit for the groundwork of the IDF's organization as a nation in arms following the struggle for independence. He appreciated, with Ben-Gurion, the need for formal discipline and for all the infrastructure of a regular army; what he lacked was the spark of inspired combat leadership—which others could and did provide.

Working through Yadin, Ben-Gurion navigated Israeli strategy through a complex set of perils—the imminence of UN intervention to internationalize the new part of Jerusalem, which the Israelis held firmly; British hostility, which culminated in an aerial clash between the Israeli and the Royal Air Forces over the Sinai at the end of the war; international sympathy for the exodus of hundreds of thousands of Palestinians displaced by the fighting. At war's end Israel, having successfully mobilized and organized a substantial military force, controlled more land than had been originally allotted under the partition resolution, and, because of the flight of large portions of the Palestinian Arab population, land in which the Jews constituted a firm majority. A Jewish state recognized by the world's great powers had come into existence, and if its borders were long and exposed, it had, nonetheless, the base it needed on which to grow and flourish.

A FINAL WARNING

Israel, like many democratic states, takes for granted a military that views itself, by and large, as the neutral servant of a modern state. It has not always or entirely been so—and indeed, without Ben-Gurion's conscious efforts, one doubts whether it would ever have become so.[68] The Palmach could easily have become, or attempted to become, an ideological Praetorian Guard for a socialist state. In fact, the senior ranks of the IDF were not and never have been quite immune from partisan politics—nor could they be, as generals retired young and often moved directly into politics. Still, the Ben-Gurionist imprint on the IDF made it an infinitely more professional and apolitical force than that of any Arab country save Jordan, with corresponding benefits in terms of military effectiveness.

Ben-Gurion was the father of the IDF in other ways. He remains even to this day a revered founding figure in the military even more than in society at large: periodically, in fact, members of the IDF high command have been known to gather for a day of study of his writings, pondering his legacy and its meaning. Throughout his retirement generals came to consult the Old Man, sometimes with scary results. When in May 1967 Rabin as chief of staff came to talk to him at Sde Boker about the imminent possibility of war, Ben-Gurion lashed out at the danger of Israel embarking upon a conflict without a single international ally.[69] Shaken, Rabin, his nerves already overstretched by anxiety, short of sleep and overdosed on the cigarettes he puffed nonstop, almost collapsed. But the old statesman knew better than most the dangers that inhere in war. Operationally the conflict turned out better than anyone could have expected, but his forebodings about the consequences even of a war handily won—in particular, the problem of what to do with a large, hostile Palestinian population—were closer to the mark than any could have anticipated.

Ben-Gurion, like other great war statesmen, combined a warm affection for soldiers and their commanders with a mistrust of military bureaucracy, he had, let it be said, a streak of near-pacifist antipathy to war as well.

> The essence of an army's existence is not democratic, not humane, not Zionist, and not socialistic, because an army exists for killing and destruction. But there is no escaping the fact that our enemies wish to annihilate us, and only through military power can we destroy the enemy's will and ability to harm us.[70]

These words come from one of his most interesting speeches, delivered on 19 June 1948; entitled "From the Haganah in the Underground to a Regular Army," it captures some of the key features of his military thought. It included, as well, his unyielding view of expert military advice:

> In military matters, as in all other matters of substance, experts knowledgeable in technique don't decide, even though their advice and guidance is vital; rather, an open mind and a common sense are essential. And these qualities are possessed—to a greater or lesser degree—by any normal man.[71]

There are no general issues [in war]," Ben-Gurion said, "only details."[72] If he is to be faulted it should be for having failed to create institutions that could sustain the kind of civilian control he exercised personally as prime minister and minister of defense, roles that he combined throughout his political career. He had brilliant protégés such as Shimon Peres, whom he put into the ministry of defense, but before long retired generals, rather than true civilians, came to exercise the real control over the conduct of Israel's military affairs. Ben-Gurion's inbred secretiveness, the result of years of semi-clandestine political work, the East European socialist political culture, and the imperative of security for a small and threatened state, impeded civilian scrutiny of Israel's military institutions by, for example, the Defense and Foreign Affairs committees of the Knesset. Some would go further, arguing that Ben-Gurion was responsible for a kind of idolatrous worship of the IDF which obscured its real weaknesses until 1973 and 1982, and which bred a kind of militarization of Israeli foreign policy. These criticisms may have some merit, but they go too far. The feat of creating an independent state under incredibly adverse political and military circumstances in 1948–49 was an astonishing achievement; to do so while inculcating the fundamentals of political neutrality and professionalism into a military forged out of disparate factions and composed of recruits from every corner of the earth, was more remarkable yet.

Ben-Gurion held one more seminar. In 1953 he once again stepped back from public responsibilities and carefully scrutinized Israeli defense policy.[73] From the end of August through mid-October—seven weeks—he decided to start over again "as if I knew nothing, just as I did in 1946."[74] Once again he interviewed commanders, read widely, and pored over intelligence estimates.

This time his conclusions were very different. He saw for Israel a window of opportunity in which a resumption of large-scale warfare was unlikely. He also noted that the traditional Arab regimes, which the Jews of Palestine thought they understood and with which they had had long-standing contacts, were being displaced by more radical nationalist regimes far less amenable to covert or tacit deals. Foreseeing a long period of hostility to the Jewish state, he began constructing a new strategy, resting on three pillars: foreign alliance (with France), the acquisition of nuclear weapons, and the temporary deferral of large-scale military expenditure in favor of absorbing the hundreds of thousands of new Jewish immigrants from Arab lands. It was another act of strategic foresight and one which, once again, did not sit well with the Israeli military establishment.

Ben-Gurion had many remarkable qualities as a military statesman, not least of which was his awareness of when to stop. In a stubborn, willful, and angry man such qualities are all the more impressive. His unwillingness to overreach at the end of the Israeli war of independence, when the IDF could probably have seized much if not all of the West Bank of the Jordan or bits of the Sinai, is a fine example of understanding what Clausewitz called "the culminating point of victory"—the point beyond which success will likely tip into failure. But most remarkable of all was his willingness and ability to think everything through afresh. That indeed was his most important message for the IDF. In the summer of 1950, less than two years after the war, he wrote an introduction to a collection of speeches published by the IDF's publishing house. He concluded with these words:

The most dangerous enemy to Israel's security is the intellectual inertia of those who are responsible for security. This simple and fundamental idea guided me from the day that I accepted, at the 22nd Zionist Congress, responsibility for the security of the *yishuv*. And this simple and fundamental thought I tried to instill in all of the comrades that worked with me on security matters before the war, during the war, and after it.[75]

This "simple and fundamental truth," as he called it, still stands as a warning to the IDF—and indeed to all military organizations today.

CHAPTER 6

LEADERSHIP WITHOUT GENIUS

THE GREAT EXCEPTIONS?

Lincoln, Clemenceau, Churchill, and Ben-Gurion each made his share of mistakes. Each, on occasion, misjudged his opponents, indulged incompetents or penalized the merely unlucky, ignored unpleasant realities and feared chimeras. Each adhered to flawed strategic views, meddled, or judged too harshly. Had their generals simply saluted and acceded meekly to their opinions, disaster would have resulted. Much of their genius lay in their ability to tolerate disagreement; even more in their ability to retreat from their own poor decisions or simply to change their minds.

Still, if in these respects they resembled normal politicians in kind, if not in degree, they clearly stand out as active statesmen—querying, prodding, suggesting, arbitrating, and on rare occasions ordering their professional subordinates. None of them lived by the "normal" theory of civil-military relations—accepting in their commanders a large sphere of professional independence into which they would not intrude. All of them drove their generals to distraction, eliciting a curious mixture of rage and affection as they did so. Yet despite their rejection of the idea of clear-cut divisions of responsibility between politician and general, we generally judge them to have succeeded, and decisively so.

To be sure, how one judges the effectiveness of statesmen (or for that matter, generals) poses an interesting analytic problem. In the conduct of affairs one searches for a standard other than that of arithmetical certainty or scientific precision. All of these statesmen failed in some respects, yet so too did their subordinates, and even more so their allies and their opponents. To what standards should one turn to judge the quality of war statesmanship?

The test of ultimate success, although one of the most important tests, is not the only one. No one can judge final results, for, as Churchill commented in his biography of his ancestor the first duke of Marlborough, "It is not given to princes, statesmen, and captains to pierce the mysteries of the future, and even the most penetrating gaze reaches only conclusions which, however seemingly vindicated at a given moment, are inexorably effaced by time."[1] Nonetheless, in each of these cases, there can be little doubt that the outcomes of these struggles—the maintenance of the American Union and the destruction of African-American slavery, the defeats of the first and second attempts to create a Germano-European Empire, and the rebirth of a Jewish state after nearly two millennia of statelessness—were the achievements of the four men discussed here. The odds in each of these cases were so finely balanced that leadership could and did make the difference. Take away each leader, and one can easily imagine a very different outcome to "his" conflict.

But what lessons can one really extract from the exploits of men who were, by all accounts, extraordinary leaders? Could lesser statesmen hope to act as these men did? Might one not reasonably suggest that these men were sui generis, and that their styles of leadership would fail the average politician in the average conflict? Even if we admit that they succeeded by what looks like meddling and micromanaging, could we not suggest that they succeeded either despite such behavior, or merely because genius knows no rules? To answer these questions, let us see what happens when the style of war leadership approximates the "normal" theory of civil-military relations, whereby politicians maintain a more distant relationship with their generals and refrain from engaging in the kind of active, harassing, interventionist probing of their military leaders about military matters that characterized these four. For better or worse, there are more than enough contemporary cases against which one may test such a proposition. Let us consider the most important, namely the United States, which from 1965 through the end of the century waged war according to the "normal" theory of civil-military relations.

"LOOSE ASSUMPTIONS, UNASKED QUESTIONS, AND THIN ANALYSES"

The Vietnam war cost the lives of nearly 60,000 young Americans, left many more maimed, and for a generation tore apart the fabric of American society. The legacy of bitterness and suspicion resulting from that war persists in America today, even as the generation of young men whose lives were most touched by it have come to maturity and beyond. It may seem odd to suggest that the United States fought in Vietnam using something like the "normal" theory of civil-military relations. Indeed, one of the war's legacies is the pervasive belief that the United States failed to achieve victory because civilian leaders "made the military fight with a hand tied behind its back," and that the key to success in the future would be soldiers given a free hand to do their jobs. This diagnosis, radically incomplete at best and downright false at worst, affects American civil-military relations to the present day. The standard account of the Vietnam conflict treats it as a prime example of civilian micromanagement of military operations, with appalling consequences. But was it really? Did a manipulative and domineering president, Lyndon Baines Johnson, and an arrogant and impatient secretary of defense, Robert Strange McNamara, act as a Churchill or a Lincoln would have but—lacking the masterly touch—with disastrous results?

That Johnson and McNamara exercised close supervision of *some* elements of the war is no doubt true. In what has come to symbolize for a generation of civilian and military leaders a gross overplaying of the proper role of a civilian commander in chief, Johnson did indeed review lists of targets to be struck by American aircraft in Hanoi and Haiphong, imposing limits on the numbers of sorties and in some cases setting rules of engagement. It is an image that has left its mark on American civil-military relations, and hence deserves closer scrutiny. Was this the unequal dialogue at work, but in the hands of an insecure and overreaching politician who, lacking the wisdom of a true statesman, made an appalling mess with the means he might have used more successfully?

Consider the prime example of overweening civilian control—Johnson's control of target selection. The most careful study of the conduct of the air war over Vietnam notes that in fact Johnson ended up approving most of the targets submitted by the Joint Chiefs of Staff.[2] To be sure, the process of approval meant a drawn-out air campaign rather than the sudden shock that is (in theory, at any rate) critical in order for air power directed against a national economic and political entity to work. Undoubtedly too, the exclusion of certain areas from bombing (early on, antiaircraft sites, but also targets in Hanoi proper and the port of Haiphong) sharply reduced the US air war's effectiveness, both as a way of bringing pressure to bear on the North Vietnamese government and in support of the nominal operational mission: cutting off supplies coming in to feed Hanoi's aggression in the South. There are, however, two mitigating arguments.

First and most important, Johnson and his advisers feared and sought to avoid an extension of the war by Chinese intervention in it.

As we now know, this was no idle fear, for in fact the Chinese sent over 300,000 troops into Vietnam and lost over a thousand killed in action.[3] At the time too, it must be remembered, the Korean war was less than fifteen years in the past, and the Cuban missile crisis less than five. Both events had taught the American decision makers that the threat of escalation by the major Communist powers was real. Korea seemingly taught the lesson that pressing too far—as the Americans had when they advanced to the Yalu River, in particular—could indeed widen the war, while restrictions on the use of military power (e.g., refraining from bombing Chinese and Soviet installations supporting Communist units in Korea) could confine it. The Cuban missile crisis demonstrated the artfully restrained use of force—while providing evidence that in some military quarters the urge to use massive violence required civilian restraint. Today historians might qualify or object to these readings of what occurred in 1950–1953 and in 1962, but at the time the lessons seemed altogether clear.

In 1964–1967 America's civilian and military leaders shared the view that Indochina was not the place to again commit US forces in a protracted Asian war with what they believed, at the beginning of the conflict, to be a solid Sino-Soviet bloc. The politicians simply shared the assumption of their military advisers that Communism indeed presented a united front against the West, and that further colored their understanding of what kind of force they could apply. Fearing that a few errant bombs might produce an international crisis and hoping to contain a war that would, in any event, be decided in South Vietnam, Johnson had his reasons to restrict US bombing. An Air Force general who commanded the Seventh Air Force in Vietnam wrote after the war that he

> deeply resented the proscription of attacks on North Vietnamese airfields, SAM and AAA sites, and other targets. Airmen are bound to resent such restraints. . . . But self-imposed restraint has been a fact in all US conflict since World War II, and obviously

our hope in the age of nuclear and thermonuclear weapons is that some restraint will be exercised by all superpowers in all future conflicts.[4]

When, a quarter of a century later and in a far more benign world environment, a mistargeted bomb struck the Chinese embassy in Belgrade—in the course of a war half a world away from Beijing and marginal to its interests—China's relations with the United States were visibly disrupted for over a year—and embittered well beyond that. Knowing that fact, one is inclined to give Johnson a bit more of the benefit of the doubt.

To be sure, the second aspect of the centrally controlled bombing of Vietnam—the modulated application of violence—resulted from a theory of strategic signaling and gradual escalation that proved calamitously false. The Communist leadership in Hanoi was simply too determined, too tough, too willing to accept suffering to yield to graduated pressure—or to "diplomatic" signals conveyed by bombs whistling their way into power stations or radar installations. Johnson and McNamara operated from a false strategic concept—a "theory of victory" that rested on a radically inadequate understanding of the opponent and, for that matter, of their own society. The argument thus becomes less a question of how they exercised civilian control than one of how well—or poorly—they thought about strategy.

The argument against their style of civilian leadership would be infinitely stronger if one could adduce evidence that Johnson's professional military advisers had a better idea of how to fight the war. That they supported the war we know. That they favored waging it more aggressively we also know. But one searches in vain for evidence that they had any strategic concept other than more intense bombing or the dispatch of even more men to the fighting front. Consider, for example, the following exchange between the president and Chief of Naval Operations Admiral D. L. McDonald at a critical White House meeting on July 22, 1965:[5]

ADMIRAL McDONALD: Sending in the Marines has improved the situation. I agree with McNamara that we are committed to the extent that we can't move out. If we continue the way we are now, it will be a slow, sure victory for the other side. But putting more men in it will turn the tide and let us know what further we need to do. I wish we had done this long before.

THE PRESIDENT: But you don't know if 100,000 men will be enough. What makes you conclude that if you don't know where we are going—and what will happen—we shouldn't pause and find this out?

ADMIRAL McDONALD: Sooner or later we will force them to the conference table.

THE PRESIDENT: But if we put in 100,000 men won't they put in an equal number, and then where will we be?

ADMIRAL McDONALD: Not if we step up our bombing . . .

THE PRESIDENT: Is this a chance we want to take?

ADMIRAL McDONALD: Yes, sir, when I view the alternatives. Get out now or pour in more men.

THE PRESIDENT: Is that all?

ADMIRAL McDONALD: Well, I think our allies will lose faith in us.

THE PRESIDENT: We have few allies really helping us now.

ADMIRAL McDONALD: Take Thailand for example. If we walk out of Vietnam, the whole world will question our word. We don't have much choice.

A decision of the first magnitude—whether to embark on a large-scale war in Vietnam—took place with remarkably crude strategic judgments by the uniformed military. As H. R. McMaster points out, "The chiefs' inability to formulate a specific proposal or estimate of the situation left the initiative for planning with the proponents of graduated pressure."[6]

Or take another example, from the account of one aide present at a meeting in November 1965 between President Johnson and the Joint Chiefs of Staff—a meeting characterized, in his recollection, by a violent explosion of presidential temper. The chiefs had come to a different political conclusion from that of their civilian superiors, albeit with no evidence to back it up:

> They decided unanimously that risks of violent Chinese or Soviet reactions to massive US measures taken in North Vietnam were acceptably low, provided we did not delay. Unfortunately, their opinions and judgments were not commonly held in the Pentagon, at least by those who were actually steering military strategy—namely, McNamara and his coterie of civilian "whiz kids."[7]

This judgment, however, reflected the chiefs' instincts, not their expertise in international politics. There is no evidence that they understood any better than the civilian leadership the mentality of friend or foe, or that they had any ideas for bringing the war to a conclusion on terms acceptable to American diplomacy and bearable for the American public. Some of the early air-war concepts (for example, an extensive program of bombing of industrial targets in North Vietnam) reflected an unthinking application of World War II–era concepts to a very different enemy.[8] The fundamental ground-war concept—attrition designed to grind the enemy into incapacity—was, as it turned out, impossible to achieve. McNamara finally left his position as secretary of defense, exhausted and embattled, in 1968. His successor, Clark Clifford, described the following conversation with the Joint Chiefs of Staff in March of that year:

> How long would it take to succeed in Vietnam? They didn't know. How many more troops would it take? They couldn't say. Were

two hundred thousand the answer? They weren't sure. Might they need more? Yes, they might need more. Could the enemy build up in exchange? Probably. So what was the plan to win the war? Well, the only plan was that attrition would wear out the Communists, and they would have had enough. Was there any indication that we've reached that point? No, there wasn't.[9]

Thus, criticism of the American military for "failing to stand up to civilian leadership"—a frequent theme in American military writing on the war—largely misses the point. They had no argument to use, no alternative to offer, no "professional judgment" that applied to the war. And indeed, decades after the Vietnam débacle, professional soldiers were still debating whether the United States could have won the war and what the proper strategy would have been. A conventionally manned and supported linear barrier running from the sea to the Thai frontier to block Northern infiltration of the South? An aggressive campaign of counterinsurgency? Massive aerial bombardment from the outset?[10] As so often occurs, the professionals disagreed, and still disagree, over the largest questions.

In fact, Johnson's and McNamara's conduct of the Vietnam war reveals the opposite of the methods of a Lincoln, a Clemenceau, a Churchill, or a Ben-Gurion. After the initial decisions to enter the war, the American civilian leadership held back from the kinds of bruising discussions with their military advisers that caused so much grief to Churchill's subordinates. It was not until October 1967 that the chairman of the Joint Chiefs of Staff joined the Tuesday lunches at which the president, the secretaries of state and defense, the national security advisor, and the president's press secretary discussed Vietnam.[11] During the period of the escalation of the commitment to Vietnam there was no comprehensive politico-military assessment of American strategy. Nor could there be. The chiefs' recommendations for an all-out effort seemed so inappropriate to the nature of the enemy and the international political circumstances that the civilian leaders decided to make war their way, without their military advisers' counsel. At some level, one might almost say that the JCS chose irrelevance rather than accepting and working within the political constraints that America's civilian leaders believed they had to live with.

To be sure, much of the blame for the ineffectiveness of the Joint Chiefs lay with an administration that chose its top military leaders for political pliability. The truth was that the military system had brought to the top generals like Maxwell Taylor and Earle Wheeler, who were either politically too close to the civilian leadership to offer it real alternatives, or too desirous of consensus to lay out sharp choices for them to make.[12] One recent student of the war goes so far as to argue that Taylor, as chairman of the Joint Chiefs of Staff, recommended senior officers for those posts who "were less likely than their predecessors to challenge the direction of the administration's military policy."[13] In any event, the civilian leadership—unlike the four leaders discussed here—did not attempt to force a discussion of the essential strategic problem of ends and means. Thus, at the Guam conference of 20–21 March 1967, when key American leaders, including the president, met with their Vietnamese counterparts and General William Westmoreland, the American commander in South Vietnam, there was little "detailed discussion or re-evaluation of the military situation." Not surprising, given General Westmoreland's view that the war was going well—a view resulting from a variety of quantitative indicators *all* of which would later turn out to be suspect.[14]

The standard indictment of civilian leadership during the Vietnam war includes a criticism of its preference for incremental uses of force rather than the sudden, massive application of power that the military would have preferred. This may have been applicable to the air war in the North, but the same could hardly be said of operations in the South; the American buildup in South Vietnam proceeded very quickly indeed and was limited as much by logistical constraints as by deliberate decisions. With one major port—Danang—there was a limit to how much US materiél South Vietnam could absorb; as it was, vast base areas soon mushroomed, stocked with huge, unusable quantities of supplies for the American forces in the field. Indeed, what is most striking is McNamara's and Johnson's willingness to write large checks on American military manpower through 1968, extending up to, but not including, a full mobilization of the reserves.

Combat developed rapidly, largely in response to increased North Vietnamese efforts against the Republic of Vietnam, but also as a result of the aggressive American military style. That style—largely unrestrained by civilian political authority—included a vast volume of firepower, the poisoning of large areas of vegetation, and a continuous effort to find the enemy and bring him to battle with American troops.

Arguably American strategy might have been better served by greater reliance on population protection and development of the Army of the Republic of Vietnam (ARVN). "One of the great mysteries of the American involvement in the Indochina wars is why the Vietnamese army failed to develop into a first-rate military force, as did the ROK [Republic of Korea] army," wrote one of America's most senior Vietnam intelligence officers.[15] It is not such a mystery, unfortunately: the development of the South Vietnamese military was not the highest priority for a US Army focused overwhelmingly on closing with the enemy. To the extent that American soldiers did focus on training the ARVN it was for the purpose of fighting a conventional war.[16] In this respect, and most notably in the development of the operational concept of "search and destroy," the military had its way.

American forces did, of course, chafe under all kinds of constraints during the Vietnam war, at least until 1970; they could not cross international borders (e.g., into Laos or Cambodia) in large numbers; they had to respect the prerogatives of corrupt local political leaders and commanders; they could not use firepower indiscriminately in densely built-up areas. But some of these restraints stemmed from humanitarian inhibitions, others from the nature of guerrilla conflict, and still others from the conditions found in all wars and particularly in coalition conflicts. In the same way that the Supreme Allied

Commander in Europe during World War II, General Dwight D. Eisenhower, found that he could not control the behavior of Free French forces nominally under his command, so too the Military Assistance Command Vietnam was infuriated at the behavior of some South Vietnamese generals. Interestingly enough, however, it was the *military* commander, General William Westmoreland, who decided not to seek a joint command that might have given the Americans greater control over the selection and promotion of officers in the ARVN. In the view of Robert Komer, "*the very massiveness of our intervention actually reduced our leverage. So long as we were willing to use US resources and manpower as a substitute for Vietnamese, their incentive for doing more was compromised.*"[17]

Westmoreland himself operated under remarkably little civilian oversight. During his four and a half years in Vietnam he received a few visits from McNamara and Johnson; he also flew to Washington. Yet his chief memory of his visit in November 1967 with President Johnson was not of analyzing strategic choices, but rather of his impression of LBJ: "I have never known a more thoughtful and considerate man than Lyndon B. Johnson."[18] McNamara certainly, and Johnson possibly, knew that the war was not going well from the beginning—as early as 1966. Yet their scrutiny of operations in Vietnam focused chiefly on the level of effort being made, not on its fundamental direction. One searches the "Pentagon Papers" (published in 1971, but compiled earlier in the war on the direction of Secretary McNamara himself) in vain for any probing of the assumptions of "search and destroy." In a conscience-wracked memoir McNamara recalls:

> Looking back, I clearly erred by not forcing, then [July 1965] or later, in either Saigon or Washington—a knock-down, drag-out debate over the loose assumptions, unasked questions, and thin analyses underlying our military strategy in Vietnam. I had spent twenty years as a manager identifying problems and forcing organizations—often against their will—to think deeply and

realistically about alternative courses of action and their consequences. I doubt I will ever fully understand why I did not do so
here.[19]

Westmoreland, the straitlaced and, on the whole, unimaginative
commander of Military Assistance Command Vietnam (MACV), would
not have lasted four and a half years in command under Lincoln. A
Clemenceau would surely have visited him more than once or twice in
his theater of war (and for just a few days). A Churchill would hardly
have let him slip away without a constant, even brutal questioning of
his strategic concept. And a Ben-Gurion would, after massive study,
have discovered the impossibly haphazard organization that divided
the air war (to take just one example) among at least three separate and
uncoordinated commands, and that prevented the American commander in South Vietnam from overhauling his ally's corrupt army.

It is striking, in retrospect, to what extent soldiers and civilians alike
avoided such critical issues as the need for a unified command in
Southeast Asia, or the need to gain control of and reform the South
Vietnamese military—an issue Westmoreland dismissed as smacking of
colonialism. He did not understand the issue even in retrospect. "We
were in Vietnam to help the Vietnamese, not do the job for them. . . . If
we did it for them, how were they to learn? Junior and senior commanders alike learn to assume responsibility only from experience."[20]
That the United States *was* in fact doing the job for the South
Vietnamese did not escape observers, and Westmoreland's peculiarly
finicky regard for local sensibilities meant that the Army of the Republic
of Vietnam remained corrupt and inept (with some notable exceptions)
for much of its unhappy existence.

The civilian leadership may have disagreed with Westmoreland's
conclusions, but they never called him to task for them. Nor did the
civilians impose, as is sometimes suggested, a numbers-driven operational understanding of the war in lieu of a more sophisticated or
traditional military view. The "body count" and similar quantifiable

systems were developed by civilian and military leaders alike, with the latter often embracing them enthusiastically. Nor was there anything terribly sophisticated in some of the military's preferred modes of operation: "The best way to defeat the enemy and to protect the South Vietnamese people was to utilize maximum force against the entire Communist system," wrote Lieutenant General Julian J. Ewell and Major General Ira A. Hunt in a study promoting the use of the body count and a counterinsurgency strategy based on attrition.[21] "Once one decided to apply maximum force, the problem became a technical one of doing it efficiently with the resources available." Not entirely coincidentally General Ewell, commanding general of the 9th Division in the Mekong River delta, acquired the nickname "The Butcher of the Delta" for his obsession with the body count.

The problem lay not in the intelligence or strength of will of Johnson and McNamara, nor yet in their desire to run the details of a war from a Washington command post. It lay first and foremost in their problematic judgment about what force could achieve in Indochina—but also in their inability to pick the right generals, to conduct a strategic (and, for that matter, operational and tactical) dialogue with them, to set priorities and maintain proportion in a secondary conflict. It lay, in short, in their lack of any sound sense of what they needed to do to run a war.

"FINALLY, THERE'S A REALIZATION . . . WHAT A MILITARY CAN AND CANNOT DO FOR A DEMOCRACY."

Vietnam bred a generation of embittered American officers, not only because their country lost a war and (in the view of many veterans) blamed them for it, but because of the pernicious effects of the war on the US military for years after. A corruption of the officer's code of honor through the numbers game of body counts, a dilution of the quality of noncommissioned and commissioned officers, a hollowing out of conventional forces in Europe and the United States—these and other problems persisted until the 1980s and even a bit beyond. They resulted, in part, from the failure of the American high command to balance the requirements of war-fighting with that of maintaining a workable Cold War military establishment. Whereas in Korea the Joint Chiefs of Staff recommended the capping of a commitment in order to build up forces in Europe—where war, they believed, might occur with little notice—in Vietnam they made no attempt to maintain a balanced force. To the end they recommended increased force, not less.

None of this in any way exculpates the civilian leadership of the Department of Defense or President Johnson for their handling of the war. Just the reverse, in fact, for they were ultimately responsible for the armed forces' performance. The point is, however, that contrary to received opinion, the fault in Vietnam was a deadly combination of inept strategy and excessively *weak* civilian control. It was a failure to understand its tasks, not its desire to micromanage, that constituted the fatal flaw of civilian leadership during the war. Some of the fault may have lain in their unwillingness to accept the notion that this was indeed a war, as opposed to a bit of violent diplomatic signaling.[22] Their arrogance may have been the hubris intrinsic to a technocratic as opposed to a political or even artistic view of the world, a view in which simple indices of success replace politico-military judgment of a more traditional type. Perhaps, and more importantly, the war was simply unwinnable.[23] But it is difficult to imagine that it could have been directed any worse than it was.

In the aftermath of Vietnam the senior leadership of the armed forces learned its lessons. The United States Army, led by General Creighton Abrams, hero of the relief of Bastogne in 1944 and the canny commander of American forces in Vietnam during the last, dismal phases of the war, supported the creation of the Total Force—a force structure in which reserve and active duty units would be intermingled.

An expanded sixteen-division Army would rely on National Guard and other reserve units in order to mobilize for conflict. "They're not taking us to war again without calling up the reserves," Abrams declared.[24] "They" were the politicians, and the object was not merely efficiency, but forging and maintaining a bond with the American people. No more wars in cold blood. No more wars without a mobilization of popular support. No more of the derision and contempt that were showered upon American soldiers returning from duty in Southeast Asia.

This was a bold move. The regular Army had always disdained the National Guard, which provided the bulk of combat units in the reserve forces. The National Guard had evolved from the old state militias and retained some of their less attractive qualities, most notably a promotion system in which political connections played a substantial role. The Guard had, moreover, served as a haven for young men who wished to escape duty in Vietnam but who were unwilling to declare themselves conscientious objectors or, more extreme yet, to flee the country. And, on top of it all, few professional soldiers believed that part-timers could ever acquire the discipline and technical competence to serve effectively alongside regulars in time of war. Still, in order to secure the tie with American society that the senior leadership of the Army believed had been ruptured, they would swallow all of these objections.

Creighton Abrams was a brave and competent soldier, a patriot and surely, in his own mind, a loyal believer in the Constitution and civilian supremacy. This was, nonetheless, an extraordinary effort by the military to limit the choices available to their civilian masters, to tie the hands of policymakers through the seemingly technical manipulation of organizational structures. Nor were the civilian leaders weak or incompetent: the secretary of defense at this time was none other than James Schlesinger, a tough-minded former analyst at the RAND corporation who had a firm grasp of the technical issues facing the Department of Defense. It does not seem to have occurred to either soldier or statesman, however, that there was something highly improper, to say the least, in allowing the armed services to thus determine the ways in which they could be used in combat. What is all the more remarkable is that the military in doing this deliberately chose to place its reliance on forces that it mistrusted. When the test came in 1990 the United States Army flinched from mobilizing the "roundout" brigades of National Guard units that it had insisted it would send into battle. The 24th Mechanized Infantry Division departed for the Persian Gulf without its third brigade—the 48th brigade of the Georgia Army National Guard—despite the promises its commanders had always made that it would only go to war with its citizen soldiers by its side.

The civilian leadership accepted the Total Force, with all of the constraints that it was intended to impose upon the politicians, because it had accepted much of the military's (incorrect) reading of what had happened in Vietnam. The military had fought "with a hand tied behind its back." The civilians had interfered and micromanaged. Political objectives were left murky and unclear. It was the "normal" theory of civil-military relations (and with it, of strategy) with a vengeance. As often happens, the clearest articulation of military views came from the mouth of a civilian. In November 1984 Secretary of Defense Caspar Weinberger, who had served under General Douglas MacArthur in the Pacific and had admired him greatly, articulated six principles for the use of force by the United States that became canonical within the defense establishment; they embodied, for a generation of officers, the "normal" theory of civil-military relations.

(1) The United States should not commit forces to combat overseas unless the particular engagement or occasion is deemed vital to our national interest.

(2) If we decide it is necessary to put combat troops into a given situation, we should do so wholeheartedly and with the clear intention of winning. If we are unwilling to commit the forces or resources necessary to achieve our objectives, we should not commit them at all.

(3) If we do decide to commit forces to combat overseas, we should have clearly defined political and military objectives. And we should know precisely how our forces can accomplish those clearly defined objectives. And we should have and send the forces needed to do just that. As Clausewitz wrote, "No one starts a war—or rather, no one in his senses ought to do so—without first being clear in his mind what he intends to achieve by that war, and how he intends to conduct it."

(4) The relationship between our objectives and the forces we have committed—their size, composition, and disposition—must be continually reassessed and adjusted if necessary. Conditions and objectives invariably change during the course of a conflict. When they do change, then our combat requirements must also change. We must continuously keep as a beacon light before us the basic questions: "Is this conflict in our national interest?" "Does our national interest require us to fight, to use force of arms?" If the answers are "yes," then we must win. If the answers are "no," then we should not be in combat.

(5) Before the United States commits combat forces abroad, there must be some reasonable assurance we will have the support of the American people and their elected representatives in Congress.

(6) The commitment of US forces to combat should be a last resort.[25]

The Weinberger rules did not survive long in practice (they represented an impossible standard of purity) but they represented an ideal to which succeeding political and military leaders pledged allegiance, often with astonishing directness. In the 1990s one retired four-star general would recall: "As a young officer, I literally carried a copy of that for ten years with me in my briefcase because I thought it was so important, and it had such a dramatic effect on me when I read it, to think, 'Holy mackerel, it's really as simple as this.' I said, 'Finally, there's a realization about what a military can and cannot do for a democracy.'"[26]

The Weinberger speech sparked vociferous opposition from another veteran of World War II, George Shultz, who as secretary of state was loath to see America's hands tied by a reduction of strategy to rules of thumb. Within the military, however, the Weinberger principles were celebrated as strategy of the soundest type. Widely reprinted, the speech appeared in the syllabi of staff colleges and became, in fact, a kind of dogma. It was reinforced by what became known as the Powell Doctrine, after the powerful and charismatic then-chairman of the Joint Chiefs of Staff, General Colin Powell (secretary of state as this goes to press), who announced his commitment to a doctrine of "overwhelming force"—not appropriate force, or force adequate to meet the objectives, but "overwhelming force." When in 1986 Congress (which also paid lip service to the conventional reading of Vietnam) strengthened the Joint Staff and the chairman of the Joint Chiefs of Staff, it reinforced these lessons. Henceforth the civilians would have one primary military adviser—the chairman of the JCS—overshadowing all others, and behind him a powerful staff under his personal control, rather than that of the services. The president and the secretary of defense would have a single authoritative source of professional military advice, and even if the chairman did not formally occupy a place in the chain of command (which ran, in theory, from the secretary of defense to theater commanders in chief) he would, in practice, act as a conduit for military advice to the president, and relay orders from him and the secretary to the military. The "normal" theory had triumphed.

"FREEDOM OF ACTION TO DO THE JOB ONCE THE POLITICAL DECISION HAD BEEN MADE."

If in American military mythology Vietnam was the dark and foreboding tale, the Gulf war of 1991 has become the opposite: a tale of war conducted as it ought, i.e., a war in which the politicians set objectives, established simple guidelines for the conduct of operations, and got out of the way. In short, the Gulf war seemed to vindicate the "normal" theory of civil-military relations. President George H. W. Bush, who presided over the war, articulated this view after it:

> [Chairman of the Joint Chiefs of Staff] Colin Powell, ever the professional, wisely wanted to be sure that if we had to fight, we would do it right and not take half measures. He sought to ensure that there were sufficient troops for whatever option I wanted, and then the freedom of action to do the job once the political decision had been made. I was determined that our military would have both. I did not want to repeat the problems of the Vietnam War (or numerous wars throughout history), where the political leadership meddled with military operations. I would avoid micromanaging the military.[27]

There can be little doubt that the first Bush administration ran the Gulf War in a considerably more hands-off fashion than the Johnson administration did the Vietnam war. This reflected to some extent the civilians' interpretation of the lessons of Vietnam; it reflected as well the extraordinary stature of the chairman of the Joint Chiefs of Staff, General Colin Powell, who accrued enormous power from a combination of charisma, bureaucratic skill, and the enhanced powers of the Joint Staff under the Goldwater-Nichols Department of Defense Reorganization Act of 1986.

Powell successfully preempted a good deal of civilian control in the Gulf war through his own highly developed political skills. This was, after all, an officer who had learned as a White House Fellow working in the Nixon White House that "you don't know what you can get away with until you try."[28] The wildly popular general—who declared himself a Republican shortly after retiring from the military, and who came close to a run for the presidency itself a year later—shared many policy outlooks with his civilian superiors. Having served as national security advisor in the Reagan administration, he understood the workings of government better than anyone else in uniform, and just as well as any of the civilians. He would need little guidance, then, in those matters.

There was, to be sure, far less need for close civilian control of the kind exercised by a Lincoln or a Churchill here. The enemy, Iraq, was utterly isolated. Its prewar patron, the Soviet Union, was collapsing; its Arab neighbors were hostile; and potential allies such as China did not as yet see the need to tip the balance against the United States. The Iraqi army was war-weary. The United States led a coalition of the richest and most powerful countries in the world, and itself brought to bear an armed forces superbly trained and equipped as a result of the Reagan-era defense buildup. The technological, tactical, and even numerical superiority of the coalition forces was overwhelming. In retrospect, although not necessarily at the time, it becomes clear that the stunning success of January/February 1991 was overdetermined.

And yet, even the story of supreme command in the Gulf war suggests something other than a vindication of the "normal" theory of civil-military relations. To begin with, it is apparent that Powell opposed war with Iraq; the dramatic account by Woodward—for which Powell apparently served as a source—makes that quite clear.[29] As Powell himself indicates in his memoirs, it took a sharp rebuke by Secretary of Defense Dick Cheney to remind him that he was supposed to execute policy, not make it.[30]

The Goldwater-Nichols legislation had made the chairman of the Joint Chiefs of Staff the primary military adviser to the president, and in Powell's hands the chairmanship became an exceptionally powerful position and one which shut off many other sources of military advice to civilian authority. Powell's jealousy of his position as the preeminent adviser erupted when he learned that Cheney had had his military assistant, Rear Admiral William Owens, canvass the Pentagon for options other than those provided by Powell—an operation that the chairman of the Joint Chiefs of Staff regarded as "freelancing" even if it came by the secretary's direction.[31] Nevertheless, the civilians managed to find unorthodox military advice, particularly when it appeared that mainline military planning was confining itself to a straightforward thrust into Kuwait.[32]

The plan for air operations in the Persian Gulf, for example, emerged from a small planning cell in the Air Staff—a military organization reporting not to the theater commander in chief, General Norman Schwarzkopf, but to the chief of staff of the Air Force and the secretary of that service. Under the leadership of Colonel John Warden, a zealous proponent of air power as the decisive arm in war, and the author of a book on air-campaign planning, a plan called INSTANT THUNDER was devised. (Warden and his staff self-consciously chose that code name in order to reject explicitly the incrementalism of the ROLLING THUNDER campaign of Vietnam.) Warden headed the Air Force's long-range war planning cell but had no place in the chain of command. Nonetheless he briefed Powell and then, two weeks after the crisis began, the theater air commander, Lieutenant General Charles Horner, on his plan. Horner, who disliked Warden, disparaged his plan at first and sent him back to Washington but retained several of his staff. In the meanwhile, however, Air Force Chief of Staff General Michael Dugan and Secretary of the Air Force Donald Rice protected Warden, who continued to support Riyadh planning efforts from his office in the basement of the Pentagon.

Powell, deeply mistrustful of the Air Force and its claims, did his best to contain the Air Staff's efforts. He may have played a role in Dugan's subsequent dismissal, after the Air Force general had incautiously commented to reporters traveling with him to the Persian Gulf that an air campaign would go after the circle immediately around Iraqi dictator Saddam Hussein, and not just against more conventional military targets. But civilian patronage for the air campaign plan, together with the transfer of some of Warden's staff to the planning operation in Saudi Arabia, and a broader concern about the prospect of large numbers of casualties in a ground war, allowed it to flourish, and indeed become a centerpiece of the war.

The development of the ground campaign plan proceeded far more slowly. Here too, a civil-military interaction was critical. In October Schwarzkopf sent his chief of staff to brief the option that had been developed for the expulsion of Iraq from Kuwait using the single corps then deployed in Saudi Arabia. Much of the civilian leadership was appalled at the proposal for a frontal assault into Kuwait, although in truth the strength of the forces available did not appear to allow for much more than that. Two key civilians—National Security Advisor Brent Scowcroft and Secretary of Defense Dick Cheney—were particularly upset.[33] President Bush quickly approved the military's request for an additional, even larger collection of heavy forces from Europe—VII Corps under Lieutenant General Frederick Franks. The size of the force, and its eventual commitment to a plan that involved a sweep around the Iraqi front lines as well as a punch through to Kuwait City proper, reflected civilian scrutiny and more than a little civil-military tension in the months leading up to the war.

Dick Cheney mastered the final plan down to a considerable level of detail. The secretary of defense, a tough Wyoming politician, had, like many politicians of his generation, been of draft age during the Vietnam war but had never served—a fact that may have colored the attitude of some of the senior officers with whom he dealt. He had become secretary of defense in difficult circumstances, in the wake of the disastrous failed nomination of Senator John Tower to that position, and he quickly made his mark by publicly (and, as it turned out, unfairly) castigating Air Force Chief of Staff General Larry Welch for unauthorized discussions with Congress and by dismissing the commander in chief of Southern Command, General Fred Woerner, and later Dugan. A palpable disdain for Cheney persisted. Welch remarked, "I've been shot at by professionals and I'm still here. So being shot at by an amateur is not likely to cause me any pain."[34] When Cheney had finished being briefed on the Gulf war plan the Joint Staff staged a ceremony at which he was awarded a "certificate stating that Richard Bruce Cheney was now an honorary graduate of all the war colleges."[35]

It was the kind of patronizing humor that one finds it difficult to imagine an officer daring with Clemenceau. Cheney made no modifications in the plans, nor does it appear that he or any other civilian leader interacted with Schwarzkopf except through Powell during the war. Indeed, with the exception of Cheney's visits to the theater, it is not clear that he and the theater commander spoke regularly during the war at all.

During the war itself, in fact, only two issues seem to have elicited political control, in both cases exercised preemptively by Powell. One involved the bombing of Baghdad. Early in the morning of 13 February 1991 (Riyadh time) American planes attacked an Iraqi command-and-control center that, unknown to coalition planners, housed a shelter for families of the Iraqi élite. Several hundred casualties resulted, according to the Iraqis, who moved swiftly to show the smoking wreckage on CNN. The result was cessation of attacks on Baghdad for several days, followed by extreme restriction of attacks thereafter, each target being personally approved by the theater commander in chief.[36] Air Force planners report that the guidance for this came directly from Powell.[37] The suspension of bombing in Baghdad did not trouble Powell or even the Air Force commander in Saudi Arabia. Neither had had high expectations of attacks on so-called "strategic" targets, preferring as they did attacks on ground forces and the infrastructure that supported them.

The second case of interaction was more serious. On the second night of the war Iraq fired eight surface-to-surface missiles at Israel. The warheads were crude and the missiles inaccurate, but the potential for damage to the coalition was severe—or at least so the leadership of the American government believed.[38] The initial air plan had called for attacks on the Iraqi launch sites for the so-called SCUD missiles (actually, Iraqi modifications of Soviet SCUD missiles), these occurred at the outset of the campaign, but planners belatedly learned that the Iraqis had shifted the missiles to mobile launchers. As a result, coalition forces began an extensive air search for the Iraqi missiles—a fruitless task that took some of the most effective aircraft in the inventory out of the broader air campaign.[39]

The impetus for an active air campaign against the Iraqi missiles came from Washington and was resisted in the field. Because the SCUD missiles were notoriously inaccurate, one general openly shrugged off the mobile missiles as being militarily unimportant—a remark that demoralized air crew and helped convince the Israelis that their concerns did not rank high with the Americans. When the secretary of defense was briefed on the handful of aircraft sorties that Central Command would throw against the missile launchers, he erupted. "Goddamn it, I want some coverage out there. If I have to talk to Schwarzkopf, I'll do it."[40] Once again, it was the politically adept Powell who stepped in before civilian leaders could communicate their displeasure directly to the theater commander. What was interesting here was the assumption that it would be odd or even improper for the secretary of defense to communicate directly to a theater commander, rather than through a uniformed intermediary who was not technically in the chain of command.

In retrospect, all three civil-military disputes—whether to go to war at all, what kind of plan to adopt, and how much effort to put into SCUD-hunting—were resolved by Powell's preemptive injection of political concerns into the directives issued to Schwarzkopf, with whom he was in daily contact by telephone. Behind this, however, lay a decisive condition: a plenitude of military power so great that commanders and politicians alike had no hard choices to make. The great and bootless SCUD-hunt did *not* mean that hundreds (or even scores) of American soldiers would die in attacks against insufficiently bombarded Iraqi positions. The decision to proceed to war despite the reservations of the military did *not* pave the way for postwar recriminations about the price of this vast expedition sent halfway around the world. The military's inability to come up with a ground-war plan that made sense to civilian leaders did *not* force a crisis at the top—it merely elicited another surge in men and machines to a theater already inundated with troops and the paraphernalia of war.

The uncertainty of civilian control, however, became clear at the end of the war. After six weeks of pounding from the air and less than four days of ground combat the Iraqi army in Kuwait and southern Iraq had disintegrated or fled. The question of when and how to terminate the war—which seems not to have been the subject of high-level discussions, although there was staff work along these lines early on—now arose. Two critical decisions had to be made: when to stop the war, and how to handle the armistice negotiations. In both cases, the military made the critical decisions—and in both cases, it appears in retrospect, they made the wrong ones.

The end of the ground war was driven by a discussion in the Oval Office on 27 February 1991. In a decision that National Security Advisor Brent Scowcroft described as "too cute by half," the cease-fire was declared to begin at midnight, so that the ground war would have lasted precisely one hundred hours.[41] General Powell made the recommendation, arguing that the president's victory conditions had been fulfilled: Bush had articulated those objectives on August 8, well before a decision to use force against Iraq had, in fact, been made.

> Four simple principles guide our policy. First, we seek the immediate, unconditional, and complete withdrawal of all Iraqi forces from Kuwait. Second, Kuwait's legitimate government must be restored to replace the puppet regime. And third, my administration, as has been the case with every president from President Roosevelt to President Reagan, is committed to the security and stability of the Persian Gulf. And fourth, I am determined to protect the lives of American citizens abroad. [42]

By all accounts, the political leadership went along with Powell's recommendation; Powell reported that Schwarzkopf, with whom he had just spoken, agreed with it. Shortly after the war General Schwarzkopf had a different version of events, telling British television interviewer David Frost that he had recommended a continuation of operations in order to complete the annihilation of Iraqi forces. Whatever the truth of the matter, the suspension of offensive operations was a mistake at two levels. First, it soon appeared that American forces had not, in fact, sealed the exits from the Kuwait Theater of Operations (KTO). And second, the most important part of the enemy force—the élite Republican Guard armored divisions—had in fact escaped intact, and were thus able to maintain the Saddam Hussein regime in power after the war.

Powell's rationale for pushing the end of the war at this juncture reflected two political judgments. He feared that pounding the Iraqi forces along the route out of Kuwait City (the so-called "Highway of Death") would hurt American standing in international public opinion, and he believed that the main objective—driving the Iraqis out of Kuwait—had been achieved. Both, of course, were not military but political judgments and both, in retrospect, appear questionable. The so-called "Highway of Death" was littered not with bodies but with the carcasses of vehicles, most of whose occupants had fled once American aircraft had begun strafing the columns of retreating Iraqi troops. No images of it had yet appeared on television, and there was nothing to indicate that any unacceptable public reaction overseas or at home was about to occur. In any case, a definition of "unacceptable" in these circumstances clearly rested with the political leadership. As for the achievement of the president's objectives, those had been narrowly interpreted to mean the physical eviction of Iraqi forces from Kuwait and their neutralization as a threat to *coalition* forces. Here a more serious error occurred.

Even the formal statement of Bush's objectives made it clear that the restoration of the Kuwaiti status quo ante was insufficient reason to terminate the war; in that text the broader objective of ensuring the stability of the Persian Gulf carries equal weight with the eviction of Iraqi forces from Kuwait. In fact, however, the crispness of Bush's statement of objectives—so much admired at the time and thereafter—was illusory. Only the first objective, driving the Iraqi forces out of Kuwait, seemed unambiguous. The restoration of the legitimate government of Kuwait was almost as straightforward, assuming that one did not insist on excessively democratic interpretations of the word "legitimate." The third objective was a vague statement of the obvious, namely that the United States cared about the stability of the world's oil supply. The objective of protecting the lives of American citizens ended when Saddam returned Western hostages before the war, an act that meant that the only lives of American citizens to be jeopardized would be those of servicemen and -women sent to war in the Gulf.

In retrospect, two implicit and unstated objectives stood out: the destruction of Iraq's program of weapons of mass destruction and the replacement of the regime. The attack on Iraq's nuclear and biological program began during the war and continued afterward through UN inspections and sanctions. As the American intelligence-collection effort directed against that program assembled and processed information about it, it loomed ever larger in the minds of political leaders. As for the ensuring of peace and stability, that clearly implied the removal of Saddam Hussein from power. Although American leaders shied away from making this an explicit objective—fearing the consequences of appearing to target an individual political leader for death or removal, and being uncertain of their ability to achieve the former—they nonetheless believed that the catastrophic war would doom Saddam's regime.[43]

The act of waging war leads—in fact, forces—statesmen to alter their objectives and purposes, thereby frustrating those who hope to reduce strategic aims to checklists. The end of the Gulf war brought in its wake new purposes, such as the permanent large-scale presence of American forces in the Persian Gulf as guarantors of order there; subsequently it also entailed the air policing of large areas of Iraq. It led to further purposes as well, including the use of the upheavals in the Gulf to bring about partial resolution of the Arab-Israeli conflict. The premature termination of the Gulf war also had consequences, still felt a decade later, after the Saddam Hussein regime had wriggled out from under an onerous United Nations weapons-inspection and sanctions regime.

The problem of the early ending of the war was compounded by the manner in which the American theater commander conducted the armistice negotiations at Safwan. After conversations with Powell (who relayed White House guidance), Schwarzkopf had, at Powell's bidding, prepared proposed military conditions for the defeated Iraqi forces to meet. Two days later, on the eve of the talks, Schwarzkopf joked that "it would be interesting to see which came first: authorization to conduct the talks, or the talks themselves." Just before the negotiations began the terms of reference came back, with the only change being that the State Department had changed the word "negotiate" to "discuss." In other words, Schwarzkopf had no guidance at all beyond the purely technical terms (e.g., requirements that the Iraqis point out minefields and biological-weapons storage sites) that he had himself drawn up.[44]

Thus, General Schwarzkopf entered the armistice negotiations with no directives from his civilian leadership. Left to his own devices, he concluded a relatively generous settlement with his Iraqi interlocutor— a relatively junior lieutenant general, whose unease at being the vanquished Schwarzkopf attempted to reduce by having himself patted down for weapons by American military police.[45] More to the point Schwarzkopf, proceeding from his narrow interpretation of the objectives of the war, then permitted the Iraqis the use of helicopters; these proved invaluable in their suppression of the Shi'ite uprisings against Saddam's régime. The subsequent massacres—which occurred in direct view of outraged American soldiers—ended the immediate threat to the continuity of the Iraqi dictator's rule.

Schwarzkopf's indulgence towards the Iraqi government reflected a deep conviction on the part of American military leaders—particularly in the Army, but shared by many civilians—that having won the war the thing to do was to declare victory and come back home for victory parades of a type not seen since the end of World War II. Indeed,

Schwarzkopf and Powell discussed having the armistice negotiations take place on the quarterdeck of the battleship USS *Missouri*, site of the Japanese surrender in 1945. This desire (thwarted, according to Schwarzkopf, by the length of time required to bring the battleship to the theater) reflected an astonishing lack of historical perspective as well as their misperception of the completeness of the military's success.[46]

The military's urge (understandable in light of its experiences in Vietnam) to define the war in purely conventional terms had led it to oppose in the most resolute way any prolonged occupation of southern Iraq or any support for an anti-Saddam resistance movement in the north (under Kurdish auspices), in the south (the Shi'ites), or any direct move on Baghdad. Ironically, the United States Army was following the 1966 advice of Senator George D. Aiken of Vermont, whose solution to the Vietnam conflict was then "to declare victory and come home." In many ways the military's predilections mirrored those of the Bush administration itself, which feared getting bogged down in Iraqi politics and which had, as it later appeared, an entirely excessive fear of the "Arab street." There was, in fact, no evidence to suggest that more robust action at the end of the war—to annihilate rather than expel the Republican Guard, to aid Kurdish or Shi'ite insurgents, or simply to insist that there could be no peace with Iraq until Saddam was removed from power—would have met with unacceptable opposition from the Arab world.

The civilian leadership appears, in some measure, not to have thought through the longer-term consequences of the war or the follow-through that even a smashing victory requires. They had come to accept, by default, the military's definition of victory as a battlefield outcome, in which the relationship with political objectives was defined as narrowly as possible. In this case that nominal political objective was the restoration of the previous government of Kuwait, but in point of fact—as soon became clear—larger, vaguer, and even more consequential purposes were entailed. The elimination of the Iraqi weapons-of-mass-destruction programs really began only after the war ended, and as ten years of cunning and determined Iraqi resistance revealed, even a decision on the battlefield could not yield final victory absent a strategy for achieving it. Within a decade UN inspections had ceased, repeated bombing of Iraq had achieved little of consequence, while sanctions and an embargo had gained the Iraqi people, if not Saddam himself, sympathy in many quarters of the world. A substantial American force was now required to police the Persian Gulf, including Iraq proper, and the victorious coalition of the Gulf war had reduced itself to the United States, Britain, and a handful of anxious and not entirely reliable local Arab allies.

The tale of the Gulf war and its aftermath is not one of usurpation of strategic control by the military but rather, in large part, one of abdication of authority by the civilian leadership. They had their reasons, of course. Like their military subordinates, they believed that civilian "micromanagement" had brought about the calamity in Vietnam; they confronted an extremely forceful, popular, and sophisticated chairman of the Joint Chiefs of Staff; they trusted the technical competence of the forces under their command; and they feared the consequences of a protracted commitment in a region that they viewed as culturally alien and of secondary importance as the Cold War ended. They yielded, finally, to the understandable temptation to bask in the admiration and approval that is the lot of successful warriors home from their wars. But war, like politics itself, almost never has a clear-cut terminus. The creation of strategy resembles Penelope's web—beautiful loom-work by day unraveling at night. Perhaps the greatest error a strategist can make, in fact, is believing in the chimerical notion of "victory"—as opposed to incremental and partial successes, which then merely give way to new (if, one hopes, lesser) difficulties. Small wonder, perhaps, that President George H. W. Bush, himself a decorated war hero, who led the United States to dazzling battlefield successes that cost only a handful of lives and virtually no treasure, whose approval ratings reached the highest levels pollsters had ever seen, found himself evicted from office less than two years later in a humiliating defeat by the governor of a small, poor Southern state—Bill Clinton, who had avoided the draft during Vietnam.

"BY GOD, WE'VE KICKED THE VIETNAM SYNDROME ONCE AND FOR ALL."[47]

Many soldiers and politicians thought that the Gulf war had put to rest the ghosts and demons of the Indochina war. Throughout the Gulf war President George H. W. Bush, by his own account, brooded about Vietnam—indeed, his exuberant declaration at the end of the war revealed how much it had preyed upon his mind. His diary for 26 February 1991, two days before the end of the war, includes a passage, "It's surprising how much I dwell on the end of the Vietnam syndrome."[48] "Vietnam will soon be behind us." He regretted that the war had not ended with a "battleship *Missouri* surrender. This is what's missing to make this akin to WWII, to separate Kuwait from Korea and Vietnam. . . ."[49] The very insistence on the "end of the Vietnam syndrome" (by which Bush seems to have meant sloppy, unsatisfying endings, internal divisions, and a hampered military) reveals, of course, just how painfully present that experience remained for him. The sloppy ending of the Gulf war—which left Saddam Hussein still in power, still a menace, and increasingly free of externally imposed sanctions a decade later—showed that the president had fallen short of his immediate objective as well.

For, in fact, the Gulf war did not end the "Vietnam syndrome" but, if anything, strengthened it. The lessons of the Gulf war learned by the American defense establishment amounted to a powerful reinforcement of deep-seated beliefs that go back to Vietnam and that amounted to a tremendous reinforcement, to the point of distortion, of the "normal" theory of civil-military relations. In the decade that followed, the twinned lessons of Vietnam and the Gulf combined to create a version of the "normal" theory of civil-military relations that ended by weakening the principle of civilian control of the military in the United States, deepening mistrust between senior officers and politicians, and even, in some measure, politicizing the officer corps.

The lessons of Vietnam and the Gulf war did not disappear with the gradual retirement of the Vietnam generation of military officers. Extensive surveys of officers conducted by social scientists from the Triangle Institute for Security Studies in 1999 asked officers whether they should be neutral, advise, advocate, or insist on control of certain elements of the use of force. The results revealed that officers believed that it was is their duty to "insist" on the adoption of certain courses of action (rather than advise or advocate), including "setting rules of engagement" (50 percent), developing an "exit strategy" (52 percent), and "deciding what kinds of military units (air versus naval, heavy versus light) will be used to accomplish all tasks" (63 percent).[50] What "insist" meant in this context was, of course, unclear. Still, something profound had changed in American civil-military relations. Officers, their self-confidence strengthened by two decades of increasing prestige and by a generally accepted version of civil-military relations marked by the morality tales of the Vietnam and Gulf wars, had come to believe that civilians had little business in probing *their* business.

The TISS survey data indicate that the post–Gulf war American military had a view of who should control the use of force very different indeed from the unequal dialogue discussed here. Nor is it the case that these views were theoretical propositions only, not reflected in action. When, for example, sources on the Joint Chiefs of Staff leaked military opposition on the conduct of the 1999 Kosovo war to the press, the stated objection was that "I don't think anybody felt like there had been a compelling argument made that all of this was in our national interest"—as if the determination was the military's to make.[51] Indeed, by the turn of the twenty-first century it was the norm for military officers to leak to the press their opposition to government policy involving the use of force. This is a far cry from the outraged but dutiful muteness with which the chiefs of staff of the Army and Navy accepted President

Roosevelt's decision to invade North Africa in 1942, against their explicit and firm advice.

In the Gulf war, and in the host of small wars since then, military "advice" has not really been "advice" at all, but something different: a preparation of options, and sometimes a single option, for the civilian leadership. American civilian decision-makers hesitated before demanding much of their military subordinates. Having earlier denounced the passivity of the first Bush administration in Yugoslavia and particularly in Bosnia, the Clinton administration in 1992 was paralyzed by military estimates that it would take 400,000 troops or more to intervene there.[52] When American forces were used, it was with virtually no cooperation and communication with—let alone subordination to—a broader political effort. Indeed, Richard Holbrooke, America's chief negotiator in the Balkans in 1995, recalls that his military counterpart, Admiral Leighton Smith, viewed himself as an independent force: ". . . he told me that he was 'solely responsible' for the safety and well-being of his forces, and he would make his decision, under authority delegated to him by the NATO Council, based on his own judgment. In fact, he pointed out, he did not even work for the United States: as a NATO commander he took orders from Brussels."[53] Smith's mulish opposition to the man charged with implementing American policy reflected the same kind of presumptuousness that, in far graver circumstances, had afflicted the relationship between Foch and Clemenceau. It was a reminder that coalition operations, now a staple of peacekeeping and limited interventions, produce their own difficulties in the area of civil-military relations.

The Somalia intervention of 1993 offered another such case. A commitment of American forces under the auspices of the United Nations allowed for the pursuit of parallel and conflicting policies, which culminated in a disastrous attempt to kidnap a Somali warlord whose cooperation was essential to any stable arrangement in Mogadishu. Here too civilian abdication, not military arrogance, was to blame. Deferring to a zealous United Nations high commissioner—

an American—neither the president nor the secretary of defense regarded American forces operating in Mogadishu as forces fighting a low-level war, but a war nonetheless, in which some effort should be made by national authority to harmonize ends and means. Far from abusing the military by micromanaging it, the Clinton administration abused it by failing to take the war seriously and inquire into means, methods, and techniques. Its civilian leadership failed (to take just the Somalia case) by refusing to ask why American forces in Somalia were operating under several different commands—commands which communicated with one another poorly and in some cases not at all.

Particularly in the years after the Gulf war, it became expected that civilian leaders, not their military subordinates, would take responsibility for military failure. Secretary of Defense Les Aspin resigned following the death of eighteen Rangers ambushed in downtown Mogadishu in 1993—even though his military advisers had not urged upon him a course of action other than that undertaken by American forces there, and had, in fact, favored the withdrawal of the one system that might have rescued the Rangers, the AC-130 aerial gunship. In a similar if less extreme vein, Secretary of Defense William Perry, confronted by the Senate Armed Services Committee, took responsibility for any failures associated with the bomb attack on the Khobar Towers in Dhahran, Saudi Arabia, that killed nineteen servicemen in 1996, while the theater commander in chief sat silently beside him. Lower-level officers might suffer for sins of omission and commission (an Air Force brigadier general was denied promotion after the Khobar attack, which he could neither have prevented nor defended against more effectively than he did), but higher commanders were not penalized. For civilian leaders to hold military leaders accountable for their operational performance far graver failures, apparently, would have to occur.

The decline in the quality of American civil-military relations at the top has coincided with the emergence of an American military edge—technological, organizational, and quantitative—that stems from the

United States' extraordinarily prosperous economy and the overall quality of its armed forces. Yet even in successes such as the 1999 Operation
ALLIED FORCE, the NATO war with Serbia led by an American, General
Wesley Clark, the failure of statesmen and commanders to come to
terms with one another had deleterious consequences. Clark, a bright,
ambitious, and politically sophisticated general, supported American
policy as articulated by the secretary of state:

> One of his colleagues asked him where his civilian pals were
> going to be if things went sour. Would they, like the civilians
> behind the Vietnam débacle, go off to write their books and take
> their big jobs, the way Mac Bundy and Bob McNamara had
> done? . . . In the military, someone who was too nimble, too
> supple with words, too facile, someone who was able to go to dif-
> ferent meetings and seem to please opposing constituencies, was
> not regarded with admiration; he was regarded with mistrust.[54]

Clark paid dearly for getting crosswise of military colleagues who had
no use for the Kosovo war or for the president who had led them into it.
But neither the president nor the secretary of defense chose to speak
with their theater commander, who found himself on the receiving end
of admonitions from a hostile chairman of the Joint Chiefs of Staff and
uncooperative generals at home. "I had little idea, and never had during
the entire crisis, how the commander in chief, or the secretary of
defense were making their decisions."[55]

For their part the civilians scrutinized target lists but generally
approved the requests of their theater commander, who faced far more
unwillingness from NATO allies. President Clinton, seeking to avoid
casualties which he felt himself peculiarly unable to justify, declared
early on that the United States would commit no ground forces to
Kosovo—an indiscretion that virtually guaranteed a prolonged air campaign, during which Serb forces could massacre the Albanian Kosovars
at leisure. This decision seems to have preceded rather than followed

any strategic discussions with military leaders. An unthinking requirement for "force protection" as the first mission for American soldiers, ahead of any objective for which they might be put in harm's way, reflects an unwillingness to come to terms with what the use of force means; today, rather than the reckless dissipation of strength, it means an only slightly less reckless conservation of it.[56]

The Kosovo war ended with no American combat casualties, and with the eviction of Serb forces from Kosovo. For this success Clark, who had no friends in the military high command and who had alienated Secretary of Defense William Cohen—a civilian leader who had absorbed the views of the Joint Chiefs of Staff—found himself unceremoniously retired early. In his place General Joseph Ralston, vice chairman of the Joint Chiefs of Staff, who had expressed all of the conventional military reservations about fighting the Serbs, moved up to become Supreme Allied Commander Europe.

"ROUTINE METHODS"

At one level, civil-military relations today are smooth and easy; senior military leaders mix far more easily with their civilian superiors than they did in Lincoln's or even Churchill's day. They attend the same meetings of the Council on Foreign Relations and converse with equal ease on political, although not often military subjects. They share offices in the bureaucracy and interact easily in interagency meetings. This superficial harmony has even led some scholars to talk of a theory of concordance as a more attractive paradigm for civil-military relations.[57] This is, however, a mirage.

During the Cold War the American military accumulated, while scarcely being aware of it, an enormous amount of power and influence. It divided the world into theaters of operation; these have mushroomed into commands whose staffs dwarf those of the immediate office of the president.[58] In order to fight a Cold War characterized by multiple and often delicate alliances, it schooled its senior officers in politics, beginning when they were cadets at the military academies, by having them serve as interns in Congress. It taught politics, under the name of strategy, in its war colleges. At the same time, particularly after Vietnam, it deprecated efforts by civilian leaders to become overly expert in the details of military affairs. As for explaining its failures or half-successes since World War II, even thoughtful general officers declared that to have victories, "You must have the political will—and that means the will of the administration, the Congress and the American people. All must be united in a desire for action."[59] If accepted, such an extreme precondition—a unity that has escaped the United States in every major war except the World Wars—means that the civilians will always disappoint the military and the soldiers will always have an excuse.

There was nothing deliberately malign in this hardening of military views about the use of force, very much along the lines of Weinberger's rules and the Powell doctrine.[60] More deeply disturbing at the end of the century were signs that the American military was increasingly willing to take sides in politics in order to preserve its own interests. This politicization occurred as much at the top of the hierarchy as it did lower down. Having successfully wooed a group of recently retired general officers to endorse his candidacy in 1992, President Bill Clinton found himself trumped by the son of the man he had defeated. George W. Bush collected a longer and more impressive list, topped by three men who had retired only weeks or even days earlier from military service: the professional chiefs of the Navy and the Marine Corps, and the commander of the American forces in the Persian Gulf.[61] The use of senior generals as props for political campaigns, and the flags' willingness to sign up as partisans, was a long way from the standards of behavior set by men like George C. Marshall, the Army's chief of staff during World War II. Marshall chose not even to vote (admittedly an extreme choice) in order to avoid any partisan taint. In 1943 he lectured a subordinate: "We are completely devoted, we are a member of a priesthood really, the sole purpose of which is to defend the republic."

Hence, he insisted, public confidence in a politically neutral military was "a sacred trust" to be borne in mind "every day and every hour."[62]

There was a paradox here. The "normal theory, which called for sealing the military off from civilian meddling in the details, had eventually given way to a military willing to involve itself, if only tentatively at first, in politics. Yet this willingness follows from the "normal" theory's unrealistic view of the use of force as something divorced from politics in all but the broadest sense of the word. The post–Cold War world being one in which the interplay of force and politics has grown ever more complex, it is not surprising that soldiers tend to engage in politics, albeit with the best of motives. The tendency to do so was reinforced by the increasing gap between traditional military values of hierarchy, order, loyalty, and self-sacrifice and a civilian world that seems increasingly egalitarian (at least in work habits), fluid, individualistic, and acquisitive. Both the steady spread of gender integration in the modern military and weakening barriers to homosexual participation in the armed forces have quietly reinforced a sense of siege among more traditionally minded officers, even as they have blurred the barriers between institution and interest group for others.[63] These subtle but powerful societal forces exacerbated a sense of civil-military tension, if not of crisis, by the time a new president took office in 2001. Not entirely coincidentally his new secretary of defense, Donald Rumsfeld, who had held the same job a quarter-century before, began his tenure with an elaborate set of defense reviews that ostentatiously excluded the active-duty military from participation save as a kind of uniformed research assistants. Until the outbreak of a new and different kind of war following the terror attacks on the United States on September 11, 2001, the Rumsfeld Pentagon exhibited levels of civil-military mistrust as bitter as anything seen in the Clinton administration.

For the leaders of America today, the strong temptation in a world dominated by American military power is to brush aside the lessons of civil-military relations hard won over a century of total wars. There is a danger that absent recent or current experience of really dangerous war—war in which the other side can inflict damage and has options—civilian and military decision-makers alike will forget the lessons of serious conflict. Those lessons are, above all, that political leaders must immerse themselves in the conduct of their wars no less than in their great projects of domestic legislation; that they must master their military briefs as thoroughly as they do their civilian ones; that they must demand and expect from their military subordinates a candor as bruising as it is necessary; that both groups must expect a running conversation in which, although civilian opinion will not usually dictate, it must dominate; and that that conversation will cover not only ends and policies, but ways and means. "Our highest civilian and military heads [must] be in close, even if not cordial, contact with each other . . .,"[64] declared a weary but wise general officer veteran of the Vietnam war.

Just before the turn of the twenty-first century, the Senate Committee on Foreign Relations was reviewing the 1999 war fought by the United States and its NATO allies against Serbia. "I was troubled," Senator Gordon H. Smith, (R-Oregon), who was chairing the hearing, remarked, "over the degree to which political considerations affected NATO's military strategy." He was disturbed that matters had gotten "even to the point where politicians . . . questioned and sometimes vetoed targets that had been selected by the military." He continued:

> I firmly believe in the need for civilian control of the military in a
> democratic society, but I also believe we can effectively adhere to
> this critical principle by clearly outlining political objectives and
> then, within the boundaries of those objectives, allowing the military
> commanders to design a strategy in order to assure the
> achievement of those objectives.[65]

The "normal" theory of civil-military relations was alive and well.

A great statesman is a rarity, and an average politician who poses as a Churchill or a Lincoln may come to grief. But it is also the case that a mediocre statesman who resorts to rules of thumb—including "defer to the professionals"—is heading, and probably by a shorter path, to ruin. Interestingly enough, General Colin Powell himself took as a life lesson, "Don't be afraid to challenge the pros, even in their own back yard. Just as important, never neglect details, even to the point of being a pest."[66] Except under uniquely favorable conditions (as, for example, in 1999 when the United States and its allies went to war with Serbia—a country whose gross national product was one fifteenth the size of the American defense budget) the outcome of civilians taking military advice without question is unlikely to be a good one.

The hopeful belief in bright dividing lines between civilian and soldier, political matters and military ones, is what Carl von Clausewitz termed a "theory of war"—a set of beliefs and doctrines that seem to make the use of force more manageable. As he also noted, however, in the absence of "an intelligent analysis of the conduct of war . . . routine methods will tend to take over even at the highest levels."[67] The "normal" theory of civil-military relations is, in effect, an effort to make high command a matter of routine. The unequal dialogue, to which we turn next, is the essence of the technique of the successful war statesman discussed in previous chapters, and the opposite of Clausewitz's "routine methods."

CHAPTER 7

THE UNEQUAL DIALOGUE

"AN AVERAGE SPECIMEN OF HUMANITY"

We have seen four great statesmen and four very different sets of problems—Lincoln searching for a general whose concept of the war mirrored his own; Clemenceau attempting to balance contradictory impulses on the part of equally competent military leaders; Churchill relentlessly probing for choices; Ben-Gurion determined to grasp the fundamentals in the midst of complexity. They dealt differently with their varied predicaments. Lincoln exercised guile masquerading as rustic simplicity; Clemenceau, the Tiger, breathed defiance and resolve; Churchill dazzled and exasperated with his genius and his wit; Ben-Gurion studied and hectored in equal measure. What did they have in common?

Interestingly enough, none of these men dictated to their subordinates. They might coax or bully, interrogate or probe, but rarely do we see them issuing orders or acting like a generalissimo. Each tolerated, indeed promoted men who disagreed with them, forcefully. Grant, Foch, Brooke, and Yadin were not weaklings, and did not hesitate to argue with statesmen whom, by and large, they admired (albeit less than did many of their countrymen). What occurred between president or prime minister and general was an unequal dialogue—a dialogue, in that both sides expressed their views bluntly, indeed, sometimes offensively, and not once but repeatedly—and unequal, in that the final authority of the civilian leader was unambiguous and unquestioned— indeed, in all cases stronger at the end of a war than it had been at the beginning. Far from the simplistic conventions of the "normal" theory of civil-military relations—which seems to reserve dialogue for only the beginning and end of a war—the practice of these men was interaction throughout a conflict.

That give and take exacted a real price, and by and large that price fell on the shoulders of the generals, who found themselves broken down by the strain of managing a war while in turn being managed by a civilian leader who treated military advice as just that—advice, not a course of action to be ratified with no more than formal consideration. Some of the lesser figures in these wars suffered under the burden of treatment that for the rest of their lives they considered unfair, sometimes brutally so. British soldiers like Field Marshals Sir John Dill and Archibald Wavell were prime cases of intelligent, well-schooled, and able men who simply could not get along with a prime minister who had greater respect for another sort of men with more evident brilliance and less stolid reserve—and, let it be added, men who had the good fortune to command an army encountering success rather than failure. Few students of the Civil War will shed a tear for the egomaniacal, self-pitying George McClellan, but it is hard to avoid feeling a twinge of sympathy for the crusty, irritable, competent George Meade, the last commander of the Army of the Potomac, who provided that outmaneuvered host with its one clear-cut victory up until the very end of the war, namely the battle of Gettysburg. After winning that epic three-day contest that left 50,000 men dead or wounded—barely a week after taking command—he learned that the president despaired of him because he had failed to *annihilate* Lee. It seemed a poor recompense when the previous history of the Army of the Potomac had consisted of defeats and one inconclusive draw at the bloody battle of Antietam, and in outrage Meade offered his resignation—which Lincoln declined. When Meade proved unwilling to venture more ghastly losses in the fall of 1863 he found himself superseded (but, perhaps even more humiliatingly, not formally replaced) by an alcoholic soldier from the West whose only virtue seemed to be his sheer determination. At war's end, Meade received precious little thanks (and less trust) from the president, and was not even present at the final surrender of Lee's forces at Appomattox Courthouse.

Even the favored generals, those who delivered victories and served loyally, did not always receive kind treatment in return. Clemenceau skewered the departed Foch in his memoirs, declaring that the general was "an average specimen of humanity whose main weakness was to imagine himself greater than he was."[1] Yigal Alon, the dashing leader of the Palmach and clearly the preeminent general of Israel's war of independence, found his military career terminated before it had fairly begun; he would comment and advise from the sidelines, and play an important role in Israeli politics, but after the age of thirty-one he would never again exercise the military leadership at which he so clearly excelled. For him, as for any ambitious and patriotic soldier gifted with the ability to lead large organizations in war, it must have been an exceptionally cruel blow.

Brooke, for confessing his true thoughts about Churchill in his memoirs—reservations coupled with lavish praise and the offering of his own enormous sense of strain as an excuse—found himself cut dead by the leading Western figure of the twentieth century. "Brooke was the only man on whom I ever saw him deliberately and ostentatiously turn his back," recalled John Colville, Churchill's secretary during the war.[2] Even Grant, operating under the broadest of guidance from a president who professed not to wish to know about his plans, was in fact under close scrutiny from his own military household, subject to minatory warnings from the amateur strategist in the White House and the strictest injunction not to exceed his orders in the slightest. Secretary of War Edwin W. Stanton's telegram to him of 3 March 1865—drafted in Lincoln's hand, with only the date, salutation, and signature being in Stanton's—read as follows:

> The president directs me to say to you that he wishes you to have no conference with General Lee unless it be for the capitulation of Gen. Lee's army, or on some minor, and purely, military matter. He instructs me to say that you are not to decide, discuss, or confer upon any political question. Such questions the president holds in his own hands; and will submit them to no military conferences or conventions. Meantime you are to press to the utmost your military advantages.[3]

All concerned knew who was master, and if each of these statesmen could offer generous praise none of them would, in the final analysis, relax his grip over his sorely tried subordinates, to the very end.

"IN ALL GREAT EMERGENCIES EVERYONE IS MORE OR LESS WRONG."

What, then, in the final analysis were the leadership qualities exercised by the statesmen described here, and in what measure can they be emulated by others? These men were not military or technical experts; we have seen that they often made mistakes in their judgment of technical matters, no matter how knowledgeable they were. Perhaps one of their strengths lay in their awareness that the experts might be equally mistaken, a knowledge that is, after all, a dark form of wisdom. That mordant observer of men in politics, Henry Adams, observed that "in all great emergencies he commonly found that everyone was more or less wrong."[4] True enough, but some of the art of leadership may lie in intuiting when others are even more wrong than oneself.

Certainly, the statesmen discussed here demonstrated a measure of what we commonly call intuition that stands well above the norm in human affairs. "Intuition" and "genius" are words that capture merely the surface of their statecraft. "What makes statesmen, like drivers of cars, successful is that they do not think in general terms—that is, they do not primarily ask themselves in what respect a given situation is like or unlike other situations in the long course of human history," writes Isaiah Berlin, in two particularly fine essays on the essence of statesmanship.[5] The gift of great political leaders "entails, above all, a capacity for integrating a vast amalgam of constantly changing, multicoloured, evanescent, perpetually overlapping data, too many, too swift, too intermingled to be caught and pinned down and labeled like so many individual butterflies."[6] The gift, he notes, is rather like that of some great novelists, and indeed there was more than a little of the artist in the temperament of several of these statesmen. "[W]hat makes men foolish or wise, understanding or blind, as opposed to knowledgeable or learned or well informed, is the perception of these unique flavors of each situation as it is, in its specific differences."[7] An awareness of the unique character of a given political situation is only part of the statesman's art, according to Berlin. What is equally important, he believes, is the ability to synthesize, to comprehend how a multiplicity of forces and conditions are interacting. The old metaphor of statesman as captain of a ship is just, but it applies best when thought of as the conning of an exceedingly complex sailing vessel sailing through awkward seas, with its multiplicity of sails, ropes, and masts, all working with and against one another and the weather in a way too complicated to be reduced to rules or maxims. Small wonder that Clemenceau remarked to Churchill in one of the crises of 1918, "I have no political system, and I have abandoned all political principles. I am a man dealing with events as they come in the light of my experience."[8] The biographer may find more of principle than Clemenceau admitted, but it is a sentiment that other political leaders have expressed. In a more extreme vein, Lincoln once wrote that "I claim not to have controlled events, but confess plainly that events have controlled me."[9] Again, it was not an entirely straightforward remark (little about Lincoln was straightforward) but neither was it simply untrue.

The eye for—indeed, the fascination with—detail displayed by the great war statesmen was, therefore, not a mere irritating trait on the part of arrogant political leaders but an essential element of their warcraft. The challenge for a supreme leader lies not in choosing at which level of guidance or abstraction to function, but rather in integrating the details with the grand themes, in understanding the forest by examining certain copses and even individual trees with great care. By way of contrast, the American politicians failed as war leaders in Vietnam not because they immersed themselves in too much detail but because they looked at the wrong details and drew the wrong conclusions from them. They did not test a strategy—a theory of victory, as some have called it—against the realities of the field; they did not ask whether the organizations at work had the right structures, the right tasks, and above all the right leaders. They did not cross-examine, test, and probe their subordinates, and they did not force them into debates with other professionals who took a different view.

In his annual message to Congress on 1 December 1862, Lincoln declared that "The dogmas of the quiet past are inadequate to the stormy present. . . . As our case is new, so we must think anew, and act anew."[10] Part of the statesman's art of perception lies in seeing, embedded in a mass of detail, that which is indeed new and different. This sense for the new—for that which does not reflect past experience or the concepts of conventional military thought—operates at multiple levels, beginning with technology. Lincoln personally tested firearms, and pushed the stodgy commander of the US Army's ordnance corps to buy the recently invented breech-loading repeating rifle; Clemenceau devoted close attention to the expansion of tank production—and French tanks in 1918 were the best in the world; Churchill had an abiding fascination with all aspects of military technology; Ben-Gurion had, among other achievements to his credit, the creation of an embryonic arms industry that even before a state existed was developing everything from small arms to light artillery pieces. These were after all curious men who, even though they did not overrate technology, nonetheless rated it highly.

A more profound sense of the new, however, may be detected in these men's appreciation of the existence of novel strategic conditions or operational problems. Lincoln's insistence on turning the Army of the Potomac against Lee's army rather than against the enemy's capital is evidence of this, as was his understanding—far earlier than most of his generals—that the war would become a revolutionary struggle which would require the shattering of the South's will to resist, not merely the defeat of its forces in the field. Clemenceau saw the need for the creation of a unified Allied command in the West, despite the doubts of his senior field commander. Churchill had a particular genius for defining the campaigns of a new kind of war. And Ben-Gurion, as we have seen, saw more clearly than any around him that the defense organization of the *yishuv* could not cope with a set of strategic challenges which it had not anticipated. In all cases, their perception alone was not enough: rather, these statesmen exercised their leadership by explaining and persuading others of its truth.

"War is an option of difficulties," declared General James Wolfe, conqueror of Quebec. One of the tasks of a war statesman is indeed to make choices among difficulties, based on the widest possible perspective, which he alone may have. "In any sphere of action there can be no comparison between the positions of number one and number two, three, or four."[11] Inevitably, a military commander's point of view must be partial, restricted in various ways but not least by a sense of responsibility for the conduct of actual operations. It is up to the statesman to find the right point of view from which to judge military action. Usually, though not always, this entails deciding when political considerations must override legitimate, even pressing military ones, and this trade-off applies in the greatest wars and in far less substantial conflicts as well. From Lincoln's willingness to appoint semicompetent or even incompetent but politically well-connected amateurs to senior positions, to the indirect pressure brought to bear on American airmen by then-President Bush and Secretary of Defense Cheney to waste sorties hunting for SCUD missiles in the Iraqi desert, statesmanship in war requires a willingness to accept military sacrifices in the name of a larger goal. To be able to do that well, however, requires a fine understanding of just how painful those sacrifices will likely be.

Here again, mastery of military detail is essential. Lincoln studying treatises on war and poring over every telegram coming in to the War Department; Clemenceau visiting the front lines and talking to soldier and general alike, even under fire; Churchill ceaselessly probing and interrogating his chiefs of staff; Ben-Gurion patiently copying in his voluminous diaries every detail down to the last bullet—these men understood that they could not lead if they did not know an enormous amount about the business of war.

Yet their detailed knowledge could not come from prodigious study alone. All of these leaders had to understand the modes of thought of their military subordinates, and needed skilled assistants to translate their wishes into directives, orders, requests, and suggestions. In the shadow of each of these figures stood a military interpreter—a Halleck, a Mordacq, an Ismay, and a Yadin—who had several features in common with his counterparts: they were highly intelligent, even bookish; highly literate, able to communicate clearly in writing; they had no strongly held political views; they had no (or had given up) aspirations to high field command; they were on decent, if not always intimate terms with other generals. During World War II, for example, Admiral William Leahy served this role by acting as chief of staff to the president. He had no operational responsibilities, no cumbersome staff to manage, no line responsibilities of any kind, in fact. He was a military assistant with only one constituency, the president. This role of military liaison is of necessity often an informal one. Senior commanders usually outrank such an assistant, who may not have a vote at the council table. Interestingly enough, modern civil-military command systems do not allow for such a role, combining as they do in the position of a chief of the General Staff (or, in the American case, chairman of the Joint Chiefs of Staff) this role with others that are incompatible with it, including managing a central joint staff, arbitrating disputes among services or field commanders, and representing institutional views to the senior politician. The two roles are necessarily in tension, and to combine them does not necessarily serve political leaders well.

The broadest views and the most expert knowledge, comprehensively gathered and effectively transmitted, helped make these statesmen successful. One must add that they required, as well, exceptional judgment of other men. For if, indeed, everyone is "more or less wrong," the truth is that all generals are more or less flawed. Much of leadership is knowing whom to select, whom to encourage, whom to restrain, and whom to replace. All four of these leaders were far more willing to dismiss their most senior generals than is the norm today, and lest that be thought a reflection of capriciousness on their part, consider the consequences of Lyndon Johnson's unwillingness to replace General William Westmoreland with someone better suited to the complex political and military challenges the United States faced in Vietnam. Generals are, or should be, disposable. Statesmen should not, of course, discard them thoughtlessly, nor need they treat them discourteously. Yet all four of these statesmen showed themselves able to treat generals in line with Gladstone's first requirement for success as a prime minister: "One must be a good butcher." Indeed, it was the most mild-mannered of the four, Lincoln, who relieved commanders most frequently.

The dismissal of a general in wartime is no light thing. As democratic politicians well know, today's disgraced commander may be tomorrow's political rival: General George McClellan ran for president in 1864, General Douglas MacArthur came close to doing so in 1952, and both Presidents Bush and Clinton understood quite well that General Colin Powell could do the same in 1992 or 1996. Parliamentary systems have their equivalent paths to power, as several Israeli generals

(Yitzhak Rabin, Ehud Barak, and Ariel Sharon) have demonstrated; ironically it may be easier for a general to become a president than a mayor or even a senator. But even in a parliamentary system like that of Great Britain, in which it is highly unlikely that a general could end up at the head of a well-organized political party, a retired military leader can nonetheless act as a political force, usually with the backing of politicians who, for a variety of motives, fling themselves into his camp. Sir Edward Carson, for example, as First Lord of the Admiralty in 1917, declared, "As long as I am at the Admiralty the sailors will have full scope. They will not be interfered with by me, and I will not let anyone interfere with them."[12] But Carson's views may have had as much to do with rivalries within the British Cabinet as with any sentiment of true conviction that the admirals had it right.

Serving as the catspaw of rival politicians or merely riding on the crest of fame, deserved or otherwise, a retired general can exercise considerable political influence, particularly once freed from the constraints imposed by active service. Such influence has a relatively brief duration, as George McClellan discovered when he ran against Abraham Lincoln in 1864, or as Douglas MacArthur found when he returned to the United States after a series of bruising battles with President Harry S Truman. This potential for influence is, nonetheless, a source of worry for politicians in wartime.

Lord Beaverbrook, who had the opportunity to view British civil-military relations at close quarters in two world wars, comments on the mood of those relations in wartime Britain in 1916.

The picture of Ministers which the Generals drew to themselves and which was reflected to some extent to the public, was something like this.

The Minister sat in a leather-bound armchair in a room where even the faintest hum of outside traffic was hushed, and pulled at a long cigar while he languidly superintended the activities of the secretaries. From this repose he would cheerfully give an order speeding "glum heroes up the line to death" by the thousands—although he knew nothing of war. He then rose to go out to dinner, with others of his colleagues who had been similarly employed. If the Minister ever did show any activity, it was of that inconvenient kind by which an ignorant civilian interfered with the superb expert efficiency exhibited by the General. And in the meantime, too, the General, instead of smoking a cigar, was daily qualifying for a Victoria Cross by the hardships he endured and the dangers he ran.

Anyone who will take the trouble to read those London newspapers of the period which reflected the Generals' standpoint, will recognize the picture.[13]

But, as Beaverbrook noted, anyone who visited the generals found them "just as snug and safe" as the politicians. Yet, down to the present day, the taunt of "armchair strategist" is often hurled at civilian political leaders, as if generals still make their decisions astride horses, cantering along a battle line. Military organizations and their leaders may suffer routine humiliation and setbacks in peace, but once war begins, their status grows enormously. To the present day, a general in wartime is an imposing figure—at least until (shortly after) the guns are silent.

To the political dangers posed by a dismissed general in wartime are added others. Will his dismissal demoralize troops in the field? Will it disrupt the continuity of command so badly that a military organization will lose its ability to fight? What consequences will flow from the time the new commander takes to learn his organization, his theater, and his task? And above all, can the right man, or merely a better man, be found for the same exacting job? Politicians, like the heads of all vast organizations at all times, find themselves perplexed by a dearth of talented leaders. The chief of the German General Staff in 1914 was Helmuth von Moltke the Younger, nephew of the great Moltke who had directed Germany's short, bloody wars of unification in 1864, 1866, and 1870–71. When he learned in 1905 that Kaiser Wilhelm II would appoint him to succeed the considerably more self-assured Alfred von Schlieffen, the gloomy general is reported to have said to his master, "So you hope to win twice in the same lottery?" It was not an unintelligent remark.

There is no uniform standard for the selection of generals. The dogged defender and the audacious attacker, the flexible and resourceful improviser and the disciplined man of method, the young and the old, the excitable and energetic, and the phlegmatic and unflappable all have their place. Leadership is contextual, and much of the art of civilian leadership in wartime resides in the ability to judge context, and not only context but character. When Lincoln and Stanton sent Charles Dana to spy on Ulysses S. Grant, they cared less about Grant's skill at maneuver than about the balance between his resolution and his intelligence, the very human flaw of his drunkenness, and the other qualities that made him a leader whom men would follow. It made far more sense to send a journalist than a soldier to judge these qualities.

The four leaders we have discussed here show in common qualities of obstinate, unyielding determination. Indeed, in the popular imagination that is how they are often remembered and celebrated: Churchill's ringing peroration to his speech of 18 June 1940, "We shall never surrender," captured a magnificent defiance that heartened a nation. Clemenceau, "the Tiger," was no less magnificent in his insistence, "*Je fais la guerre*"—"I make war." Ben-Gurion's sturdy determination carried the day when many of his political colleagues were prepared to step back from independence at the very last moment. And gentle, melancholic Lincoln was possibly the toughest of them all, unyielding in his insistence in the crisis of December 1860 following his election that "the tug has to come, & better now than any time hereafter," and in his sober readiness to fight the war to the end. The words of his Second Inaugural Address, containing though they did an outstretched hand of reconciliation, included as well these words:

> Fondly do we hope—fervently do we pray—that this mighty scourge of war may speedily pass away. Yet, if God wills that it continue, until all the wealth piled by the bondman's two hundred and fifty years of unrequited toil shall be sunk, and until every drop of blood drawn with the lash, shall be paid by another drawn with the sword, as was said three thousand years ago, so still it must be said, "the judgments of the Lord are true and righteous altogether."

The resolution these men embodied was not the impetuous all-or-nothing of youth; it was the hard will of men who confronted the single great task of their lives, old men (as even the youngest of them, Lincoln, described himself before taking office) who had seen much and who did not necessarily expect to survive the struggles upon which they embarked.

Nations are led and ruled by words, and each of these men, deeply read in history, politics, and literature, had mastered the arts of speech and writing on a level beyond all but the most gifted orators and authors. These skills help explain, perhaps, the attention that their defiant rhetoric has attracted; a contemporary reader marvels, wistfully perhaps, at their command of the spoken and written word. The word "rhetoric" has, in our time, taken on the meaning of empty, indeed deliberately misleading rhodomontade. Its truer meaning, persuasive political speech, is reflected in the skill of these leaders, who understood that groups and nations—democratic nations above all—are led by the carefully wrought word. They did not leave the writing of their speeches to staffs of junior officials, and they understood far better than their counterparts today the importance not only of words that rouse, but of those that depict, clarify, and explain. The thick volumes of speeches by these war leaders reveal an interesting fact: the celebrated passages familiar to all are but a tiny fraction of the work. To a far greater extent than television-driven politicians today, these men used the spoken word to explain, at great length and in sometimes surprising detail, the meaning and course of their war. Compare, for example, Churchill's "Give us the tools and we will finish the job" speech of 9 February 1941 with President George W. Bush's speech of 7 October 2001 announcing the commencement of military operations in Afghanistan. Bush's speechwriters borrowed a line from Churchill's speech: "We shall not fail or falter; we shall not weaken or tire" became, sixty years later, "We will not waver; we will not tire; we will not falter; and we will not fail." But Bush's speech was a fraction the length and not nearly as detailed as Churchill's speech; it did not promise hardships, and it described the enemy only in general terms.

Churchill and statesmen of his ilk did not give away future operations or more than hint at the course they intended to follow, but they went to great pains to explain the path they had followed thus far, the dominant tendencies and turning points, and the nature of the national predicament as they understood it. There is, indeed, something almost professorial in their description of campaigns and battles, in their recitation of statistics, and in their judicious summing up of trends and patterns. We have also seen in previous chapters that their mastery of the subtler arts of communication, of the pointed memorandum and the concise telegram, not to mention the ability to listen that is so rare at the pinnacle of any great institution, was no less critical to their success. Without complete mastery of the written and spoken word, demonstrated equally on a podium before tens of thousands, a parliament of hundreds, or a meeting room containing fewer than a dozen, they could not have led.

"THE TRUEST CONSISTENCY"

The great speeches of implacable determination still ring. But they mask, unfortunately, the quality all four exhibited, and without which they could not have succeeded: moderation. That word may seem strange when applied to a Ben-Gurion or a Clemenceau, duelists in spirit—and, in the case of Clemenceau, in practice was well. Of all of them Churchill—so often derided as the bully and hothead—captured most vividly the essence of political moderation. "A statesman in contact with the moving current of events and anxious to keep the ship on an even keel and steer a steady course may lean all his weight now on one side and now on the other."[14]

Sometimes moderation appears in a natural form, as advocacy of restrained measures, or as simple tolerance—thus, for example, Clemenceau's generally easy relations with Catholic generals, despite his own strongly anticlerical views.

> Monsieur Clemenceau came to Bombon unexpectedly one morning and asked to be shown to the Marshal [Foch]. Captain Boutal told him that he was at church, adding, "I will go at once and tell him you are here." "Do not interrupt him for anything in the world—it agrees with him too well," answered the witty old heathen, quite willing to take a chance even with the Almighty if France could be benefited.[15]

What each of these men had, however, was a deeper quality, a moderation that lay not in gentle speech but rather in two qualities: the ability to discipline his passions, and an understanding of when and how to counteract a trend. What Clemenceau and Churchill put in a grimly humorous way, Aristotle and others had already described in their more philosophical treatment of moderation as being not a course in and of itself, but the product of tilting first in one direction, then another.[16]

Seeming contrariness, even perversity, may reflect not stubborn pursuit of dogma or mere willfulness, but a deliberate throwing of one's weight to the opposite side of a listing ship. Clemenceau's alternate throwing of his weight to Foch and Pétain is an ideal example of this. So too was Ben-Gurion's support for the politically isolated veterans of the British army in the *yishuv*. More importantly, the war objectives of each of the four men reflected core principles, but also flexibility and self-restraint in the pursuit of ultimate objectives. Lincoln would wage war to save the Union, but would offer the Southern states restoration of their privileges and position on far easier terms than would the dominant Republicans of the North. Clemenceau would fight Germany to the death, but he would not fall in with Foch and much of French opinion in attempting to wrest France's security from a defeated foe by force of arms, in opposition to France's allies. Churchill, who described the moral of his World War II memoirs as "In war: resolution; in defeat: defiance; in victory: magnaminity; in peace: good will," was prepared for a generous peace with Germany even as he saw, earlier than any other Western statesman, the rising threat of the Soviet Union. Ben-Gurion, who would not yield on the creation of a Jewish state, fended off the wishes of successful generals to carve out a larger territory for Israel on the West Bank of the Jordan.

In the conduct of operations, Clausewitz once wrote, armies reach a culminating point of victory—a moment at which they have achieved the maximum of their potential, and beyond which they run the risk of exhaustion and defeat. All four statesmen intuitively understood this notion and applied it on the largest scale. Leaders intoxicated with military success usually bring disaster upon themselves and their nation, be they men of genius like Napoleon Bonaparte or merely successful thugs like Saddam Hussein. This is a trap, however, into which more timid and less bloodthirsty politicians fall as well—as the Soviet leadership proved in Afghanistan in the 1980s.

This understanding of limits is reflected in the way in which these four leaders dealt with one of the most difficult strategic challenges of their wars: the security of their capital cities. Each of them faced the possibility of seeing his capital cut off or even occupied by the enemy. The symbolic importance of Washington, Paris, London, and Jerusalem loomed large for these war leaders. Lincoln and Ben-Gurion believed that the loss of these capitals would doom their chances of sustaining their young nations. For that reason—and not because of a case of nerves or an inability to see beyond their immediate security—they forced their militaries to devote all resources necessary to their defense. And yet, when later in the Civil War and the Israeli war of independence the tide had turned, their attitude changed. Lincoln was angered by Jubal Early's raid on Washington in 1864, but his coordination of the Union response to it was aimed at speeding the destruction of Lee's army by rendering the Shenandoah Valley useless to the Confederates as a granary and eliminating this exposed fraction of the Army of Northern Virginia. He did not, as Robert E. Lee had hoped, panic and draw off vast forces from the siege of Petersburg, which was slowly but relentlessly strangling the Southern capital and its army. Similarly, once Ben-Gurion believed that the bulk of Jerusalem was secure in Israeli hands he turned his attention, and the resources of the Israel Defense Forces, to operations in other theaters of war.

For Clemenceau and Churchill, on the other hand, leaders of solidly established nation-states, the prospect of losing their capitals was grievous but hardly intolerable. "I will fight before Paris; I will fight in Paris; I will fight behind Paris," Clemenceau declared on 14 June 1918.[17] Churchill, on 14 July 1940, declared that "The vast mass of London itself, fought street by street, could easily devour an entire hostile army; and we would rather see London laid in ruins and ashes than that it would be tamely and abjectly enslaved."[18] They were willing to sacrifice those cities in climactic battles that, even if lost, would not decide the outcome of the war. Both, however, were determined to keep life as normal as possible in cities besieged from the air and, in the case of Paris, under very long-range artillery fire as well.

Finally, moderation manifested itself in all four of these men in the way their emotional state contrasted with that of those around them. Lincoln understood, sooner than most of those around him, that the Civil War would last a very long time indeed. Clemenceau was staunch through his war but gloomy in the evening of his life, foreseeing, one must think, the catastrophe that would sweep over France once he was gone. Churchill's dogged good cheer during the dark days of the Battle of Britain buoyed up an élite, large elements of which thought itself defeated. And yet in 1944 he deprecated the excessive optimism of his colleagues, and in 1945 he gazed ahead with foreboding. Ben-Gurion was "a mourner among those rejoicing" when the UN voted for partition and the state of Israel was declared, yet he was also far more confident than his colleagues of ultimate success.

Moderation is compatible with ruthlessness, and each of these leaders had a deep, dark streak of willingness to do terrible things. In June 1940, only days after Britain's battered ally had succumbed to German invasion, the British Cabinet, at Churchill's insistence, decided to destroy the French fleet where it lay at anchor at Oran. Churchill wrote grimly: "This was a hateful decision, the most unnatural and painful in which I have ever been concerned. . . . On the other hand, the life of the state and the salvation of our cause were at stake. It was Greek tragedy. But no act was ever more necessary for the life of Britain and for all that depended upon it. . . . It was made plain that the British War Cabinet feared nothing and would stop at nothing."[19] True enough; the killing of some 1,300 French sailors reassured President Franklin D. Roosevelt, who was wondering whether Britain would, in fact, stick to the war alone.[20]

Indeed, for all the ruthlessness that they expended on their countries' enemies, what is almost as striking is the hardness with which they could deal with wavering allies or internal opposition. Clemenceau had no hesitation about arresting domestic political opponents and even shooting those engaged in peddling defeatism or German influence in Paris. Ben-Gurion remained, to the end of his life, defiantly convinced that the sinking of the *Altalena* with its cargo of arms, and the attendant deaths of Jewish fighters headed for the newly independent state of Israel, was supremely correct. And Abraham Lincoln, devoted though he was to the Constitution, was also more than willing to suppress the right of *habeas corpus*, impose martial law, and see politicized courts-martial created to stamp out a spirit of defeatism in the Army of the Potomac. Moderation, in other words, is entirely compatible with steel.

These statesmen did not have placid temperaments. Even Lincoln, the gentlest among them, suffered bouts of melancholy and despair—sometimes at moments (like Ben-Gurion) when those around him were most elated—one thinks of his reaction to the battle of Gettysburg, for instance, or his mournful comment to a secretary at the end of 1862, "The bottom is out of the tub." But they remained confident in the darkest hours, and did not hesitate to articulate their fears in the false dawns that they experienced. Churchill had his "black dog," and Ben-Gurion his fits of illness; what lurked behind the mask of the Tiger's glaring defiance we will never know. They knew better than their contemporaries the nature of the struggles upon which they embarked. They faced, moreover, acute opposition from within their own camps, taking the form of votes of no confidence (faced by Churchill in 1942), denunciation in parliament (Clemenceau), internal intrigue (Ben-Gurion), and effective opposition in elections (Lincoln). Their grip on power was far from certain, even as the outcome of their wars was in doubt to the end.

The quality that allowed each to persist was courage. "Courage is what makes the grandeur of man," said Clemenceau, who knew whereof he spoke.[21] "Courage is rightly esteemed the first of human qualities . . . because it is the quality which guarantees all others," Churchill said.[22] They all had physical courage, of course, which may be a more common commodity than one thinks; each was quite willing to expose himself to physical danger, and far more often than their staffs would allow. More important, however, was the kind of courage that Napoleon once called "three-o'clock-in-the-morning courage," and which he described as an essential quality in a general. Not the courage of the impetuous gambler, or the heedless daring of the desperate man, but the courage of a statesman blessed and cursed with the ability to see things as they are, "without illusions" as Dana wrote of Lincoln. In war to see things as they are, and not as one would like them to be, to persevere despite disappointments, to know of numerous opportunities lost and of perils still ahead, to lead knowing that one's subordinates and colleagues are in some cases inadequate, in others hostile, is a courage of a rarer kind than a willingness to expose oneself to the unlucky bullet or shell. Without it, all others would be in vain.

APPENDIX
The Theory of Civilian Control

"A BODY OF MEN DISTINCT FROM THE BODY OF THE PEOPLE"

The issue of civil-military relations is one of the oldest subjects of political science. Plato's *Republic* discusses the difficulties inherent in creating a guardian class who would at once be "gentle to their own and cruel to enemies," men who, like "noble dogs," would serve as the ideal city's guardians.[1] Fear of military dictatorship plagued English and American political philosophers, who saw in both classical and recent history the threats to civil liberty that could arise from large standing armies. As a British parliamentarian put it in the eighteenth century: "[soldiers] are a body of men distinct from the body of the people; they are governed by different laws, and blind obedience, and an entire submission to the orders of their commanding officer, is their only principle . . . it is indeed impossible that the liberties of the people in any country can be preserved where a numerous standing army is kept up."[2] Despotism often wears a uniform, and even in republics such as early twentieth-century France statesmen urgently pondered ways and means of reducing military autonomy and ensuring adequate civilian control of the armed forces of the state. Despite the relatively small size of the peacetime military establishment of the United States, civil-military relations in this country have experienced periodic crises—most notably during the Civil War, when on more than one occasion President Abraham

Lincoln found himself deeply at odds with his generals. The overall record of the American military, however, remains one of complete "subordination and loyalty" to the Constitution.[3] For the United States, and indeed for most democracies, the central problem of civil-military relations has *not* been the most fundamental one—that of preventing a military takeover of the state. For many reasons, including the acculturation of the military itself and the presence of numerous countervailing forces and institutions, that specter has never seriously haunted American statesmen. But the adjustment of relations regarding the preparation and use of force to serve the ends of policy has proven a very different matter.

The notion that if there is no fear of a coup there can be nothing seriously amiss with civil-military relations is one of the greatest obstacles to serious thinking about the subject. The proper roles of the military in shaping foreign policy, in setting the conditions under which it acts, in creating the kind of forces most appropriate for its tasks, in mobilizing civil society to support its activities—these are all contentious issues. The military is almost invariably the largest single element of national government; it claims a vast chunk of its discretionary spending, and it has a monopoly on the legitimate use of force. There is nothing obvious or inevitable about the subordination of the armed forces to the wishes and purposes of the political leadership.

Almost half a century ago, in what became a classic work of political science, Samuel P. Huntington set out a theory of civil-military relations to guide both civilians and soldiers in their relationships. *The Soldier and the State* has ever since set the terms of debate about civil-military relations in this country. A simplified secondhand version of the book has come, in fact, to be commonly viewed as the "normal" theory of civil-military relations—the accepted theoretical standard by which the current reality is to be judged.[4] Like most classics *The Soldier and the State* is more cited than read, and many of its subtleties have been lost on those who have admired it most. But extraordinarily influential it remains.

Huntington begins with an analysis of officership as a profession, much like medicine or the law. Like those vocations, he writes, officership is distinguished by *expertise* in a particular area of human affairs, a sense of *responsibility* that lends an importance transcending monetary rewards to one's work, and *corporateness* or a sense of community and commitment to members of one's group.[5] For Huntington, the central skill of the soldier is the "management of violence," the arts of planning, organizing, and employing military force, but not applying it. At least in ground and naval warfare, officers orchestrate and coordinate the use of force: they do not, except *in extremis*, fight themselves. To be sure, this may mean that "not all officers are professional military officers" in the restricted sense of the term.[6] Those who specialize in career areas not directly related to the management of violence are not truly professional according to this admittedly narrow set of criteria. Neither, by implication, are those whose specialty is the direct *application* of violence rather than its management and planning.

Huntington believes in the distinctiveness of the military mindset. It is, he says in a notable passage, "pessimistic, collectivist, historically inclined, power-oriented, nationalistic, militaristic, pacifist, and instrumentalist in its view of the military profession. It is, in brief, realistic and conservative."[7] To be sure, this is an ideal type. But he maintains that it is powerful nonetheless, and that this military ethos is a source of great strength not merely for the military but for society more broadly. In *The Soldier and the State*'s concluding pages he draws a striking contrast between the appearances and the inner realities of the United States Military Academy at West Point and the neighboring town of Highland Falls, New York—appearances that reflect cultural differences. The austerity and purposefulness of the military order has something to teach, or at least complement, the dazzling heterogeneity and anarchy of democratic society.

Huntington offers a recipe for ensuring civilian dominance over the armed forces, arguing as he does for a sharp division between civilian and military roles. "Objective control"—a form of civilian control based on efforts to increase the professionalism of the officer corps, carving off for it a sphere of action independent of politics—is, in his view, the preferable form of civil-military relations. He contrasts "objective control" with what he calls "subjective control," which aims to tame the military by civilizing it, thus rendering it politically aware, or by controlling it from within with transplanted civilian elites. In the contemporary world those who support this latter means of control are "fusionists" who believe that the old categories of political and military matters are difficult to distinguish.[8] In a previous age these fusionists would have asserted civilian control by keeping officership the preserve of the ruling social class; in the current era they seek to blur the autonomous nature of military professionalism. "The essence of objective civilian control," by way of contrast, "is the recognition of autonomous military professionalism."[9] There is good news here: soldiers not only respect the bounds of democratic politics when subject to objective control, they also fight more effectively. When politicians leave purely military matters to officers, and when they draw clear distinctions between their activities and those of civilians, outstanding military organizations emerge. Officers motivated by dedication to a politically sterile and neutral military ideal—"the good soldier," and "the best regiment"—will turn in a performance superior to those motivated by ideology or merely personal drives such as ambition or vainglory.[10]

This view has profound implications for strategy. Huntington quotes approvingly a Command and General Staff College 1936 publication:

Politics and strategy are radically and fundamentally things apart. Strategy begins where politics ends. All that soldiers ask is that once the policy is settled, strategy and command shall be regarded as being in a sphere apart from politics . . . The line of demarcation must be drawn between politics and strategy, supply, and operations. Having found this line, all sides must abstain from trespassing.[11]

This sharp separation is possible because military expertise is, indeed, definable and isolatable. "The criteria of military efficiency are limited, concrete, and relatively objective; the criteria of political wisdom are indefinite, ambiguous, and highly subjective."[12] Political leaders enhance their control by making the military austerely professional, while reserving to themselves alone the passing of judgments on matters of policy as opposed to technical military matters.

Many democratic politicians and even more of their fellow citizens find the understanding of strategy as craft reassuring. To believe that war is a professional art is to believe that it is not subject to the errors and follies, the bickering and pettiness, the upsets and unpredictabilities that characterize politics. Military expertise, in this view, is a constant.

> The peculiar skill of the military officer is universal in the sense that its essence is not affected by changes in time or location. Just as the qualifications of a good surgeon are the same in Zurich as they are in New York, the same standards of professional military competence apply in Russia as in America and in the nineteenth century as in the twentieth.[13]

Such a belief offers reassurance to perplexed politicians and anxious citizens. As many an injured or sickly patient in desperate straits yearns to trust a doctor with a soothing bedside manner, so too many civilians look to put their reliance in generals who cultivate a calm or dominating demeanor and an attitude of command. Paradoxically, perhaps, it is in matters of life and death that many people become more rather than less trustful of the professionals. And indeed this, in Huntington's view, is how the United States did so well during the Second World War: "So far as the major decisions in policy and strategy were concerned, the military ran the war."[14] And a good thing too, he seems to add.

A simplified Huntingtonian conception of military professionalism remains the dominant view within the American defense establishment.

In the mid-1980s the Congress conducted a debate on military reforms that led to the Goldwater-Nichols Department of Defense Reorganization Act of 1986, which substantially increased the power of the Joint Staff and the chairman of the Joint Chiefs of Staff at the expense of the military services and even, to some extent, that of the office of secretary of defense.[15] Not only did the originators of that legislation explicitly endorse Huntington's reading of American military history; they saw their responsibility as one of providing more and better centralized, autonomous military advice to civilian leaders.[16]

Huntington's theory has particular importance in a period during which the United States finds itself chronically resorting to the use of force. The concept of "objective control" offers a way of coping with the dangers that military organizations pose for democracies—what Tocqueville described as "a restless, turbulent spirit" that "is an evil inherent in the very constitution of democratic armies, and beyond hope of cure.[17] Objective control offers a simple formula for the guidance of politicians and the education of officers and it promises not merely civilian control and constitutional governance but strategic success.

And yet the theory of objective control does not suffice as a description of either what does occur or what should. Scholarly critics have taken issue with its assumptions about the nature of military professionalism and, as we shall see, these views have some foundation. Furthermore, an examination of recent history—including even the relatively successful Gulf war—suggests that the Huntingtonian model of desirable civil-military relations does not characterize conflict. The most successful cases of wartime leadership in a democratic state—Lincoln's stewardship of the Union cause in the American Civil War, Winston Churchill's conduct of British affairs during World War II, or David Ben-Gurion's skillful handling of Israeli war policy during the country's struggle for existence—reveal nothing like the rigid separations dictated by the "normal" theory of civil-military relations.

CRITICS OF THE "NORMAL" THEORY

The standard conception of military professionalism, despite its general acceptance, nonetheless attracted criticism from a number of sources. Historian Allen Guttmann contended that Huntington had misinterpreted American history in constructing his argument.[18] Rather than being isolated from the American polity in the late nineteenth and early twentieth centuries and during the interwar years, Guttmann argued, American officers were in fact quite representative of it. And rather than adhering to a conservative world view at odds with that of the broader society, they shared the pragmatic and democratic views of American society generally. Huntington detects and approves of a deep tension between civil and military values, and asserts the value of military detachment from society. Guttmann rejects that assessment and deprecates Huntington's endorsement of it.

Huntington's ideal officer is a well-defined aristocratic type—a Helmuth von Moltke, to take a Continental example—who is at once patriotic and yet, in some fashion, almost above patriotism in his sense of membership in the brotherhood of arms. Where Huntington noted and celebrated the honor of soldiers as a central aspect of the military way, Guttmann points out the stubborn pragmatism of American generals. Guttmann observes that such quintessentially American figures as Stonewall Jackson had little sense of the punctilious chivalry that European officers admired, and that (in his view) characterize Huntington's theory.[19] When a Confederate colonel reporting on the successful and bloody repulse of a Yankee attack expressed his admiration for the enemy's bravery and his regret at having to kill such courageous foes, Jackson replied, "No. Shoot them all. *I* do not wish them to be brave."[20] Other observers of the American military, taking a somewhat different tack but arriving at a similar conclusion, note the conventionality of its officer corps, which is solidly middle class in its values and aspirations and thus firmly anchored in the society from which it emerges.[21] Huntington's hopes for creative tension between civilian and military values find no resonance in a military that watches the same television programs and listens to the same music as society at large.

Sociologist Morris Janowitz and others have made a similar if more contemporary argument. The traditional notion of professionalism has weakened, they contend, as war itself has changed. "As a result of the complex machinery of warfare, which has weakened the line between military and nonmilitary organization, the military establishment has come more and more to display the characteristics typical of any large-scale organization."[22] While Huntington's concept of "objective control" may have made sense in the age of the World Wars, the nuclear revolution gave birth to "a convergence of military and civilian organization." Janowitz proposes what he calls a "constabulary concept" of officership—one dedicated to the limited use of force in carefully defined circumstances.[23] He draws a distinction between "heroic leaders, who embody traditionalism and glory, and military 'managers,' who are concerned with the scientific and rational conduct of war."[24] There is little doubt in his mind that it is the modern military managers who are winning out, and a good thing too, he seems to believe. Janowitz thus appears to have accepted Huntington's definition of military professionalism but to have smoothed off its rough edges: where Huntington anticipates—indeed welcomes—a divergence between civilian and military values as a by-product of professionalism, Janowitz sees no such necessity.

Other military sociologists have gone even further. In 1977 Charles Moskos suggested that the military had begun a slow, but steady transformation from an institution—"legitimated in terms of values and norms"—to an occupation—"legitimated in terms of the marketplace, i.e., prevailing monetary rewards for equivalent competencies."[25] The increasing harmonization of military and civilian pay scales, the reduction of special military perquisites (e.g., the PX and the commissary) seemed to him to weaken the distinctiveness of the military way of life. Implicitly, at any rate, all militaries exist under some form of what

Huntington would call "subjective control." Indeed, one optimistic scholar proposes a theory of "concordance" in which "the very idea of 'civil' may be inappropriate."[26] It is a theory of "dialogue, accommodation, and shared values or objectives among the military, the political elites, and society."[27] In some ways, this practically defines away the problem of civil-military relations.

Disagree as they might, Huntington and these critics of his ideas both deliver reassuring if conflicting messages. For Huntington the good news lies in his discovery that those elements of the military persona and outlook that liberal America finds unsettling (indeed, he contends that "liberalism does not understand and is hostile to military institutions and the military function")[28] are, in fact, not merely functional but desirable. For Guttmann, Janowitz, and Moskos the good news was just the reverse: the military *resembles* America, shares its élite's values and, increasingly, parallels its social origins and way of life. As the all-out conflicts of the nineteenth and twentieth centuries gave way to more limited struggles, the military internalized civilian views of how it should conduct military operations. The stark differences between the military and civilian mind, so central to Huntington's theory, have blurred.

For neither Huntington nor his critics, however, is there anything intrinsically problematic about combining civilian control and military effectiveness, in peace or in war. Indeed, for more than one writer the term "civilian control" is a faintly absurd echo of dark popular fantasies like the 1964 film *Seven Days in May*, in which the military tries to take over the government.[29] "The concept of civilian control of the military has little significance for contemporary problems of national security in the United States,"[30] wrote one author in 1961—a dubious assertion, it now appears, at the beginning of a decade that spawned some of the most destructive tensions between civilians and soldiers the United States has ever seen. Similarly, in 1985 Congressional staff drawing up legislation aimed at enhancing the power of the military declared that "instances of American commanders overstepping the bounds of their authority have been rare. . . . None of these pose any serious threat to civilian control of the military."[31]

Neither Guttmann nor Janowitz nor Moskos, we should note, delve into civil-military relations in wartime. They accept much though not all of Huntington's characterization of America's military history in war. Indeed, some of the most influential writings on civil-military relations criticizing Huntington barely mention warfare at all.[32] And, in fact, most of the civil-military-relations literature, with the exception of Huntington, has somewhat oddly steered away from close examination of what happens during wartime.

An exception is British scholar S. E. Finer, whose critique of Huntington is very different from his American counterparts'. He argues that Huntington has severely *under*estimated the problem of civilian control. Blessed with the advantages of centralized command, hierarchy, discipline, and cohesion, and embodying virtues (bravery, patriotism, and discipline, for example) that civil society finds attractive, the military can resist civilian control effectively.[33] Noting that one of the armies that Huntington has praised as the most professional—the German—has repeatedly intervened in politics, Finer suggests that military professionalism could in fact incline militaries to engage in politics rather than not.[34] And in wartime in particular civilians are often too insecure about their knowledge, too fearful of public opinion, and too overawed by their military's expertise to exercise much control at all. "'War is too important to be left to the generals.' Few civilians seem to have agreed with this and still fewer generals," Finer writes.[35] A difference in national experience may have been at work here as well. In the United States the archetypal civil-military conflict was between the imperious general Douglas MacArthur and the doughty president Harry Truman, a confrontation crisply decided by the dismissal of the former by the latter. For British authors, the Curragh mutiny (or, as some would prefer, "incident") of 1914, in which a group of cavalry officers (fifty-seven out of seventy in one brigade) offered their resignations rather than suppress Ulster loyalists determined to keep Northern Ireland part of the United Kingdom, presents a more typical and a more disturbing threat to civilian control.[36] More instructive yet in the British experience is the struggle between civilian and military leadership during World War I. Prime Minister David Lloyd George believed himself thwarted and even endangered by a military clique resting on an alliance between the Chief of the Imperial General Staff, Sir William Robertson, and the commander of British forces in France, Field Marshal Sir Douglas Haig, aided by docile civilian politicians and journalists.[37] Finer contends that by construing civilian control too narrowly, as the formal subordination of the military to the civilian power, and particularly in peacetime, one may underestimate the difficulty of controlling the use of military power in wartime. Precisely because, unlike most other students of civil-military relations, Finer has looked at war, he has a considerably more pessimistic view of the prospect for civilian control.

A DISSENT: STRATEGIC NIHILISM

There is yet another school of thought, rarely taught in war colleges or countenanced in the corridors of power, which rejects the normal theory root and branch. If believed, this view would undermine the very possibility of civilian war leadership, because it is a doctrine of *strategic nihilism*, which denies the purposefulness of war, and of *anthropological determinism*, which substitutes an understanding of the officer as warrior for that of the officer as professional. Huntington and his critics understand the use of force as an activity subject to rational control: they disagree about the importance of professionalism understood as isolation from civil society and the nature of controlled violence in the nuclear age. This third school of thought actively rejects the premise of rationality.

The most famous of strategic nihilists is Leo Tolstoy. Although many of his readers have found his philosophy merely a diversion from his tale of the Bolkonskys and the Rostovs, his masterwork, *War and Peace*, represents a serious and coherent meditation on war by one who had witnessed it close up and studied it at length.[38] When Tolstoy's heroes encounter battle they learn that it has none of the regularity and form that they had expected. Pierre Bezukhov, his hero, comes to the field of Borodino and is baffled: he "could not even distinguish our troops from the enemy's."[39] As he soon learns at first hand, actual fighting is infinitely more chaotic than even the preliminary chaos of these initial deployments suggests.

Bezukhov's friend, the doomed Prince Andrei Bolkonsky, is a professional soldier whose dreams of high command wither as he learns the truth about war. After aspiring to imitate, in some measure, his hero and his country's enemy Napoleon, Andrei gradually realizes that military genius is a fraud. He declares that "there was not and could not be a science of war, and consequently no such thing as military genius." When asked why, he replies:

What theory or science is possible where the conditions and circumstances are unknown and cannot be determined, and especially where the strength of the active forces cannot be ascertained? . . . You can't foresee anything. Sometimes—when there is not a coward in front to cry: "We are cut off!" and start running, but a brave, spirited man who shouts "Hurrah!"—a detachment of five thousand is worth fifty thousand, as at Schöngraben, while at other times fifty thousand will flee from eight thousand, as at Austerlitz. What science can there be in a matter in which, as in every practical matter, nothing can be determined and everything depends on innumerable conditions, the significance of which becomes manifest at a particular moment, and no one can tell when that moment will come?[40]

Tolstoy, at times, dispenses with his characters and lectures his readers directly on this score, telling them that Napoleon and Alexander of

Russia had no real control of the unfolding of the terrible war between France and Russia, "because their will depended on that of millions of men who actually had to do things.. . . . A king is the slave of history. . . ."[41] The notion that millions of soldiers were killed or maimed because of politics is absurd, in Tolstoy's view, in part because the causes are so trivial and the actual events so monstrous.[42] Shortly before his death Prince Andrei learns that generals are only called geniuses because of the prestige of their positions, and because of mankind's overwhelming propensity to flatter those in power. "The best generals I have known were, in fact, stupid or absent-minded men," Prince Andrei concludes. And, indeed the most successful general of them all, Kutuzov, is notable in Tolstoy's account chiefly for his unwillingness to act in any way like a conventional, purposive strategist.

For Tolstoy the falsehood of military history lies in its necessary reductionism, its deceitful attempt to merge a myriad of actions by individuals or very small groups into larger coherent aggregates. There is, he observed bitterly, "the necessity of lying" when one discusses the actions of thousands of fearful men spread over several miles of ground.[43] The account of the course of a battle, and no less of the course of a campaign as described by the military historians, is nothing more or less than a fraud, imposed by rationalists on a world that escapes understanding.[44] Yet historians and contemporaries alike regard battles as the building blocks statesmen and generals use to build a strategic edifice. By showing the essential component of strategy—the battle, with its unities of time, place, and action—to be a tissue of lies, Tolstoy calls into question the very notion of strategy itself.[45]

One might say that a novelist's account of war is bound to underplay the role of strategy, if only because his story focuses so keenly on the individual rather than the collective predicament. Yet Tolstoy's views resonate in the writings of formidable military historians as well. Gerhard Ritter, the great German historian of civil-military relations and war planning; Russell Weigley, one of the foremost American military historians of the last half century; and John Keegan, perhaps the most widely read of late-twentieth-century military historians; each in different ways questions or even repudiates strategy in our sense of harnessing war to political ends. By so doing they make the problem of civilian wartime leadership out to be insuperable. Theirs is a counsel of despair, but worth examination nonetheless.

Ritter, in his crowning work *The Sword and the Scepter: The Problem of Militarism in Germany*, sympathizes with the Clausewitzian desire to subordinate war to politics, but argues that the Prussian theorist substantially underestimated the difficulty of doing so. Ritter agrees with Finer in this, saying, "In wartime, politicians always have a hard time gaining and maintaining authority against successful generals."[46] He attributes some of the intrinsic tension between soldiers and statesmen from Moltke to Bismarck to a difference in perspective, with the former seeking to achieve the maximum possible with the means at hand, the latter to build and preserve order, albeit through the use of military means.[47] The problem of civil-military relations lies in harmonizing "the military stance and the principle of constructive peace," which are intrinsically at odds. Ritter makes a narrower and more empirical observation as well. The harmonization of war and politics runs afoul of human nature, which is considerably less lofty and disinterested than Clausewitz assumes.

> Clausewitz's theory of war predicates statesmen whose characters are utterly pervaded by impulses of grandeur, heroism, honor, national power, and freedom, men who are motivated by calm political reason far above petty intrigue or advantage rather than by blind hatred. He further presupposes soldiers accustomed to regard themselves as loyal servants of their supreme commander, never in danger of being ruled by political ambitions or jealousies, military men to whom the thought does not even occur that they might oppose their sovereign warlord or exploit popular support for their own purposes. Not in a single line does Clausewitz even so much as hint that the situation might be very different.[48]

Here is an argument quite different from Huntington's ascription to the officer corps of a conservative, and to (democratic) politicians, a generally liberal outlook—different world views to be sure, but both serious and coherent intellectual positions and moral commitments. In Germany's master concept for the opening stages of the First World War, the Schlieffen Plan, Ritter saw a tragic and more typical case of strategy dragging policy along with it.[49] Politicians had a vague concept of what the plan entailed (although the German Foreign Ministry did not learn of it from the General Staff until December 1912—at least seven years after its inception), but were unable or unwilling to deal with its political implications.[50] As appalling a case as the Schlieffen Plan was, the course of German civil-military relations throughout World War I was even more dramatic testimony to the difficulty of forging strategy. Mediocre statesmanship and a blinkered, aggressive military class are the norm, Ritter seems to say, which means that Clausewitzian strategy is unlikely to succeed.

Weigley, following Ritter, rejects strategy as a near impossibility. Indeed, he cites with approval Ritter's conception of "the essentially demoniac character of power," as a nearly insuperable obstacle to the practical implementation of political control in war.[51] Weigley believes that "the logic that drives war toward remorseless revolutionary struggle" almost prevents it from being usable as an implement of policy.[52] Indeed, in the twentieth century "warfare sets its own purposes."[53] No regime, he argues, be it democratic, monarchical, or totalitarian, has been able to make war "a disciplined tool of policy rather than an autonomous force."[54] To be sure, there have been exceptional civilian leaders like Lincoln who came close to the classical ideal of a statesman who could make war serve political ends. But even he was stretched to the limit, too burdened with responsibilities "to spend much of his time practicing the art of military strategy."[55] More typical is the sinister tendency of war to militarize civilians, to make them succumb to the logic of military operations, forfeiting long-range political calculations for the imperatives of campaigning today. Thus, even cases of apparently effective control by civilian politicians over the exercise of military force are deceiving: statesmen serve as no more than spokesmen for the gods of battle.

Ritter and Weigley do not necessarily deplore the attempt to forge and implement strategy. For Weigley the search for strategy in the eighteenth century reflected an understandable but futile desire to avoid the calamities of chronic warfare that had bedeviled seventeenth-century Europe. "The quest for decisive battle was the educated soldier's rationalist effort to make war cost-effective, the promptness of the decision through battle promising to prevent an inordinate drain upon the resources of the state."[56] Yet this eighteenth-century quest, which persisted through the nineteenth and twentieth, failed. Attrition and exhaustion, not harmonious adjustment of ends and means, have decided war's outcomes. War may conceivably avert some developments—it could block the French or German attempts to achieve Continental hegemony, for example—but it can achieve no positive purpose.[57] It is the crudest of the tools that statecraft has at its disposal. Carl von Clausewitz once said that war has its own grammar (combat) but not its own logic (politics). In the strategic nihilist's view, that grammar overwhelms all but the simplest logic.

John Keegan rejects the possibility of strategy based on a Huntingtonian relationship of ends and means for yet a third reason, namely, that strategy is incompatible with the nature of the men who wage it. He is, if anything, more acerbic and definitive than his fellow antistrategists. "I am increasingly tempted towards the belief that there is no such thing as 'strategy' at all."[58] Or, "Politics played no part in the conduct of the First World War worth mentioning."[59] But his reasons for rejecting strategy differ from those of Tolstoy or Ritter and Weigley. "War is wholly unlike diplomacy or politics because it must be fought by men whose values and skills are not those of politicians or diplomats."[60] Keegan contends that there is a distinctive military way, one that in many respects transcends cultures ("there is only one warrior culture") and is inimical to politics. Profoundly ambivalent to soldiers themselves, Keegan argues that societies have attempted to tame warriors by putting them in the mold of what he calls "the regimental soldier." These "artificially preserved warrior bands" have served important roles in modern states, but Keegan believes that their day is waning—and he has said as much for some time. In his first and best known book, *The Face of Battle*, he suggested that classic battle, and with it, the classic warrior, was heading down the path to obsolescence. The last sentence of that work, in fact, has it that "the suspicion grows that battle has already abolished itself."[61]

Keegan rejects what he terms the Clausewitzian model of war—one which involves the rational control of violence to serve political ends—because he believes that the human implementers of strategy, and not simply the instrumentality of battle, are intrinsically unsuited to their task. The warrior spirit is ineluctably opposed to politics and will take war in directions that make no political sense. Keegan recognizes the admirable qualities of the warrior, and would seek to retain the best of his virtues, but believes that this can be done only by transforming the traditional military function. In making this argument Keegan falls back on a long tradition that celebrates the martial virtues while deploring their manifestation in war, an urge that seeks to retain such values as courage, fidelity, and audacity but to redirect them. William James calling for the "moral equivalent of war" in strenuous public service or modern students of the martial arts celebrating "the new warrior" each, in different ways, have attempted to carry through Keegan's project.[62]

Keegan would regard both Huntington's and Janowitz's conception of military professionalism as naïvely optimistic. Much of Keegan's argument rests on an attack on—one might almost say a visceral detestation of—the classical Clausewitzian view of the relationship between war and politics. "War . . . need not imply politics, since the values of many of those who make war—warriorism and warriors respectively— reject deterrence and diplomacy for action."[63] According to Keegan, Clausewitz views military power as a mere scalpel in the hand of a statesman-surgeon, but fails to understand that "warrior values can and do supplant those of politics."[64] Strategic nihilists, like nihilists generally, do not offer practical prescriptions, of course, but the implications of their views—not altogether unfounded—further undermine the assumptions required to make Huntington's prescription for sound civil-military relations work.

THE EXCEPTIONAL PROFESSION

Despite these various rebuttals of Huntington's argument, his general concept still stands and retains its popularity. Military life has witnessed many changes, but it nonetheless remains a way apart—a point brought home to the Clinton administration in 1993, when the president attempted to lift the US military's ban on homosexuals serving in uniform. Journalist Tom Ricks may have said it best when he described life in today's military as "what Lyndon Johnson's Great Society could have been. . . . It is almost a Japanese version of America—relatively harmonious, extremely hierarchical, and nearby always placing the group above the individual."[65] With its distinctive way of life on self-contained bases, a perhaps anachronistic commitment to service, discipline, and honor continue to pervade an institution that, for example, will still penalize a senior officer for adultery—a sin usually overlooked by the civilian society around it.

Those who predicted a mere constabulary role for the military, hence its transmutation into a kind of heavily armed police force, have also been proven wrong. Two real wars—Vietnam and the Persian Gulf—have been fought between the time those predictions appeared and the present day. The rarity of large wars is not, of itself, an indication of the obsolescence of the military profession understood as the management of large-scale force. There are other explanations including the configuration of international politics in which one country, the United States, dominates all others, and the possession of overwhelming power by the status quo dominant nations. Even so, Keegan's curious declaration that "the suspicion grows that battle has already abolished itself"[66] rings hollow, followed as it has been by conventional conflicts such as the Falklands, Lebanon, Persian Gulf, and Yugoslav wars, to name only the larger ones.

Furthermore, and contrary to what proponents of the "constabulary function" of the military suggest, the minor interventions, demonstrations of force, and peacekeeping operations of today do not diverge from the norms of the past. Soldiers and Marines of a bygone era suppressed hostile Indians and Nicaraguan rebels; their counterparts today have returned to Haiti, invaded Grenada, overthrown a Panamanian dictator, dueled with Somali tribesmen, and suppressed Serb paramilitaries. The differences do not look all that great. As intellectually intriguing as the arguments of the strategic nihilists might be, they too have proven ultimately unconvincing. Some wars and lesser uses of force clearly achieved their objectives (for example, Egypt's October 1973 campaign which broke the Arab-Israeli peace deadlock, or the Gulf war). Beyond this, nihilism is ultimately a doctrine of irresponsibility that provides no standards of conduct for either statesman or soldier. Even Finer's dispute with Huntington seems to be confounded by the apparent deference of military leaders to their civilian superiors. With the sole exception of the MacArthur controversy, and perhaps not even that, the Western world has not recently witnessed the kind of virulent antipathy between "brass hats" and "frocks" that in 1914–1918 characterized civil-military relations in both Britain and France.

There is, however, another possible critique of Huntington's theory, and that rests on his and his critics' conception of professionalism. Put simply, it is that although officership is a profession, it differs in many respects from all others: in some of the most important respects it does not, in fact, resemble medicine or the law. Indeed, the Huntingtonian construct represents a concept of professionalism prevalent in the 1950s, but since challenged in many spheres as unrealistically pristine; "incomprehensibility to laymen, rather than rationality, is the foundation of professionalism," in the acid words of a scholar writing in the more cynical 1970s.[67] Officership differs in a number of important ways from other professions. Unlike law, medicine, or engineering, it binds its members to only one employer, the government, and has only one fundamental structure—the large service branch. But other differences are more important, in particular those bearing on the goals of the professional activity and the nature of the expertise involved.

All professional activities present difficulties of moral choice and ultimate purpose to those who practice them. The wrenching choices involved in the treatment of terminally ill patients are well known; so too are the ethical dilemmas of a lawyer who becomes privy to knowledge of the criminal activities of his client. But by and large in the professions of law and medicine, on which the classic conception of professionalism is based, the ultimate goals are fairly straightforward. They are, for the doctor, to cure his patients of their diseases, or at least to alleviate the pain they suffer. Occasionally, of course, these two imperatives conflict. For the lawyer they are, at least within the American legal system, to achieve the best possible result (be it acquittal, or, in civil cases, maximum financial and other forms of redress) for his clients.

The soldier's ultimate purposes are altogether hazier: they are, as Clausewitz and others insist, the achievement of political ends designated by statesmen. But because political objectives are just that—political—they are often ambiguous, contradictory, and uncertain. It is one of the greatest sources of frustration for soldiers that their political masters find it difficult (or what is worse from their point of view, merely inconvenient) to fully elaborate in advance the purposes for which they have invoked military action, or the conditions under which they intend to limit or terminate it. The "professional" concept of military activity, moreover, depicts political purpose in war as purely a matter of foreign policy; and yet in practice the "high" politics of war is suffused as well with "low" or domestic politics. President Lincoln wants a victory at Atlanta in the summer of 1864 in order to crush the

Confederacy—but also to boost his own chances of reelection, which in turn is necessary for the ultimate victory of the Union. President Roosevelt dismisses professional military advice and orders an invasion of North Africa in 1942 rather than a landing in France in 1943—this, he explains, in order to engage American public opinion in the fight in the European theater, rather than in hopes of achieving an early end to the war. President Johnson limits air attacks on Hanoi and Haiphong in 1965–1968 in part to preserve his ability to launch the Great Society, but also to limit the chances that China will enter the war.

The traditional conception of military professionalism assumes that it is possible to segregate an autonomous area of military science from political purpose.[68] In many ways one can. Frequently, however, a seemingly sharp separation crumbles when it encounters the real problems of war. Consider the question confronted by the Allies in the late summer and fall of 1944 in France: whether to advance on a wide front or to concentrate scarce logistical resources behind a northern thrust along the French, Belgian, and Dutch coasts (directed by a British general) or a southern thrust into central Germany (directed by an American general). One might say that there was a military "best answer," assuming that the ultimate objective was simply the defeat of Germany—which in turn incorrectly assumes that the word "defeat" lends itself to a simple definition. But in fact the political objectives of even the Second World War were far more complex than that; they involved questions of cost in lives and treasure, minimization of damage to Allied civilian populations (including Londoners under threat from V-2 missiles launched in Holland), and matters of national prestige. These were not political modifications to a "military" objective of defeating Germany, but essential to it. "The distinction between politics and strategy diminishes as the point of view is raised. At the summit true politics and strategy are one."[69] Careless readers of Huntington have missed his awareness that these kinds of mixed political-military decisions do indeed occur; in truth, they occur even more frequently than the "normal" theory would suggest.

That the good military officer requires technical expertise no one would deny. But is it indeed true that "the peculiar skill of the military officer is universal" across time, nationality, and place? The qualifications of a good North Vietnamese infantry officer in Indochina in 1965 would surely have differed in some important respects from those of a good American officer opposing him. The Vietnamese would have needed a ruthless disregard for his own men's suffering and casualties that would have rendered an American not merely morally unfit to command, but a likely candidate for "fragging"—assassination—by his own men. He could have easily remained ignorant of large areas of technical knowledge (for example, the employment of close air support, or planning procedures for heliborne movements) that the American required. More than one author has suggested that the Vietnam failure stemmed at least in part from the stubborn resistance of American officers to adapting their conception of professionalism to the war before them. And American bafflement when facing unconventional opponents like Somalia's Muhammad Farah Aideed reflects, in part, the American military's reluctance to walk away from an essentially conventional conception of what it is to be "a professional."[70]

Huntington's assertion that, in the modern age at any rate, professional armies are better armies may require at least some revision, although it is a belief in which many regular armies take comfort.[71] The more research is done on one of the most formidable fighting machines of all time, the German Wehrmacht, the greater the role of its ideology appears to be.[72] For a generation after World War II scholars attributed the fighting abilities of the Germans in World War II to neutral, professional characteristics: small-unit cohesion and careful practices of officer and noncommissioned officer selection and recruitment.[73] More prolonged and careful investigation, however, has revealed that the permeation of the German army by Nazi ideology made it a better fighting force.[74] Not only did it instill in a large proportion of its men a fanatic determination to fight—it also contributed indirectly to the maintenance of tactical effectiveness. The ruthlessness of the Nazis allowed for the harshest possible repression of dissent or doubt. The Germans, who had executed forty-eight of their own men during World War I, shot somewhere between 13,000 and 15,000 during World War II; the comparable numbers for the British army were 356 in World War I and 40 in World War II.[75] At the same time, the Hitler Jugend provided a reserve of junior officers and leaders while Nazi ideology reinforced the central virtues of military leadership, including selflessness, physical courage, and initiative.[76] Perhaps the greatest proof of the contribution of ideology lies in the record of the units of the Waffen-SS, which by war's end constituted no less than a quarter of Germany's army, and which repeatedly turned in an outstanding fighting performance. Of Theodor Eicke, the leader of one of the most successful of the Waffen-SS divisions, the *Totenkopf* (Death's Head), one historian notes: "Eicke's style of leadership differed little in practice from the methods he had used to administer the prewar concentration camp system. . . . What he lacked in formal training, imagination, and finesse, he attempted to overcome through diligence, energy, and a constant effort to master the baffling technical intricacies of mechanized war."[77] Eicke was a successful military leader not in spite of those characteristics that would have earned him a trial for his numerous crimes against humanity had he survived the war, but because of them.

Nor is the German experience unique. Ideological armies—the Chinese People's Liberation Army, the international brigades in the Spanish Civil War, and the preindependence Palmach in Palestine are all examples—have often turned in superior tactical performances against larger and better equipped regular forces. The ideologically motivated fighter may make a good junior officer—he often embodies the self-sacrifice, integrity, and drive the leaders of soldiers in battle require. More than a few higher-level commanders as well have—like Eicke, albeit in very different causes—demonstrated high orders of ability.[78]

If the content of military professionalism is, as Huntington contends, the "management of violence," that is a definition that excludes large areas of military activity (logistics, for example) which often have considerable civilian analogues and yet are indispensable to military operations.[79] Many of these skills are readily transferable to or from the civilian world. It is no accident that the US Army's chief logistician in the Persian Gulf, Lieutenant General Gus Pagonis, became, immediately upon retirement, an extremely successful executive at Sears, in the same way that the military rapidly promoted civilian executives to high military rank during the World Wars. Moreover, although all serious modern military organizations devote a great deal of effort to schooling and training, history is filled with examples of soldiers taken up from civilian life who very quickly master the essentials of military affairs. The World Wars offer examples of great soldiers who spent only brief peacetime periods of their life in regular military organizations, and then flourished in times of actual war. General Sir John Monash, one of the best generals of World War I, was a civil engineer whose prewar experience consisted solely of militia duty. Yet he rose to command perhaps the most formidable of all Allied units, the Australian Imperial Force.[80] There are hardly any accounts, even a century ago, of self-taught or part-time doctors and engineers performing nearly so well.

Military professionalism is job-specific, much as business management is. Brilliant entrepreneurs may prove utterly unable to cope with the problems of running the corporations their creative genius brought into the world. Skilled managers of a long-established high-technology firm like IBM would probably find it difficult to assume equal responsibilities in an entertainment company like Disney. There is, to be sure, enough commonality in management experience to make it plausible to put a former manufacturer of repeating rifles in charge of a large ice cream company (Ben & Jerry's), but that does not guarantee success. The ruthless churning of higher management in many companies reflects what might be thought of as "wartime" conditions—a ceaseless turnover of executives who, though qualified by training and experience for the highest office, nonetheless prove unfit for their tasks, exhausted by their previous work, or merely, but fatally, unlucky. In this above all they resemble generals in an intense war. This should not surprise us, for in some sense businesses fight their "wars" every day, unlike military organizations.

This observation suggests a deeper problem with the notion of expertise in the management of violence as the essence of the military profession. Where lawyers continually appear in court or draw up legal instruments, where doctors routinely operate or prescribe medication, where engineers build bridges or computers, soldiers very rarely manage violence, or at least not large-scale violence. They prepare to manage violence; they anticipate its requirements; they study past uses of violence, but they very rarely engage in the central activity that defines their profession. In the words of one British general writing after World War I:

> Imagine an immense railway system, created but not in use, held in reserve to meet a definite emergency which may emerge on any indefinite date, a date certain (with the British) to be fixed by the Directors of another, and a rival, system, instead of by its own. Once a year, and once a year only, the railway is allowed to be partially opened to traffic for a week (maneuvers): for the remaining fifty-one weeks not only are there no train services, but the locomotives are stripped, many of their essential parts being stacked in out-of-the-way parts of the Kingdom. Yet, let the signal be given, and in four days' time the parts of the engines have to be assembled, wheels have to be fixed to dismantled trucks, cushions have to be fixed to the first-class carriages, the personnel must be at their posts, the coal—mountains of it—has to be on the spot, and a huge, complicated, most rapid and crowded process of transportation and movement comes straightway into being—provided—the rival company has not sandbagged the manager or dropped a few bombs upon the terminus.[81]

Many, perhaps most, officers spend entire military careers without participating in a real way in war. And even those who do fight in wars do so for very small portions of their careers, and very rarely occupy the same position in more than one conflict. A lawyer may try hundreds of cases, or a doctor treat hundreds or even thousands of medical problems, of an essentially similar type during the course of several decades; a soldier will usually have only one chance to serve in a particular capacity. There are few generals who have had the experience of being divisional or corps commanders—let alone theater commanders or chiefs of general staffs—in more than one war. As a result then, particularly at the beginning of a war, a country's most senior leaders—nominally the most seasoned veterans—are in a professional position as close to that of the novice lawyer or doctor as to that of the senior partner in a law firm or the chief surgeon in a hospital.

The lack of practice military people have in their profession at the highest level is only one factor in the astounding, and by no means infrequent, catastrophic errors made by supposedly competent military organizations.[82] The errors of the Schlieffen Plan were not merely political but logistical: those who concocted it had assumed away problems of supply and marching endurance that made it nearly impossible of execution. The highly skilled tacticians of Germany launched in March 1918 the ruinous MICHAEL offensive, which shattered the German army and made inevitable their country's defeat. The pioneering air generals of the US Army Air Forces in World War II embarked upon a ruinous, unescorted daylight precision-bombing campaign against Germany that collapsed in the Schweinfurt débacles of 1943. The Israelis in 1973 adhered to a doctrine of tank warfare that proved utterly unsuited against modern hand-held anti-tank weapons, and as a result suffered heavy losses in the first days of fighting against Egyptian infantry armed with portable missiles and rocket-propelled grenades. The United States Army in Vietnam, led by experienced and able veterans of World War II, adopted a strategy of "search and destroy" predicated on entirely false assumptions about its ability to control the loss rates of the Vietnamese Communists.[83] These and other calamities stem not from incompetence as normally understood, but from the features that make the

waging of war different from other professions: the distorting psychological effects of fear, hatred, and the desire for glory; the nature of a
reacting opponent; and the absence of rules that bound the activity
concerned. As Clausewitz observed, "every war is rich in unique
episodes. Each is an uncharted sea, full of reefs."[84] Each age has its
"own theory of war, even if the urge has always and universally existed
to work things out on scientific principles."[85] War is too varied an
activity for a single set of professional norms.

THE UNEQUAL DIALOGUE

One should not carry such arguments against a rigid division of "professional" and "political" too far. Clearly, no one fresh from the office
or the classroom can command an aircraft carrier or an armored division, much less pilot a fighter plane or repair an infantry fighting
vehicle. The politician who plans his own commando operation will
almost surely regret it. More than one group of revolutionary leaders,
from Bolshevik commissars in 1919 to Iranian mullahs over half a
century later have, willy nilly, turned to officer experts whom they
may not have trusted but whose services they required. Enough of the
officer's code survives, despite the allure of a materialistic culture, to
make concepts like honor distinguishing characteristics of the military
way. "The officer's honor is of paramount importance," write founding
members of the Army's Center for the Professional Military Ethic.[86]
That a profession of arms exists—even though a more amorphous
one than one might at first think—cannot be doubted. Even at the
height of the Cold War an eminent British officer could detach the
purposes of warfare from professionalism: "I suppose there are some,
in Western countries, who have become professional fighting men to
fight Communism, though I hope not."[87] It is a remark instantly comprehensible to other professional soldiers, if not perhaps to most
citizens.

Besides, a repudiation of "objective control" carries with it grave risks. To reject Huntington's idea of sequestering issues of policy from those of military administration or operations is to open the way to a military that is politicized and, by virtue of its size and discipline, a potentially dominant actor in the conduct of foreign and internal affairs. In states with less-established democratic traditions such changes would open the path to direct military intervention in politics. Huntington is correct in his contention that such partisanship will eventually diminish military proficiency.

But the "normal" theory still requires emendation in its understanding of the military profession and hence in its understanding of civilian control. If, as argued above, officership is a unique profession, military expertise is variable and uncertain, and if the boundaries between political ends and military means are more uncertain than Huntington suggests, civilian control must take on a form different from that of "objective control," at least in its original understanding.

ACKNOWLEDGMENTS

This book took far too long to write, for reasons which need not be discussed here. That it finally saw the light of day is due to the support and assistance of many friends, colleagues, and co-workers. Above all others, I owe a debt to my wife, Judy, who nudged without nagging, and whose faith in this book and its author kept him pledged to its completion. A string of research assistants, who have gone on to various exciting endeavors after helping with source-sleuthing, footnote-chasing, and editing, were indispensable: particular thanks go to Luli Aguilera, A. Heather Coyne, Richard Do, Scott Douglas, Daniel Ginsberg, Lyle Goldstein, Lawrence Kaplan, Gal Luft, Peter McCormick, Sean McDonald, Johanna Moehring, Tammy Schultz (an indefatigable proofreader as well), Jonathan Schwarz, Kevin Tehan, William Young, Kimberlee Zeppegno, and Laurence Zuriff. Donna Vandish, Gina Johnson, and Thayer McKell, program coordinators for the Strategic Studies program which I direct, did their best to protect my time for scholarship.

To my students, and in particular to those who took "Soldiers, Statesmen, and the Use of Force," I owe a debt of gratitude for stimulation and constructive disagreement. Tom Donnelly, Tom Ehrhard, and Mike Vickers have always been particularly ferocious and distressingly cogent in argument. "I have learned much from my teachers, more from my colleagues, and most from my students," said an ancient rabbi, and from them and so many others I can now confirm the truth of that statement.

Writing is a lone task, but not so the sharing of scholarship. Mike Abramowitz, Andy Bacevich, Dick Betts, Tami Biddle, Tom Keaney, Dick

Kohn, Bill Kristol, Wick Murray, Doug Porch, Tom Ricks, Alex Roland, and Stephen Rosen read this manuscript, discussed its ideas with me, and improved it in many ways with their criticism and suggestions. I am fortunate indeed to have such colleagues and more, such friends.

The Woodrow Wilson International Center for Scholars provided the leisure and resources for the writing of much of this book, for which I am particularly grateful to Lee Hamilton, Robert Litwak, and Sam Wells. The Smith Richardson Foundation funded a good deal of the research: Devon Cross and Marin Strmecki there have been steadfast friends and supporters throughout. Several research institutions over-seas were most helpful, including the Public Record Office, of course, for British records, and the Liddell Hart Centre for Military Archives of King's College Library. There, Kate O'Brien and Patricia Methven were particularly kind at any early stage of my researches. The Library of Congress is one of mankind's great treasures, and its staff have been invariably helpful, as its resources have been unfailingly astounding. The Ben Gurion Research Center at Sde Boker provided me with much fascinating material. Its director, Tuvia Friling (now Archivist of the State of Israel), and his staff were not merely helpful, but hospitable in their desert home.

At The Free Press I managed to outlast not one but two editors—the long-suffering Bob Wallace, who spent years waiting for the manu-script, and Chad Conway who secured its speedy publication. Bruce Nichols guided me through final production, together with his assis-tants and copy editors: it has been a pleasure to work with them all.

Johns Hopkins University's Paul H. Nitze School of Advanced International Studies has been, throughout, a congenial place from which to think through the problems discussed herein. The character-istic SAIS mixture of historically informed scholarship, commitment to rigorous policy analysis, and exposure to the daily politics of Washington has been invaluable in shaping my thinking about the issues treated here. Many thanks to my colleagues and to its deans, George Packard and Paul Wolfowitz, for their encouragement, and to interim dean Stephen Szabo, who gave me the last bit of teaching relief needed to complete the manuscript. The library staff headed by Peter Promen and Linda Carlson have been superbly efficient, and I am most grateful to them.

I conducted preliminary work on this book at two other exceptional institutions, the Naval War College in Newport, Rhode Island, and the Olin Institute for Strategic Studies at Harvard University. At the latter, I was inspired as a student and novice scholar by Samuel P. Huntington, ever a wise and generous mentor. This book challenges, or rather suggests a large modification to, one of his theories. That is in the spirit of his teaching and indeed his example of the academic life, which upholds the pursuit of truth as the highest good, and vigorous debate as both a means of getting there and a source of pleasure in its own right. This book is, in many respects, a tribute to him.

I conceived this book at the Naval War College, where colleagues and staff (particularly the able librarians led by Bob Schnare) helped me get started on this project. No one played a more important role in launching this book than Al Bernstein, chairman of the strategy department, who lured me to Newport and inspired me with his brilliance as a teacher and a leader. We worked together there and in Washington, and he always asked after the book, even when other cares lay heavily upon him. We shared one of life's great friendships, cut short by his untimely death. I dedicate this book to his memory.

NOTES

PREFACE

1. Henry A. Kissinger, *The White House Years* (Boston: Little, Brown and Co., 1979), p. 1299. The reference is to Anwar Sadat.
2. Samuel Eliot Morison, "History as Literary Art," in *By Land and By Sea: Essays and Addresses by Samuel Eliot Morison* (New York: Alfred A. Knopf, 1953), p. 298.
3. Edmund Wilson, "Re-examining Dr. Johnson," in *Classics and Commercials: A Literary Chronicle of the Forties* (New York: Farrar, Straus and Giroux, 1944), p. 248.

CHAPTER 1: THE SOLDIER AND THE STATESMAN

1. Livy, *Histories*, Book XLIII, Alfred C. Schlesinger, trans. (Cambridge: Harvard University Press, 1951), Vol XIII, pp. 159–63.
2. Bill Gertz, "Ex-commander in Somalia hits second guessing," *Washington Times*, 22 October 1993, p. A8.
3. *Washington Post*, 21 October 1992, p. B1.
4. Lloyd J. Matthews, "The Politican as Operational Commander," *Army* (March 1996): 36.
5. Samuel P. Huntington, *The Soldier and the State* (Cambridge: Harvard University Press, 1957).
6. Martin Gilbert, *Winston S. Churchill*, Vol. VIII, *Never Despair* (Boston: Houghton Mifflin Co., 1988), p. 1329.
7. Carl von Clausewitz, *On War*, Michael Howard and Peter Paret, eds. and trans. (Princeton: Princeton University Press, 1982).
8. Ibid., I:1, p. 87; emphasis added.
9. Ibid., VIII:6, p. 608.
10. For one example see Eliot A. Cohen, "Playing Powell Politics," *Foreign Affairs* 74:6 (November/December 1995): 102–10.
11. See S. W. Roskill, *The War at Sea* (London: HMSO, 1954), Vol. I, pp. 457–58.
12. War Cabinet, Chiefs of Staff Committee, minutes of meetings to 1946. CAB 79/88. C.O.S. (43) 325, 130th meeting, 23 June 1943.

13. Stephen P. Rosen, *Winning the Next War* (Ithaca: Cornell University Press, 1991), p. 19. See also Stephen P. Rosen, *Societies and Military Power: India and Its Armies* (Ithaca: Cornell University Press, 1996), pp. 266 ff.

14. Ariel Sharon with David Chanoff, *Warrior: The Autobiography of Ariel Sharon* (New York: Simon & Schuster, 1989), p. 286.

15. Charles de Gaulle, *The Edge of the Sword*, trans. Gerard Hopkins (London: Faber and Faber, 1960), pp. 98–99. This book was first published in French in 1932. A perceptive and generally similar set of perceptions may be found in Pat C. Hoy, "Soldiers and Scholars," *Harvard Magazine* (May–June 1996): 64–70.

16. Winston S. Churchill, *The Gathering Storm* (Boston: Houghton Mifflin, 1948), p. 462. Churchill continued, "During the war, as will be seen, I forced long staff studies of various operations, as the result of which I was usually convinced that they were better left alone."

17. Scott Cooper, "The Politics of Airstrikes," *Policy Review* 107 (June/July 2001). Web version. http://www.policyreview.org/jun01/cooper.html

18. The regular practice of placing soldiers on active duty as Assistant to the President for National Security Affairs dates to the appointment of Vice Admiral John Poindexter in the Reagan administration. On the use of military officers for political tasks in Congress (including writing "an operation manual for new Republican members"), see Dana Priest, "Pentagon to Review Hill 'Fellowships,'" *Washington Post* (10 October 1996), pp. 1, 19.

19. Aleksandr A. Svechin, *Strategy*, Kent D. Lee, ed., trans. unknown (1927; Minneapolis, MN: East View Publications, 1991), p. 145.

20. Harry D. Train, "An Analysis of the Falklands/Malvinas Islands Campaign," *Naval War College Review* 41:1 (Winter 1988): 50. Emphasis in the original.

21. Bernard Brodie, *War and Politics* (New York: Macmillan, 1973), p. 496.

CHAPTER 2: LINCOLN SENDS A LETTER

1. Roy P. Basler, ed., *The Collected Works of Abraham Lincoln* (New Brunswick, NJ: Rutgers University Press, 1953–55), Vol. VII, p. 324.

2. T. Harry Williams, *Lincoln and His Generals* (New York: Knopf, 1952), pp. 7–8, 13.

3. Charles A. Dana, *Recollections of the Civil War: With the Leaders in Washington and in the Field in the Sixties* (New York: D. Appleton and Company, 1898), p. 188. Lincoln asked Dana to head for the field on 6 May 1864.

4. See James M. McPherson, *Abraham Lincoln and the Second American Revolution* (New York: Oxford University Press, 1990), pp. 68–89. Joseph T. Glatthaar, in his *Partners in Command: The Relationships Between Leaders in the Civil War* (New York: Free Press, 1994), on p. 265 takes issue with the Williams thesis, but only briefly.

5. Basler, ed., *Works*, Vol. IV, p. 316.

6. This interpretation of Lincoln, treated more broadly, may be found in a recent scholarly biography: David Herbert Donald, *Lincoln* (New York: Simon & Schuster, 1995).

7. See General Scott's Memorandum for the Secretary of War, 17 March 1861, in *The War of the Rebellion: A Compilation of the Official Records of the Union and Confederate Armies*, 70 volumes, 128 books (Washington, DC: US Government Printing Office, 1881–1901), Series I, Vol. I, pp. 200–201; henceforth cited as *OR*.

8. On Meigs' role in the attempted relief of Fort Sumter see Russell Weigley, *Quartermaster General of the Union Army: A Biography of M. C. Meigs* (New York: Columbia University Press, 1959), pp. 138–53.

9. Abraham Lincoln to Lyman Trumbull, 10 December 1860, in Basler, ed., *Works*, Vol. IV, pp. 149–50.

10. For a good analysis see Steve E. Woodworth, "Davis, Bragg, and Confederate Command in the West," in Gabor Boritt, ed., *Jefferson Davis's Generals* (New York: Oxford University Press, 1999), pp. 65–83.

11. Basler, ed., *Works*, Vol. VI, pp. 78–79; emphasis in the original. The letter appears to have been given to Hooker at a personal interview at the White House.

12. Ibid., Vol. VII, p. 499, letter to Ulysses S. Grant, 23 August 1864.

13. Ibid., Vol. VI, p. 357. "Order of Retaliation," 30 July 1863.

14. See Webb Garrison, *The Lincoln No One Knows: The Mysterious Man Who Ran the Civil War* (Nashville, Tennessee: Rutledge Hill Press, 1993), pp. 124–25.

15. Dana, *Recollections*, p. 183.

16. William H. Herndon, *Life of Lincoln* [1888] (New York: Da Capo Press, 1983), pp. 269–70.

17. A. Lincoln, "Opinion on the Draft," in Basler, ed., *Works*, Vol. VI, p. 445. This entire document is a cold assessment of the need and case for conscription by the Union. It may have been intended to serve as the basis of a speech, but it was never used for that purpose.

18. Carl von Clausewitz, *On War*, Michael Howard and Peter Paret, trans. (Princeton: Princeton University Press, 1982), I: 6, p. 118.

19. Nicolay and Hay, *Lincoln*, Vol. IV, pp. 75–76.

20. See J. F. C. Fuller, *The Generalship of Ulysses S. Grant* (New York: Dodd, Mead, 1929), pp. 43–62, for some of the earliest debates about the impact of the rifle on the war. These are brought up to date by Grady McWhiney and Perry D. Jamieson, *Attack and Die: Civil War Military Tactics and the Southern Heritage* (University, AL: University of Alabama Press, 1982). A contrary view may be found in Paddy Griffith, *Battle Tactics of the Civil War* (New Haven, CT: Yale University Press, 1987). See as well Edward Hagerman, *The American Civil War and the Origins of Modern Warfare: Ideas, Organization, and Field Command* (Bloomington: Indiana University Press, 1988).

21. Roger Hannaford at the battle of Waynesboro, 2 March 1865, quoted in
     Stephen Z. Starr, *The Union Cavalry in the Civil War,* Vol. II, *The War in the East
     from Gettysburg to Appomattox, 1863–1865* (Baton Rouge: Louisiana State
     University Press, 1981), p. 373. Note that the cavalry charged on foot, as
     occasionally occurred. See also Starr's description (p. 123) of a Union cav-
     alry brigade's defense against Kershaw's infantry division at Cold Harbor,
     which was decided in five minutes by the fire of repeating arms. More gen-
     erally, see the discussion on p. 89.

22. The standard account, on which I have relied here, is Robert V. Bruce,
     Lincoln and the Tools of War (Indianapolis: Bobbs-Merrill, 1956).

23. US Department of Commerce, Bureau of the Census, *Historical Statistics of
     the United States: Colonial Times to 1970* (Washington, DC: US Government
     Printing Office, 1975), Part II, p. 731. The standard work on the subject
     remains George Edgar Turner, *Victory Rode the Rails: The Strategic Place of the
     Railroads in the Civil War* (Lincoln: University of Nebraska Press, 1953).

24. For a good account see Charles R. Shrader, "Field Logistics in the Civil
     War," in Jay Luvaas and Harold W. Nelson, eds., *The U.S. Army War College
     Guide to the Battle of Antietam* (Carlisle, PA: South Mountain Press, 1987),
     pp. 255–84.

25. Turner, *Victory Rode the Rails,* p. 280.

26. See also Thomas Weber, *The Northern Railroads in the Civil War, 1861–1865*
     (New York: Columbia University Press, 1952).

27. Ibid., pp. 282–96.

28. Jack K. Bauer, *The Mexican War* (New York: Macmillan, 1974), pp. 237, 396.

29. Robert L. Thompson, *Wiring a Continent: The History of the Telegraph Industry
     in the United States, 1832–1866* (Princeton: Princeton University Press,
     1947), p. 217. The discussion of the growth of the telegraph is drawn from
     Thompson, including the charts in *Wiring a Continent,* pp. 241, 394, 408.

30. The standard source is William R. Plum, *The Military Telegraph During the
     Civil War in the United States,* 2 vols. (Chicago: Jansen, McClurg, & Co.,
     1882). Plum says that in 1871 the Prussian forces in France operated barely
     one tenth of that amount of military telegraph wire.

31. Ibid., Vol. II, pp. 141, 238.

32. Report to the Secretary of War by the Chief, U.S. Military Telegraph, 31
     October 1864, *OR,* Series III, Vol. IV, p. 842.

33. Nicolay and Hay, *Lincoln,* Vol. IV, pp. 352–54.

34. David Homer Bates, *Lincoln in the Telegraph Office: Recollections of the United
     States Military Telegraph Corps During the Civil War* (New York: The Century
     Co., 1907), pp. 94, 134–36. Bates was manager of the telegraph office in the
     War Department from March 1862 to the end of the war. His superior,
     Thomas T. Eckert, was chief of the telegraphic staff and was subsequently
     made assistant secretary of war.

35. Report to the Secretary of War by the Acting Signal Officer of the Army, 31
     October 1864. *OR,* Series III, Vol. IV, p. 820.

36. Bates, *Lincoln in the Telegraph Office*, pp. 42, 123.
37. For an example, see the discussion of Halleck's communications with Hooker in Kenneth P. Williams, *Lincoln Finds a General: A Military Study of the Civil War*, 5 vols. (New York: Macmillan, 1949–1959), Vol. II, pp. 635–36.
38. An excellent brief discussion of Civil War logistics is C. R. Shrader, "Field Logistics in the Civil War," in J. Luvaas and H. W. Nelson, eds., *The U.S. Army War College Guide to the Battle of Antietam*, pp. 255–84.
39. Letter to Orville Browning, 22 September 1861, in Basler, pp. 531–33.
40. Letter to James C. Conkling, 26 August 1863, in ibid., Vol. VI, p. 407.
41. Letter to Joseph Hooker, 10 June 1863, in ibid., Vol. VI, p. 257.
42. See, for example, his memoranda for a plan of campaign of 27 July 1861 and 1 October 1861, in ibid., Vol. IV, pp. 457–58, 544–46.
43. Letter to Horace Greeley, 22 August 1862, in ibid., Vol. V, p. 338.
44. McPherson, *Lincoln*, p. 41; emphasis in the original.
45. For a discussion of the role of raiding in Civil War strategy see Archer Jones, *Civil War Command & Strategy: The Process of Victory and Defeat* (New York: Free Press, 1992), pp. 84 ff. and passim. Jones takes this argument too far, however.
46. See Charles Royster, *The Destructive War: William Tecumseh Sherman, Stonewall Jackson, and the Americans* (New York: Alfred A. Knopf, 1991) and Mark Grimsley, *The Hard Hand of War: Union Military Policy toward Southern Civilians 1861–1865* (Cambridge: Cambridge University Press, 1995).
47. McPherson, *Lincoln*, pp. 91 ff.
48. Emory Upton, *The Military Policy of the United States* (New York: Greenwood, 1968), p. 236 (reprint of 1904 edition, published posthumously).
49. On Butler and technology see Robert V. Bruce, *Lincoln and the Tools of War* (Indianapolis: Bobbs-Merrill, 1956), pp. 72–73, 137, 122–23, 290, 283–84 and passim.
50. The inclusion of Sherman in this indictment may seem strange to some, but see Albert Castel, *Decision in the West: The Atlanta Campaign of 1864* (Lawrence, KS: University Press of Kansas, 1992).
51. Proclamation Revoking General Hunter's Order of Military Emancipation of May 9, 1862, in Basler, ed., *Works*, Vol. V, pp. 222–23.
52. Letter to General Joseph Hooker, 10 June 1863, in ibid., Vol. VI, p. 257.
53. Letter to Major John J. Key, 26 September 1862, in ibid., Vol. V, pp. 442–43.
54. Letter to Major John J. Key, 24 November 1862, in ibid., p. 508.
55. Endorsement concerning John J. Key, 27 December 1862, in ibid., Vol. VI, p. 20.
56. Nicolay and Hay, *Lincoln*, Vol. VII, p. 278.
57. Letter to George G. Meade, 14 July 1863, in Basler, ed., *Works*, Vol. VI, p. 328.
58. See Gabor Boritt, "'Unfinished Work,'" in Gabor S. Boritt, ed., *Lincoln's Generals* (New York: Oxford University Press, 1994), pp. 81–120.

59. Lorenzo Thomas and Ethan Allen Hitchcock to Edwin Stanton, 2 April 1862, in *OR*, Series I, Vol. 12, Part I, pp. 228–29. See also Hitchcock's report to the president of 30 March 1862, pp. 229–30.

60. See Lincoln's memorandum for the record of 8–9 July 1862 on these conversations in Basler, ed., *Works*, Vol. V, pp. 309–12.

61. See Abraham Lincoln to Joseph Hooker, 14 May 1863, in ibid., Vol. VI, p. 217.

62. See the discussion in R. M. Epstein, "The Creation and Evolution of the Army Corps in the American Civil War," *Journal of Military History* 55:1: 21–46.

63. Dana, *Recollections*, p. 1.

64. Ibid., p. 20. It should be noted that Stanton made it clear that Lincoln, and not the secretary of war alone, read Dana's reports closely. Other evidence corroborates this, including the fact that Lincoln personally dispatched Dana to Grant a second time in May 1864. See also P. H. Watson to C. A. Dana, 27 November 1863, *OR*, Series I, Vol. XXXI, Part III, p. 256, informing Dana that "both [Stanton and Lincoln] receive your dispatches regularly and esteem them highly."

65. Dana, *Recollections*, p. 33.

66. Ibid., p. 235.

67. Charles Dana to E. M. Stanton, 12 October 1863, *OR*, Series I, Vol. XXX, Part I, p. 215.

68. On Grant's alcohol problem see William S. McFeely, *Grant: A Biography* (New York: W. W. Norton, 1981), pp. 132 ff.

69. Charles Dana to John Rawlins, 15 July 1864, as quoted in John Y. Simon, ed., *The Papers of Ulysses S. Grant*, Vol. XI, *June 1–August 15, 1864* (Carbondale: Southern Illinois University Press, 1967), p. 253.

70. Edwin M. Stanton to Ulysses S. Grant, 3 March 1865, in Basler, ed., *Works*, Vol. VIII, pp. 330–31.

71. Sherman's account, including the original terms and his subsequent snub of Stanton, may be found in William Tecumseh Sherman, *Memoirs of General William T. Sherman* (New York: Library of America, 1990), pp. 842–66.

72. According to Dana, who was there, Stanton did not offer his hand either. Rather he merely made a "slight forward motion of his head, equivalent, perhaps, to a quarter of a bow." Dana, *Recollections*, p. 290.

73. There is an interesting description of Lincoln's guidance to Grant in advance of that speech, given in Nicolay and Hay, *Lincoln*, Vol. VIII, p. 341.

74. Ulysses S. Grant to Abraham Lincoln, 19 July 1864, in Simon, ed., *Grant Papers*, Vol. XI, p. 280.

75. See, inter alia, *OR*, Series I, Vol. XXXVII, Part II, pp. 65 ff.; Dana, *Recollections*, pp. 229–32; Basler, ed., *Works*, Vol. VII, pp. 424–76.

76. This episode is well covered in Glatthaar, *Partners in Command*, pp. 211–16.

77. Letter to Ulysses S. Grant, 3 August 1864, in Basler, ed., *Works*, Vol. VII, p. 476.

78. See, for example, his concise and insightful dispatch to General David Hunter, 23 July 1864, in ibid., p. 456.

79. Quoted in Stephen Ambrose, *Halleck: Lincoln's Chief of Staff* (Baton Rouge: Louisiana State University Press, 1962), p. 157.

80. Williams, *Lincoln Finds a General*, Vol. V, at pp. 271–82 has an interesting assessment of Halleck, of whom the author declares he has altered his views (for the better) more than his views of any other Civil War figure. See also a generally favorable biography: Ambrose, *Halleck*, cited at note 82 below.

81. Howard K. Beale, ed., *Diary of Gideon Welles*, 3 vols. (New York: W. W. Norton, 1960), Vol. I, pp. 216, 364.

82. Halleck rarely receives kind treatment from students of the war. See, however, two biographical studies: Stephen E. Ambrose, *Halleck: Lincoln's Chief of Staff* (Baton Rouge: Louisiana State University Press, 1962), and Curt Anders, *Henry Halleck's War* (Carmel, Indiana: Guild Press of Indiana, 1999).

83. Ulysses S. Grant to Julia Dent Grant, 30 April 1862, in Ulysses S. Grant, *Personal Memoirs of U. S. Grant* (New York: Library of America, 1990), p. 1006.

84. The best biography is Benjamin P. Thomas and Harold M. Hyman, *Stanton: The Life and Times of Lincoln's Secretary of War* (New York: Alfred A. Knopf, 1962).

85. Quoted in ibid. at p. 385. For a general assessment of their relationship, see pp. 381–91.

86. Ibid., pp. 402–18.

87. See William B. Hesseltine, *Lincoln and the War Governors* (New York: Alfred A. Knopf, 1955).

88. Ulysses S. Grant to Charles A. Dana, 15 July 1864, in Simon, ed., *The Papers of Ulysses S. Grant*, Vol. XI, *June 1–August 15, 1864* (Carbondale: Southern Illinois University Press, 1967–2001), p. 251. "I am sorry to see such a disposition to condemn a brave old soldier as Gen. Hunter is known to be without a hearing." Yet one author describes him as "a prime example of Lincoln's inability . . . to select officers for high command"; see Ezra Warner, *Generals in Blue: Lives of the Union Commanders* (Baton Rouge: Louisiana State University Press, 1962), p. 244.

89. Nicolay and Hay, *Lincoln*, pp. 359–60.

CHAPTER 3: CLEMENCEAU PAYS A VISIT

1. Winston S. Churchill, *Amid These Storms: Thoughts and Adventures*, "A Day with Clemenceau" (New York: Charles Scribner's Sons, 1932), pp. 173–74, 176.

2. Quoted in David S. Newhall, *Clemenceau: A Life at War* (Lewiston, ME: Edwin Mellen, 1991), p. 318.

3. I have used two reference works for most of the statistics in this chapter: Patrick H. Hutton, Amanda S. Bourque, and Amy J. Staples, eds., *Historical Dictionary of the Third French Republic, 1870–1940,* 2 vols. (New York: Greenwood Press, 1986), and Randal Gray with Christopher Argyle, *Chronicle of the First World War,* 2 vols. (New York: Facts on File, 1990).

4. See Alistair Horne, *The Price of Glory: Verdun 1916* (London: Macmillan, 1962), pp. 327–28.

5. See the scathing summary in John Keegan, *The First World War* (New York: Alfred A. Knopf, 1999), pp. 367–69.

6. Jean-Baptiste Duroselle, *Clemenceau* (Paris: Fayard, 1988) p. 108.

7. Newhall, *Clemenceau,* pp. 48–50.

8. Duroselle, *Clemenceau,* p. 445.

9. André Beaufre, "Foch," in Michael Carver, ed., *The War Lords: Military Commanders of the Twentieth Century* (Boston: Little, Brown, 1976), p. 126.

10. Duroselle, *Clemenceau,* p. 596.

11. Quoted in Newhall, *Clemenceau,* p. 322.

12. Quoted in ibid., p. 195.

13. Jere Clemens King, *Generals & Politicians: Conflict Between France's High Command, Parliament and Government, 1914–1918* (Westport, CT: Greenwood, 1951), pp. 11 ff. On the state of French civil-military relations before the war, which is indispensable to understanding the tension between civilians and generals during it, see Douglas Porch, *The March to The Marne: the French Army, 1871–1914* (Cambridge: Cambridge University Press, 1981).

14. Ibid., pp. 115 ff.

15. Edward Spears, *Prelude to Victory 1917* (London: Jonathan Cape, 1939), p. 435.

16. Figures on death and prison sentences from Guy Pedroncini, *Pétain: Le Soldat, 1914–1940* [*The Soldier, 1914–1940*] (Paris: Perrin, 1998), p. 122. Total numbers of mutineers from Gray and Argyle, *Chronicle,* Vol. 2, p. 40.

17. Martin Gilbert, *The First World War: A Complete History* (New York: Henry Holt & Company, 1994), p. 385.

18. Jean Jules Henri Mordacq, *Le Ministère Clemenceau: Journal d'un Témoin* [Minister Clemenceau: Journal of a Witness], Vol. I, *Novembre 1917–Avril 1918* (Paris: Librairie Plon, 1930), p. 13.

19. Ibid., p. 205.

20. Ibid., Vol. II, p. 54.

21. Ibid., p. 62.

22. Ibid., Vol. I, p. 233.

23. This and other data taken from Anne Blanchard et al., *Histoire Militaire de la France* [*Military History of France*], Vol. 3, *De 1871 à 1940* ed. Guy Pedroncini, (Paris: Presses Universitaires de France, 1992–1994), Chapter 7, "L'armée française et la Grande Guerre," [The French Army and the Great War,"] pp. 161–202).

24. Ibid., p. 170.

25. Much of what follows is based on the journal of General Mordacq, who kept a detailed diary throughout the war and beyond. Since Clemenceau destroyed his own papers, Mordacq's are our primary souce for the Tiger's activities.

26. Mordacq, *Journal,* Vol. I, p. 6.

27. Edward Spears, *Assignment to Catastrophe,* Vol. II, *The Fall of France 1940* (New York: A. A. Wyn, 1955), p. 98. Spears was serving, as he had in World War I, as a liaison officer with the French.

28. Quoted in Bertrand Favreau, *Georges Mandel ou la passion de la République* (Paris: Fayard, 1996), p. 476.

29. See Mordacq, *Journal,* Vol. I, pp. 174 ff.

30. Ibid., Vol. II, p. 55. He describes this process, pp. 70–72.

31. Ibid., Vol. I, pp. 148, 174 ff.

32. Ibid., pp. 114 ff.

33. Ibid., p. 141.

34. Ibid., p. 172.

35. His receipt of the bouquet is described in Mordacq, *Journal,* Vol. II, p. 105.

36. Guy Pedroncini, *Pétain le Soldat,* p. 226.

37. Ferdinand Foch, *The Principles of War,* trans. J. de Morinni (New York: H. K. Fly, 1918). For a very perceptive analysis see Gideon Y. Akavia, *Decisive Victory and Correct Doctrine: Cults in French Military Thought Before 1914* (Stanford, CA: Stanford University Center for International Security and Arms Control, 1993).

38. Ferdinand Foch, *The Memoirs of Marshal Foch,* trans. T. Bentley Mott (New York: Doubleday, 1931), p. 179.

39. For a useful revisionist view of Foch, see Damien Fenton, "Unjustly Accused: Marshal Ferdinand Foch & the French 'Cult of the Offensive,'" *WaiMilHist* 1:4 (July 1999). *WaiMilHist* is an electronic journal of military history produced by the History Department of the University of Waikato, Hamilton, New Zealand. Its Web site is www.waikato.ac.nz/wfass/sub-ject/history/waimilhist/1999/contents.htm.

40. See Jean Autin, *Foch, ou le triomphe de la volonté* [*Foch, or the Triumph of the Will*] (Paris: Librairie Académique, 1987), p. 129 passim.

41. Quoted in ibid., p. 192.

42. Ibid., p. 129.

43. Jean-Jules-Henri Mordacq, *Clemenceau* (Paris: Les Éditions de France, 1939), p. 209.

44. Ibid.

45. Quoted in Donald Smythe, *Pershing: General of the Armies* (Bloomington: Indiana University Press, 1986), p. 73.

46. Foch, *Memoirs,* p. 185.

47. Ibid., p. xiv.

48. Ibid., p. xxvi.

49. Pétain's biographer, Guy Pedroncini, emphasizes this side of his subject, perhaps to excess. See Guy Pedroncini, *Pétain: le soldat*, pp. 10ff. and passim.

50. Quoted in Alastair Horne, *The Price of Glory: Verdun 1916* (London: Macmillan, 1962), p. 134. There is a good summary of Pétain's career and character at pp. 132–41.

51. Pedroncini, *Pétain le soldat*, pp. 117–22.

52. Foch was picked at the Doullens conference on 26 March 1918 to coordinate the activities of the Allied armies; he acquired the title of supreme commander on 14 April, with his responsibility extended to include Italy on 2 May and the Belgian army—anomalously left out of his scope of control—on 9 September.

53. William Robertson, *Soldiers and Statesmen 1914–1918*, 2 vols. (London: Cassell, 1926), Vol. II, pp. 296–97.

54. For an interesting account of this see the memoir of the ubiquitous Maurice Hankey, who as secretary to the War Cabinet knew all about it: Maurice Hankey, *Supreme Command 1914–1918*, 2 vols. (London: Allen & Unwin, 1961), Vol. II, pp. 775–84.

55. For a good description see G. C. Wynne, *If Germany Attacks: The Battle in Depth in the West* (1940; Westport, CT: Greenwood, 1976).

56. For accounts see Jean-Jules-Henry Mordacq, *Le commandement unique: comment il fut realisé* [*The Unified Command: How It Was Achieved*] (Paris: Éditions Jules Tallander, 1929), pp. 46–47 and passim; Pedroncini, *Pétain le soldat*, pp. 197 ff.

57. For a general discussion see Tim Travers, *The Killing Ground: The British Army, the Western Front and the Emergence of Modern Warfare 1900–1918* (London: Allen & Unwin, 1987).

58. Interestingly, Foch admired Germany's monumentally complex and audacious Schlieffen Plan even after World War I; see Raymond Recouly, *Foch: My Conversations with the Marshal*, trans. Joyce Davis (New York: D. Appleton, 1929), p. 15.

59. Georges Clemenceau, *Grandeur and Misery of Victory*, trans. F. M. Atkinson (New York: Harcourt, Brace, 1930), p. 76.

60. Mordacq, *Journal*, Vol. II, p. 8.

61. Raymond Poincaré, *Au Service de la France: Neuf Années de Souvenirs* [In the Service of France: Nine Years of Memories] (Paris: Librairie Plon, 1928), Vol. X, *Victoire et Armistice 1918* [Victory and Armistice: 1918], p. 213.

62. See Mordacq, *Journal*, Vol. I, p. 115.

63. Ibid., pp. 139–41.

64. For the dispute seen through American eyes, see David F. Trask, *The AEF and Coalition Warmaking, 1917–1918* (Lawrence, KS: University Press of Kansas, 1993), pp. 33–36.

65. See Autin, *Foch*, pp. 214–16.

66. See the discussion in Foch, *Memoirs*, p. 440.

67. See Pedroncini, *Pétain, Général en Chef* [*Pétain: General in Chief*] pp. 210–30.

68. Mordacq, *Journal*, Vol. I, p. 240.

69. Described in ibid., Vol. II, pp. 38–77.

70. Clemenceau, *Grandeur and Misery*, p. 48.

71. Ibid., p. 61.

72. Ibid., p. 75.

73. Foch, *Memoirs*, p. 185.

74. Quoted in ibid., pp. 434–35.

75. Recouly, *Foch*, pp. 39–40.

76. Ibid., p. 436.

77. Smythe, *Pershing*, pp. 237, 229 passim.

78. Clemenceau, *Grandeur and Misery*, p. 124.

79. Mordacq, *Journal*, Vol. II, p. 284.

80. Holger H. Herwig, *The First World War: Germany and Austria-Hungary, 1914–1918* (London: Arnold, 1997), pp. 425 ff.

81. Woodrow Wilson, *War and Peace: Presidential Messages, Addresses, and Public Papers 1917–1924*, 2 vols., edited by Ray Stannard Baker and William E. Dodd (New York: Harper, 1927), Vol. I, pp. 161–62.

82. Mordacq, *Journal*, Vol. II, p. 293.

83. Recouly, *Foch*, pp. 39–40.

84. See King, *Generals and Politicians*, pp. 196 ff.

85. See Mordacq, *Journal*, Vol. II, pp. 284–85; see also Mordacq's study of the armistice negotiations, *La Vérité sur l'armistice* [*The Truth About the Armistice*] (Paris: Éditions Jules Tallandier, 1929), pp. 70 ff.

86. Recouly, *Foch*, pp. 39–40.

87. Quoted in Foch, *Memoirs*, p. 456.

88. Mordacq, *La Vérité*, p. 71.

89. Quoted in Recouly, *Foch*, p. 45.

90. Ibid., p. 41.

91. Mordacq, *Journal*, Vol. II, p. 339.

92. Recouly, *Foch*, pp. 176–77.

93. The main work on the subject is Jere Clemens King, *Foch versus Clemenceau: France and German Dismemberment, 1918–1919* (Cambridge, MA: Harvard University Press, 1960). See also Newhall, *Clemenceau*, pp. 447 ff.

94. See Recouly, *Foch*, pp. 193–99.

95. William Maxwell Aitken, *Men and Power 1917–1918* (New York: Duell, Sloan and Pearce, 1956), p. 150 and passim.

96. Miquel, *Clemenceau*, p. 318 ff.

97. This episode is described at Mordacq, *Journal*, Vol. III, pp. 226–31.

98. G. Ward Price, "Historic Interview with Marshal Foch," *The Daily Mail*, April 19, 1919.

99. Miquel, *Clemenceau*, pp. 360 ff.

100. Ibid., p. 362. Miquel's account rests heavily on André Tardieu, *The Truth About the Treaty* (Bloomington: Bobbs Merrill, 1921), available at the Web site : www.ukans.edu/~libsite/wwi-www/treatytruth/tardieu00tc.htm. For

the specific discussion, see Chapter 5, "The Left Bank of the Rhine," at www.ukans.edu/~libsite/wwi-www/treatytruth/tardieu05.htm#V.

101. Mordacq, *Journal*, Vol. III, p. 259.

102. Paul Mantoux, *The Deliberations of the Council of Four (March 24–June 28, 1919): Notes of the Official Interpreter Paul Mantoux*, 2 vols., trans. and ed. by Arthur S. Link (Princeton: Princeton University Press, 1992), Vol. II, p. 466.

103. Ibid., p. 468.

104. Ibid., pp. 474–75.

105. Clemenceau, *Grandeur and Misery*, p. 11.

106. Ibid., p. 7.

107. Maxime Weygand, *Le Maréchal Foch* (Paris: Flammarion, 1947), p. 293.

108. Mantoux, *Deliberations*, Vol. I, p. xxviii. (From Link's Introduction.)

109. Clemenceau, *Grandeur and Misery*, p. 239; emphasis in the original.

110. Ibid., pp. 403, 405.

111. Charles de Gaulle, *The War Memoirs of Charles de Gaulle*, Vol. II, *Unity, 1942–44*, trans. Richard Howard (New York: Simon & Schuster, 1959), p. 351.

CHAPTER 4: CHURCHILL ASKS A QUESTION

1. Winston S. Churchill, *The Second World War*, Volume II, *Their Finest Hour* (Boston: Houghton Mifflin Co., 1949), pp. 184–85.

2. Ibid., p. 185.

3. R. V. Jones, *The Wizard War: British Scientific Intelligence 1939–1945* (New York: Coward, McCann & Geoghegan, 1978), pp. 107–8.

4. Churchill, *Their Finest Hour*, pp. 386–87. See as well F. H. Hinsley et al., *British Intelligence in the Second World War: Its Influence on Strategy and Operations*, Vol. I (London: Her Majesty's Stationery Office, 1979), pp. 550–56.

5. G. R. Elton, *Political History: Principles and Practice* (New York: Basic Books, 1970), p. 71.

6. John Charmley, *Churchill: The End of Glory* (New York: Harcourt Brace, 1993).

7. Liddell Hart Centre for Military Archives, Alan Brooke Papers, 5/9, entry of 10 September 1944.

8. Bernard Fergusson, ed., *The Business of War: The War Narrative of Major-General Sir John Kennedy* (New York: William Morrow, 1958), p. 115.

9. Sir Hastings Ismay to Sir Leslie Hollis, 18 February 1957, Ismay papers, King's College, London, I/14/60.

10. David Fraser, *Alanbrooke* (New York: Atheneum, 1982), p. 532; Alex Danchev, *Very Special Relationship: Field Marshal Sir John Dill and the Anglo-American Alliance 1941–44* (London: Brassey's, 1986), takes a similar view.

11. David Reynolds, "1940: The Worst and Finest Hour," in Robert Blake and Wm. Roger Louis, eds., *Churchill* (New York: W. W. Norton, 1993), p. 255.

12. Martin Kitchen, "Winston Churchill and the Soviet Union During the Second World War," *Historical Journal* 30:2 (June 1987): 435.

13. Sheila Lawlor, "Greece, March 1941: The Politics of British Military Intervention," *Historical Journal* 25:4 (December 1982): 933.

14. Kitchen, "Winston Churchill."

15. Warren F. Kimball, "Churchill and Roosevelt," in Robert Blake and William Roger Louis, eds., *Churchill* (New York: W. W. Norton, 1993), p. 306.

16. Fergusson, *The Business of War*, p. 60.

17. Ibid., p. 157.

18. John Colville, *The Fringes of Power: 10 Downing Street Diaries, 1939–1945* (New York: W. W. Norton, 1985), 23 October 1940 entry, p. 275.

19. Alex Danchev, "'Dilly-Dally,' or Having the Last Word: Field Marshal Sir John Dill and Prime Minister Winston Churchill," *Journal of Contemporary History* 22 (1987): 37.

20. Ibid., p. 29.

21. Michael Howard, "The End of Churchillmania? Reappraising the Legend," *Foreign Affairs* (September/October 1993), p. 145. This extended review essay stresses, interestingly, the negative portrayals of Churchill over the positive.

22. Charles Wilson, *Churchill Taken from the Diaries of Lord Moran: The Struggle for Survival 1940–1965* (Boston: Houghton Mifflin Co., 1966).

23. John Colville, *The Churchillians* (London: Weidenfeld and Nicolson, 1981), p. 191.

24. The scholarly view began to shift against Churchill with such works as A. J. P. Taylor, ed., *Churchill Revised: A Critical Assessment* (New York: Dial Press, 1968), and continues with more recent studies—including even the more moderate Robert Blake and William Roger Louis, eds., *Churchill* (New York: W. W. Norton, 1993).

25. Quoted in Martin Gilbert, *In Search of Churchill* (New York: John Wiley & Sons, 1994), p. 216.

26. Ibid., p. 184.

27. Winston S. Churchill, *The Second World War*, 6 vols., Vol. I, *The Gathering Storm* (Boston: Houghton Mifflin Co., 1948), p. 421. Jeremy Campbell, *Winston Churchill's Afternoon Nap* (New York: Simon & Schuster, 1986), pp. 210 passim, describes the physiology of circadian rhythms that made (and make) hour-long naps of this type a natural recourse "to enter the ancient sleep-ability gate as soon as it opened."

28. Churchill, *Their Finest Hour*, memorandum to General Sir Hastings Ismay, chief of the Imperial General Staff, and Sir Edward Bridges, 19 July 1940, pp. 17–18.

29. Lecture to Imperial Defense College, October 1949, Ismay Papers III/4/12.

30. Ismay letter to Anthony Eden, 7 January 1964, Ismay Papers IV/Avon/16a.

31. Winston S. Churchill, *Marlborough: His Life and Times* (New York: Charles Scribner's Sons, 6 vols., 1933–38, Vol. I (1933), p. 94. Churchill described Halifax as "the foremost statesman of these times."

32. Winston S. Churchill, *My Early Life*, Winston S. Churchill, *Painting as a Pastime* (New York: McGraw-Hill, 1950), p. 331.

33. See Churchill's essay, "Consistency in Politics," in Winston S. Churchill, *Amid These Storms: Thoughts and Adventures* (New York: Charles Scribner's Sons, 1932), pp. 39–50.

34. Churchill, *Marlborough*, Vol. II, p. 35.

35. Winston S. Churchill, *The River War*, rev. ed. (London: Longmans Green, 1902), p. 162.

36. Churchill, *The World Crisis*, Vol. I, *1911–1914* (New York: Charles Scribner's Sons, 1924), pp. 125–48.

37. Those interested should read on this subject, Maurice Ashley, *Churchill as Historian* (London: Secker & Warburg, 1968).

38. Churchill, *Marlborough*.

39. Churchill, *Marlborough*, Vol. V, p. 246.

40. Winston S. Churchill, *A History of the English-Speaking Peoples*, 4 vols. (New York: Dodd, Mead & Co., 1956), Vol. IV, *The Grand Alliance*, pp. 149–263.

41. Churchill, *Second World War*, Vol. III, *The Grand Alliance*, p. 608.

42. Winston S. Churchill, speech to Congress, 19 May 1943, in Robert Rhodes James, ed., *Winston S. Churchill: His Complete Speeches*, Vol. VII, *1943–1949* (London: Chelsea House Publishers, 1974), p. 6783.

43. Winston S. Churchill, *Painting as a Pastime* (New York: McGraw-Hill, 1950).

44. Martin Gilbert, *Winston S. Churchill*, Vol. VII, *Road to Victory, 1941–1945* (Boston: Houghton Mifflin, 1986), p. 20.

45. Paper of 16 December 1941, composed for Churchill's first wartime meeting with Roosevelt, in Warren F. Kimball, ed., *Churchill and Roosevelt: The Complete Correspondence* (Princeton: Princeton University Press, 1984), Vol. I, p. 303.

46. Churchill, *The World Crisis*, Vol. I, *1911–1914*, p. 174.

47. Churchill, *Marlborough*, Vol. VI, p. 600.

48. I have discussed Churchill's view of strategy in "Churchill at War," *Commentary* 83:5 (May 1987): 40–49.

49. Harold Macmillan diary entry of 16 November 1943, as quoted in Gilbert, *The Road to Victory*, p. 554.

50. Gilbert, *Road to Victory*, p. 759.

51. James Leasor, *War at the Top* (London: Michael Joseph, 1959), p. 173.

52. Norman Brook to Hastings Ismay, 27 January 1959, Ismay Papers I/14/8. Liddell Hart Centre.

53. Churchill, *The World Crisis*, Vol. IV, *1916–1918*, Part II (1927), p. 247.

54. See, for example, Tim Travers, *The Killing Ground: The British Army, the Western Front and the Emergence of Modern Warfare 1900–1918* (London: Allen & Unwin, 1987).

55. Churchill, *World Crisis,* Vol. III, 1916–18, pp. 194–95.

56. Churchill, *World Crisis,* Vol. II, *1915,* p. 284.

57. Ibid., p. 164.

58. Personal Minute D185/3, 14 October 1943. Prime Minister's Office, Operational Papers 3/336/3; henceforth cited as PREM.

59. Brooke Diary, entry for 5 June 1944.

60. C.O.S. (41) 334, Minute 4, 26 September 1941. CAB 79/86 (confidential annexes to COS meetings).

61. See R. Stuart Macrae, *Winston Churchill's Toyshop* (Kineton: The Roundwood Press, 1971). Macrae's discussion of Churchill on pp. 166–69 is of particular interest, and supports a number of the points made above. Macrae, then a colonel in the British Army, was the deputy director of this operation (M.D. 1) throughout most of the war.

62. Winston S. Churchill, speech of 15 February 1942, *Winston Churchill: His Complete Speeches, 1897–1963,* ed. Robert Rhodes James (London: Bowker, 1974), Vol. VI, p. 6584.

63. Winston S. Churchill, Minute of 8 April 1943, quoted in Michael Howard, *Grand Strategy,* Vol. IV (London: HMSO, 1970), p. 369.

64. Winston S. Churchill, Minute to the Cabinet, 16 December 1939, quoted in Churchill Prime Minister's Office: Operational Papers, *The Second World War,* Vol. I, p. 547.

65. Hastings L. Ismay, *The Memoirs of General Lord Ismay* (New York: Viking, 1960), p. 166.

66. Prime Minister's Serial D 114.1, PREM/3/496/4.

67. Prime Minister's Serial D 136/1, PREM 3/496/4.

68. This in part on the strength of Cunningham's memoirs; admirals and generals, no less than prime ministers, have benefited from well-written recollections of their service in government.

69. S. W. Roskill, *Churchill and the Admirals* (New York: William Morrow, 1978), p. 188.

70. For other discussions of Churchill and the admirals see Arthur J. Marder, *From the Dardanelles to Oran: Studies of the Royal Navy in War and Peace* (London: Oxford University Press, 1974).

71. PREM 3/322/5/6.

72. Note from paymaster general to prime minister, "The Post-War Fleet," 5 July 1944, reprinted as WP (44) 764, 29 December 1944, PREM 3/322/5/6.

73. Prime Minister Personal Minute M 767/3 to First Sea Lord, 1 November 1943, PREM 3/322/5/6.

74. See the data in S. W. Roskill, *The War at Sea,* Vol. I (London: HMSO, 1954), p. 576. In June 1943 the Royal Navy and Royal Marines together numbered 660,000; in the same month of the following year they numbered 778,000, the peak for the war. By November 1943, the date of the controversy described here, they were probably somewhere in between these two

numbers; moreover, since some of the increase occurred in the Marines, who were not covered by Churchill's strictures, it would appear that he won a considerable victory.

75. See the memoranda, which are reprinted in John Ehrman, *Grand Strategy*, Volume V, *August 1943–September 1944*, pp. 398–403.

76. Gilbert, *Road to Victory*, p. 865.

77. Norman Brook in John Wheeler-Bennett, ed., *Action This Day: Working with Churchill* (London: Macmillan 1968), p. 22.

78. Prime Minister to Secretary of State for War, 21.11.42, PREM 3/54/7. All of the correspondence referred to on this matter is taken from this file.

79. John Colville, *The Fringes of Power: 10 Downing Street Diaries 1939–1955* (New York: W. W. Norton, 1985), p. 433.

80. F. H. Hinsley et al. *British Intelligence in the Second World War*, Vol. II (New York: Cambridge University Press, 1981), pp. 655–57.

81. See, for example, Ismay's comment on Dill's 6 May 1941 memorandum arguing against sending tanks to the Middle East: letter to John Connell, 13 September 1961 in Ismay Papers/IV/Con/4/6a.

82. Ibid.

83. Quoted in Danchev, "'Dilly-Dally'": 27.

84. See Philip Warner, "Auchinleck," in John Keegan, ed., *Churchill's Generals* (New York: Grove Weidenfeld, 1991), p. 138.

85. Letter of 26 June 1941, cited in J. R. M. Butler, *Grand Strategy*, Vol. II, *September 1939–June 1941* (London: HMSO, 1957), pp. 530–31.

86. Walt W. Rostow, *Pre-Invasion Bombing Strategy: General Eisenhower's Decision of March 25, 1944* (Auston: University of Texas Press, 1981).

87. PREM 3/334/4.

88. Churchill, *Second World War*, Vol. VI, *Triumph and Tragedy* (1953), p. 456.

89. Warren F. Kimball, *Churchill & Roosevelt: The Complete Correspondence* (Princeton: Princeton University Press, 1984), Vol. II, pp. 389–402.

90. Dwight D. Eisenhower to George Catlett Marshall, FWD 18345, 30 March 1945. In Alfred Chandler, ed., *The Papers of Dwight David Eisenhower: The War Years* (Baltimore: Johns Hopkins University Press, 1970), Vol. IV, p. 2561.

91. Americans as well as Britons were "kept in the picture," it should be noted. See the remarkable tribute by Edward Mead Earle in his introduction to his seminal edited volume, *Makers of Modern Strategy: Military Thought from Machiavelli to Hitler* (Princeton: Princeton University Press, 1943), p. vii.

CHAPTER 5: BEN-GURION HOLDS A SEMINAR

1. Quoted in Michael Bar Zohar, *Ben-Gurion: A Biography*, trans. Peretz Kidron (New York: Adama Books, 1978), p. 198.

2. Ben-Gurion knew, with varying degrees of fluency, Hebrew, Yiddish, Russian, Polish, English, German, French, Turkish, and Arabic. His military-history library comprised, as one might expect, an extensive collection on World War II, but also on other conflicts, including an impressive group of books about the American Civil War, featuring standard works such as Freeman's *Lee's Lieutenants* and the collected works of Lincoln.

3. See Shabtai Teveth, *Ben-Gurion and the Holocaust* (New York: Harcourt Brace, 1996).

4. Michael Bar Zohar, *Ben-Gurion: The Armed Prophet* (Englewood Cliffs, NJ: Prentice Hall, 1968), pp. 129 ff.

5. Figures on the Arab population vary, and much depends upon one's definition of Palestine: All of the Mandate area? The area assigned to the Jewish state under the partition plan? Or the area that subsequently became Israel? (The remnants of the portion assigned to Palestine's Arabs were absorbed by Egypt and Jordan.)

6. A short account of the end of the British Empire after World War II is Wm. Roger Louis, "The Dissolution of the British Empire," in Judith M. Brown and Wm. Roger Louis, eds., *The Oxford History of the British Empire*, Vol. IV, *The Twentieth Century* (New York: Oxford University Press, 1999), pp. 329–56.

7. The most comprehensive biography of David Ben-Gurion is appearing in multiple volumes by Shabtai Teveth. The first volumes have been translated into English as Shabtai Teveth, *Ben-Gurion: The Burning Ground, 1886–1948* (Boston: Houghton Mifflin, 1987). Despite its title, the book ends early in the Second World War, but it is a magnificent study nonetheless.

8. A particularly useful scholarly edition of Ben-Gurion's war-of-independence diary is Gershon Rivlin and Elchanan Oren, eds., *The War of Independence: Ben-Gurion's Diary*, 3 vols. (Tel Aviv: Ministry of Defense Publishing House, 1982), which covers the period October 1947 to July 1949 (Hebrew). The Ben-Gurion Research Center is publishing edited versions of earlier parts of the diary, as noted below.

9. See Shabtai Teveth, *Ben-Gurion and the Palestinian Arabs: From Peace to War* (Oxford University Press, 1985), passim.

10. See, for example, Ben-Gurion's remarks on 3 April 1947: David Ben-Gurion, *Chimes of Independence: Memoirs (March–November 1947)*, ed. Meir Avizohar (Tel Aviv: Am Oved, 1993, in Hebrew),. p. 150. Note that this work is not a memoir but rather an edited version of Ben-Gurion's diaries.

11. Ben-Gurion, *Chimes*, p. 198.

12. The organization of the Haganah is described in Meir Pa'il, *The Emergence of ZAHAL (I.D.F.)* (Tel Aviv: Zmora, Bitan, Modan, 1979, in Hebrew); see in particular organization chart 5 at the end of the book. Note that the translation of the title is incorrect: more accurate would be "From the Haganah to the Israel Defense Forces."

13. Data from Susan Hattis Rolef, ed., *Political Dictionary of the State of Israel*, 2nd ed. (New York: Macmillan, 1993), pp. 136–37.

14. Ben-Gurion, *Chimes*, p. 142. A two-paragraph summary of his assessment of both problems and remedies is to be found in the entry for 27 May 1947, p. 192.

15. Ibid., p. 148.

16. See, for example, the diary entry of 4 June 1947, p. 290.

17. Ibid., 10 April 1947, p. 159.

18. Ibid., 10 April 1947, pp. 171–72.

19. Ibid., 22 April 1947, p. 176.

20. Record Group 319, Records of the Army Staff, Army Intelligence Document File 1944–1955. National Archives at College Park, College Park, Maryland. File 435169, "Foreign Report," 28 January 1948. See also File 456080, "Arab and Jewish Military Forces in the Middle East, 25 January 1948," and File #455109, "Preliminary Report on Palestine Visit," 20 March 1948. Deliberate deception may well have been at work.

21. Ben-Gurion, *Chimes*, 2 May 1947, p. 181.

22. Ibid., 30 May 1947, p. 201.

23. See Yosef Avidar oral history, 13 March 1977, Ben-Gurion Archives—Oral Histories, Ben-Gurion Research Center, Ben-Gurion University, pp. 12–13. Henceforth cited as BEN-GURION-OH.

24. Ben-Gurion, *Chimes*, 30 April 1947, p. 180; 2 May 1947, p. 181.

25. David Ben-Gurion, *The War of Independence: Ben-Gurion's Diary*, Gershon Rivlin and Elhanan Oren, eds., 3 vols. (Tel Aviv: Ministry of Defense, 1983), Vol. I, p. 53 (Hebrew: henceforth cited as *War Diary*).

26. For a generally unsympathetic but interesting view of Ben-Gurion's relationship with Galili, see Anita Shapira, *The Army Controversy 1948: Ben-Gurion's Struggle for Control* (Tel Aviv: Hakibbutz Hameuchad, 1985, Hebrew), pp. 12–13.

27. *War Diary*, Vol. I, 23 October 1947, p. 421.

28. Neil Asher Silberman, *A Prophet From Amongst You: The Life of Yigael Yadin: Soldier, Scholar, and Mythmaker of Modern Israel* (Reading, MA: Addison-Wesley, 1993), pp. 82 ff.

29. Ibid., pp. 80–82.

30. Ben-Gurion, *Chimes*, 4 June 1947, pp. 290–91, 8 June 1947, p. 300.

31. See Mordechai Naor, *Laskov* (Jerusalem: Keter, 1989, Hebrew), pp. 169–85.

32. Ibid.

33. The standard work is Yoav Gelber, *The Kernel of a Regular Jewish Army: The Contribution of British Army Veterans to the Creation of the IDF* (Jerusalem: Yitzchak ben Zvi Foundation, 1986, Hebrew).

34. A very interesting discussion of this comparison may be found in Jehuda Wallach, *Called to the Colours: The Creation of a Citizen Army in War Time* (Tel Aviv: Ministry of Defense, 1997, Hebrew).

35. Zahava Osterfeld, *An Army Is Born: Main Stages in the Buildup of the Army under the Leadership of David Ben-Gurion*, 2 vols. (Tel Aviv: Ministry of Defense, 1994, Hebrew), Vol. II, p. 821.

36. Ibid., p. 835.

37. This speech, like others of this period, is reprinted in David Ben-Gurion, *When Israel Fought in Battle* (Tel Aviv: Am Oved, 1950, Hebrew; reprint 1975).

38. See diary entry for 18 October 1947 in Ben-Gurion, *Chimes*, pp. 406–7.

39. *Wisdom of the Fathers*, 2:1, trans. Avrohom Davis (New York: Metsudah, 1986), p. 41.

40. Ben-Gurion, *Chimes*, p. 503.

41. In fact Israeli aircraft shot down five RAF Spitfires in one aerial clash during this fighting.

42. On the complicated Arab politics of the time, see Uri Bar Joseph, *The Best of Enemies: Israel and Transjordan in the War of 1948* (London: Frank Cass, 1987), and P. J. Vatikiotis, *Politics and the Military in Jordan: A Study of the Arab Legion, 1921–1957* (London: Frank Cass, 1967).

43. Jon and David Kimche, *Both Sides of the Hill: Britain and the Palestine War* (London: Secker & Warburg, 1960), p. 12.

44. *War Diary*, Vol. I, p. 415 (entry of 14 May 1948).

45. Ibid., pp. 196 ff. (entry of 31 January 1948).

46. Ibid., pp. 330–31 (entry of 31 March 1948).

47. There is an account of this episode in Silberman, *Prophet*, at p. 119. He doubts that it happened as Yadin described it.

48. For a brilliant account of the memory of Latrun—extraordinarily contentious to this day—see Anita Shapira, "Historiography and Memory: Latrun, 1948," in *Jewish Social Studies: The New Series* (Fall 1996) 3:1, pp. 20–61.

49. See Ben-Gurion's 16 June 1948 speech to other members of the government, "In the Days of the Truce," in his *When Israel Fought in Battle*, p. 129. At this point, when the road to Jerusalem had been secured, the city was demoted to a second priority, after the Negev desert.

50. For a description of this episode see Bar Zohar, *Ben-Gurion*, pp. 181 ff., *War Diary*, Vol. III, p. 712.

51. David Ben-Gurion, speech to the Cabinet, 27 September 1948, in his *War Diary*, Vol. III, p. 726.

52. "How shall we deal with coming things?" 11 September 1948, in Ben-Gurion, *When Israel Fought in Battle*, p. 230.

53. Yitzhak Rabin, *Service Notebook*, 2 vols. (Tel Aviv: Maariv, 1979, Hebrew), Vol. I, p. 79.

54. *War Diary*, entry of 18 June 1948, Vol. II, p. 534.

55. Ibid., pp. 528–34.

56. A detailed account of the absorption of the IZL into the IDF may be found in Ostfeld, *An Army is Born*, Vol. II, pp. 622–79.

57. For an overall view of the *Altalena* affair see Shlomo Nakdimon, *Altalena* (Jerusalem: Edanim, 1978, Hebrew).

58. The *Altalena* affair still reverberates in Israeli politics. See Menachem Begin, *The Revolt*, trans. Samuel Katz (Tel Aviv: Steimatzky, 1951), pp. 154–176 for his account; Bar Zohar, *Ben-Gurion*, pp. 170–75 gives what is, in essence, Ben-Gurion's view.

59. Ben-Gurion, *Chimes*, diary entry of 5 November 1947, p. 464.

60. The best account is Yoav Gelber, *Why the Palmach was Dissolved: Military Power in the Transition from* Yishuv *to State* (Jerusalem: Schocken, 1986, Hebrew).

61. Shapira, *Army Controversy*, pp. 33–36.

62. See Ben Dunkelman's interesting autobiography, *Dual Allegiance* (New York: Crown, 1976).

63. Ibid., p. 206.

64. The best account of this investigation is Shapira, *Army Controversy*.

65. Ibid., p. 103.

66. David Ben-Gurion, "Letter to a comrade in the Palmach," 17 October 1948, in Ben-Gurion, *When Israel Fought in Battle*, pp. 273–82.

67. See for example Yitzhak Rabin's account in his *Service Notebook*, Vol. I, pp. 83–88.

68. The two best books on Israeli civil-military relations are Yoram Peri, *Between Battles and Ballots: Israeli Military in Politics* (Cambridge: Cambridge University Press, 1983), and Yehuda Ben Meir, *Civil-Military Relations in Israel* (New York: Columbia University Press, 1995).

69. Rabin, *Service Notebook*, Vol. I, pp. 150 ff.

70. Ben-Gurion, "From the Haganah in the Underground to a Regular Army," 19 June 1948, in his *When Israel Fought in Battle*, p. 151.

71. Ibid., p. 152.

72. Ben-Gurion, speech to *Mapai* secretariat, 30 October 1947, in his *Chimes*, p. 446.

73. See the fascinating reprint of his conclusions in David Ben-Gurion, "Army and State," *Ma'archot* (May 1981, Hebrew): 2–11.

74. Ibid., p. 2.

75. Ben-Gurion, *When Israel Fought in Battle*, p. 11.

CHAPTER 6: LEADERSHIP WITHOUT GENIUS

1. See Winston S. Churchill, *Marlborough: His Life and Times*, 6 vols. (New York: Charles Scribner's Sons, 1938), Vol. VI, p. 600.

2. Mark Clodfelter, *The Limits of Air Power: The American Bombing of North Vietnam* (New York: Free Press, 1989). I have relied heavily on this excellent work.

3. The most recent work on this subject is Qiang Zhai, *China and the Vietnam Wars, 1950–1975* (Chapel Hill: University of North Carolina Press, 2000).

4. William M. Momyer, *Air Power in Three Wars* (Washington, DC: US Government Printing Office, 1978), p. 388.

5. Taken from Larry Berman, *Planning a Tragedy: The Americanization of the War in Vietnam* (New York: W. W. Norton, 1982), pp. 112–13.

6. H. R. McMaster, *Dereliction of Duty: Lyndon Johnson, Robert McNamara, the Joint Chiefs of Staff, and the Lies That Led to Vietnam* (New York: HarperCollins, 1997), p. 147.

7. Charles G. Cooper, "The Day it Became the Longest War," *Proceedings of the US Naval Institute* (May 1996): 78. Cooper was then a young Marine officer in charge of holding the map for the JCS.

8. Clodfelter, *Limits*, pp. 100–101.

9. Stanley Karnow, *Vietnam: A History* (New York: Viking, 1983), p. 555, interview with former secretary of defense Clark Clifford.

10. See, inter alia, Andrew F. Krepinevich, *The Army and Vietnam* (Baltimore: Johns Hopkins University Press, 1986), and Harry Summers, *On Strategy: A Critical Analysis of the Vietnam War* (Novato, CA: Presidio, 1982). For good overall summaries of the debate see Jeffrey Record, "Vietnam in Retrospect: Could We Have Won?" *Parameters* 26:4 (Winter 1996–1997): 51–65, and Dale Andrade, "Rethinking the Years After Tet," *Joint Force Quarterly* (Autumn/Winter 1999–2000), pp. 107–8, or see www.dtic.mil/doctrine/jel/jfq_pubs/2123.pdf.

11. Clodfelter, *Limits*, p. 85.

12. See Bruce Palmer, *The 25-Year War: America's Military Role in Vietnam* (Lexington, KY: University Press of Kentucky, 1984), p. 35. Palmer was the number two commander in Vietnam, and later vice chief of staff of the Army.

13. McMaster, *Dereliction of Duty*, p. 331.

14. *The Pentagon Papers: The Defense Department History of United States Decisionmaking on Vietnam*, Senator Gravel edition, 4 vols. (Boston: Beacon Press, 1975), Vol. IV, pp. 424–25.

15. George Allen, *None So Blind: A Personal Account of the Intelligence Failure in Vietnam* (Chicago: Ivan R. Dee, 2001), p. 99.

16. Robert W. Komer, *Bureaucracy Does Its Thing: Institutional Constraints on U.S.-GVN Performance in Vietnam* (Santa Monica, CA: RAND, 1972), R-967-ARPA, pp. 40 passim. A slightly revised version is *Bureaucracy at War: U.S. Performance in the Vietnam Conflict* (Boulder, CO: Westview, 1986).

17. Komer, *Bureaucracy at War*, p. 34.

18. William C. Westmoreland, *A Soldier Reports* (New York: Doubleday, 1976), p. 307.

19. Robert S. McNamara, *In Retrospect: The Tragedy and Lessons of Vietnam* (New York: Vintage, 1995), p. 203.

20. Westmoreland, *A Soldier Reports*, p. 171. See the vehement disagreement by his civilian deputy, Robert W. Komer, in his study, *Bureaucracy Does Its Thing*, see also the book version of this report, *Bureaucracy at War*.

21. Julian J. Ewell and Ira A. Hunt, *Sharpening the Combat Edge: The Use of Analysis to Reinforce Military Judgment* (Washington, DC: Department of the Army, 1974), pp. 227, 228.

22. Stephen Peter Rosen, "Vietnam and the American Theory of Limited War," *International Security* 7:2 (Fall 1982): 83–113.

23. Jeffrey Record judges the war unwinnable in his thoughtful article, "Vietnam in Retrospect."

24. Quoted in Lewis Sorley, *Thunderbolt: General Creighton Abrams and the Army of His Times* (New York: Simon & Schuster, 1992), p. 364.

25. www.amsc.belvoir.army.mil/ecampus/gpc/prework/strategy/use.htm; speech given at National Press Club 28 November 1984; reprinted from *Defense* (January 1985): 1–11.

26. General Howell Estes, Jr., in "Give War a Chance," *FRONTLINE*, PBS Program #1715, aired: May 11, 1999; see also www.pbs.org/wgbh/pages/frontline/shows/military/etc/script.html

27. George H. W. Bush and Brent Scowcroft, *A World Transformed* (New York: Random House, 1998), p. 354.

28. Colin Powell, *My American Journey* (New York: Random House, 1995), p. 167.

29. Bob Woodward, *The Commanders* (New York: Simon & Schuster, 1991).

30. Colin Powell with Joseph E. Persico, *My American Journey* (New York: Random House, 1995), pp. 465–66. For a critical look at Powell's fascinating memoir, see my "Playing Powell Politics," *Foreign Affairs* 74:6 (November/December 1995): 102–10.

31. Ibid., pp. 238–39.

32. Henry Rowen, "Inchon in the Desert: My Rejected Plan," *The National Interest* 40 (Summer 1995): 34–39. Rowen was assistant secretary of defense for international security affairs.

33. For a description of this period, see Michael R. Gordon and Bernard E. Trainor, *The Generals' War: The Inside Story of the Conflict in the Gulf* (Boston: Little, Brown, 1995), pp. 123–58.

34. Bob Woodward, *The Commanders*, p. 79.

35. Powell with Persico, *My American Journey*, p. 503.

36. For a short summary of this episode, see Thomas A. Keaney and Eliot A. Cohen, *Revolution in Warfare? Air Power in the Gulf* (Annapolis, MD: Naval Institute Press, 1995), pp. 58–59, also pp. 130, 185, 214, 222. This book summarizes Eliot A. Cohen, ed., *Gulf War Air Power Survey* for 1991–93, 5 vols. (Washington, DC: US Government Printing Office, 1993).

37. See Williamson Murray et al., *Operations*, in Cohen, ed., *Gulf War Air Power Survey*, Vol. II, Part I, p. 221.

38. In retrospect it is far from certain that Israeli participation in the war would have caused the coalition to fall apart; even if several members had withdrawn, it is not clear that the United States would have had to terminate the war.

39. Keaney and Cohen, *Revolution in Warfare*, pp. 74–78.

40. Gordon and Trainor, *The Generals' War*, p. 234 and passim.

41. Bush and Scowcroft, *A World Transformed*, p. 486.

42. George H.W. Bush, "Address to the Nation Announcing the Deployment of United States Armed Forces to Saudi Arabia," 8 August 1990; see also bushlibrary.tamu.edu/papers/1990/90080800.html.

43. Bush admitted his mistake ten years later. See Jeff Franks, "Ex-President Bush Says He Underestimated Saddam," Reuters, 23 February 2001, and user.tninet.se/~qkl782y/report5/z0224e14.htm.

44. Norman Schwarzkopf, *It Doesn't Take a Hero* (New York: Bantam, 1992), pp. 479–80.

45. Ibid., p. 484.

46. Ibid., p. 473.

47. President George H. W. Bush, "Remarks to the American Legislative Exchange Council," March 1, 1991; See www.bushlibrary.tamu.edu/papers/1991/91030102.html. (Note: In many accounts the word "kicked" is rendered "licked.")

48. Bush and Scowcroft, *A World Transformed*, p. 484.

49. Ibid., pp. 484–85.

50. Peter Feaver and Richard Kohn, "The Gap: Soldiers, Civilians, and Their Mutual Misunderstanding," *The National Interest* 61 (Fall 2000): 29–37.

51. Bradley Graham, "Joint Chiefs Doubted Air Strategy," *Washington Post*, 5 April 1999.

52. See Rowan Scarborough, "Chiefs Sound Bosnia Alarm; Chaos Seen for U.S. troops," *Washington Times*, 12 August 1992.

53. Richard Holbrooke, *To End a War* (New York: Random House, 1998), p. 118.

54. David Halberstam, *War in Time of Peace: Bush, Clinton, and the Generals* (New York: Scribner, 2001), p. 416.

55. Wesley K. Clark, *Waging Modern War: Bosnia, Kosovo, and the Future of Combat* (New York: Public Affairs, 2001), p. 341.

56. See R. Jeffrey Smith, "A GI's Home is His Fortress: High-Security, High-Comfort U.S. Base in Kosovo Stirs Controversy," *Washington Post*, 5 October 1999.

57. Rebecca L. Schiff, "Civil-Military Relations Reconsidered: A Theory of Concordance," *Armed Forces & Society* 22:1 (Fall 1995): 7–24.

58. See a series of articles on the theater commanders in chief by Dana Priest in the *Washington Post*, 28–30 September 2000.

59. Anthony C. Zinni, "A Commander Reflects," *Proceedings of the US Naval Institute* (July 2000): 34. Zinni was at the time commander in chief of Central Command.

60. For an interesting account of how a less Vietnam-dominated theater commander felt these pressures, see Clark, *Waging Modern War*.

61. See Steven Lee Myers, "Gore's Service Does Not Keep Vets from Bush," *New York Times*, 21 September 2000.

62. Quoted in Forrest C. Pogue, *George C. Marshall*, Vol. 3, *Organizer of Victory, 1943–1945* (New York: Viking, 1973), pp. 458–59.

63. The most comprehensive recent study of American civil-military relations is Peter Feaver and Richard Kohn, eds., *Soldiers and Civilians: The Civil-Military Gap and American National Security* (Cambridge, MA: MIT Press, 2001).

64. Palmer, *The 25-Year War*, p. 201.

65. Remarks of Senator Gordon Smith (R.-Oregon), "The War in Kosovo and a Postwar Analysis," US Senate, Committee on Foreign Relations, 106th Cong., 1st sess., April 20, September 28, and October 6, 1999 (Washington, DC: US Government Printing Office, 2000), p. 77.

66. Powell, *My American Journey*, p. 109.

67. Carl von Clausewitz, *On War*, trans. Michael Howard and Peter Paret (Princeton: Princeton University Press, 1982), II: 4, p. 154.

CHAPTER 7: THE UNEQUAL DIALOGUE

1. Georges Clemenceau, *Grandeur and Misery of Victory*, trans. F. M. Atkinson (New York: Harcourt Brace, 1930), p. 404.

2. John Colville, *The Churchillians* (London: Weidenfeld and Nicolson, 1981), p. 143.

3. Roy P. Basler, ed., *The Collected Works of Abraham Lincoln* (New Brunswick, NJ: Rutgers University Press, 1953), Vol. VIII, pp. 330–31.

4. Henry Adams, *The Education of Henry Adams* (New York: Library of America, 1983), p. 818.

5. Isaiah Berlin, "Political Judgment," in Henry Hardy, ed., *The Sense of Reality: Studies in Ideas and their History* (New York: Farrar, Straus & Giroux, 1996), p. 45. See also Berlin's "The Sense of Reality" in the same volume.

6. Ibid., p. 46.

7. Berlin, "The Sense of Reality," in Hardy, ed., *The Sense of Reality*, p. 24.

8. In Winston S. Churchill, *Clemenceau*, in *Great Contemporaries* (London: Thornton Butterworth, 1937), pp. 311–12.

9. Basler, *Collected Works of Lincoln*, Vol. VII, p. 281.

10. Ibid., Vol. V, p. 537.

11. Winston S. Churchill, *The Second World War*, Vol. II, *Their Finest Hour* (Boston: Houghton Mifflin, 1949), p. 15.

12. Quoted in Lord Beaverbrook (William Maxwell Aitken), *Men and Power 1917–1918* (New York: Duell, Sloan and Pearce, 1956), p. 151.

13. Lord Beaverbrook (William Maxwell Aitken), *Politicans and the War* (New York: Duell, Sloan and Pearce, 1960), pp. 238–39.

14. Winston S. Churchill, "Consistency in Politics," in his *Amid These Storms: Thoughts and Adventures* (New York: Charles Scribner's Sons, 1932), p. 39.

15. Ferdinand Foch,*The Memoirs of Marshal Foch*, intro. and trans. by T. Bentley Mott (New York: Doubleday, 1931), p. xxv. Mott was Foch's American liaison officer.

16. See, for example, Aristotle's *Nichomachean Ethics*, Book II.

17 Jean-Jules-Henri Mordacq, *Le Ministère Clemenceau: Journal d'un Témoin* Vol. II, *Mai 1918–11 Novembre 1918* (Paris: Librairie Plon, 1930, French), p. 61.

18. Robert Rhodes James, ed., *Winston S. Churchill: His Complete Speeches 1897–1963* (New York: Chelsea House Publishers, 1974), Vol. VI, p. 6249.

19. Churchill, *Their Finest Hour*, pp. 232, 238.

20. Robert Sherwood, *Roosevelt and Hopkins: An Intimate History* (New York: Harper & Bros, 1948), p. 149.

21. Quoted in Jean-Jules-Henri Mordacq, *Clemenceau* (Paris: Les Éditions de France, 1939, French), p. 209.

22. Quoted in Colin R. Coote, ed., *A Churchill Reader* (Boston: Houghton Mifflin, 1954), p. 386. Coote ascribes this quotation to Churchill's *Great Contemporaries*.

APPENDIX

1. Allan Bloom, *The Republic of Plato* (New York: Basic Books, 1968), Book II, 375a–d, pp. 52–53.

2. Quoted by "Brutus," one of the leading anti-Federalists, in "On the Calamity of a National Debt that cannot be Repaid, and on Standing Armies," *New York Journal*, 10 January 1788, reproduced in Bernard Bailyn, ed., *The Debate on the Constitution* (New York: Library of America, 1993), p. 734.

3. Richard Kohn, "The Constitution and National Security," in Richard Kohn, ed., *The United States Military Under the Constitution of the United States, 1789–1989* (New York: New York University Press, 1991), p. 87.

4. For evidence of the durability of Huntington's views, see, for example, Sam C. Sarkesian and Robert E. Connor, Jr., *The US Military Profession into the Twenty-First Century: War, Peace and Politics* (London: Frank Cass, 1999), and Don M. Snider, John A. Nagl, and Tony Pfaff, "Army Professionalism, the Military Ethic, and Officership in the 21st Century" (Carlisle Barracks: US Army War College Strategic Studies Institute, 1999). A particularly interesting document, largely Huntingtonian in tone, is the US Army's Field Manual 100-1, *The Army*, periodically revised and now available on the World Wide Web (www.adtdl.army.mil/cgi-bin/atdl.dll/fm/100-1/toc.htm); the current edition is dated 14 June 1994.

5. Samuel P. Huntington, *The Soldier and the State: The Theory and Politics of Civil-Military Relations* (Cambridge, MA: Harvard University Press, 1959), pp. 8–11.

6. Samuel P. Huntington, "Power, Expertise, and the Military Profession," *Daedalus* (Fall 1963): 785–86.

7. Huntington, *Soldier and the State*, p. 68.

8. Ibid., pp. 80 ff., 351–60.

9. Ibid., p. 83.

10. Ibid., p. 74.

11. Ibid. p. 308.

12. Ibid., p. 76.

13. Ibid., p. 13.

14. Ibid., p. 315.

15. See United States Senate, Committee on Armed Services, *Defense Organization: The Need for Change*, Senate Print 99-86, *Staff Report to the Committee on Armed Services*, 99th Cong., 1st Sess. (Washington, DC: US Government Printing Office, 1985).

16. United States. Congress. Senate. Committee on Armed Services. *Defense Organization: The Need for Change: Staff Report to the Committee on Armed Services*, United States Senate. Washington, DC: GPO, 1985, p. 36, quotes Huntington on World War II. For a list of the broad problems the Senate staffers—who played the largest role in drafting the legislation—saw, see the list on pp. 3–10.

17. Alexis de Tocqueville, *Democracy in America*, J. P. Mayer, ed., George Lawrence, trans. (New York: Harper & Row, 1969), Vol. II, Part III, Ch. 22, p. 653. Chapters 22–26, pp. 645–666 treat this issue more broadly.

18. See Allen Guttmann, "Political Ideals and the Military Ethic," *American Scholar* 34:2 (Spring 1965): 221–37, and Allen Guttmann, *The Conservative Tradition in America* (New York: Oxford University Press, 1967), Ch. 4, "Conservatism and the Military Establishment," pp. 100–122.

19. Ibid., p. 108.

20. The story is told in Douglas Southall Freeman, *Lee's Lieutenants: A Study in Command* (New York: Charles Scribner's Sons, 1943), Vol. I, p. 424, emphasis in the original. Guttmann is not entirely fair, since Jackson was nothing if not punctilious in his treatment of federal wounded, prisoners, and civilians—rather more important marks of military chivalry.

21. See Sam Sarkesian, "Military Professionalism and Civil-Military Relations in the West," *International Political Science Review* 2:3 (1981): 283–97.

22. Morris Janowitz, *The Professional Soldier: A Social and Political Portrait* (New York: Free Press, 1971), p. 15.

23. Ibid., p. 418.

24. Ibid., p. 21.

25. Charles C. Moskos, "From Institution to Occupation: Trends in Military Organization," *Armed Forces and Society* 4:1 (Fall 1977): 41–54.

26. Rebecca L. Schiff, "Civil-Military Relations Reconsidered: A Theory of Concordance," *Armed Forces & Society* 22:1 (Fall 1995): 7.

27. Ibid., p. 12.

28. Huntington, *Soldier and the State*, p. 144. Liberal military policy is, he said, the blunt injunction to the armed forces: "Conform or die," p. 155.

29. Note, however, that the military coup theme continues to be a vehicle for serious discussion of civil-military relations. See Charles J. Dunlap, Jr., "The Origins of the American Military Coup of 2012," *Parameters* 22:4 (Winter 1992/93): 2–20.

30. Gene M. Lyons, "The New Civil-Military Relations," *American Political Science Review* 55:1 (March 1961): 53.

31. *Defense Organization*, p. 42. Note that this report defined three types of threat to civilian control: "the man on horseback" seizing power; the "benign takeover" when civilian government collapses; or the "commander taking actions on his own initiative," as in Stanley Kubrick's classic movie, *Dr. Strangelove*—a particular anxiety of the nuclear era—see p. 28. As we shall see, this narrows excessively the scope of the problem of civilian control.

32. See, for example, Lyons, "The New Civil-Military Relations."

33. S. E. Finer, *The Man on Horseback: The Role of the Military in Politics* (New York: Praeger, 1962), pp. 7–10.

34. Ibid., pp. 207 ff.

35. Ibid., p. 72.

36. See the discussion in Kenneth Kemp and Charles Hudlin, "Civil Supremacy over the Military: Its Nature and Limits," *Armed Forces and Society* 19:1 (Fall 1992): 7–26.

37. See the gripping, if perhaps overdrawn, description of the tension between "frocks" and "brass hats" in Lord Beaverbrook (William Maxwell Aitken), *Men and Power 1917–1918* (New York: Duell, Sloan and Pearce, 1956), in particular pp. 186 ff.

38. See Isaiah Berlin, *The Hedgehog and the Fox: An Essay on Tolstoy's View of History* (New York: Simon & Schuster, 1953), for an able defense of Tolstoy as a philosopher of history.

39. Leo Tolstoy, *War and Peace*, trans. Anne Dunnigan (New York: Penguin, 1968), III.2.21, pp. 915–16.

40. Ibid., III.1.11, pp. 774–75.

41. Ibid., III.1.1.

42. Ibid., III.1.1.

43. Ibid., p. 128, excerpt from an 1868 essay by Tolstoy.

44. See the discussions in Berlin, *Hedgehog and the Fox*, also James T. Farrell, "Leo Tolstoy and Napoleon Bonaparte," *Literature and Morality* (New York: Vanguard, 1946), pp. 103 ff.

45. For a masterly survey of this debate, brought up to date, see Richard K. Betts, "Is Strategy an Illusion?" *International Security* (Fall 2000): 5–50.

46. Gerhard Ritter, *The Sword and the Scepter: The Problem of Militarism in Germany*, trans. Heinz Norden (Coral Gables: University of Miami Press, 1969–1973), Vol. III, p. 486.

47. Ibid., Vol. I, pp. 70–75. Note that much of Ritter's judgment of the military striving for maximum achievement applies chiefly to the German military of the late nineteenth and early twentieth centuries.

48. Ibid., Vol. I, p. 68.

49. See Gerhard Ritter, *The Schlieffen Plan: Critique of a Myth*, trans. Andrew and Eva Wilson (New York: Praeger, 1958).

50. Ibid., p. 91, and Ritter, *Sword and Scepter*, Vol. II, p. 210.

51. The citation is to Ritter, *Sword and Scepter*, Vol. I, p. 49.

52. Russell Weigley, "Military Strategy and Civilian Leadership," in Klaus Knorr, ed., *Historical Dimensions of National Security* (Lawrence, KS: University Press of Kansas, 1976), p. 69. For a critique of Weigley see Christopher Bassford, *Clausewitz in English: The Reception of Clausewitz in Britain and America 1815–1945* (New York: Oxford University Press, 1994), pp. 24 and passim.

53. Russell Weigley, "The Political and Strategic Dimensions of Military Effectiveness," in Allan R. Millett and Williamson Murray, eds., *Military Effectiveness*, Vol. III, *The Second World War* (Boston: Allen & Unwin, 1988), p. 341.

54. Ibid., p. 39.

55. Ibid., p. 42.

56. Russell Weigley, *The Age of Battles: The Quest for Decisive Warfare from Breitenfeld to Waterloo* (Bloomington: Indiana University Press, 1991), p. 536.

57. Ibid., p. 539.

58. John Keegan, *The Mask of Command* (London: Penguin, 1987), p. 7.

59. John Keegan, *A History of Warfare* (New York: Knopf, 1993), p. 21.

60. Ibid., p. xvi.

61. John Keegan, *The Face of Battle* (New York: Viking, 1976), p. 336.

62. William James, "The Moral Equivalent of War" (1910), reprinted in *William James: Writings 1902–1910* (New York: The Library of America, 1987), pp. 1281–93; for examples of the latter, see Forrest E. Morgan, *Living the Martial Way: A Manual for the Way a Modern Warrior Should Think* (Fort Lee, NJ: Barricade Books, 1992), and Richard Strozzi Heckler, *In Search of the Warrior Spirit* (Berkeley, CA: North Atlantic Books, 1992),. An older but no less useful account, published in Japanese in 1905, is Inazo Nitobe, *Bushido: The Soul of Japan* (Rutland, VT: Charles E. Tuttle, 1969).

63. John Keegan, letter to the editor, *Times Literary Supplement* (UK), 23 April 1993, p. 15.

64. Ibid.

65. Thomas E. Ricks, "The Great Society in Camouflage," *Atlantic Monthly* (December 1996): 24.

66. John Keegan, *The Face of Battle* (New York: Viking, 1976), p. 336.

67. See Edward Layton Jr., *The Revolt of the Engineers* (Cleveland: The Press of Case Western University, 1971), p. 4. On professionalism more generally, see Talcott Parsons, "Professions," in David L. Sills, ed., *International Encyclopedia of the Social Sciences* (New York: Macmillan, 1968), Vol. 12, pp. 536–57. Parsons says that the rise of the professions "probably constitute[s]

the most important change that has occurred in the occupational system of modern societies."

68. See, for example, Huntington, *Soldier and the State*, pp. 56, 255.

69. Winston S. Churchill, *The World Crisis, 1915* (New York: Charles Scribner's Sons, 1923), p. 6.

70. See A. J. Bacevich, "The Use of Force in Our Time," *Wilson Quarterly* 19 (Winter 1995): 50–63.

71. See, for example, Richard Holmes, *Acts of War: The Behavior of Men in Battle* (New York: Free Press, 1985), pp. 281–90. Holmes makes the standard arguments against ideology as a motivating force, but (a) excludes counterexamples, and (b) identifies ideology only in terms of the hatred of the enemy, which is surely too simple a description of its effects.

72. See in particular Omer Bartov, *Hitler's Army: Soldiers, Nazis, and War in the Third Reich* (New York: Oxford University Press, 1991), and among the volumes of the German official history of the Second World War a particularly powerful essay: Jürgen Förster, *"Das Unternehmen 'Barbarossa' als Eroberungs- und Vernichtungskrieg"* ["The 'Barbarossa' Campaign as a War of Conquest and Destruction"], in Horst Boog et al., *Das Deutsche Reich und der zweite Weltkrieg* [The German Government and the Second World War], Vol. IV, *Der Angriff auf die Sowjetunion* [The Attack on the Soviet Union] (Stuttgart: Deutsche Verlags-Anstalt, 1983), pp. 413–47.

73. The classic article, published shortly after the war, was Edward Shils and Morris Janowitz, "Cohesion and Disintegration in the Wehrmacht in World War II," reprinted in Morris Janowitz, *Military Conflict: Essays in the Institutional Analysis of War and Peace* (Beverly Hills: Sage, 1975), pp. 177–220. Extremely influential too was Martin van Creveld, *Combat Power: German and US Army Performance, 1939–1945* (Westport, CT: Greenwood, 1982).

74. A careful reading of some of the older literature would have made this point as well. For example, Shils and Janowitz note that the primary groups of the Wehrmacht were built around a "hard core" of committed men—many of them dedicated Nazis.

75. Bartov, *Hitler's Army*, p. 96.

76. See Jürgen Förster, "The Dynamics of *Volksgemeinschaft*: The Effectiveness of the German Military Establishment in the Second World War," in Millett and Murray, eds., *Military Effectiveness*, Vol. III, pp. 180–220.

77. Charles W. Sydnor, Jr., *Soldiers of Destruction: The SS Death's Head Division, 1933–1945* (Princeton: Princeton University Press, 1977), p. 274.

78. Think, for example, of the outstanding Israeli commander of the 1948 war of independence, Yigal Alon, former commander of the Palmach, or for that matter Leon Trotsky, the Russian Revolution's "organizer of victory."

79. On the management of violence as the essence of military professionalism, see Huntington, *The Soldier and the State*, p. 11; Huntington estimated that 80 percent of regular officers and 20 percent of reservists fit that criterion

("Power, Expertise, and the Military Profession," p. 785), but this greatly underestimates the number of officers whose expertise is nonmilitary (logisticians, doctors, lawyers, communicators, chaplains, air-traffic controllers, and the like).

80. For a capsule biography see Malcolm Falkus, "Monash," in Michael Carver, ed., *The War Lords: Military Commanders of the Twentieth Century* (Boston: Little Brown, 1976), pp. 134–43.

81. Ian Hamilton, *The Soul and Body of an Army* (New York: George H. Doran, 1921), p. 25.

82. John Gooch and I have discussed this at some length in our book, *Military Misfortunes: The Anatomy of Failure in War* (New York: Free Press, 1990).

83. See Andrew F. Krepinevich Jr., *The Army and Vietnam* (Baltimore: Johns Hopkins University Press, 1986).

84. Clausewitz, *On War*, I:7, p. 120.

85. Ibid., VIII:3, p. 593.

86. Snider, Nagl, and Pfaff, "Army Professionalism," p. 38.

87. John Hackett, *The Profession of Arms* (London: Times Publishing Co., 1963), p. 47.

INDEX

Abdullah, King of Transjordan, 181, 187–188
Abrams, Creighton, 215–216
Adams, Henry, 245
Afghanistan, 255, 257
Afrika Korps, 149
Aideed, Muhammad Farah, 283
Aiken, George D., 230
Aisne River, 90
Allen, Ethan, 48
Alon, Yigal, 189, 193, 195, 244
Alsace, 65, 68, 76, 97
Altalena affair, 191–192, 259
American Allied Expeditionary Air Force, 150
American Civil War, 174
  Anglo-American relations in, 35
  Churchill on, 124–125
  navy in, 29, 35
  quality of military officers in, 39–43
  railroads in, 29–31, 33
  telegraph in, 31–33
  weaponry in, 27–29, 33, 42
  see also Lincoln, Abraham
American Expeditionary Force (AEF), 63, 87, 94
American Telegraph Company, 32
Anglo-American Commission of Inquiry, 158
Anglo-American relations
  in American Civil War, 35
  in Second World War, 115–116, 131, 133–134
Anthropological determinism, 272
Antietam, battle of, 29, 48, 244

Anzio, landing at, 132
Appomattox Courthouse, 41, 244
Arab Legion, 181, 183, 184, 186–187
Arab Liberation Army, 182
Arab Revolt, 157
Argonne offensive, 88, 92
Aristotle, 256
Army of the Republic of Vietnam (ARVN), 211–213
Aspin, Les, 235
Atlantic, battle of the, 120, 131, 132–133
Atlantic convoys, 11
Auchinleck, Claude, 149
Austerlitz, battle of, 33
Australian Imperial Force, 285
Austria-Hungary, 95, 96

Baghdad, 70, 224
Balkans, 70, 234
Banks, Nathaniel, 41
Barak, Ehud, 251
Bastogne, 215
Battle of the Atlantic Committee, 131, 133
Beauregard, Pierre, 42
Beaverbrook, Lord (William Maxwell Aitken), 101–102, 116, 251–252
Beersheba, 179
Begin, Menachem, 192
Belgium, 71, 78, 79, 89, 96, 97
Belgrade, Chinese embassy in, 206
Ben-Gurion, David, 5–8, 12, 154–199, 201–202, 213, 248, 249, 253, 256–257, 260

Ben-Gurion, David – *contd*
  age at command, 7
  Altalena affair and, 192, 259
  atomic weapons and, 6
  Churchill and, 7
  in First World War, 162
  "From the Haganah in the
      Underground to a Regular
      Army" by, 198
  frugality of, 162
  Haganah and, 156, 158–159,
      165–178, 193, 194
  Hebrew language and, 190
  Israel Defense Forces and, 190,
      192–193, 195, 187, 198
  Israeli war of independence and,
      178–189, 193–196, 199, 258,
      267
  Laskov and, 173–174
  military technology and, 247–248
  Palmach and, 171, 192–195
  political background of, 163–164
  reading by, 155–156
  retirement of, 154–155
  as state-builder, 189–190
  statehood objective of, 156–165,
      257, 259
  Yadin and, 8, 186, 194, 195–196,
      242–243
Ben-Gurion, Paula, 154, 162
Berlin, 95–97, 104, 152
Berlin, Isaiah, 246
Bevin, Ernest, 161
Biltmore program, 165
Bismarck, Otto von, 275
Black Hawk war, 21
"Black Sunday", 159
Bletchley Park, 132, 147–148
Bliss, Tasker Howard, 88
Blockade, in American Civil War, 29,
      36
Boer war, 81
Bolo Pasha affair, 68–69
Bolshevik revolution, 101, 288

Bonar Law, Andrew, 103
Bosnia, 234
Bracken, Brendan, 116
Bragg, Braxton, 22
Briand, Aristide, 69
Britain, battle of, 111, 132–133, 259
Brook, Norman, 128, 143–144
Brooke, Alan, 8, 113–114, 130, 137,
      138, 139, 141, 148, 150,
      242–243, 244
Browning, Orville, 35
Buchanan, James, 56
Buell, Don Carlos, 40
Buena Vista, battle of, 21
Bull Run, first battle of, 29, 30, 32,
      37
Bull Run, second battle of, 40
Bundy, McGeorge, 236
Burnside, Ambrose, 24, 40, 45
Bush, George H. W., 4, 220, 223, 226,
      227–228, 230–232, 234, 249,
      250
Bush, George W., 238, 255
Butler, Ben, 41–42, 52
Butterfield, Daniel, 42

Caillaux, Joseph, 74
Cambodia, 211
Cameron, Simon, 20, 32
Caporetto, battle of, 70
Carmel, Moshe, 168–169, 169–170
Carson, Sir Edward, 101–102, 251
Center for the Professional Military
      Ethic, 288
Chamberlain, Joshua Lawrence, 41
Chamberlain, Neville, 116, 121
Champagne offensive, 70
Chancellorsville, battle of, 40, 41, 48
Charmley, John, 113
Chase, Salmon P., 24
Chattanooga, battle of, 22, 30, 40, 47,
      50
Chemical weapons, 87, 143
Chemin des Dames, 90

Cheney, Richard Bruce, 221, 223–224, 249
Cheyl mishmar (CHIM), 177
Chickamauga, battle of, 22, 39
China, 206, 204–205, 221, 282, 284
Churchill, Winston, 5–8, 14, 71, 110–153, 176, 177, 178, 201–202, 213, 246, 256, 259, 260, 267
  age at command, 7
  on American Civil War, 124–125
  art of interrogation of, 136–153, 249
  atomic weapons and, 6
  biography of Marlborough by, 124, 126, 202
  Brooke and, 8, 113–114, 138–139, 148, 150, 242–243, 244
  Clemenceau and, 7
  coalition warfare and, 79, 133–136
  in colonial campaigns, 123
  communism and, 133, 135
  on courage, 260
  First World War and, 60–62, 123–124, 127–129
  French fleet, destruction of, 259
  front line visits of, 60–62, 147
  health of, 118
  historical critique of, 112–119, 129–131
  History of the English-Speaking Peoples by, 124
  intelligence operations and, 142–143, 147–148
  Ismay and, 121, 137
  memoirs of, 117, 257
  Middle East commanders and, 149
  military technology and, 247
  naval judgement of, 141–142
  as painter, 125
  on Palestine, 160
  peace aims of, 151–152
  political rhetoric of, 152–153, 253, 255

  as popular icon, 117–118
  regimental patches issue and, 144–147
  The River War by, 123
  Roosevelt and, 115–116, 127, 131, 134
  Royal Air Force and, 121
  Royal Navy and, 141–142
  staff of, 119–121
  war strategy and, 113, 125–136, 248, 258
  work habits of, 116, 119–120
  The World Crisis by, 124, 126, 151
Civil War *see* American Civil War
Clark, Wesley, 236, 237
Clausewitz, Claus von, 8–10, 25, 58, 150, 151, 199, 218, 241, 257, 275, 277, 278–279, 281, 282
Clemenceau, Georges, 5–8, 60–109, 178, 201–202, 213, 246, 248, 253, 258–259
  age at command, 7
  Alsace and Lorraine and, 65, 68, 76
  Churchill and, 7
  coalition warfare and, 82–83, 87–88, 91–94
  on courage, 260
  death of, 108
  Dreyfus affair and, 66
  Foch and, 63, 65, 67, 77, 79, 89–94, 97–107, 234, 242–243, 244, 256, 257
  front line visits of, 60–62, 74–76, 88–89, 91, 249
  Grandeur and Misery of Victory by, 105
  Lincoln, respect for, 7, 65
  military advisers to, 73–74, 88
  military technology and, 247
  peace and armistice negotiations and, 63, 64–65, 94–97, 101–104, 106–108
  personal discipline and organization of, 72–73, 74

Clemenceau, Georges – *contd*
  Pétain and, 63, 65, 77, 88–91, 103, 105, 256
  political background of, 63, 65, 68
  politics of, 65–66, 246
  purging of army and, 74, 91
  style of command of, 65, 71–72, 74–76, 257, 258
  suppression of domestic opposition to war, 74, 76, 259
Clifford, Clark, 208–209
Clinton, Bill, 232, 234–235, 236–237, 238, 250, 279
Coalition warfare, 82–84
  Churchill and, 79, 133–136
  Clemenceau and, 83, 87–88, 91–94
Cohen, William, 237
Cold Harbor, battle of, 27, 43
Cold War, 215, 231, 237–238, 288
Collective settlements (*kibbutzim*), 154, 163
Colville, John, 244
Commune, 65, 66
Communications revolutions, 6–7, 26
Communism, 133, 136, 152, 161, 205, 206, 288
Constitution of the United States, 216, 263
Cooper, Scott, 15
Council of Four, 102, 104
Council of Foreign Relations, 237
Cox, Jacob, 41
Crossbow Committee, 133
Cuban missile crisis, 205
Cunningham, Sir Alan, 140–141, 148–149
Curragh mutiny, 271–272
Czechoslovakia, 152, 176

Dahlgren John A., 29
Dana, Charles, 25, 49–52, 253, 260
Danang, 210
Danchev, Alex, 117
Dardenelles, 70, 118, 128

Davis, Jefferson, 21–22
Dayan, Moshe, 195
D-Day, 133
Defense in depth, 85–86, 90
De Gaulle, Charles, 13–14, 109, 136
Deir Yasin massacre, 191
Dill, Sir John, 116–17, 140, 148, 149–150, 243
Directive Number 4, 85
Dr. Strangelove, Or: How I Learned to Stop Worrying and Love the Bomb (movie), 15
Dori, Ya'akov, 172, 173, 195
Doullens conference of 1918, 79, 90
Dreyfus, Alfred, 66
Duchêne, General, 90–91
Dugan, Michael, 222, 223
Dunkelman, Ben, 193–194
Duroselle, Jean-Baptiste, 66

Early, Jubal, 48, 50, 53–54, 55, 57, 258
École Supériuere de la Guerre, 67, 81
Edward VIII, King of England, 118
Egypt, 123, 179–185, 189, 192, 280
Eicke, Theodore, 284
Eilat, Israel, 195
Eisenhower, Dwight D., 1, 134, 152, 212
El Arish, 195
Elton, G. R., 113
"Empire's Post-War Fleet, The", 141
Esterhazy, Ferdinand, 66
Etzion settlement, 184
Ewell, Julian J., 214

Face of Battle, The (Keegan), 278
Falklands War, 16, 280
Feinstein, Ze'ev, 169, 172
Finer, S. E., 271–272, 275, 280
First World War, 127–128, 136, 272, 285
  Ben-Gurion in, 162

casualties in, 63, 64, 70, 88
Churchill and, 60–62, 123–124,
    127–129
coalition warfare, 79–80, 83–84,
    87–88, 91–94
defense in depth, 85–86, 90
MICHAEL offensive, 287
peace and armistice negotiations,
    63, 64–65, 95–105, 107–108
Schlieffen Plan, 276, 287
weaponry in, 87
see also Clemenceau, Georges
Foch, Ferdinand, 63, 65, 67, 77–80,
    81, 82, 84–86, 89–94, 95,
    97–107, 234, 242–243, 244, 256,
    257
Fort Pickens, 20
Fortress Monroe, 48
Fort Sanders, 28
Fort Sumter, resupply of, 20, 48
Fourteen Points, 95, 96, 100
Franks, Frederick, 223
Free French, 109, 136, 212
Frémont, John C., 35
French Revolution, 8, 174
"From the Haganah in the
    Underground to a Regular
    Army" (Ben-Gurion), 198
Frost, David, 226

Galilee, 167, 180, 186, 187
Galili, Israel, 169, 172, 173, 193
Gandhi, Mahatma, 155
General Orders 252, 24
Goerge Catlett Marshall Medal, 4
Gettysburg, battle of, 29, 39, 40, 41,
    46, 124–125, 243, 260
Gladstone, William, 250
Goldwater-Nichols Department of
    Defensive Reorganization Act of
    1986, 220, 221, 267
Goltz, Rüdiger von der, 77
Grandeur and Misery of Victory
    (Clemenceau), 105

Grant, Ulysses, 17–19, 20–21, 24, 38,
    40, 41, 42, 43, 44, 47–54, 55,
    57–58, 66, 242–243, 244–245,
    253
Great Society, 282
Greece, 129, 134, 136, 138–139, 149,
    152
Greeley, Horace, 49
Greenbaum, Yitzchak, 194
Grenada, 280
Grigg, P., 145–146
Guam conference of 1967, 210
Gulf war, 1, 3, 217, 219–233, 249,
    267, 279, 285
Guttmann, Allen, 268, 270, 271

Habeas corpus, suppression of, 259
Haganah, 156, 158–159, 165–178,
    191–193
Haifa, 167, 179, 181
Haig, Sir Douglas, 63, 64, 83, 84, 89,
    95, 272
Haiphong, 204, 282
Haiti, 280
Halifax, Lord, 122
Halleck, Henry, 33, 44, 45, 47, 53,
    54–55, 57, 73, 249
Hancock, Winfield Scott, 39
Hanoi, 204, 206, 282
Harel brigade, 193
Haupt, Herman, 29–30, 42
Hay, John, 58–59
Hebrew language, 190
Hebron, 157, 188
Heintzelman, Samuel, 39–40
Herndon, William, 25
Hinderburg Line, 85
Histadrut, 162
History of the English-Speaking Peoples
    (Churchill), 124
Hitchcock, Ethan Allen, 48
Hitler, Adolf, 74, 80, 108, 121, 131,
    133, 136, 143, 157, 160, 176
Hobart, Percy, 116

Holbrooke, Richard, 234
Holocaust, 160
Hooker, Joseph, 22–23, 24, 40, 42, 44, 48, 49
Hopkins, Harry, 131, 134
Horner, Charles, 222
Howard, Michael, 117–118
Howard, Oliver Otis, 40, 42
Hunt, Ira A., 214
Hunter, David, 44, 57
Huntington, Samuel P., 4–5, 263–272, 276, 279–285, 289
al-Hussaini, Abd el-Kadr, 185, 186
al-Husseini, Haj Amin, 159–160
Hussein, Saddam, 222, 227–230, 257

Independence Day (movie), 4
India, 123, 135, 160
International Churchill Society, 117
Iraq, 70, 181, 183, 188, 189, 221–232
Irgun Zvai Leumi (IZL), 158, 159, 163, 170, 179, 191–192
Ismay, Hastings, 114, 121, 128, 137, 148, 249
Isonzo, twelfth battle of, 70
Israel Defense Forces (IDF), 169, 174, 175, 177, 179, 184, 186, 187, 188, 191–200
Israeli war of independence, 178–189, 193–196, 199, 244, 258
Italian campaign, 127, 130, 132, 134

J'accuse (Zola), 66
Jackson, Stonewall, 23, 29, 41, 268
Jaffa, 179
James, William, 278
Janowitz, Morris, 269, 270, 278
Jena, battle of, 33
Jerusalem, 167, 179, 180, 181, 183, 185–189, 191, 192, 193, 196, 257, 258
Jewish Agency, 162, 168, 181
Jewish Quarter, 187

Joffre, Joseph-Jacques-Césaire, 75
Johnson, Lyndon B., 204–212, 214, 215, 250, 282
Johnston, Joseph, 29, 52, 56
Joint Chiefs of Staff (JCS), 204, 208–210, 215, 219, 220, 231, 233–234, 236, 237, 267
Joint Intelligence Committee (JIC), 142–143
Jones, R. V., 110–112
Jordan, 161, 184, 187–189, 197, 199
Jordan River, 188, 257
"Journals of a Witness" (Mordacq), 73
Jutland, battle of, 141

Kastel, 186
Katyn Forest massacre, 152
Katznelson, Berl, 154, 155
el-Kawukji, Fawzi, 182
Keegan, John, 274–275, 277–279
Kennedy, John F., 152
Key, John J., 44–46
Key, Thomas M., 44
Khobar Towers bombing, 235
Killer Angels (Shaara), 41
Kimball, Warren, 115–116
Kimche brothers, 183
King, Jere Clemens, 69
King David Hotel, Jerusalem, 159
Kitchener, Lord, 123, 129
Komer, Robert, 212
Korean war, 205, 215, 232
Kosovo war, 233, 236–237
Kubrick, Stanley, 15
Kurds, 230
Kuwait, 222, 223, 226, 227–228, 230

Laos, 211
Laskov, Haim, 173–174
Latrun, 186–187, 190
Leahy, William, 249
Lebanon, 12, 181, 183, 280
Lechi (Lohamei Herut Yisrael), 158, 159, 170, 179, 191

Lee, Robert E., 22, 23, 30, 38, 39, 41, 42, 46, 47, 52, 57, 58, 243, 245, 248, 258
Libya, 149
Liddell Hart, Basil, 196
Lincoln, Abraham, 5–8, 17–59, 73, 112, 155, 156, 178, 201–202, 213, 246–247, 250, 259–260, 262–263, 267, 276, 281–282
  assassination of, 50
  cabinet of, 23–24
  Clemenceau's respect for, 7, 65
  Dana and, 49–52, 253
  education of, 24–25
  emancipation and, 44
  firearms and, 28–29, 247
  Grant and, 17–19, 20–21, 44, 47–54, 242–243, 244–245, 253
  habeas corpus, suppression of, 259
  Hooker and, 22–23, 44
  intellect of, 24–25
  Key and, 44–46
  McClellan and, 24, 44, 45, 251
  Meade and, 24, 46–47, 243–244
  oversight of military operations by, 19–21, 24–25, 34, 43–54, 248–249, 257–258
  qualifications as commander in chief, 21–26
  Second Inaugural Address of, 253–254
  Sherman and, 20–21
  slavery and, 34, 36
  Stanton and, 55–56
  strategic concept of, 34–38, 43–44, 58–59
  telegraph and, 32–33
Lincoln and His Generals (T. Harry Williams), 18
Lincoln Finds a General (Kenneth P. Williams), 18
Lindemann, Frederick (Lord Cherwell), 116, 120–121, 128, 141

Link, Arthur, 107
Livy, 3
Ljubljana gap, 118
Lloyd George, David, 60, 63, 100, 104–105, 272
Logan, Jon, 41, 42, 57
Logistical revolution, 26
Lohamei Herut Yisrael (Lechi), 158, 159, 170, 179, 191
Longstreet, James, 23, 27–28, 30
Lorraine, 65, 68, 76, 89, 97
Lucius Aemilius, 2–3
Luftwaffe, 139

MacArthur, Douglas, 217, 250, 251, 271, 280
Makleff, Mordechai, 193
Manassas, first battle of, 29, 30, 32, 35
Mandel, Georges, 73–74
Mapai (*Mifleget poalei yisrael*), 164, 166, 168
Marcus, Mickey, 187
Marlborough, Duke of, 121–122, 124, 126, 202
Marne, battles of the, 78, 90
Marshall, George C., 128, 238–239
McClellan, George, 24, 32, 40, 43, 44, 45, 46, 48, 49, 243, 250, 251
McDonald, D. L., 206–207
McDowell, Irwin, 24
McMaster, H. R., 207–208
McNamara, Robert Strange, 204, 211, 212–213, 214, 236
McPherson, James, 36, 38
Meade, George, 24, 30, 46–47, 52, 243–244
Meigs, Montgomery C., 20
Menzies, Robert, 114
Mexican war, 31, 39
MICHAEL offensive, 287
Miles, Nelson, 41
Military Assistance Command Vietnam (MACV), 212, 213

Millerand, Alexandre, 69
Minié ball, 21, 27, 57
Mishmar HaEmek, 180
Mishmar Hayarden, 184
Moltke, Helmuth Johannes Ludwig
    von, 252–253
Moltke, Helmuth Karl Bernhard von,
    77, 81, 252–253, 268
Monash, Sir John, 285
Montenegro, 96
Monterey, battle of, 21
Montgomery, Sir Bernard Law, 147
Moran, Lord, 118
Mordacq, Jean-Jules-Henri, 73, 74, 88,
    90, 94, 98, 102, 103–104, 249
Moses, 155
Moskos, Charles, 269, 270
Mott, T. Bentley, 80
Moyne, Lord, 158

Napoleon Bonaparte, 8, 23, 26, 65,
    78, 79, 81, 104, 257, 260
Napoleon III, 65
National Guard, 216, 217
Nazi ideology, 108, 283, 284
Negba, 180
Negev desert, 154, 180, 187, 195
Netherlands East Indies, 132
Nicolay, John, 58–59
Nivelle offensives, 68, 70, 85
Normal theory of civil-military
    relations, 5–8, 15, 18, 34, 36, 76,
    201–203, 217, 220, 232–233, 239,
    240, 243, 263, 267, 282, 289
Normandy invasion, 130, 134,
    150–151
North Africa, 77, 127, 134, 149, 234,
    282
North Atlantic Treaty Organization
    (NATO), 234, 236, 240
Norway, 118, 132, 136, 140

Objective control, theory of, 4–5,
    264–267, 269, 289

Old City, 187, 188
Omdurman, battle of, 123
On War (Clausewitz), 8
Operation ALLIED FORCE, 236
Operation DRAGOON, 134
Operation HUSKY, 134–135
Operation INSTANT THUNDER, 222
Operation JUPITER, 132
Operation NACHSHON, 186
Operation ROLLING THUNDER,
    222
Operation VICTOR, 137–140
Oran, Algeria, 136, 259
Ottoman Turks, 70
Owens, William, 221

Pagonis, Gus, 285
Paget, General, 145–146
Painlevé, Paul, 68–69
Palestine, 70, 154, 155, 156–165, 172
    see also Ben-Gurion, David
Palmach, 12, 167, 170, 171, 173, 175,
    182, 190–195, 196, 244, 284
Panama, 280
Paris, France, 64, 71–72, 86, 90, 258
Passchendaele, battle of, 64
Pearl Harbor, 125
Pedrocini, Guy, 64
"Pentagon Papers", 212
People's Liberation Army (China),
    284
Peres, Shimon, 198
Perry, William, 235
Pershing, John J., 63, 80, 84, 87–88,
    92–94, 95, 97
Persian Gulf war, 1, 3, 217, 219–233,
    249, 267, 279, 285
Pétain, Philippe, 63, 65, 77, 80–82,
    84–91, 95, 99, 102, 103, 105,
    256
Petersburg, siege of, 50, 58, 258
Plato, 262
Poincaré, Raymond, 63, 69, 81, 88,
    95, 97, 101, 103, 104

Poland, 87, 96, 136
Pope, John, 24
Portal, Sir Charles, 141, 148
Pound, Sir Dudley, 140, 149
Powell, Colin, 219, 220–230, 241, 250
Powell Doctrine, 219, 238

Quayle, Dan, 117

Rabin, Yitzhak, 189, 192, 193, 195, 197, 251
Railroads
    in American Civil War, 29–31, 33
    in Second World War, 151
Ralston, Joseph, 237
Rawlins, John, 42, 52
Rawlinson, Henry, 61
Reagan, Ronald, 1, 226
Recouly, Raymond, 105
Red River expedition, 41
Republican Guard (Iraq), 227, 230
Republic (Plato), 262
Reynolds, David, 115
Reynolds, John, 39
Rhine River, 65, 97, 100, 101, 102–103, 107, 147
Ribot, Alexandre, 69
Rice, Donald, 222
Richmond, Virginia, 35, 42, 48, 66
Ricks, Tom, 279
Rifle, rise of, 27–29, 33
Ripley, James W., 29
Ritter, Gerhard, 274, 275–277
River War, The (Churchill), 123
Robertson, Sir William, 83–84, 272
ROK (Republic of Korea) army, 211
Romania, 71, 96
Roman Republic, 2–3
Rommel, Erwin, 149, 192
Roosevelt, Franklin D., 115–116, 121, 127, 131, 134, 136, 152, 226, 233–234, 259, 282
Rosecrans, William, 39, 40, 50–51

Rosen, Stephen, 12
Roskill, S. W., 140
Royal Air Force, 11, 110, 111, 121, 132, 139, 150, 196
Royal Navy, 119, 124, 140, 141–142
Rumsfeld, Donald, 239
Russo-Japanese war, 81

Sadeh, Yitzhak, 168, 173
Salonika, 70
Sarrail, Albert, 79
Saudi Arabia, 222, 223, 224, 235
Schlesinger, James, 216
Schlieffen, Alfred von, 253
Schlieffen Plan, 276, 287
Schwarzkopf, Norman, 3, 222, 223, 224, 225, 226–227, 229–230
Schweinfurt débacles, 287
Scott, Percy, 119
Scott, Winfield, 19, 20, 31, 38, 43, 48
Scowcroft, Brent, 223, 226
SCUD missiles, 224–225, 249
Sde Boker kibbutz, 154, 197
Second World War, 11, 14, 64, 174, 212, 238, 249, 266, 282, 283–284, 285
    Anglo-American relations in, 115–116, 131, 133–134
    railroads in, 151
    Schweinfurt débacles, 287
    weaponry in, 132, 133
    see also Churchill, Winston
Sedan, 94
Senate Committee on Foreign Relations, 240
Serbia, 96, 236, 237, 240, 241, 280
Seven Days in May (movie), 270
7th Brigade, 193
Seward, William, 23–24, 35, 56
Shaara, Michael, 41
Sharon, Ariel, 12–13, 251
Sharpsburg, battle of, 45
Shaw, George Bernard, 124
Sheridan, Philip, 53–54

Sherman, John, 55
Sherman, William Tecumseh, 20–21,
     30–31, 38, 40, 43, 52, 55, 56, 57,
     58
Shi'ites, 230
Shiloh, battle of, 43, 51
Schultz, George, 219
Sicily, 127, 134
Sickles, Daniel, 41
Sinai peninsula, 180, 183, 188, 195,
     196, 199
Singapore, 133
Slavery, 34, 36
Smith, Gordon H., 240
Smith, Leighton, 234
Sneh, Moshe, 169
Soldier and the State, The
     (Huntington), 4–5, 263–267
Somalia, 234–235, 280, 283
Somme campaign, 70, 78, 128
Soviet Union, 131, 133, 134–135,
     136–137, 149, 152, 163, 176,
     182, 188, 189, 221, 257
Spanish Civil War, 284
Spears, Edward, 63, 69
Stalin, Joseph, 16, 121, 135
Stanton, Edwin W., 23, 24, 30, 32,
     33, 48, 49–56, 245, 253
Strategic nihilism, doctrine of,
     272–279
Stuart, E. B. J., 23
Subjective control, concept of, 265,
     269–270
Switzerland, 136
Sword and the Scepter: The Problem of
     Militarism in Germany (Ritter),
     275
Syria, 161, 182, 184, 188

Taylor, Maxwell, 210
Tedder, Arthur, 151
el-Tel, Abdullah, 181
Tel Aviv, 155, 167, 168, 178, 179,
     181, 183, 190

Telegraph, in American Civil War,
     31–33
Temple Mount, 187
Thailand, 207, 209
Thatcher, Margaret, 117
Thomas, George, 39, 51
Thomas, Lorenzo, 48
Tiberias, 179
TIGER convoy, 140
Tirpitz (battleship), 142
Tocqueville, Alexis de, 267
Tolstoy, Leo, 272–274, 277
Total Force, 215, 217
Totenkopf (Death's Head) division,
     284
Tower, John, 223
Train, Harry, 16
Transjordan, 181, 187
Trent affair, 35
Triangle Institute for Security
     Studies, 233
Truman, Harry S., 112, 251, 271
Turing, Alan, 147
Turkey, 94–95, 128, 140
Turner, George Edgar, 30
Turner, Levi C., 45
24th Mechanized Infantry Division,
     217
Twenty-Second Zionist Congress
     (1946), 160–161, 200

U-boats, 140, 142
United Nations, 172, 178, 179, 196,
     234, 259
   Resolution 181, 185, 187, 188
   Special Committee on Palestine
     (UNSCOP), 158
US Army Signal Corps, 32
US Military Telegraph, 32
US Navy, in Civil War, 29, 35
USS Missouri, 230, 232
United Workers' Party (Mapam), 163,
     194
Upton, Emery, 38–39, 40, 41

Verdun, battle of, 64, 70, 81, 85, 86
Vichy regime, 74, 80
Vicksburg campaign, 50
Vienna, 118, 152
"Vietnam syndrome", 232
Vietnam war, 3, 16, 64, 203–219, 222, 230, 231, 232, 247, 250, 279, 283, 287
Viviani, René, 69

Waffen-SS divisions, 284
War and Peace (Tolstoy), 273–274
Warden, John, 222
War of the Spanish Succession, 124
Washington, George, 156
Washington, raid on, 48, 50, 53, 57–58, 258
Washington conference of 1942, 134
Wavell, Archibald, 149, 243
Weaponry
    in American Civil War, 27–29, 33, 42
    in First World War, 87
    in Israeli war of independence, 175–176
    in Second World War, 132, 133
    weapons of mass destruction, 87, 143, 228
Weigley, Russell, 274, 276–277
Weinberger, Caspar, 117, 217–219, 238
Weizmann, Chaim, 164
Welch, Larry, 223
Welles, Gideon, 55

West Bank, 188, 199, 257
Western Wall, 185
Westmoreland, William, 210, 212–213, 250
Weygand, Maxime, 106
Wheeler, Earle, 210
White Paper of 1939, 157, 158, 176
Wilderness, battle of the, 50
Wilhelm II, Kaiser, 253
Williams, Kenneth P., 18
Williams, T. Harry, 18
Wilkie, Wendell, 116
Wilson, James, 40
Wilson, Woodrow, 93, 95, 96, 97, 100, 102, 105, 107
WINDOW, 11
Wingate, Orde, 116
Woerner, Fred, 223
Wolfe, James, 248
Woodward, Bob, 221
World Crisis, The (Churchill), 124, 126, 151
World War I *see* First World War
World War II *see* Second World War

Yadin, Yigal, 8, 173, 186, 194, 195–196, 242–243, 249
Yad Mordechai, 180, 184
Yalu River, 205
Yugoslavia, 234, 280

Zemach, 184
Zionist program, 156–157, 160–165
Zola, Émile, 66